THOMAS HUGHES

THOMAS HUGHES IN 1857

THOMAS HUGHES

THE LIFE OF THE AUTHOR OF
TOM BROWN'S SCHOOLDAYS

by

EDWARD C. MACK

and

W. H. G. ARMYTAGE

LONDON
ERNEST BENN LIMITED

First published 1952

Published by Ernest Benn Limited
Bouverie House, Fleet Street, E.C.4
Printed in Great Britain by
Richard Clay & Company, Ltd., Bungay, Suffolk

Acknowledgements

IN the composition of a biography of this kind, where the material is so dispersed, we have been greatly assisted by the courtesy and co-operation of a number of friends. The late Mr. George Hughes of Topeka, Kansas, kindly put at our disposal the great mass of his father's letters and papers. Miss Jeanie Hughes of Garden City, Long Island, Mr. Walter Hughes of Devonshire, Mrs. Dorothea Hughes Simmons of Jamaica, Mr. Ambrose Roberts of Chester, Mr. H. Rutter, Mr. K. Sutton, Mrs. Dorrie H. Taylor, Mr. E. W. Huson, Mr. Frank Tyrrell, Mrs. Aubrey W. Long, Colonel Arthur Churchill and Mrs. W. Radcliffe all helped with information.

The British Museum, Macmillan and Company, Rugby School, Harvard University, Princeton University, the New York Public Library, the Morgan Library, and the Cooper Union Library have been most generous in affording us the hospitality of their material, and Mrs. W. T. Walton has allowed us to use the rich collections at Rugby, Tennessee.

Unsparing assistance has been given by Miss Jean Macalister, Reference Librarian at the Columbia University Library, and by Mrs. Florence Poris in garnering information. Professors Emery Neff and Garrett Mattingley have read the manuscript and made invaluable criticisms and suggestions. And for our wives' contribution, even the dedication seems an inadequate tribute.

Contents

Illustrations

FOR RUTH *AND* FRANCES

CHAPTER ONE

Old England, 1822–1833

MOST ancient and famous of all the figures cut in the sides of the chalk downs of southern England is the White Horse near Uffington. Some say that it is the original of the heraldic dragon on the arms of England. Others point to its resemblance to the horse engraved on the earliest of British coins 2,000 years ago. Local tradition, built up around the queer attenuated shape, long nose, and gigantic body, has christened its setting Dragon's Hill, the place where the dragon was killed by St. George.

Certainly the turf which surrounds, and periodically obscures, the snowy outline, springs with history. For along the breezy top of Dragon's Hill once ran an old British trackway, while at its feet was built the Roman road. It cradled King Alfred, whose victory over the Danes was commemorated by a heap of sarsen stones less than a mile away. Like the moss which wrapped the stones, local tradition blurred the facts of its creation, and, by a process which tantalised and exasperated the scientific historian, it became known as Wayland Smith's Cave.

The vale itself was unique. Drayton, who toured England in the time of Queen Elizabeth, declared:

'This White Horse all the vales of Britaine would o'erbeare,
And absolutely sit in th'Imperiall chaire',

and Chesterton, 300 years later, declared:

'Before the gods that made the gods
Had seen their sunrise pass,
The White Horse of the White Horse Vale
Was cut out of the grass' [1]

I

Mary Ann Watts loved the White Horse, for father, grandfather, and great-grandfather had all held the living of Uffington. Mary Ann Watts would have held it too, had she been a man, but, being a woman, she did the next best thing, and married a clergyman. Him she persuaded to transfer from a canonry at St. Paul's to settle with her in Uffington. When she was barely twenty she bore a son, whom she determined should also live in the Watts tradition at Uffington.

Her husband, the Rev. Thomas Hughes, was middle-aged when she married him, and much wedded to London life. So, though they spent six months of each year in White Horse Vale, they spent the other six months in London. If the Canon was the rector, his young wife was the director, and ran both house and parish with an iron hand. Her good works, thrift (she helped only those who could show evidence of helping themselves), and capacity for making friends earned her the friendship of Walter Scott, who first shook her by the hand with 'a grip' she could 'only compare with a blacksmith's vice'; of R. H. Barham, to whom she suggested, not only the utilisation of his curious gift of rhyming, but also some of the subjects of the *Ingoldsby Legends*; of Harrison Ainsworth, who pursued the romance of the past with a zest which they all shared; and of the actress Mrs. Siddons and the poet Southey.

In such a literary climate her only son John spent his youth. Only ten years old when the nineteenth century began, he was never quite at home in the new century, and neither Westminster nor Oriel fired him with any desire to escape from under the parental wing. When he married, he settled down as a scholarly dilettante near his mother at Uffington. His wife, Margaret Wilkinson, daughter of Thomas Wilkinson of Stokesley Hall, Yorkshire, duly presented him with eight children: George, Tom, John, Walter Scott, Jane Elizabeth, William Hastings, Henry, and Arthur. The first five of these were born at Uffington.

Tom, the second son, was born on 20 October 1822 near the White Horse. It impressed him all his life; and was not only the subject of his second novel, but intruded itself into everything he wrote.[2]

2

Mary Ann Watts lived till her grandson Tom was thirty-one. Both from Uffington rectory and from her London house in Amen Corner she was a dominant influence, whether knitting worsted socks for his 'unwilling little feet', or making fish-nets to sweep the dace and chub from the streams. She saddled Tom's brother with the name of Hastings to secure the patronage of Sir Thomas Hastings. Once, when Tom dropped a gold sovereign, given to him by the Duchess of Buckingham, out of the carriage window, Mary Ann retrieved it. Instead of returning it, she bought him a pocket edition of Milton's poems inscribed with the words 'Thomas Hughes from the Duchess of Buckingham': thus virtually precluding him from admiring the great Puritan.

But going up to see her in London had its charms. Meeting and boarding the London coach was one of them. Years later the image was still fresh in Tom's mind:

'I can still vividly recall the pleasing thrill of excitement which ran through us when we caught the first faint clink of hoof and roll of wheels, which told of the approach of the coach before the leaders had appeared over the brow of the gentle slope some two hundred yards from the cross-roads where, recently deposited from the phaeton (dog carts not having been yet invented) we had been waiting with our trunk beside us in joyful expectation. Thrice happy if, as the coach pulled up to take us on board, we heard the inspiring words "room in front", and proceeded to scramble up and take our seats behind the box, waving a cheerful adieu to the sober family servant as he turned his horse's head slowly homeward, his mission discharged.' [3]

Nor was the ride with the coachman, Bob Naylor, any less thrilling than the anticipation, for Bob had a good voice and ear, and a great fund of songs and stories. As the coach swung into the gloom of Kensington, Tom, at the age of five, would imagine that it was indeed an Arabian night, as he saw the vases in a shop gleaming green and red and blue.

The quietude of Amen Corner, behind its big timber gates, with Fleet Street on one side and Newgate on the other, was emphasised by the distant murmurs which these two streets diffused. At times such quietness almost frightened him: on the day he visited Barham he wondered 'how any human being could live there during those bright autumn days', and only the hope of meeting Hood and Paul Pry at dinner led him to stay.[4] But there was always Henry New, the ex-prizefighter, Tom's first hero, to tell the boys stories of fairs and wakes, to take them to the Zoo, and teach them riding, boxing, and wrestling. At Amen House there was Sir Walter Scott, lion of them all.[5] And when other diversions palled, his grandfather would admit him to the study to enjoy the forbidden pleasures of melting lead, cooking apples, and moulding putty.

Such jinks and jaunts were great events, for most of Tom's life was spent at Uffington. 'Nothing pleased me so much as playing with the village children,' he confessed. White Horse Vale was insular, wild, and primitive; much removed from the civilised pleasures of the Kennet Valley. Till he was eleven he spent most of his time under the easy hand of his father, who wrote essays for *Blackwood's* under the *nom de plume* of 'Buller of Brasenose' (which his critics altered to 'Duller of Pewternose'), and *Ainsworth's Magazine*. His *Boscobel Papers* were praised by Mary Russell Mitford as uniting 'the most careful and accurate historical research with the rarer power which holds attention fixed upon the page'. 'Legend for legend, tale for tale, wisdom for wisdom, song for song, jest for jest,' she declared, he was a match for Geoffrey Chaucer.[6] A polyglot and artist, a story-teller and a mimic, he had all the qualities which enabled him to use his leisure to the full. Sir Walter Scott thought highly of him, and in the preface to *Quentin Durward* had praised his *Itinerary of Provence and the Rhone*.

Just as he could bring around him all the wild cattle of High Clare by calling from the box of his carriage, so he endeavoured to keep the country in order. According to his son, who idealised him as Squire Brown in *Tom Brown's Schooldays*, John Hughes had 'true popular sympathies'. He had played cricket and football all his life with his villagers, and proudly boasted that only one man from Uffington had joined the gangs of rick-burning rioters. Nevertheless, 'servants were servants,' the old Tory told his wife, 'bound not only to diligence but strict obedience and deference to the wishes of master and mistress.' Though he had once saved a Dissenter's house from burning, he regarded them as 'stiff necked and perverse'. From earliest years he commended industry as a Christian duty, since 'it usually pleases God so to dispose of the course of events, that those best qualified to be useful to others in their generation have the best prospect of success in it'.[7]

In accordance with such sentiments, it was but natural that Tom should read Maria Edgeworth's moral tales, then at the height of their popularity. He and his brother each wrote a letter to the little Irishwoman after reading *Frank and Rosamund*, asking her the contents of the remaining drawers in the wonderful Indian cabinet. To Tom aged six, and George his brother, then aged seven, Maria Edgeworth wrote a reply:

'I am glad that you can write as well as read; your two letters were both very well written, and I had pleasure in reading them. . . . I wish I could tell you anything more that would entertain you about the other nine drawers of the Indian cabinet; but what I am going to tell you will disappoint you I daresay, and I cannot help it. When Rosamund opened the 4th drawer she found in it —nothing—but a sheet of white paper at the bottom of the drawer, and on the paper was written only the word *China*. The writing was in a large round hand, like that in which your letter to me was written. Rosamund shut this drawer and opened the next, which was the 5th—empty! On the paper at the bottom of this drawer, in the same handwriting, was *Constantinople*. The 6th, the 7th, the 8th which she opened, were all empty! On the paper in the 6th drawer, which was very deep, was written *The North Pole and Iceland—Norway— Sweden and Lapland*. In the 8th drawer was written *Rome and Naples—Mount Vesuvius and Pompeii*. At the bottom of the 9th drawer, *Persia—Arabia and India*.

Then on the paper in the 9th drawer was written in small-hand and cramped writing without lines, and as crookedly as might be expected from a first attempt without lines, what follows:—

"I, little Matt. (which is short for Matthew), promise my dear good kindest of all aunts, Aunt Egerton, whom I love best in the world, that when I am grown up *quite* to be a great man, and when I go upon my travels as I intend to do when I am old enough and have money enough, I will bring her home all the greatest curiosities I can find for her in every country for these drawers. I have written in them the names of the countries I intend to visit, therefore I beg my dear aunt will never put anything in these 9 drawers till my curiosities come home. I will unpack them myself . . . ." '

Tom had no need to emulate Matt, for his own life was as happy as anything in fiction. As he roamed the countryside, he saw backswording, jingling, wrestling, jumping, and learned the strains of country ballads. Little wonder he 'loved every stone and turf' of the country where he was born and bred, and could write in *Tom Brown*:

'There's nothing like the old countryside for me, and no music like the twang of the real old Saxon tongue, as one gets it from the veritable chaw of the White Horse Vale'.[8]

3

According to Hughes himself, the most important single early influence on his life was that of his brother George. Thirteen months older than Tom, George was never separated from his brother for more than a week until he went up to Oxford in 1841; when, a year later, Tom joined him there they either shared the same rooms or were on the same staircase:

'Looking back over all those years, I can call to mind no single unkind, or un-worthy, or untruthful, act or word of his; and amongst all the good influences for which I have to be thankful, I reckon the constant presence and example of his brave, generous, and manly life as one of the most powerful and ennobling.' 9

Tom surely exaggerated the strength and virtues of a brother who preferred Tom when he was helpless and 'beholden' to him, and who subsequently achieved so little that he was overcome, like his father, by deep depression. But it is understandable that George should have seemed a tower of strength to the youthful Tom Hughes. Unlike his brother, who was shy and retiring in company, Tom loved talking to his father's guests, and was flippant, saucy, and sociable from his earliest years—qualities that immensely aided him later in adjusting to life. But he was, rather surprisingly, beset by fears. He was afraid to fire at rooks or to ride a horse bareback; he was poor at games. George, on the other hand, even resented being led by a leading-rein to his first hunt, and welcomed being 'blooded' at a fox-hunt. A half-century later Tom still remembered a dream in which a bear attacked his brother and himself. George got over the fence 'as easily as we should have done out of dreamland, while I, though I managed to catch hold of the top, had lost all power of scrambling up, and hung by my hands until I almost felt the big beasts' breath on my back'. George was the buckler and shield, protector of Tom when at school, participator in his pleasures when at home or at Amen Corner. Under his inspiration Tom conquered fear.

Their grandmother treated them both alike.

'She used to take me and my brother out shopping in the early morning, and our excursions extended as far as Billingsgate fish market, then at the height of the career which has secured for it an unenviable place in our English vocabulary. It was certainly a strange place for a lady and small boys, and is connected with the most vivid of my childish memories. Toddling after my grandmother to the stall where she made her purchases, we came one morning on the end of a quarrel between a stalwart fish-hag and her fancy man. She struck him on the head with a pewter pot which flattened with the blow. He fell like a log, the first blood I had ever seen, gushing from his temples, and the scene is as fresh as ever in my memory at the end of half a century. The narrow courts in that neighbourhood are still my favourite haunts in London.' 10

4

In contrast to Tom's rich contacts with people and places, the influence of books on his life before he went to Rugby seems to have been small. Symbolically, his freshest memory pertaining to reading was the unfortunate Milton episode. He did, however, read some poetry—more than anything else—and was familiar with *Robinson Crusoe, Pilgrim's Progress, Sandford and Merton*, as well as the books of Maria Edgeworth. These highly moral and instructive volumes, the conventional educational fare of the day, were supplemented by old ballads like 'Roland the Brave' and 'Durandarté', sung to him by a relative when he was ten, and by such books as Charles Waterton's *Wanderings in South America*, with its stories of how the 'mighty Cayman was caught and ridden, how the young boa constrictor was vanquished and carried home'.

5

In 1830, when he was eight years old, Tom and his brother George were sent to a private school at Twyford near Winchester. Here he met the first of his contemporary friends—the strange Charles Mansfield, later famous as the distiller of benzol from coal, and his partner in the great adventure of Christian Socialism. This school was ahead of the times in at least two respects: it gave prizes for gymnastics and extra marks for reading and learning poetry by heart, a custom called 'standing up'.

'We were allowed (within limits) to choose our own poets, and I always chose Scott from family tradition, and in this way learned the whole of the "Lady of the Lake", and most of the "Lay of the Last Minstrel" and "Marmion" by heart, and can repeat much of them to this day.' 11

Thus emerged the first of the intellectual influences that were to help shape Tom Hughes' beliefs, an influence to which he owed many of his views about the squirearchy, the Church, and the virtues of the traditional life of the countryside. But it was many years before books were to play a leading role in Tom Hughes' life. Even later on he tended to approach ideas through personalities rather than through literature. And he always showed a predilection, acquired in youth, for action and common sense as against theory, and for character as against intellect.

When Tom was eleven years old, his grandfather died. His grandmother promptly moved to Kingston Lisle, where she raised mustards and peppers of the Dandy Dinmont breed from dogs given her by Sir Walter Scott, and where Harrison Ainsworth, as her guest, wrote *Jack Sheppard* and *Guy Fawkes*. John Hughes, freed at last from the maternal apron-strings, took the opportunity to buy Donnington Priory, near Newbury, and there the family moved in 1833. Donnington was an ideal setting for a patriarchal squire such as John Hughes more and more aspired to be. The anxiety of these days was felt even amid the spacious life of Donnington, with its hunting and its gay parties. Now Margaret Hughes began to keep a school where the children of Donnington might learn the catechism, the three Rs, and 'good plain morals'. With her daughter Jane Elizabeth (Tom's sister) she tended the sick and helped the old. John forsook his hunting, and sent his pink hunting-coat to be dyed black. But the dyer made a mess of it, and traces of the original pink still showed along the seams.[12]

Even with all his efforts John Hughes was more and more haunted by his inability to find himself, and was increasingly pursued by a 'morbid consciousness of his own sin'. Not so his son. Tom learned to love Donnington Priory, a fine old mansion at the foot of the Castle hill, as much as he had Uffington. Near the Priory was Donnington Castle, where the Craven Hunt met, and near Donnington was Newbury, where two battles of the Civil War were fought. But here, for Tom, no battles were ever fought except on the archery green or the hunting-field. It was the setting of the happiest period of his life, the country where, ten years later, he was to court his future wife.

NOTES

[1] S. M. Ellis, *Wilkie Collins and Le Fanu* (London, 1931), 211–22.
[2] (T. Hughes) *The Scouring of the White Horse* (Boston, 1859), preface.
[3] *Lippincott's Magazine*, April 1876, 458.
[4] *New York Tribune*, 6 Sept. 1866.
[5] E. E. Brown, *True Manliness*, vi.
[6] M. R. Mitford, *Recollections of a Literary Life* (London, 1852), 488 and 500.
[7] T. Hughes, *Memoir of a Brother* (London, 1873), 13–14.
[8] *Tom Brown's Schooldays*, By an Old Boy (New York, 1928), 16.
[9] T. Hughes, *Memoir of a Brother*, xii.
[10] Brown, *True Manliness*, vi.
[11] *ibid.*, v.
[12] *Cornhill Magazine*, lviii (1925), 280, 'Fragments of Autobiography', ed. H. C. Shelley.

CHAPTER TWO

Rugby, 1833–1842

HAD his two sons been ready for school five years earlier, it is doubtful whether John Hughes would have sent them to Rugby. They might not have been sent to a public school at all, such was the low estimation of their value. Whether old, like Eton and Harrow, or new, like Shrewsbury and Rugby, such schools were backwaters in a fast-flowing time. The indictments against them had been mounting up, and the batteries of critics had been assaulting their antiquated curricula, barbarous conditions, and lack of adaptability.

Not that such arguments would weigh very heavily in John Hughes' mind, for, though a cultured and scholarly man alive to the mood of the times, his innate conservatism would probably have induced him to send the boys to his own old school: Westminster.

But in 1833 Dr. Thomas Arnold, a friend of his Oxford days, had been headmaster of Rugby for five years, and though, in his son's words, he was 'considerably exercised by the Doctor's politics, he shared that unhesitating faith in his character and ability which seems to have inspired all his contemporaries'.

I

Shortly after Tom arrived at Rugby he was invited to breakfast by Arthur Penrhyn Stanley, then about to leave school in the blazing glory of a Balliol scholarship.[1] Stanley was the embodiment of Arnold's deepest wishes: a scholar of intellectual honesty imbued with an almost painful moral earnestness and sense of responsibility. With C. J. Vaughan, who obtained a Trinity scholarship at the same time, these two set the pattern which A. H. Clough and Arnold's own sons Thomas and Matthew tried to follow, and to which Hughes' contemporary, John Conington, added much. The Arnoldian contingent at Oxford was an active cell in the forces of reform, taking, at the turn of the half-century, a lead in liberalising those ancient foundations.

But to Tom such boys were no patterns. He 'looked on them more as potential providers of extra half-holidays than with the enthusiasm of hero-worship'. Emulation was reserved for the

'Kings of the Close round whom clustered legends of personal encounters with drovers at the monthly cattle-fairs . . . or the navvies who were laying down the first line of the London and North-Eastern Railway, or the game-keepers of a neighbouring squire with whom the school was in a state of open war over the right of fishing in the Avon.' [2]

Stanley, who had arrived at Rugby in 1829, before Arnold's work had any appreciable effect, seems to have known little of the roughness so characteristic of the school, escaping the taunts of bullies no less than the worst of fagging, and winning respect for his individuality and privacy from old and young alike. Such treatment was 'unparalleled' in those days, as Stanley realised when he read *Tom Brown's Schooldays* and found it an 'absolute revelation', opening up 'a world of which, though so near to me, I was utterly ignorant'. Even five years later, when there had been much improvement, Rugby was still a 'very rough, not to say brutal place', as Tom Hughes, who led no charmed life, discovered. 'A small boy might be, and very frequently was, fagged for every moment of his play hours day after day; and there was a good deal of a bad kind of bullying.' Commenting on this passage in the *Memoir of a Brother*, the *Saturday Review*, Hughes' inveterate enemy, said that the bullying must certainly have been bad if an 'athletic Christian' like Hughes calls it bad.[3] The indiscriminately worshipped kings of the close were a 'rough and hard set of task-masters, who fagged us for whole afternoons, and were much too ready with the cane'.[4] These words of Hughes are corroborated by others, including Clough, who could write that 'even here at Rugby, the best of all public schools which are the best kind of schools, even here there is a vast deal of bad', and by Dr. Arnold himself, who was ever conscious of 'the wickedness of young boys', a wickedness that 'would be surprising, if I had not my own school experiences and a good deal since to enlighten me'.[5] The worst single incident of bullying mentioned by Hughes is Flashman's roasting of Tom Brown before the fire when he wouldn't sell a lottery ticket; but though, according to Jelfe, authorities agree that such roastings had occurred, they were certainly exceptional, and it is notable that Hughes nowhere mentions the incident in works of non-fiction. The more usual persecutions took the form of bullying at football, blanket-tossing, striking those who tried to say their prayers openly—the prayer incident in *Tom Brown* was based more or less on fact—and in general making life onerous for small boys. The prayer question was still acute in 1834, Hughes wrote in 1895, 'especially in one large bedroom' in Arnold's own house, which was 'dominated by two notorious bullies who set their faces against boys kneeling by their bedsides'. When a new boy, the future Lord Portsmouth, tried to pray, 'the brutes I have alluded to held him down on his knees and "slippered him".' No one interfered; 'in fact the other ten or eleven were quite small, and the "præpositer" of the room had not come up as it was before 10 o'clock'.

However, even in 1834 such incidents were exceptional and disapproved of by public opinion in the school. The Lord Portsmouth episode had in fact a beneficent effect. 'Several small boys took to saying their prayers openly,' mainly, Hughes believed, because of it. [6] Indeed, if we can believe what Hughes wrote over half a century later, fear of persecution was, in general, far worse than the reality.

'In my first three days, before the upper school came back, [I] imbibed dreadful notions of the life of slavery which lay before us. Study fagging and night fagging in the House, and all manner of outside fagging, would soon make me a sadder as well as wiser lower-school boy. I noticed that my informants showed few symptoms of the crushing tyranny of which they spoke, but nevertheless awaited with some misgivings the arrival of our taskmasters. Well, they came; and though House fagging was not pleasant, it was endurable, and as for outside fagging, I certainly enjoyed it for the first seven or eight weeks.' [7]

The worst ordeal seems to have been Island fagging, which, described vivaciously for us by Hughes, was characteristic of old customs preserved by generations of innately conservative public-school boys long after they have become meaningless. As Hughes says in *Tom Brown*, 'There are no such bigoted holders by established forms and customs be they never so foolish or meaningless, as English School-boys.' Apparently there had once been school gardens, inspected by trustees and visitors on Speech Day, which had been sold when boarding-houses were built there. But the garden procession on Speech Day had to go on, so the Island farce was invented. Four weeks before Easter, eighty or ninety boys— half the sixth form took no part and exempted their fags from doing so too—would line up in the Close and run for the bridge to the Island. The first six to get there and those able to jump the moat, were excused the job of digging up the sixth-form plots, into which the Island was divided, ostensibly in preparation for planting. The unfortunates were usually the younger boys, who rarely won, despite their handicap. They were given no tools but sticks—Hughes found a handle of a broken fives bat—with which to turn over ground packed hard by rain and from which the soil had all been washed away, leaving only stones and weeds. Punctuated by squabbles and tricks whenever no one watched, this useless and demoralising work lasted till second calling over— that is, through the whole of free time. And it was repeated on every ensuing half-holiday for four weeks, until even fags were ready, like the Roman plebeians, to mutiny against the 'unspeakable' patricians of the sixth. In the last week before Easter the beds were supposed to be ready for planting and had to be turfed round. The sixth rode in the carts, and the fags pulled in relays to where turf could be found; 'this was taken (without leave), cut into squares, and dragged back'. Hughes and his fellow sufferers got some revenge one day by running away with the cart and over-turning it. Next came the job of filling the neat borders.

'Our master simply gave us the order to "get flowers" without a hint as to how this was to be done. We had no money to buy with, and no friends to borrow from. Only one alternative remained, and to this we had recourse, I fear, without the compunction which we ought to have felt.'

They placed themselves opposite a gap in the hedge of a 're-spected Rugby solicitor', and, when the coast was clear, stole primroses and violets. On Speech Day everybody stood around in his best clothes, including the Doctor and the masters, and listened to the great ladies and others pay compliments 'to our VIth Form tyrant, instead of us, to whom all the credit (if any) was due'. The compliments, Hughes added, could hardly have been sincere, as the turfing was inartistic, and the 'flowers showed unmistakable signs of not having grown naturally in their place of exhibition'. 'The following year (1835) Speech Day was changed to summer, when cricket was on, and no one would have thought of Island fagging as possible. I have always thought that the Doctor got wind of the methods by which the Island was made suddenly to blossom with spring flowers at Easter', and that that was one of the reasons for the change.[8]

2

Like Tom Brown, whom he so much resembled in being 'sturdy' and 'competitive' rather than 'terrifying', 'sensitive', or 'imaginative', Tom Hughes made good at Rugby. As Tom Brown's friend East remarked, if a boy's 'got nothing odd about him and answers straightforward and holds his head up, he gets on'. And Tom Hughes got on. He made friends. He developed self-reliance, courage, and sportsmanship out of the rough games, pranks and escapades which the relatively free life of the unreformed public school permitted. Above all, he enjoyed himself.

Big Side Hare and Hounds was typical of an activity both onerous and pleasurable. It occurred in February and March, and was compulsory for all but the sixth, of whom there were too many not 'to make a bolt on the way to the meet a perilous adventure'. Tom had, however, no desire to make a bolt, enjoying the start with its scent-boys going ahead, 'then the stripping of the crack hounds, whose jackets were confided to boys with orders where to meet the owners at the end of "the run in",' 'the waiting, and then the forward', after which 'compulsion was at an end'. 'In the second or third field the tailing off began, and all but the cracks fell out by twos or threes, the studious to get back to their studies, and the rest of us to go "pecking" along the hedge rows, or to strike the road, and patter along it to Bilton, Brownsover, Newhold, or wherever the run in might be'.[9]

Rugby football was, as any reader of *Tom Brown* knows, the heart of public-school life for Hughes. 'This is worth living for; the whole sum of schoolboy existence gathered up into one straining, struggling half-hour, a half-hour worth a year of common life.' The feast after the victory was an occasion of gargantuan proportions, with its 'jolly boys', its piles of food, its songs and toasts, and its climactic speech—'plain, strong, straight like his play'—by that gaunt Achilles, Old Brooke, who summed up for his eager listeners the lesson of the occasion in one phrase: 'we've union, they've division'. Never, the parting hero asserted, would there again be 'eight such years' of happiness, and generations of boys and men have believed him.

In time Tom Hughes became, as captain of 'Bigside' at football and head of the cricket eleven, an Old Brooke himself. He led the school eleven in a memorable match against an M.C.C.

team captained by Lord Charles Russell, half-brother to the famous Lord John; going in first 'to give his men pluck' and making the highest score for his side. He also stumped one man and bowled another. This match, played in the Close at Rugby on 17 June 1841, was undoubtedly the source for 'Tom Brown's last match'. Tom Arnold has drawn him for us attractively at fifteen, just before he became a leader. He was

'tall for his age; his long thin face, his sandy hair, his length of limb, and his spare frame, gave him a lankiness of aspect which was the cause, I suppose, that the boys gave him the extraordinary nickname of "executioner". No name could be less appropriate, for there was nothing inhuman or morose or surly in his looks, and still less in his disposition, the temper of a bully was utterly alien from him, and he was always cheerful and gay.'

A good runner, it was a pleasure to see him as a hare,

'lightly clad, and with a bag of "scent" strapped round him. He was too keen-eyed and observant to be specially popular, but all the small boys liked him because he was kind and friendly to them.' [10]

3

They were stirring times to be at school. The disturbance which the navigators caused in the school was nothing to the excitement which the railway promoters caused in the country at large. A mania gripped the public, and in the year 1836–1837 alone 1,000 miles of track was firmly promoted. The coach which used to carry Tom and his brother down to London was supplanted by the train. The boys used to board it and behave with high spirits; climbing down amongst the luggage and between the carriages with reckless abandon. 'Most reckless of all', recorded Tom Hughes, not without sly humour, 'was W. P. Adam'— later to be Chief Whip of the Liberal Party from 1874 to 1880.

There were other outside events to excite the boys. The great Nassau balloon, which had been exhibited to the inhabitants of London in repeated ascents from Vauxhall Gardens, made an experimental voyage on 7 November 1836 with Green, Holland, and Monck-Mason in the car. Having been for eighteen hours in the air, the three balloonists descended safely at Weilburg in the Duchy of Nassau. A month later, Tom's brother George wrote home saying:

'There has been a great balloon mania in the school lately; everybody has been making a balloon. We set them off with spirits of wine lighted under them, and then run after them. They generally go about five miles, and we recover them after a hard run. I have cut one out myself from tissue paper, and I will bring it home that I may have the pleasure of setting it off before Jenny.'

4

Studies are hardly ever mentioned in *Tom Brown's Schooldays*. The 'Head of Bigside', Tom wrote in 1881, 'has very little time to give to inferior industries, such, for instance, as the cultivation of Greek Iambics or Latin Alcaics'.[11] Besides, public-school Latin grammar seemed to Tom discouragingly difficult from the first, and he easily slipped into the comfortable assumption that there was nothing he could do to raise himself above the 'unpromising three-quarters' of the school. Both Tom's tutor, Cotton (the young master of *Tom Brown*, who later became headmaster of Marlborough and then bishop of Calcutta), and Dr. Arnold himself showed astonishing 'patience and forbearance' with their incorrigibly idle pupil. Arnold, Hughes later asserted, was willing to kick an unpromising pupil twenty yards yet would stick with him so long as he fell back only nineteen. Day after day he laboriously corrected Hughes' 'frightful copies of verses, and Greek and Latin prose', encircling each false concord or quantity with a black line or 'picture frame'. He did this 'slowly and grimly, his under lip seeming to grow out as the pen went deliberately round the wretched words, and one did not feel good during the operation'.[12]

Despite Arnold's patience, Tom might 'have been advised to go elsewhere early in my career but for a certain fondness for history and literature which Arnold discovered in me and which (I fancy) covered a multitude of sins'. Stimulated in Cotton's 'pupil room' by accounts of the fights between patricians and plebeians in ancient Rome, this was first discovered by Arnold when, at a monthly examination of one of the lower forms, he

'asked the head boy why it was the Romans had so specially rejoiced over the terms of a certain treaty with the Parthians (we were reading Horace, I think). It came all down to the lowest bench, where I was, and I said 'because they got back the eagles taken from Crassus' and sent a gleam of pleasure into the Doctor's face which was getting rather grim. Up I went to the top of the form, and from that time he often asked me questions outside the textbook and specially by way of illustration from Scott's novels, to which he was fond of referring.'

Only once, to his grief and humiliation, did Tom fail the Doctor. Arnold had asked the head of the school—Tom was now in the sixth form—to illustrate from Scott's novels Aristotle's remark that old age was absorbed in petty interests. The able scholars, including young Matthew Arnold, all failed, much to Arnold's chagrin, since there was a distinguished visitor present. Turning to Tom, 'the Doctor paused for several seconds with a confident look. But no response came and he passed on, "and I was left lamenting". I shall always remember the sore feeling at having disappointed him whom of all men I most wished to please.' [13]

5

Tom, idle as he was, had learned to love and respect the great headmaster. The image of Dr. Arnold—'the tall, gallant form, the kindling eye, the voice, now soft as the low notes of a flute, now clear and stirring as the call of the light infantry bugle'—that lifts *Tom Brown's Schooldays* so far above the average school story, was already forming in young Tom's mind. For the rest of his life Tom Hughes was to feel that no one was a greater teacher than Dr. Arnold, who, he said over fifty years later, gave education 'a soul and a purpose which it had wanted since Elizabeth's day'.[14] Nor, as he came later to believe, was anyone—with the possible exception of Maurice and Shaftesbury—a sounder guide on the social questions agitating Christendom. But there is no evidence that the great headmaster had corresponding feelings about Tom while he was at school. Though Arnold might be patient with his recalcitrant pupil's faults and appreciative of his virtues, Tom Hughes was not the sort of boy who could belong to Dr. Arnold's inner circle. Readers of *Tom Brown's Schooldays* who remember it as the story of Dr. Arnold will be surprised to find on re-reading how small a part the headmaster plays. Until near the middle of the book he is entirely off-stage, the reputed strong man putting down bad customs. His first appearance is as God, the father, preaching inspiring words from the pulpit. Later, when Tom does have personal contacts with him, they are never intimate ones: Arnold is lenient to Tom after his misbehaviour during Hare and Hounds thus inducing shame at a loss of reputation for steadiness; and—after thrashing him for breaking rules—Arnold lectures him once on the need of developing a sense of duty. If Tom Brown is eventually won to love of Arnold and a vision of work in God's service, his transformation comes not directly through Arnold, but through the agency of the weak Arthur, whom Tom defends and who gets Tom to stop cribbing and warring on the masters. Tom does not even realise until just before he leaves school that Arnold had planned his relationship to Arthur.

Tom Hughes' failure to achieve intimacy with Dr. Arnold (along with the qualities of his personality that precluded such intimacy) saved him from the soul-shattering experiences that Clough, Stanley, and even Matthew Arnold underwent. Dr. Arnold, who hated childishness, could not help putting pressure on his favourites to grow up prematurely, to develop an intellectual awareness and spiritual drives that were almost morbidly intense. As a consequence they were torn asunder when, without Dr. Arnold's aid, they had to face the realities of an adult world. Clough in particular found himself emotionally at sea when his beliefs were challenged at Oxford and he could find no outlet for his desire to reform the world. Matthew Arnold's 'Dover Beach' and 'Rugby Chapel' show how deeply the acids of modernity bit into those most devoted to Dr. Arnold and how desperately they needed the master's presence.

Hughes never felt such a need. Indeed, he was never, during most of his time at school, completely won over to discipleship of Arnold, no matter how much he might admire him. Tom did not become an intellectual; he was 'furiously on the other side' when Arnold expelled his brother George, though later he came to believe that George 'was in the wrong'; and when he was captain of 'Bigside', he at least once aligned himself with the 'customs and traditions as to discipline, which are almost sacred to the boys, but scarcely recognised by the masters'. Tom had control of the cricket and football funds, which were traditionally used to pay for the School House supper, but which Arnold had decreed could not be used for this purpose, since they belonged to the whole school. But the boys rebelled and had a select supper without leave, smuggling in wine and spirits, on which some got drunk and destroyed a few library books, made a row in the bedrooms, and damaged the furniture. Hughes not only gave the money, but also attended.

23

6

Nevertheless, Arnold's influence on Hughes, which increased each year, was pervasive and profound. Through the classroom, the Chapel services, the few personal contacts, and the sort of planning from afar recorded in *Tom Brown*, Arnold gradually exerted command over Tom's spirit. Tom could not, as he says movingly in *Tom Brown*, but be touched by one who 'Sunday after Sunday' witnessed and pleaded 'for his Lord, the King of righteousness and love and glory, with whose Spirit he was filled, and in whose power he spoke'. Even the irreligious felt the power of 'a man speaking' not with a 'cold clear voice' from 'serene heights', but as one fighting 'by our side' and 'calling on us to help him and ourselves and one another' to strive 'against whatever was mean and unmanly and unrighteous in our little world'.

Perhaps Arnold's historical comments and digressions deepened the social insights of his otherwise unrewarding pupil. His weekly history lesson to the sixth form enabled him to dilate on the rift between the Norman upper classes and their Saxon inferiors: a rift as plain in the eighteen thirties (according to Arnold) as ever, and becoming wider as increasing wealth estranged the classes. Arnold was never tired of teaching social wisdom through his lessons: subjects were for him mere vehicles for ideas. The social bearing of these ideas is plain to anyone who reads the thirteen letters which he addressed to the *Sheffield Courant* in 1833. But to Hughes the social bearing of such ideas was only revealed when he was able to stand outside the school and take stock of his position. And it was Stanley's *Life of Arnold*, published in 1844, which was the agent of this revelation.

There was little doubt, however, about the immediate influence of Arnold's behaviour in the affair of the football funds. When Tom admitted his presence at the dinner, Arnold did not punish him, but wrote him a friendly letter, telling him how shocked he was, how he had assumed, because he was used to being confident of his sixth form, that Tom wasn't there, and how the future of the school depended on the reliability of the sixth. Hughes dates his final allegiance to Arnold, to whom he now felt he owed more than he could ever repay, to this letter. And he forever revered the wisdom of the master who could turn a 'moral breakdown' into 'a source of strength in later years'.[15]

While he remained at school, Tom was Arnold's faithful lieutenant in the war of the sixth against the louts of the fifth form and the bad customs of the school. For the rest of his life he retained the impress of Arnold's beliefs and the memory of his personality as a symbol of those beliefs. Arnold did not give Hughes the habit of merciless intellectual probing, but he endowed him with an open-mindedness that made for tolerance and a willingness 'to change an old opinion the moment I can get a better one'. He increased Tom's democratic leanings. Even at school Tom resented the 'insolent airs with which casual intruders in fustian or corduroy were extruded' from the Close, and opened the cricket-fields on summer evenings to the best players of the town, with whom he organised matches. Above all, Arnold gave Tom 'faith in and loyalty to Christ' and the desire to engage in the big fight against evil, 'which would last all our lives, and try all our powers, physical, intellectual, and moral, to the utmost'.

Arnold did not unsettle and remake Hughes' life; but he gave it breadth and meaning. 'You may well believe', Hughes said years later, 'what a power Rugby has been in my life.' The years from ten to eighteen are the most important in a boy's life, and 'I passed all those years under the spell of this place and Arnold, and for half a century have never ceased to thank God for it'.[16]

NOTES

[1] Lt.-Col. S. Selfe, *Notes on the Characters and Incidents depicted by the Master Hand of Tom Hughes in Tom Brown's Schooldays* (Rugby, 1909), 5, quoted Fanny Hughes as saying that the two did not meet until *Tom Brown* had been published.

[2] T. Hughes, *The Manliness of Christ* (London, 1894) (1879), 232, 'Address at Rugby'.

[3] *Saturday Review*, 3 May 1873, 593.

[4] Brown, *True Manliness*, vii ff.; Hughes, *Memoir of a Brother*, 21; *Manliness of Christ*, 232.

[5] Old Rugbeian, *Recollections of Rugby* (London, 1848); *Parents' Review*, November 1895; Clough, *Poems and Prose Remains*, i, 56-57; Stanley Arthur Penrhyn, *The Life and Correspondence of Thomas Arnold* (New York, 1846), 168.

[6] Letter from Hughes, 6 March 1895, in possession of Rugby School. See also *Parents' Review*, November 1895, 641, 834.

[7] *Sybil*, 1890, 5 ff., 'The Island in 1834'.

[8] *ibid.*

[9] *ibid.*

[10] Arnold, Thomas, *Passages in a Wandering Life* (London, 1900), 32.

[11] Hughes, Thomas, *Rugby, Tennessee* (London, 1881), 133.

[12] Hughes, *Manliness of Christ*, 213 ff.

[13] Hughes, *Manliness of Christ*, 216, 1892, 'Address at Rugby'; Hughes, Thomas, *Vacation Rambles* (London, 1895), 376.

[14] Hughes, *Manliness of Christ*, 1892, 'Address at Rugby', 209, 220.

[15] *ibid.*, 216–220.

[16] Brown, *True Manliness*, x, xi; *A Layman's Address to Rugby School, Quinquagesima Sunday* 1891, 8 Feb. (London, 1891).

CHAPTER THREE

Courts and Courting, 1842–1848

TOM was 'much averse' to going to Oxford: 'dreadfully loath to leave Rugby'. 'I knew', he confessed, 'that my scholarship was too weak to allow me to take anything like high honours.' But his father was an Oriel man: over thirty years before, he had not only won a prize for reciting a Latin verse entitled *Herculaneum*, but had also been selected to speak before the great Duke of Wellington in 1814. Tom's brother George was already in residence, and was a member of the Oriel boat which went to the head of the river—the only time during the century—in the very year he came up.[1]

He lived on his brother's staircase, and naturally was drawn to the sporting circle in which George moved with such commanding mastery and distinction. The intellectual centre of gravity of the University was passing from Oriel to Balliol: Keble had resigned, Newman was at Littlemore, and the Provost, Dr. Hawkins, cold, stiff, and punctilious, had condemned *Tract XC* in the previous year. Now, in Hughes' words, he was 'high and dry . . . very methodical, very conservative, who looked even on his old friend Arnold with some misgiving'.[2] Hawkins' anti-tractarian zeal ate deeply into the routine work of the college, which suffered accordingly. Thus, though Oriel had once led the class lists, now the mere appearance of an Oriel name during the decade calls for comment. So, as Hughes said, 'with the exception of Christ Church, there was at this juncture probably no college in Oxford less addicted to reading for the schools, or indeed to intellectual work of any kind'.[3]

I

Of the fifty or so undergraduates in residence, half a dozen were gentlemen commoners, who paid double fees and battell bills, for the privilege of wearing silk gowns and velvet caps (adorned with gold tassels for the sons of peers), foregoing lectures, and dining at five in the evening with the fellows. These gentlemen commoners

'dressed gorgeously; hunted in the two winter terms; and, in the summer, drove tandem, frequented the Bullingdon and Isis Clubs, and the not very respectable premises of Milky Bill, the dog fancier, where their bull terriers drew badgers and they shot pigeons.'

Between this and another minority of scholars, the remaining three-quarters of the undergraduates were strenuous athletes. 'As regards this important department of education,' wrote Hughes, 'no accomplished young Aristotelian could have joined a more distinguished school.' The football eleven played colleges twice its size; the rowing eight was at the head of the river. Some of the men, like James Mackie (later to be M.P. for Kirkcudbrightshire), a schoolfellow of Tom's, were of great strength and stature. Of all the sports in which the vast majority of its undergraduates engaged, none was so popular as boxing. Hughes called Oriel 'the accepted home of the noble science of self-defence', and continued:

'It almost supported a retired prize fighter, who had been known in the ring as "The Flying Tailor" (a first rate teacher of boxing, however moderate his sartorial talents might have been), and cordially welcomed any stray pugilist who might be training in the neighbourhood and was in need of a pound or two. There were regular meetings in some of the largest rooms two or three times a week, at which our college men, of all weights from eight stone upwards, might find suitable matches; and occasional public gatherings at the Weirs, or Wheat Sheaf, promoted by Oriel men for the benefit of one or other of these professionals.' [4]

Even the youngest don, James Fraser, was both a dandy and sportsman. With blue frock-coat of perfect cut, light waistcoat, and lavender trousers, he owned one of the best horses in the University, and whenever the Berkshire Hunt met near Oxford, would ride over to join them. Fraser's hold upon the undergraduates, too, depended not so much on his wrestling with metaphysics, as his success against James Mackie, whom he encountered by accident in a dark corridor. By evading Mackie's bear-like grip, and giving as good as he got, Fraser won respect.

Of other dons, or other contemporaries, we hear little from Hughes. Of 'vastiest' Goldwin Smith, of John Conington with his green-cheese, bespectacled face, or Thorold Rogers, of William Stubbs, of E. A. Freeman, all of whom were contemporary with Tom at the University, scarcely a word is mentioned. For in his first half-year Tom was picked to play cricket for the University against Cambridge.

The match, seventh of the series in which both sides had so far each won three, was played at Lord's on 12 June 1842 on an intensely hot day. Tom went in fifth wicket down and was one of five to make a duck in the first innings. He redeemed this, however, by carrying his bat in the second innings as top-scorer with fifteen. Oxford lost by 162 runs. On the very same day, his brother George was rowing in the Oxford boat against Cambridge. Tom, with filial loyalty, bet £5 that Oxford would win, for they were losing the cricket match.

Rowing, in fact, was coming into its own, and George Hughes did much to raise its popularity by his dramatic part in the University boat race of 1843 when he stroked an Oxford crew of seven (the bow oar being vacant) to beat Cambridge. The crowd went mad with excitement, and 'a small, decorous, shy man in spectacles, who had probably never pulled an oar in his life' led a mob of Oxford undergraduates in pulling down a heavy toll-bar gate and throwing it in the river.[5]

In the term following this triumph, Tom rowed number 2 in the intercollegiate four-oar races, eating the half-cooked meat then prescribed as training-food. In his first race he was unfortunate enough to catch a crab in the second stroke after the start. But, fortunately for him, his brother's presence of mind got the prow of the boat into the centre of the river once more, and they chased the fast-vanishing Balliol boat. Oriel drew level as they came to the Cherwell, and Tom had the pleasure of passing his old schoolfellow, T. Walrond, who was rowing bow in the Balliol boat. Oriel won by a few feet, and the following day went on to beat the cup-holders, University College.

Except for this feat, Tom's first year at Oxford was, as he later wrote, 'utterly wasted'. Work was easy, and, falling into an 'idle, fast set', he made a fool of himself 'in the usual ways'. This dissipation was melodramatised in *Tom Brown at Oxford*, which, though substantially accurate as an account of unreformed Oxford, is not always reliable as autobiography. In the novel, Tom, no introvert like his schoolfellow, Clough, becomes bosom friends with the aristocratic Drysdale and his *nouveau riche* hangers-on— the impoverished, supercilious Piers St. Cloud and the snobbish

Chanter, whose father sold bad rails to the railway companies. From these, Tom Brown learned to swear, to gamble, and to keep late hours. The novel was spiced with sex, Tom Brown enjoying the friendship of a barmaid. After participating for weeks in Drysdale's rather stale orgies, he was persuaded by the more serious Hardy to desist from taking her to Abingdon Fair:

'If you go to Abingdon Fair with her in the company of Drysdale and his mistress', Hardy concludes, 'or, I believe in any company, you will return a scoundrel, and she ——; in the name of the honour of your mother and sister, in the name of God, I warn you.'

2

The flesh of the real Tom Hughes 'never much enjoyed that kind of thing and got very sick of it' by the time he had taken his little-go. Especially was this so after 10 August 1843, when he became engaged to Frances Ford. 'This pulled me up short,' he confessed; it was 'the most important event of my life'. Like Tom Brown of his novel, who met the heroine Mary in the vacation, Tom Hughes became disgusted with the billiards, steeplechasing, and tandems of his friends, who, he now saw were slaves to their passions.

Just as Mary's father was opposed to the engagement in the novel, so James Ford, Fanny's father, 'very properly said we were silly young people and must not see one another for years, or correspond that we might see whether we really knew our minds'. James Ford, who became Prebendary of Exeter in 1849, was confirmed, if not animated, in his decision by his wife—a former Miss Frances Nagle, whose snobbish pretentions, derived from a connection with the family of Edmund Burke, were reinforced by expectations of property in Shropshire. Two of Fanny's aunts were of the nobility: one being a sister of the tenth Lord Cranstoun, and the other the daughter of the Earl of Essex. Her uncle, who married both these ladies in turn, was Richard Ford, gourmet, wit, anecdotist, art-critic, and connoisseur: generally credited with the introduction of Amontillado sherry and the works of Velasquez into England.[6]

'I went back to Oxford a new man', declared Hughes. He cut his expenses, lived decently, and took his degree as soon as possible without coaching. From 21 August 1843—ten days after he had become engaged—he began to keep a journal in which he entered the experiences he was forbidden to communicate. This brought Fanny, he felt, 'nearer to myself. . . . I can almost fancy you are looking over my shoulder; even though you should never see this book, it will always be a satisfaction to me to read it over and to remember the feeling with which I wrote it.' [7] He did not write down everything: politics would not interest her, and besides, there were some things which it was not proper for her to hear. Were he to annotate everything, 'I should fill the book in a couple of days'.[8]

They had first become acquainted in the winter of 1842–1843, when everyone got 'so conveniently ill and we used to take those long rambles together by the Old Castle'. In the spring he was writing to her, gossiping about friends, telling stories of Oxford, which forbade boys and girls to walk *tête-à-tête*, lecturing her on Byron and Shakespeare. By April he was asking for 'a little hair of some other person . . . I daresay you can guess whose I mean . . . however I must not say anything more about it I fear, so must live in the hope of one day or other *finding* a lock by the wayside'.[9]

Fanny's response was immediate and favourable. She sent a fine auburn tress, which still survives. She welcomed his letters, and confessed in the very first one she wrote that she was glad he still possessed 'the little faded rosebud'. She didn't 'at all object to reading "hard stuff" with you'; disliked most young men because they tried to be 'witty and sentimental at once' and 'tease me in every way as they all see Papa watches me'. Her complaints about Papa were both spirited and tolerant:

'I heard Papa and Uncle agree that no young lady should go out under 18, I am only just 17, and indeed then I doubt my going out as I know Papa likes to have me completely *under him*, until he has "formed my character" and I fear I have not much to form; and even if I had, the great thing with him is to do all I am told; I never look cross at anything.'

She preferred Donnington, where she can 'do what I like pretty much (except *some few* things) as he does not think so much about me away from home. How I am longing for that time!'

When her parents had enforced the separation, Fanny was courageous and romantic, ready without reserve to pledge her faith in an uncharted future. The ban, she wrote in her second letter,

'does seem *very* hard, but I shall try to bear it well and look forward to the future, for I have such perfect trust in you that unless I hear from your own mouth that you repent of the letter you wrote to me last week tho it may be more than a year before we meet I shall believe you feel the same and I do sincerely hope that you will put the same trust in me and believe (whatever others may say) that I love you, (always shall do so) more than anything in the world. I dread Tuesday very much, but after all, time passes very fast and we can think of one another, for that no one can prevent, and no doubt the time will come when we shall laugh at all this together tho it is rather sad now.

This will show you that *I* consider (whatever you may say) myself *engaged* to you tho I am not so, and do not and never shall repent of not returning the letter, on the contrary the contents of it gave me the greatest possible happiness.' 10

Tom bore the separation with stoicism. He had been visiting the Fords when her father announced that Fanny and Tom must see each other no more. Tom was thus deprived of 'the last day' of Fanny's company. To make matters worse, Tom met her on the stairs as he was leaving.

'Dear Fanny you don't know how nearly your swollen eyes upset me; however I managed to walk to the gate, looking back over my shoulder all the time at your window; why did not you look out? But I can guess, poor Fanny.'

Her father walked down the hill with Tom, and spoke 'very kindly on the whole', shaking hands with him 'very heartily at the gate'.

'I was never very desponding, and always look on the bright side of things', Tom confessed, and the journey home soon showed it. He managed 'to play far the best knife and fork of the two' (his friend Vicary was the other) at 'some very tough beef stakes' (they were as tough as stakes, he added wryly) 'and eggs and bacon', to which he sat down soon after. Next morning it rained, and Tom had to walk thirty miles to Dartmoor:

'I was quite wet through, but as jolly as possible and by the time I got half way across I began singing to the great astonishment of two old farmers, whom I likewise disgusted by remarking what a fine day it was, at the ninth milestone I sat down and positively laughed for I had been picturing to myself what jolly old people we shall be if we live long enough, and also I had been making vows to myself to purchase a large musical box that played waltzes that we might waltz undisturbed when we meet again—whew! Why should they keep us apart; we shall not be such fools as to marry without their consent, and separating us can answer no other end but the prevention of such a step.'

The following morning Tom wrote to assure Fanny's father that he would obey him to the letter, 'as if I had not promised you would have been continually harassed and compelled to show your letters'. After talking the matter over with his own father, Tom even agreed—though he did not regret his step or offer to retrace it—that it had been somewhat unfair to Fanny to tie her, who must bear the brunt, to a long engagement:

'God knows that this very thought has been paining me ever since I knew how I felt towards you. . . . Whatever may be the result of our probation may God grant that you may not suffer in spirits by it. . . . I do not think you will give in to melancholy thoughts, while you are sure that I am the same and on that point dear, you need never doubt.' 11

Fanny's parents were not, however, willing to take any chances on the lovers' good sense; for, in spite of Tom's promises, they opened and read Fanny's mail, nearly causing Tom to break his word.

Even James Ford's defences were finally broken down, however, by the patience and determination of the lovers. Though Tom did hear from Fanny through her correspondence with his sister Jeannie, and Fanny once saw the Journal, in October 1844, they faithfully kept their promises, and their love for one another but increased. So in May 1845, a few days after Tom finished his final examinations at Oxford, and ten months before the ban was supposed to be lifted, the old man began to relent.

'I have heard such news dear Fanny,' Tom wrote in his Journal, 'that I can scarcely contain myself, or credit it; my father has forwarded me a letter of your fathers, in which he sends me his kindest regards and talks quite as if he had made up his mind *to the worst*; besides which, a few days ago Mary Potter showed me a letter of yours containing a conversation with your mother in which she talks calmly of our engagement: Can such things be? I think after this you *must* be allowed to come to Donnington at Christmas and then ! and then ! ! and then ! ! ! but I won't anticipate.'

Though Tom and Fanny had two more years to wait before they were finally united, by October they were permitted to correspond with 'all restrictions taken off' (the last Journal entry is September 21st) and Fanny did come to Donnington at Christmas. For starved lovers this seemed a plentiful crop of happiness, and Tom averred—only half-seriously since he knew that she was 'having the *bitters* of our probation to bear'—that he now 'didn't care a pin if we wait till 1849'. In case she protested, 'What the deuce am I to be doing all this time?' Tom had his answer ready: 'Learning to make puddings and mend stockings'. The future, he was confident, would take care of itself.

C

33

3

The Journal is most complete for the time that Tom spent at Donnington, which includes two three-month periods from August to October 1843 and from December 1844 to March 1845, when he was reading for his degree. Because he had the leisure to write and because Fanny would, he knew, be interested in all the domestic gossip, Tom has recorded every detail of the gay, comfortable, secure life of his home, a life that accounts so largely for his confidence in himself and his characteristic good nature, no less than for some of his limitations.

At Donnington, even more than at school and college, sports of one kind or another were the chief occupation of the day. Tom played cricket for a local team, fished with his brother, swam, punted, shot snipe, wood-pigeons and moorhens, rode horseback, and did gymnastics. There was also much leisurely strolling into Newbury, occasional visits to church, where Tom at least once gave more thought to Fanny, he was 'ashamed to say', than to Mr. Slocock's sermon, and a great deal of sociability. Brothers, uncles, and friends were constantly dropping in for an hour, a day, or a week, to dine, to play whist, or to gossip and reminisce. Occasionally there were local theatricals, native revels, and dances.

Once, because her name was Fanny and because she was his cousin, Tom permitted himself a slight flirtation with a girl named Fanny Wilkinson. He sat *tête-à-tête* with her in the greenhouse smoking a cigar and talking of the other Fanny, he danced a cotillion, played blind man's buff, and took long rides with her, and even kissed her on one occasion, dutifully reporting everything to his fiancée. But he soon found out that cousin is a dangerous relationship. Though Tom claimed that he 'never said a word to her but what I should have *wished* you to hear', the lady and her mother took him seriously, and, when they found he was engaged, wrote him a letter that made Tom feel smaller than he had ever felt in his life. As a curious sort of self-punishment Tom sent Fanny Wilkinson a pencil case that he 'particularly valued' because it was meant for Fanny Ford.

4

In these years at Donnington, however, Tom began also for the first time to read with some avidity and to cultivate his literary talents in a modest way. Mostly he read the current best-sellers or the standard classics: *Peter Priggins* (a new novel of college life), Dickens's *Christmas Carol*, just out, *Pride and Prejudice* ('the character of Elizabeth is very like you dear'), *The Taming of the Shrew*, Pope's *Iliad*, and the family friend, Scott, whom he re-read almost daily. But there were also historical and religious works. The Journal specifically mentions Stevens's *Travels in Arabia Petrœa*, read as material for a college poem, *Evelyn's Memoirs* ('a most graphic picture' of the most interesting times 'of our national history, save the last 60 years'), Southey's *Book of the Church*, Evans's *Scriptural Biography*, and, above all, the writings of Dr. Arnold. Tom's Rugby tutor, Cotton, had given him Arnold's *Sermons on Christian Life* of 1841, when he left for Oriel, and he read it carefully and constantly. The Journal for 22 December 1844, records his finishing one of Arnold's 'most beautiful sermons'; how much, he adds, 'not only I but all who were his pupils' owe to him.

Arnold died in 1842, and shortly afterwards appeared Stanley's famous life of the headmaster.

'I am reading Arnold's life,' the Journal says on November 12, 1844, 'which is a most delightful book, it gives such a picture of the active and enquiring mind whose every energy is devoted to God's service; no man I should think ever did more good in his generation.'

It is probable, too, as *Tom Brown at Oxford* says (though the Journal is silent on these matters), that Tom pursued his interest in Roman history in these years and began to read the political economists and social thinkers, especially Carlyle, whose style and ideas so much influenced the mature Hughes. *Past and Present*, the most widely read of mid-nineteenth-century social tracts, appeared in 1843, and there is no reason to doubt that Tom Hughes, like Tom Brown, read it on its appearance. Years later, Hughes wrote that he had had the 'Carlyle fit' while at Oriel, and that the 'old man' had done him and his contemporaries much good 'when we were raw youths'.[12]

The writing at which Hughes tried his hand during his college days was of the strictly amateur sort, interesting chiefly because it indicated that Tom was attracted in that direction long before he turned out *Tom Brown's Schooldays*, itself written, be it remembered, as the casual occupation of an idle day. Besides college exercises (a poem called *The Nile*, another called *Petra*, and some English verses on the Norman conquest—the only lines he ever had read out in hall while at Oxford), Tom mentions writing an 'absurd farrago in imitation of the Noctes Ambrosianae' (such a farrago was to appear in print fourteen years later), a short story called 'Columbia', and a number of imitations of English songs and poems. Tom had a characteristic English dislike of foreign, especially Italian music, because of what he called its 'flourishes', and actually frowned on Fanny's listening to much of it. But he was *very* fond of simple airs when coupled with good words'. Tom Moore was naturally a favourite poet, and Tom began the following, he says, 'in a state most completely Tommy Moorish', though 'I found my pen running into nonsense immediately'.

> 'Waking or sleeping
> Thine image I see,
> Laughing or weeping
> Thou art ever with me;
> When the spray leaves the fountain
> As it roars down the line,
> When the mist, on the mountain
> No more shall be seen,
>
> When on Dartmoor no rain falls
> When Pengreep is not dull,
> When at Barley no ass calls
> To pester and fool,
> When all that is joined now
> In sunder shall be;
> Then dearest, thine image
> Shall wander from me.'

He also quoted in the Journal his parody of one of Mrs. Butler's (Fanny Kemble's) poems, taken from a book of hers given him by his grandmother, which contained, he felt, 'the best verses of the sort I have seen [in] a long time'.

> 'Good night! I hope thour't fast asleep
> Thy bedgown buttoned round thy neck fast,
> And mind you rise at Morn's first peep
> With a good appetite for breakfast.
>
> Good night! I'm off, but not for waking,
> And if I dream I give you warning,
> T'will be most probably of making,
> A thundering breakfast in the morning.' [13]

This practice of casual verse-writing he continued, as is indicated by some rather better and more serious lines he inserted in a letter to his wife in 1848 with a lock of her hair:

> 'As along life's road we stray—
> God! if sages tell us true
> Tis a dirty toilsome way,
> But Fanny between I and you
> We needn't credit half they say;
> But suppose it sooth they tell us,
> We've a friend, to her we'll fly
> Cheerer of the broken spirit.
>
> Hail, enchanting memory—
> Youth's bright faces, brighter hours
> Cheer again our wearied eyes,
> Moments worth an age of sorrow
> Waken'd, at her bidding rise—
> May each hair a rivet be
> In the chain of memory
> Calling back such scenes to thee.'

He was also thrown, during these years, into contact with the literary great and near great. On 9 January 1844, the Journal tells of his dining in London at Barham's, where he met the comic writer Thomas Hood, 'who punned to an awful extent'. Barham, a friend of his grandfather's, Tom knew well, and his death in 1845 Tom felt as 'a great loss indeed to me, and the first blank but one [a schoolfellow named Walrond] that I have felt irreparable'. On 4 January 1844, Tom called on Albert Smith, a writer for *Punch*, who took him to the Ainsworths, where there was much conjuring and joking presided over by the great Charles Dickens 'in wild spirits'. On 6 January he called on Lockhart, and on the 11th on 'Miss Edgeworth . . . who is very entertaining and agreeable and particularly civil to me as I have given her little grandnephew Walter Fox introductions to several boys at Rugby'. The previous September, Tom had spent an evening with Professor Wilson, the Christopher North of *Blackwood's Magazine*, where there was much singing of Scottish songs and eating of 'stewd oysters . . . compounded in an apparatus . . . called a conjuror', and another with Alexander Blackwood himself, who took him to see 'De Quincy, a famous character in the Noctes Ambrosianae in the Magazine and a great original'.

5

The visits to Wilson and Blackwood occurred on a trip to Scotland which Tom took in the long vacation of 1844 as chaperon for a young man named Harry Duffield. Occasional jaunts to London had heretofore been Tom's only excursions beyond home or school, and even when he left college he had seen little of the world. 'But yesterday', he wrote in 1845, 'I was the *man* who had never been to the opera, to races or to Brighton.' So he welcomed this chance to travel, though his companion was hardly the one he might have chosen. 'His whole understanding, and little enough there is of it, seems to be centred in horses and dogs.' Despite Tom's efforts to do him 'some good', young Harry steadfastly refused even to look at the sights, caring less, as Tom said, for the 'cottage where Burns was born, the inn where he caroused, the Brigs, and banks, and braes which he has sung . . . than if they were rabbit holes'. Tom, on the other hand, showed himself a natural born tourist. He saw everything, met everybody, had all the expected reactions of an Englishman travelling abroad, and enjoyed himself hugely and continuously.

On the famous eleven-mile ride from Carlisle to Glasgow he sang Burns's songs with a jolly Scotsman, and wished Fanny could see the beautiful Clyde scenery. Glasgow, though its cathedral had reminders of scenes in *Rob Roy*, was not of much interest: its quays were not as good as those of London, and its university was a dark, ugly hole, unlike 'little' Oriel. Its church services were disgusting. There were no prayers from the congregation, which lounged and stared while the minister prayed. As soon as the service was over 'the barbarians put their hats on and stump out'. Once during the trip Hughes found a preacher who delivered a 'very good sermon for a Presbyterian', but he was still thankful for two good Episcopalian services: 'What a treat in Scotland.' Stirling Castle suggested *The Lady of the Lake* and offered a sunset that blended mountains and clouds 'in a beautiful *misty glow* of colour' that made Tom fancy himself in 'Fairyland'. Dalkeith had a palace, admittance to which Tom secured 'for two very nice people, one of them such a bonnie Scotch lassie, without the least affectation or nonsense of any sort'. On top of Ben Venue Tom made a big 'Fan' out of stones, which he hoped would last till they went there together; Fingal's Cave was too terrifically grand even to think of Fanny. Ayr, where there was a festival with 2,000 guests to dinner, was full of memories of Burns, and Abbotsford of Scott:

'The house although not so large as I expected was even more interesting than I had hoped but the *ould* woman who shows it and who makes thro Sir Walter's generosity more than 500 pounds a year hurried us over it shamefully when I could have stayed a week.'

Nearly everywhere Tom met someone: a notable like De Quincey, a Rugby schoolmate, a 'very pretty girl' from Nova Scotia, or 'tufts' such as Lord Cranstoun, whom 'we had the honour of viewing . . . at a distance' on the packet for Skye and 'breakfasting with . . . next morning'. There was, of course, swimming, fishing, rowing, riding, and tennis wherever opportunity offered. The trip ended with two visits to Tom's relations, the George Wilkinsons at Hasperley, where there were masquerades, harvest suppers, dancing, and play-acting. The gathering played *Tom Thumb* and made a hash of it, the villain retiring without being killed and the queen and others dying, amidst fits of laughter, in the way of the scenery, so that they couldn't pull the curtain without a general movement of dead bodies.

6

On the hot and memorable day when Tom Hughes played cricket for Oxford at Lord's before a crowd of middle-class spectators, another virile personality was holding the attention of a far greater, and more serious, assembly of working-men on the highest point in Lancashire. To reach this latter meeting, thousands of working-men had trudged for distances as far as twenty miles, to stand under the blazing sun to be seared by the oratory of Feargus O'Connor. Their playgrounds had fast been swallowed up. Bolton, with a population rising to 50,000, lost nearly 400 acres of its green lungs by the enclosures of the first three decades of the century. Oldham, in the same period, lost nearly 500 acres in a similar manner, Gateshead 600, while some towns, like Sheffield, had lost more than 7,000 acres in less than fifty years.[14]

On 2 May 1842, a month before the university cricket match, Feargus O'Connor, who had utilised his nine months' liberty from prison to organise the National Charter Association, inspired the presentation of a gigantic petition to parliament. This petition, the largest yet presented on behalf of universal suffrage, contained 3,317,702 signatures and was over six miles long—so long, indeed, that when it was carried to the House of Commons by a procession, the debate on its reception inspired some sharp retorts. Macaulay denounced universal suffrage as 'incompatible with the very existence of civilisation', and Roebuck denounced O'Connor as 'a fierce, malignant, and cowardly demagogue'. The House declined to hear the petitioners by a majority of 238 votes.

In the following months the grievances of the workers in the industrial towns became too hard to bear. The unemployed, suspicious of the new machines which were displacing them, fearful of the workhouses which offered them such grisly tasks as the grinding of bones, banded together, arming themselves with any weapons that came to hand. At Stalybridge 20,000 of them marched on Manchester. Elsewhere smaller groups roamed about the empty factories, removing the boiler-plugs. The government acted with promptness and severity. Staffordshire, Cheshire, and Lancashire were placed under three commissions which transported or imprisoned the leaders.

These were also times of spiritual upheaval, dramatically highlighted at Oxford by the Tractarian Movement under John Henry Newman. When W. G. Ward, the rotund, persuasive bursar of Balliol, published his *Ideal of a Christian Church* in 1844, the whole university was in an uproar. Though many sympathised with its Romanism, still more were incensed at the boast it contained, which set the Established Church at defiance:

'Three years have passed', wrote Ward, 'since I said plainly, that in subscribing the Articles I renounce no one Roman doctrine; yet I retain my fellowship which I hold on the tenure of subscription, and have received no Ecclesiastical censure in any shape.'

But in February 1845 that 'Ecclesiastical censure' descended. By a majority of 391 (with 1,163 voting) the university condemned Ward's position. Hughes wrote in his Journal on the 17th of that month:

'It is really not credible that in a Protestant university a man should act up and declare that he holds every doctrine of the Roman Church and yet obtain 400 votes. It is a sad omen of the days that are coming.'

And so it was. A number of Tractarians left their Oxford fellowships and vacated their college livings. In October, John

Henry Newman resigned his fellowship at Oriel to enter the Roman Catholic Church. As Disraeli said, the Church reeled under the blow.

Surely *Tom Brown at Oxford* exaggerates the degree to which Tom was, at college, affected by these social and spiritual disturbances. It is there suggested that, deeply moved by the loss of religious faith in the world around him, and by the 'condition of England' in the hungry 'forties, he first flirted with Malthusian and Benthamite doctrines, was then attracted to the Tractarians, who concerned themselves with social matters at least to the extent of organising a school for the poor, at which Tom taught, and finally became a complete democrat, 'little better', indeed, than a physical force Chartist. His serious friend, Hardy, finally saved him from such excesses, pointing out to him, with arguments drawn straight from Carlyle, that the ballot would not produce the best leaders, and that his articles for a radical journal were merely a one-sided expression of vanity.

Actually, Tom Hughes suffered no deep unrest during his college days; never hung suspended, like his friend Clough and so many others, between two worlds—one dead, the other powerless to be born. The Tractarians left him cold: the nearest he came to teaching in their schools being, he admitted shamefacedly, to read the works of Scott to a 'broken-down old jockey' to 'keep him from the public house'.[15] He hated their 'Gothic mouldings' and 'man millinery', their asceticism and exclusiveness, and declared:

'I'm as fond of the church as any one of them, but I don't want to be jumping up on her back every minute, like a sickly chicken getting on the old hen's back to warm its feet whenever the ground is cold, and fancying himself taller than all the rest of the brood.'

And Dr. Arnold had fortified him against their theology, so that 'I and many others passed through that time unscathed'.[16]

Of the deeper social issues he was, if we can believe certain of his later statements, blissfully unconscious. He 'attended more to cricket and rowing and boxing' than to 'lectures on ethics and politics', and confined his reading of *The Times* to the pages which reported the cricket matches and the debates on the Corn Laws. From poverty and its impact he was cushioned by his experiences in Berkshire, where his mother and the parson's wife 'knew every poor person in the parish'.[17]

Hughes' own intimate Journal confirms this impression. He told Fanny: 'One feels so out of the world at Oxford, as if nothing that one could say would interest or amuse'. Most of its pages are full of examinations, ceremonies (which Fanny could not attend), of town and gown rows, and of Tom's election to the Druids, 'the only secret that there will ever be between us'. The rest is mere boating talk, climaxed by an account of a great supper at which Tom sang, amid rapturous applause, a song which he had composed with the help of his brother, George, who winged his 'hobbling lines'. The last of the eleven verses illustrates, more than a chapter of analysis, his outlook at this time:

> 'Our maundering critics may prate as they please
> Of glory departed and influence flown—
> Row and work, boys of England, on rivers and seas,
> And the old land shall hold, firm as ever, her own.' [18]

7

Yet this last impression, too, is exaggerated. The influence of his old school-fellow, Arthur Hugh Clough, especially from the year 1843, when he became a tutor of Oriel, was strong. Clough was rooted in the north (his father was a Liverpool cotton merchant) and, as a friend of Carlyle, responded to the tensions of the times in London. James Fraser, too, for all his riding to hounds and dandified appearance, was sensible to the changes going on around him, and preceded Clough in departing from the cloistered calm of the Oriel quadrangle.

Both helped to nourish hatred of the 'insolence of undergraduate life' and sentiments of democracy in Hughes' heart. When two young Lincolnshire farmers settled in the neighbourhood—'nice gentlemanly sensible fellows whom I shall cultivate if opportunity offers'—Tom wrote:

'When one turns from such men as these to the present race of young nobility it is quite sad to see the contrast; the latter must mend, or we must look for great changes in the country, but I wouldn't say this to everybody.'

Experiences beyond the cloistered calm of Oriel sharpened these sentiments, and he wrote:

'It is awful to think of numbers of poor creatures who are exposed to the bitter cold of a December night, and when one asks oneself what trials have I to bear in comparison to these, and why I am so much more favoured than others . . . it makes one positively ashamed.

'Dr. Arnold used to say that the most blessed sight on God's earth was to see a young man surrounded by all the comforts of our high civilisation which riches can procure, and in the vigour of mind and body, turning in earnest to the high duties which his position imposed upon him from conscientious motives; I think there is one more blessed, and that is to see a poor man labouring under the privations that our high state of civilisation necessarily brings, with little comfort for his body, and no resources in his mind to which to turn, labouring on in cheerfulness and content, in the hope of sharing in a better world the comforts which he cannot share in this.' [19]

His trip to Scotland in the summer of 1844 crystallised his political opinions. In Lancaster, county town of the shire which had been the centre of disturbance two years before, he was finally argued out of his Toryism by some fellow-travellers whom he met in a commercial hotel, so that, as he wrote, 'before I returned to Oxford for Michaelmas Term I had become a good free-trader'. His Liberalism, marching with the intellectual development of other old Rugbeians at Oxford, was made explicit when one of them, A. P. Stanley, published his *Life of Dr. Arnold* in that very year. This, in Hughes' own words, threw

'a white light upon great sections, both of the world which we have realised more or less through the classics, and the world which was lying under our eyes, and all around us, and which we now began, for the first time, to recognise as one and the same.'

Tom was haunted by one of Arnold's doctrines: 'If there is one truth short of the highest for which I would gladly die, it is democracy without Jacobinism'. Little wonder, therefore, that he confessed 'the noble side of democracy was carrying me away'; and that 'the people's charter was beginning to have strange attractions for me'.[20]

He left Oxford, as he later claimed, a 'Radical'. This caused the first serious rift between him and his brother George, whose 'reverence for national life, and for the laws, traditions, and customs, with which it is interwoven and of which it is the expression' were as much strengthened by Dr. Arnold as were Tom's hopes for reform.

Animating and sustaining this tender growth was a rich subsoil of religious experience. This nourished not only the other-regarding pulses of his politics, but also the flowering of his love for Fanny Ford.

'What would our relation to one another be', he wrote in one of many similar passages, 'were it not that what is begun here may last forever . . . I would not for millions of worlds have loved one whose image I could not have carried with me in thought into that life for which, by God's grace, we are now preparing.' [21]

It armed him, too, against the flood of geological speculation which was then sapping the foundations of many another's belief. Minnie Senior, daughter of the great political economist Nassau William Senior, one of the big guns of the *Edinburgh Review*, shocked him by saying that 'she didn't believe in love and that she didn't intend to marry any man under 3,000 pounds a year'.[22] When she read *The Vestiges of Creation*, Tom was even more pained:

'It is a most dangerous and immoral work; I wonder very much at Minnie's having read it,' he wrote. 'I should have thought any girl would have closed it in disgust, but it is the fashion I suppose, as it seems to be to read Goethe's works, the first of which sickened me. I am very sorry that Minnie reads such works, it must lower her mind; if I get a chance I will tell her my opinion though she cut me for it.' [23]

As for Minnie's agnostic brother, Nassau John, Tom Hughes nearly caused a mortal feud between them: first by endeavouring to convert him, and then, when Nassau John wanted to marry Tom's sister Jeannie, by trying to prevent it.

'I would give anything to be able to make Nassau serious,' he wrote in his Journal, 'for no man can be a real friend unless he is so.' [24]

Even after the engagement was announced in the spring of 1846, Tom wrote him a letter questioning his fitness to guide a 'young and innocent and religious woman', and warning him that if he did not learn self-denial and self-discipline, God might take Jeannie away from him.

Fortunately for both of them, the letter was never sent.

8

As early as January 1844, Tom Hughes decided to become a barrister. He still felt, and was long to continue to feel, the attraction of being ordained. 'What a delightful life a country clergyman's must be,' he exclaimed after writing an ordination sermon for a friend of his brother's; 'I find I take very naturally to the work.' But his lot, he was convinced, was 'cast in a different sphere; may God enable me to do my duty in it, to his glory'.[25]

By January 1845 he was keeping his first term at Lincoln's Inn, and by April his second. After shuttling back and forward between Donnington, Oxford, and London, he settled down at Kingston Lisle, where his grandmother, Mary Ann Hughes, was now living. By June he reported, 'Stephen's commentaries are yielding rapidly'. He pressed on with his studies, rejecting his father's suggestion that he should travel abroad to learn French and German, for he was anxious to qualify as soon as possible, in order to marry Fanny.

On 7 July he went up to read in Coulson's chambers and took 'small rooms on the third floor at No. 15 Lincoln's Inn Fields at a rent of £30 a year'. From his windows he could look out on the fields themselves. These he furnished with a legacy of £200 from a great-aunt, and with an annuity of £200 from his father, he was able to live frugally, saving £100 a year.

'My engagement was a constant stimulus to work and economy, and made me indifferent as to society.' With a good housekeeper from Fanny's own county of Devonshire—a 'glorious old woman' named Roxworthy—to look after him, he would rise at seven, breakfast at eight, and work in chambers from ten to five. In the evenings he would eat and walk before returning to his books again from eight to eleven. The week-ends—Saturday night and Sunday—were spent either with the family of Nassau Senior, or with Tom Arnold, 'an excellent fellow and a great friend of mine'.[26]

'Even when we are apart', he told Fanny, 'I don't suppose there are two people in England who have more to be thankful for.' 'What earthly claim have I to be one of the happiest men in England at this minute?' he asked. 'During the last month I felt several times uncommonly ashamed of myself at night for having been so perfectly happy during the day.'[27]

Tom could, after all, see her now, which seemed a great deal, though one refuses to take literally his assurance to her that 'had you only been my sister I should not have differed in anything material at least I hope not'.[28] When she was absent he could dream and plan. Before her arrival at Donnington for that long-awaited Christmas party, he charmingly pictured her there in imagination:

' "The governor" has just told some good story deserving a pinch of snuff, which he is accordingly taking to the discomfiture of Squab and Harry [two of

Tom's brothers] whose helps of turkey are delayed during the operation, and look at the sly old Major how he is nodding and rubbing his hands over that pretty speech he has just made to Fanny Manning, and there's my mother half amused and half annoyed at the Dutchman's extraordinary attempts to carve the tongue, which notwithstanding his natural steadiness of character and a pair of Holland's best spectacles he is massacring as never unfortunate tongue was massacred before, and Mr. Tom and Miss Fanny squeezing hands under the table, what, at your old tricks! It ought to be all above board now.' 29

On another occasion he drew a delightful sketch of their prospective married bliss. He would read Sterne's *Sentimental Journey* to her

'soon after we are married it wouldn't quite do for a lady to read by herself I am sorry to say but there is so much good feeling in it that everyone ought to have had the pleasure of hearing it and so you shall dearest, fancy our drawing in two luxurious arm chairs (or *our* sofa by the bye that's better now I think of it) round the fire in the little back room which we are to keep sacred . . . *our slippers* made up and on a comfortable foot stool, the kettle all ready for tea or chocolate at eight—on the little table by the door the (oh for shame) whiskey bottle in case we should like a tumbler before retiring.'

This life would be interrupted only for occasional tours around England, on which Tom would teach Fanny fly-casting. They would not travel abroad: the places might be all right, but 'getting from one to the other must be horrible. I don't like any foreign nation much from the little I know of them, and I am certainly a most thoroughly prejudiced John Bull.' Then, too, there might be the interruption of children, and Tom wondered 'if I shall ever have any of my own if so what models they will be, won't they dearest'.30

Sometimes Tom's dreams would take more practical turns. Perhaps for a time, he told Fanny, they might have to live in lodgings,

'but I trust I should never have been selfish enough to engage you had I not been able to offer you a better prospect than lodgings; we will be looking out for a house and doing everything in a most orderly and methodical way for the next year or two. I intend to save enough while I am a student out of my allowance, (and with a help perhaps by occasionally writing in periodicals) to buy a decent law library, which is the great expense when a man is called, and besides this I intend to get a little *good* furniture and some *silver forks and spoons* (what a joke) so that there will not be any great outlay on our outset in life.' 31

Inevitably, too, Tom's thoughts sometimes grew solemn. His very happiness, which overawed him and made him feel guilty, increased his feeling that 'we are not sent into this world to do nothing but enjoy ourselves'. Love seemed less and less 'a short dream of bliss on this earth which has self for its foundation and its endings', and more and more a glorious 'moving of two souls together towards a heavenly home'. 'Alas how weak and sinful we all are . . . how necessary then must it be to have continually by one's side a mentor and fellow labourer whose hope is one with ours.' [32]

Tom's seriousness was increased by the sights he witnessed in London.

'You may imagine', he wrote later, 'the effect upon me of a sudden plunge into what was then one of the worst quarters of London. My rooms were in Lincoln's Inn Fields, and I passed daily, twice at least, through the horrible nests of squalor and vice which then stood on the site of the New Law Courts. I soon found that (with the exception of thieves and beggars) these nests were peopled by shop workers—poor men, women and children, who, if their employers could have flogged them, would have been in a far worse case than any negro slave. I say that the competitive struggle for life had brought them to this pass: and yet the most approved teachers, in reviews and newspapers, which I had begun to read, and even in Parliament, were insisting on "free competition" as a corollary to "free trade", and a necessary pillar of industrial prosperity.' [33]

His social conscience was aroused by an experience one evening in these early days. While strolling between Soho and Regent Street in his evening clothes, he came upon a battle between some labourers and a policeman who had arrested a rag-picker. Tom had been reading in *The Times* of recurrent beatings of policemen by Irish labourers and thieves, and since this had outraged 'all my public school notions of fair play', he had decided, in characteristically practical fashion, to help the next officer he met with his fists. Here was his opportunity. He promptly jumped into the fight and succeeded in keeping the mob at bay until police reinforcements arrived. But the sequel was disillusioning. The police, assuming without proof that the sick and undernourished ragpicker was a thief, began pummelling him. So when six of the labourers returned and started shouting at Tom, he felt ashamed and in a most unchristian temper. After feebly defending his class against the blanket denunciations of demagogues, he swallowed his pride, apologised, and promised to go to court and testify in the morning. If all men were as innately just and educable as Tom Hughes, moral suasion might, as Tom never ceased believing, solve a great many social problems. [34]

But he found few outlets for his new-born convictions. On one occasion he made the gesture of letting the ragged children of the neighbourhood into the gardens of Lincoln's Inn. But the beadle was scandalised, and got the trustees to say that the key to No. 15 would be taken away if the practice did not stop; this alarmed Mrs. Roxworthy, and Tom had to desist. In 1847 he helped collect money for the sufferers from the Irish famine, with, as we shall see, momentous results for him. But for the most part he merely grumbled and worried.

His law work really kept him busy. Not that preparation for the law was the exacting task it is today. As Goldwin Smith wrote, 'I duly ate my dinners at Lincoln's Inn. A course of dinners was the curriculum in those days.' [35] But it was dull, 'a jungle of antiquated fooleries kept up by the pedantry and the interest of those who profited by it', according to Frederic Harrison.[36] And Hughes never took to it, however optimistic he may have felt when he earned his first fee in the spring of 1846: two and a half guineas for getting signatures against the railroad. 'I read hard at the law,' he wrote, 'but it was very much against the grain', and only partially successful. He might have liked common and criminal law, but 'conveyancing and real property law had no attractions for me, beyond the determination, if I could, to make a living by them'.[37] Nor did he ever outgrow this feeling. He constantly expressed a predilection for the clerical life, though he kept telling himself that law was a noble calling and he had 'no business to wish or hope for anything else and do not'. Even after seven years of practice he was still finding the 'vocation of barrister . . . difficult to be swallowed' and longing for the ministry.

'I don't think I am quite so sure as you that one oughtn't to change,' he wrote his friend Lord Goderich [later Earl de Grey and Ripon and finally the Marquess of Ripon], 'and often feel strongly tempted to turn parson (if any Right Rev. would do the needful for me). I think that Fanny would be a wonderful parsoness, and after all if a man is ever prompted to it can he ever safely turn from the work which was Christ's special work on earth? I have long intended to lay a case before the Prophet [Maurice] on this subject, but I hate trying to shift responsibility from my own shoulders. Meantime you and I will most likely grind on to our graves making and administering feeble and flabby laws, having at any rate the comfort that our lives, as they ought to be, are battles, tho' it be but with mud dragons and desolate parchment wastes, wherein it don't much matter if we get licked, seeing as how "so thou but strive thou soon shall see Defeat itself is victory".' [38]

Fortunately for Tom, he read law with an able and kindly man who found that his strength lay in preparing deeds such as appointments of new trustees. These needed a long recital of facts and only a simple common form for their operative part. So determination finally brought its reward, and on 28 January 1848 he was admitted to the Bar, having migrated to the Inner Temple ten days earlier. When called, he said later, he was 'probably about as fit for that ceremony as the average of my contemporaries'.[39] He certainly never won distinction. According to his friend Ludlow, he was 'quick to see a point, but perhaps did not always sufficiently see all around'. Moreover, he always started by thinking his client the 'most injured man in the world on the strength of his brief', but had been disillusioned so often that he took to assuming he was a rogue until the contrary was proved.[40] But, as the legal journal, *The Green Bag*, said, he was a sound equity lawyer.[41] He enjoyed 'almost exclusively quiet respectable family solicitors' as clients, who had 'half a dozen suits a year each'.[42] With some assistance from other sources he made an adequate living out of practice in Chancery.

This legal training was to be invaluable in other spheres.

9

Coterminous with the end of his legal apprenticeship was the end of his engagement. It was announced publicly at Christmas 1846, at which time, Tom said in November, Ann MacKenzie might find 'her high opinion of me as an affectionate brother . . . considerably diminish'. After Christmas events moved more rapidly than either had hoped was possible, though they were already becoming, as Tom said, 'lovesick (what a horrid word to be applied to such a dear sensible old couple as we are)'.[43]

They were married on 17 August 1847, five months before Hughes was called to the Bar. In the prayer that Tom wrote for his wedding day he asked for no new blessings of 'riches health honour, friends or any happiness as the world reckons happiness', but only for 'humble hearts and consciences alive to every effort of our great adversary'. God, he trusted, would know their needs and lead the way 'which conducted to the gates of "Thy heavenly kingdom" '.

At the time of their marriage Tom and Fanny had but £400 a year to live on (though a £500 legacy from his grandmother was accumulating for Tom), and their friends thought they were mad. But, settling in tiny lodgings in London, they always managed to pay their way, and were very happy. Three months after their marriage Fanny wrote to Tom, 'I am sure I never talked to you, wrote to you or loved you half as much till I became your own wife'. The long engagement was good, since they now knew one another so well; while he was away she led the retired life proper for a young lady under the circumstances, and was happy just thinking of him.[44]

'Though I admit the experiment was a risky one,' Hughes wrote in his old age, 'I have never repented it.' [45] Fanny must know, he told her in 1867, 'after the twenty years of our joint life, always getting more and more into a single life, that I do live only when with you, and always do what you tell me.' [46] This was not perhaps entirely accurate, since Hughes travelled far more, unaccompanied by his often-ailing wife, than was strictly necessary. And he worked overtime, despite her disapproval (he claimed she agreed with him 'in the abstract'), bringing about social reforms and building 'the new Jerusalem' in England.[47] But on the whole the Hugheses were a devoted couple through a long life together. If Fanny occasionally smothered his exuberance, this was but needed protection against his volatile idealism. His pointed denial that his 'capacity for enjoying anything has been diminished through you' suggests that she may have sensed some such feeling on his part. Fanny Hughes' feet were firmly planted on the ground. Tom Hughes was as fortunate in his marriage as were his father and his grandfather.

NOTES

[1] T. Hughes, *James Fraser, Second Bishop of Manchester* (London, 1889), 27.
[2] *ibid.*, 25.   [3] *ibid.*, 26.   [4] *ibid.*
[5] W. Tuckwell, *Reminiscences of Oxford* (London, 1900), 114; T. Hughes, *Memoir of a Brother*, 66–71; *The Times*, 18 June 1946.
[6] Letter of Fanny Hughes to Alexander Macmillan (undated); R. E. Prothero, *The Letters of Richard Ford* (New York, 1905), Preface and 134, 155; Brown, *True Manliness*, xi–xiii.
[7] Hughes' Journal, 21 Aug. 1843.
[8] *ibid.*, Jan.–April 1844, 18 July 1844, 23 Feb. 1845.
[9] Letters, Hughes to Fanny Ford, 5 March, 22 April 1843; 23 Nov. 1845; Journal, 20 Jan. 1844.
[10] Letters, Fanny Ford to Hughes (undated).
[11] Journal, 23, 27 Aug. 1843.

[12] Ripon Papers, British Museum Add. MSS. 43,531. Hughes to Ripon, 19 May 1881; 9 March 1883.

[13] Journal, 12 Sept. 1843; 18 Jan. 1844; Jan.–April 1844; 9, 22, 23 Aug.; 3 Sept. 1845.

[14] J. L. & B. Hammond, *The Bleak Age* (Pelican Books, 1947), 80; Barbara Hammond, 'Two Towns' Enclosures' in *Economic History*, ii (London, 1933), 258–266.

[15] *Economic Review*, vii (London, 1895), 309–310.

[16] T. Hughes, *The Manliness of Christ*, 229; Address at Rugby, 1892.

[17] *Cornhill Magazine*, lviii, 472, *Address on the Occasion of a Presentation* . . . . (Manchester, 1885), 5.

[18] Severn, *Almanac of English Sports* (London, 1868); T. Hughes, *Memoir of a Brother*, 79.

[19] Journal, 12 Dec. 1844.

[20] T. Hughes, *Memoir of a Brother*, 72, 88; Brown, *True Manliness*, xi–xiii; *Cornhill Magazine*, lviii, 564.

[21] Journal, 23 Aug. 1845.   [22] *ibid.*, 30 Sept. 1845.   [23] *ibid.*, 21 Sept. 1845.

[24] *ibid.*, 30 Aug. 1845; letters, Hughes to Fanny Ford, 29 Oct. 1945; Hughes to Nassau John Senior, 9 Nov. 1846.

[25] Journal, 10 Jan.; 3 May; 13 Nov. 1944; letter, Hughes to Fanny Ford, 23 Oct. 1845.

[26] Journal, 4 June, 1845; *True Manliness*, xii, xiii.

[27] Hughes to Fanny Ford, 14 Dec. 1845; 29 Jan. 1846.

[28] Hughes to Fanny Ford, 26 Nov. 1846.

[29] Hughes to Fanny Ford, 2 Nov. 1845.

[30] Hughes to Fanny Ford, 29 Oct. 1845; 15 Nov.; 13 Dec. 1846.

[31] Letter, Hughes to Fanny Ford, 16 Nov. 1845.

[32] Letter, Hughes to Fanny Ford, 29 Oct. 1845.

[33] Brown, *True Manliness*, xiv.

[34] *Cornhill Magazine*, cviii, 'Fragment of Autobiography', 73.

[35] Haultain, Arnold (Editor); *Goldwin Smith Reminiscences* (New York, 1910), 121.

[36] Harrison, Frederic, *Autobiographic Memoirs* (London, 1910), i, 149.

[37] Brown, *True Manliness*, xv.

[38] Wolf, Lucien, *The Life of the First Marquess of Ripon*, 2 vols. (London, 1921) i, 152–153; letter, Hughes to Ripon, 25 Aug. 1855.

[39] Brown, *True Manliness*, xv.

[40] *Economic Review*, vi, 1896, 303.

[41] *The Green Bag*, Sept. 1896, 375.

[42] Ripon Papers, Letter, Hughes to Ripon, 1 June, 1869, British Museum, Add. MS. 43,520.

[43] Letters, Hughes to Fanny Ford, 25, 28 Nov. 1846.

[44] Letters, Fanny Hughes to Hughes, 14, 24 Nov. 1847.

[45] Brown, *True Manliness*, xv.

[46] Letter, Hughes to Fanny Hughes, 23 Sept. 1867.

[47] Letter, Hughes to Fanny Hughes, 8 Jan. 1869.

CHAPTER FOUR

New Horizons, 1848–1853

IN the late summer of 1846, Hughes went to chapel at Lincoln's Inn. The preacher impressed him so much that he wrote to Fanny on 6 November:

'We had an excellent sermon from Morris (*sic*) the reader, on the character of Esau, from 12th Hebrews, the afternoon's lessons. His views nearly co-incide with Arnold's in one of his sermons in the 4th vol., which I will bring you at Xmas, but he brought out a new point to me, viz. how impossible it was for Esau to obtain the blessing after he had sold his birthright.' [1]

A month later he was glad not to have missed 'a capital sermon from Morris on the text I was quoting to you the other day, I mean "all flesh is grass" '.

'There was somehow a reality about the service which was new,' he confessed. 'I went again to satisfy a want, and if I overslept myself I found that I had lost something—that my day had not started right. . . . if I missed morning chapel I had an uncomfortable feeling till eleven or twelve o'clock, as if I had not had my breakfast or had put on a dirty shirt.' [2]

Twelve years later the ascendancy had grown so much that he began:

'to doubt whether there has been his like since St. Paul. I used to think Luther as great a man, but I begin very much to doubt this—those that live longest will see most but if our prophet doesn't do as great a work under far harder circes it won't be because God has not raised up the right man and spoken by him but because an adulterous and perverse generation will not be hindered from going to the devil.' [3]

Hughes' prophet was Frederick Denison Maurice, and his analogy was an apt one. For Maurice had also travelled alone, breathing out threatening and slaughter against the Thirty-nine Articles, but saw the light, on his dusty Unitarian road, and had been converted to a belief in Christ, to become a chosen vessel to bear God's name before the Gentiles of London. Now forty-one years old, he couched the analysis of a professor in the apocalyptic language of prophecy. 'Behind the grey bricks and crowded streets and bewildered busy people, he discovered the pouring of vials, and the loosening of the great winds of heaven, and the thunder of the trumpets of the night.' [4]

'To listen to him', wrote one, 'was to drink spiritual champagne.' Tom's friend, Matthew Arnold, said that Maurice 'passed his life beating the bush with deep emotion, but never starting the hare'. The metaphysic of Maurice eluded others too: Gladstone, who had known him at Oxford, 'got little solid meat from him' and found him 'difficult to catch, and still more difficult to hold'; Aubrey de Vere said that listening to him was 'like eating pea soup with a fork'.[5] But to Tom Hughes his winged words flew straight to the heart.

Tom needed those words. Launched into a doubtful career in the turbulent world of 1848, he was in danger, now that Arnold was dead, of succumbing to the doubt, inertia, and conventionalism that overwhelm so many well-brought-up young men in a time of trouble. Maurice gave him the support of a renewed faith in a beneficent spiritual universe outside of time and space, and in the Anglican Church as a rod of salvation and the instrument of a high social mission. He offered him the challenge of action to reform the world as the road to happiness. And he introduced him to the cause—Christian Socialism—that was to serve as the means to this action. For fifty years Tom Hughes was to be a disciple of Maurice.

I

To others, too, of his youthful audience at Lincoln's Inn, Maurice was an inspiration. One of them was a small, slightly built conveyancer, then in his middle twenties, who had been practising at Lincoln's Inn since 1843: J. M. Ludlow. Ludlow, a descendant of one of Cromwell's major-generals, had never known a public school, nor yet a father's control. Born in India, and educated in Paris, he was endowed with gifts and accomplishments unusual for a barrister of those times. His Continental training had sharpened his capacity for detached and objective observation, and he soon became, not only a friend, but also an active reagent on the thought of Maurice. For Ludlow as a boy of nine had seen one revolution in Paris, and as a student he had drunk deep of the Fourierian spring. Fourier, for the young French intellectual of the eighteen-thirties, had much the same effect as Lenin had on the European intellectual a century later.

France was the seed-bed of socialistic enterprise, and Ludlow during his life in Paris had reaped some of these wild oats to sow in England. Ludlow was, however, no irresponsible revolutionary. His mind, well stored and tidy, was early exercised in the logistics of social change. He met Maurice soon after the latter had assumed the chaplaincy of Lincoln's Inn, and had just lost his wife. Maurice was aching for friendship, and looked to Ludlow, himself unmarried, for that self-dependency which he so sorely lacked.

Ludlow's roots in England had not yet struck deep. He returned to Paris in February 1848, when the revolution seemed to menace the safety of his two sisters. While he was there, further experiments in Socialism which he witnessed moved him to write to Lincoln's Inn urging that unless such a force was Christianised it would shake Christianity to its foundations. Maurice, to whom the letter was addressed, was profoundly moved. He circulated copies of it to his friends, and the following Sunday he preached a sermon on the theme. In the sermon, he said:

' We must understand the power and privilege of saying "Our Father . . . Thy will be done on earth, as it is in heaven." . . . This prayer does not treat the projects of men for universal societies, unbounded pantisocracies, as too large. It over reaches them all with these words "as in Heaven".'

That Ludlow had released hidden springs of action in Maurice, Maurice was the first to see. 'God Himself is speaking to us,' he wrote ; 'if we ask Him what He would have us do, we shall be shown.' [6]

2

They were. France had sneezed, and England caught a cold. At the time Maurice was preaching in Lincoln's Inn Chapel the Chartists were collecting their strength for a gigantic demonstration on Kennington Common. They had collected thousands of signatures to a petition, which was to be presented to Parliament by Feargus O'Connor, their fiery fifty-four-year-old leader who had recently become an M.P. The demonstration had been so widely publicised in O'Connor's own paper, the *Northern Star*, that the Government armed the civil service, barricaded all offices, and enrolled over 150,000 special constables to supplement the troops deployed all over London. Tom Hughes was one of these special constables, but he volunteered, as he said, 'with shrewd misgivings in my own mind that the Chartists had a great deal to say for themselves'.

On 10 April 1848, assembling on the south side of the Thames on Kennington Common, a force of Chartists, estimated by *The Times* to number 20,000, marched towards Westminster. At their head was the monster petition which, they claimed, weighed five tons and contained over five million signatures.

Meanwhile, another orator was exciting the crowd in Trafalgar Square, where Hughes and his friends ('The Devil's Own' as Hughes called them later) were on duty. The orator certainly roused Hughes, who objected to some of his remarks, and a scuffle took place. Blood was up, and to prevent it flowing, the real police came up and arrested Hughes and his friends: marching them off to the jeers of the crowd to lodge them in a stable in St. Martin's Lane.[7] Farther off, in the quieter reaches of Harley Street, a small, headstrong young clergyman some three years older than Hughes had come up from his country living of Eversley to call on Maurice, the godfather of his son. Maurice was principal of Queen's College, where Kingsley hoped to teach, and since Queen's College was in Harley Street, Kingsley went there to look for him.

But Maurice, like England, had caught a cold, and instead of going out with Kingsley, gave him a letter of introduction to, and urged him to call on, Ludlow, who had returned from Paris. Kingsley went along to Lincoln's Inn, and spent the rest of the morning in Ludlow's company. In the afternoon both went off to Kennington, but, on reaching Waterloo Bridge, discovered that the procession had not been allowed to cross the Thames, and that the much-publicised five-ton petition had been conveyed to Westminster in three hansom-cabs.

In the drizzling rain of that evening, Kingsley, Maurice, and Ludlow discussed the whole affair. Kingsley, removed from the restraining influence of his wife, was as eager and passionate as a child to help these poor underdogs whose great demonstration had been such a fiasco. In burning phrases, all the brighter from the darkness of the night, he fired the graver Ludlow and energised the more hesitant Maurice. The evangel was born: Christians must give an answer to the social problem. So the three of them decided to write a new set of *Tracts for the Times*, social in orientation. And, as the placard written by Kingsley, posted up the following day, asserted:

'The Charter is not bad *if the men who use it are not bad*. . . . There will be no true freedom without virtue, no true science without religion, no true industry without the fear of God and love to your fellow citizens. Workers of England, be wise, and then you *must* be free, for you will be fit to be free.' [8]

Well might Canon Raven claim that this was 'the first manifesto of the Church of England, her first public act of atonement for half a century of apostasy, of class-prejudice and political syco-phancy'.

3

The little group were soon joined by Maurice's brother-in-law and Charles Mansfield, the distiller of benzol from coal, an old school friend of Tom Hughes. To illuminate the difficult path of the working class they decided to produce a paper to be called *Politics for the People*. A friend of Kingsley's undertook to publish it, and the first number appeared on 6 May, less than a month after their first resolution. A weekly with sixteen pages to an issue, it lasted for two months: Ludlow writing no fewer than thirty-eight articles for its double-columned pages. In the twelfth of these he sounded the organ-notes of the movement:

'Democracy must mean, not the letting loose all the accumulated selfishness of the many, but the giant self-control of a nation, ruling itself as one man, in wisdom and righteousness, beneath the eye of God.'

And

'Let each man learn to govern himself, not in solitude, but in fellowship with others, and from fellowship to fellowship, from circle to circle, the privilege of the few ever widening to admit the many, the collective self-government of English democracy is achieved.'

It was this concept of fellowship, or association, which Ludlow had seen operating in France in the Société des amis des pauvres, which led the group to undertake the civilising of the inhabitants of Great Ormond's Yard, a black spot near Maurice's own house. When *Politics for the People* ceased publication, the group dropped their pens and trudged through this derelict area to teach in a night school they had founded. It was a task which called, not so much for learning, as sheer moral courage. Maurice had invariably to be attended by another member to keep order, while even the stoutest of them never walked across the yard unaccompanied. So it is little wonder that Maurice one day told the group that he had secured another helper who would be invaluable in such work. When he disclosed the name, there was general laughter, and someone said, 'We are not going to start a cricket club!' But Maurice was so obviously proud of his new recruit that the new-comer was admitted, and proved 'an immediate success'. His 'knightlike loyalty, humane geniality, and simple Christian faith' made him, as the historian of Christian Socialism says, in a sense 'the centre of the movement'. That new recruit was Thomas Hughes.[9]

4

'I am not much of a thinker or projector. . . . I think it is more fit that I should take my full whack as executor and if necessary, of endurer', wrote Hughes, with characteristic modesty, yet perfect truth.[10] For 'an executor and endurer' was precisely what the group lacked. Maurice, the leader, needed a devoted executive officer; for, as he confessed, his own nature was 'very prickly and disputatious'; while his habit of speaking with bowed head and in low tones led Kingsley playfully to inquire, 'What shall it be done to the prophet who prophesieth into his first waistcoat pocket?' Kingsley himself was rooted in his study at Eversley, where, pen in hand, he was a power; but placed before an audience of working men, his characteristic stammer never failed to assert itself: as when he said, 'I am a Ch-Ch-Ch-Church of England parson and a Ch-Ch-Ch-Chartist.' Ludlow was, if anything, too self-effacing and efficient: immersed in the architecture of ideas and the organisation of activity rather than in active life. Some of the others, able as they might be in their own spheres, were too odd to be effective, and too unworldly to be taken seriously. Charles Mansfield, for instance, with his cotton cloth shoes and 'strange sad life' full of 'almost incredible moral complications'; Furnivall, with his vegetarianism and explosive temper, and A. M. Campbell, with his phonetic fads and schemes for reforming the English language: all fringed the movement from the grim economic realities of the times.

Hughes was the 'blue', the John Bull amongst them. For him, the name of action was not lost, nor sicklied o'er with the pale cast of thought, and the yearnings and aspirations of the prophets became practicable. With genial, blue-eyed empiricism, he realised he was among 'restless and eccentric persons' whose vagaries even 'the marvellous patience, gentleness and wisdom of our beloved president were not enough to counteract or control'.[11] But he was not a cricket blue for nothing. The group had recruits from every walk of life: a scholar, a politician, a doctor, an architect, an astronomer, a tractarian clergyman, a Young England swell, a poet, a critic, a couple of publishers, and five working men. He made them a team.[12]

Unlike all the rest, there was no element of felinity in his nature. All the rest were prone to criticise either themselves or each other, but Hughes radiated goodwill and tolerance. When Kingsley was prejudiced and reckless and Ludlow complained, Hughes calmed them both. Kingsley acknowledged it by saying, 'You are nearer to God than I am, I see well'. Frances Kingsley, who had no love for the more disreputable elements among the group, agreed that Hughes was 'the best fellow on earth'.[13] When Maurice and Ludlow disagreed with E. V. Neale, an older and wealthier recruit to the movement, for his freedom of thought and lavish expenditure, Hughes defended him, at times alone. Indeed, Hughes once called him a 'Knight of the Round Table', a saint who had 'done more' than any other man 'to spread sound views of social economy'.[14] Of Lord Goderich, another recruit, Hughes was the intimate confidant, the man to whom Goderich turned 'more often and with more affection' than 'to anyone else'.[15]

When *Politics for the People* suspended publication on 29 July 1848, Hughes threw himself into the various pilot projects of his new associates. He helped a scheme to waylay Prince Albert with a memorial on the sanitary condition of Jacob's Island, Bermondsey. He taught twice a week in the classes in Ormond's Yard, where his muscular presence was invaluable; his 'wonderful faculty' of 'inventing and keeping up games' prevented the recurrence of such scenes as one lecturer encountered: 'the gas turned out and his hat knocked over his eyes by one of his boys'.[16]

Also, he attracted others, like Septimus Hansard, the curate of Marylebone, where Hughes kept open house.[17] Hansard was an old Rugbeian, a gruff, blunt, toad-like man, who in turn introduced a member of his congregation, the musician George Grove. Hughes also brought in other old Rugbeians: his brother George, and G. G. Bradley, who was then a master at the school. By December of that eventful year regular meetings had begun at Maurice's house every Monday evening to read the Bible. The 'heart of the movement', as Ludlow later called it, had begun to beat.

5

Maurice's sermons in Lincoln's Inn Chapel drew others. William Cooper, who had been a Chartist and much influenced by the rationalist strain of Robert Owen, was persuaded to listen. It took four sermons to convince him that the group had something to offer to others of his class, and he consented to bring together a number of his fellow workmen at the Cranbourne Coffee Tavern on 23 April 1849. To break the ice, Kingsley stuttered his famous declaration: 'I am a Ch-Ch-Ch-Church of England clergyman and I am a Ch-Ch-Ch-Chartist.'

There, by lecture, debate, and discussion, the Christian Socialists fostered the confidence of Cooper's associates. A former Owenite, Lloyd Jones, who had been a constant witness to secular socialism for the previous two decades, gave them the benefit of his experience in journalism and co-operation as well as a knowledge of industrial England which few possessed. Joseph Millbank and Thomas Shorter, also ex-Chartists, followed, together with Charles Sully, who had fought on the barricades, and Gerald Massey, the Chartist poet.

It was at one of these meetings with the workers at the Cranbourne Coffee Tavern—Hughes gives the specific date as 12 June 1849—that the determination grew 'to take some active, practical steps towards combating the fearful evils' of trade.[18] And it was at another, in August 1849, that Hughes appeared to speak, with Septimus Hansard in the chair. At the end of this meeting the National Anthem was played, and several revolutionary Chartists hissed. Hughes sprang on to a chair and in a voice that all could hear, announced that the first man who hissed the Queen's name would have personally to settle accounts with him. 'As Mr. Hughes' fist was well known as one not to be despised, this gave a moment's pause.'[19] The pianist struck up once more, and the hisses were drowned in loyal singing. George Jacob Holyoake, commenting on the scene, remarked dryly that had a republican acted in that way it would have been considered ruffianly.[20]

During these discussions Ludlow once more went to Paris,

where he inspected the Association Ouvrières of Buchez. He returned with information that he published in the fourth of the *Tracts*. In November, a Frenchman, also a believer in such associations, joined the group. This interesting man, A. L. Jules le Chevalier (known as St. André from this time onwards), has been described as 'handsome, literally smooth-faced, and mellow: he was quite globular, and when he moved he vibrated like a locomotive jelly'.[21] His Gallic enthusiasm, coupled with popular indignation against slum conditions and an outbreak of cholera, galvanised the discussion group at the Cranbourne Tavern, and in the autumn of 1849 they worked to relieve the sufferings resulting from the epidemic. Kingsley came up from Eversley to publish *Cheap Clothes and Nasty*.

To Ludlow the answer seemed clear. Relief work among the tailors was not enough. Associations on the Buchez model should be established among them. But Maurice was not to be convinced by the babel of expedients which his flock pressed upon him, and it was not until 2 January 1850 that he was able to write to Kingsley:

'Competition is put forth as the law of the universe. That is a lie. The time has come for us to declare that it is a lie . . . I see no way but by associating for work instead of for strikes.'

Six days later, at his house, the first meeting of what was to become the Working Tailors' Association was held. By April 1850, under Walter Cooper's management, and financed by the group, twenty-four tailors were working in a co-operative workshop on the Paris model. They were started, as Hughes wrote, on very little money—£300—'with a slop-worker who had been in prison as manager, and some dozen associates of kindred opinions (Chartists) in the workroom'.[22] Nevertheless, the shop proved immediately successful, the twelve associates grew to thirty-four, and eventually a branch was set up in the ready-made trade, hitherto notorious for its sweating of labour. Others followed, founded both by loans from the group (now called the Council of Promoters, with Hughes, Furnivall, and Neale as treasurers) and sustained by their custom: Another tailors' association, two builders' (one of which built a house for Neale, and the other a hall for the Society), a printers' (which produced the pamphlets and propaganda of the Society), a bakers' (which catered for the gatherings and conferences), a needlewomen's, a pianoforte-makers', and a smiths'. Southampton followed, with a tailors' and hatters'.

The spirit in which these associations were established was that the workers were to manage and own their workshops, and divide the profits among themselves. By being their own masters they would end exploitation, and gain a realistic education in the principles of freedom, brotherhood, and self-sacrifice. Socialism would thus be Christianised and Capitalism socialised. But to ensure that the money of Neale and others was not wasted in the initial stages, a Central Board of the manager and working-class representatives of each association was established to arbitrate between members, sustained in turn by weekly contributions from each member.

By June 1850 the Society for Promoting Working Men's Associations was set up to foster the work. Working through a Council of Promoters (the Christian Socialist leaders) and this Central Board, it afforded an avenue for Hughes' activities which proved eminently satisfying. Its creed was strenuous, challenging, and offered infinite possibilities of social renewal. 'Here we had found the solution of the great labour question,' Hughes reminisced; 'we had nothing to do but to announce the solution' and 'found an association or two in order to convert all England and usher in the millennium at once.' [23]

Hughes' views at this time are illustrated by an article he wrote on 2 November 1850 for the *Christian Socialist*, a newspaper issued by the promoters and printed by a 'diminutive one-eyed costermonger' who had been in prison as a Chartist leader. This article, one of only six he contributed to the paper, was a satire on the outlook of some contemporary manufacturers, written in the form of a letter by Plugson of Undershot, a creation of Carlyle's. Written in vigorous language it was originally intended for *Punch* as the first of a series entitled 'Punch's Intercepted Letter-bag':

'I was born', Plugson begins, 'an operative, and am now one of the labour lords, Sir, of this great nineteenth century, thanks to a free and enlightened competition, whereby I've ruined two brothers-in-law, and made my wife's uncle blow his brains out—thanks to the glorious laws of supply and demand, the only natural laws of society—thanks to the Patent Plugson Economic Screw Jenny, the invention of an operative of mine, who sold it to me for 2 pounds 14s, which has enabled me to dispense with adult male labour in my factory.' Now along come co-operatives 'in defiance of all the laws of political economy, to see whether they could not help cutting one another's throats, and one person (Parson Lot, I think they call him) had been telling them it was alright. Fancy that, Sir! fancy the Established Church, one of the institutions of the country, telling a parcel of working men that it's all right to form co-operative associations. Perhaps you don't know, Sir, what co-operative associations are; why, co-operative associations are Socialism, Sir—Socialism and nothing less! I'm a liberal, Sir; I like my working men to have rational liberty; when I drop my wages from 8s. 6d. to 7s. 6d., I wouldn't force one of them to take the 7s. 6d., not if you'd pay me; if the man won't take it, why, he's free to starve, Sir—and so he should be, whether in the workhouse or out of it.' 'I tell you, Sir, I'm a liberal; I like a good strike now and then, Sir, that I do; many a time it has relieved me of a glut of stock, whilst the working men have been supporting themselves out of their own means, instead of my paying wages to them.' But this socialism, with its equality, its price and wage fixing, its retailing at cost. . . . Soon a man with capital would have no choice but to take his money and go to the 'land of free and enlightened competition, the only place where the rights of property are understood, where a man can wallop his own nigger—the States of America, Sir.'

Hughes never lost his early faith in Christian Socialism even though he professed to be amused by it. Long after the original movement was a blurred memory in the minds of men, Hughes was founding and urging others to found producers' associations. Co-operation, or Christian Socialism as he preferred to call it half a century later, 'is the crusade of the twentieth century. Other heights on the great battlefield against the world, the flesh, and the devil, will bring more fame and pudding, but the trade stronghold is the key to the position, and, therefore, the place in front for those who are in deadly earnest'.[24]

6

Promoting Christian Socialism was very strenuous work. At six o'clock in the morning Hughes would have to attend meetings of the Promoters—at 458 New Oxford Street until the autumn of 1850, and afterwards at 76 Charlotte Street—walking up from Marylebone as dawn was breaking. There the business of the various associations would be discussed, the position of the managers elaborated, and the loans made. Then Hughes would walk on farther to his chambers in 3 Old Buildings, Lincoln's Inn, which he shared with Neale, and later with Ludlow, for, as a Templar, Hughes could not hold the rooms in his own name.

And in the midst of it all, he could still find time to take Matthew, son of his old headmaster, and then private secretary to the Lord President of the Council, swimming at 6 o'clock in the morning. They once stayed in for an hour, with swans looking at them.

Neale was twelve years older than Hughes, and also an old Oriel man. He had an imagination of quicksilver, with a mind as fertile as his financial resources seemed unlimited. He maintained a large country house in Warwickshire, together with the house in Hill Street which had been 'improved' by the Builders' Association. Under the spell of his associates, he threw all he had into the movement, losing, by a conservative estimate, £60,000 in three years.

To Hughes' chambers flocked people of all shades of opinion and colour. The quarrels and inefficiencies of the managers, as Hughes confessed, 'kept the legal members of the board (none of whom was overburdened with regular practice) pretty fully occupied'.[25] The best of the managers, Walter Cooper of the first association of tailors, who had been made vicar's warden of a West-End church, falsified his books and destroyed his association. Others resented reserving profits, or refused to divide them equitably, drank heavily, borrowed money outside the movement, and broke the rules of trade.

'We were young, saucy, and so thoroughly convinced we were right, that we cared, shall I say, not a d—n,' Hughes remarked. Friends 'prophesied that my prospects at the Bar would be ruined by my crochets', he went on.

'No doubt I lost business by these "crochets" . . . but other business came, as I was wonderfully punctual at Chambers and soon got to be friends with my few clients, who even got to pardon, with a shrug of their shoulders, the queer folk they often found there. And queer no doubt they were for a Chancery Barrister's Chambers.'

He really suffered only one loss. A dear old gentleman, a family friend, induced a solicitor, 'head of a firm which could have made any young barrister's fortune', to take a brief to Hughes. The solicitor duly arrived at 3 Old Buildings, Lincoln's Inn, and was told to wait. That itself was bad enough. But when Hughes' door opened 'and a full blown black person (lately from the West Indies in quest of advice and aid for the freedmen there) walked out', it proved too much for the solicitor. He 'hurried away, saying that he would call again'. Hughes never saw his brief again, nor him.[26]

Not all his visitors were so discouraged. W. E. Forster, who married Dr. Arnold's daughter Jane in 1850, came to talk, and left saying, 'Well, for a set of revolutionists, I must say you are the pleasantest ones I know.'[27] So, too, did John Stuart Mill, who 'quite overcame his earlier prejudice'. Perhaps the strangest of all was the German V. A. Huber, whom they introduced to co-operators throughout the kingdom, and who in turn has left, in the journal of his tour, a characteristic description of a great cricket match played between Price's Factory at Belmont and an eleven composed of Christian Socialists.[28]

Such lightheartedness was characteristic of the group as a whole. Kingsley was like a boy, subject, in Hughes' phrase, to 'Rabelaisian fits'. Coming up from Eversley one day to his father's rectory in Chelsea, he sent a rhymed invitation to Hughes at Lincoln's Inn 'to get his gullet greased' at the 'jawshop in the East', concluding:

> 'So come, you thief, and drop your brief,
> At six o'clock without relief;
> And if you won't may you come to grief,
> Says Parson Lot the Socialist Chief
> Who signs his mark at the foot of the leaf.'

Hughes set out with Kingsley's publisher, but when they reached Hyde Park Corner, a dense fog came up and they were delayed. Kingsley seized the occasion to moralise: life was like that, only just enough light to get home. With a Borneo missionary, the four talked far into the night, while Kingsley preached on every subject that came into his mind. The missionary decided to go home at two in the morning, and left with a link-boy. Hughes, more accommodating, accepted a bed on the floor.[29]

7

But Hughes travelled farther afield than Chelsea to make friends. In January 1851 he accompanied Maurice through Lancashire to encourage the formation of producer co-operatives. Thanks to the efforts of such bodies as the Redemptionist Society and the National Association of United Trades, the north of England looked promising ground for such experiments, and Hughes, as the historian of the first association in London, was just the person to answer questions. On 3 January, 800 people attended a tea-party in the New Town Hall at Bury to hear the two Londoners. So good an impression did they make that not only did they receive the thanks of the assembly, but also the offer of £150 to start a cotton-mill. Four days later a similar meeting was held in the Mechanics' Institute, Manchester.

A working man described the impression created on his class:

'It was a cheering sight,' he told the *Christian Socialist*, 'to see so many people meeting as equals to inquire into the causes of bigotry without being stigmatised as Atheists or Communists.' 'Ah! Sir, I have often thought that parsons and rich men were a cruel and heartless set, when I have seen a poor uneducated ragged little boy dragged by the policeman before those whom he was told to look upon as his betters, to receive sentence for some petty theft, or rather for having been neglected in his childhood, for being the victim of evil influences over which he as a child had no control. . . . But when I see such men as Mr. Maurice and your Promoters stepping out from their own class, to lead the uneducated, and to use that education which more fortunate circumstances have given to them, on behalf of the poor ignorant serfs; then indeed I have hopes in the future, and I bear ill-will to none.' [30]

In September, Hughes and Ludlow went farther afield, this time covering Yorkshire as well. They visited thirteen societies, but found little to encourage them except friends at Leeds and possibilities at Bury. The northern spirit was harder and more realistic: joint-stock, not co-operation, was the basis of their planning, and adulteration was not unknown. Of the few real producer co-operatives, not one was paying its way.

Impressed by his contacts with consumer co-operation in the north, Hughes threw himself into the establishment of a Central Co-operative Agency for the whole movement. This was an attempt to provide an outlet for the products of the producing societies and an inlet for consumers' societies. St. André's facile genius inspired it, and Neale's wealth sustained it. Hughes became a trustee, and in the autumn served on a committee which tried to educate the trade unions in the purposes of the agency. Soon after this he assumed the editorship of the *Journal of Association*—which was the *Christian Socialist* under a new name.

This brought about a rift in the group. Ludlow was prejudiced against Neale's Central Co-operative Agency, regarding it as mere machinery, of no moral value to the participants. He was also angry because it neither paid a bonus to members nor stressed the Christian element in its composition. Hughes sided with Neale, agreed that Chartists should be admitted to the executive committee, and set out to woo trade union support. He confessed that this was 'the only serious difference that ever existed between us, though it never impaired our friendship'.[31]

Hughes' close friendship with Neale led him to volunteer to act with him and three others as a trustee of a proposed co-operative iron works at Liverpool. This, an outcome of the recent amalgamation of the iron workers into the Amalgamated Society of Engineers, was an attempt to utilise their large reserve funds. But unfortunately the great strike and lock-out of the engineers which began in January 1852 drained much of that capital. Nothing daunted, Neale transferred his energies to Southwark, and financed a similar organisation at Mile End Road, for which Hughes also became a trustee, and another at Southwark Bridge.

In the great lock-out of 1852, Kingsley, Maurice, and Ludlow were only lukewarm supporters of the A.S.E.: Kingsley in fact wrote a letter to Hughes urging him to leave these highly paid workers to wage their own battles. But Hughes loved a fight. He wrote vigorously in the *Journal of Association* on behalf of the men. In January he was trying to persuade the employers to submit to arbitration. Later he urged the workers to bear the strike with fortitude until public opinion could be rallied. But after the strike had lasted a month and there was no indication that the employers would ever permit workers to join a union, Hughes boiled with indignation. 'Which metal rings truest?' he cried. By April the strike was crushed, and Hughes, loyal to the last, rallied with Vansittart (Neale's cousin) to raise funds to enable thirty of the men to emigrate to Australia.[32]

This bitter experience made Hughes a lifelong supporter of the trade union movement. And it earned him a name amongst the trade unionists and won him the friendship of such men as William Allan, the Mustos, and William Newton—architects of the 'new unionism'.

8

Perhaps the least dramatic yet most useful of Hughes' activities for the movement began in 1850, when he established yet another friendship with a barrister at Lincoln's Inn who was, like himself, interested in social work. This barrister, R. A. Slaney, was twenty years older than Hughes, and had first entered Parliament for Shrewsbury when Hughes was leaving his cradle. Slaney was the author, among other books, of *A Plea for the Working Classes*; a keen observer and naturalist, he was well versed in the processes of parliamentary committees, having served as the chairman of two in 1838 and 1840.[33]

The early morning sessions of the Council of Promoters had convinced Hughes and Neale that the existing state of the law was unfavourable to the further growth of co-operative associations of producers and consumers, since it left them entirely at the mercy of their trustees. As long as those trustees were Christian Socialists there was little fear of their converting moneys to their own use. But since the whole object of the associations was to enable the working men to govern their own workshops, there should be some legal avenue of redress for such associations as found themselves saddled with dishonest trustees. By the existing law (the result of a series of Friendly Societies Acts in the 'thirties and 'forties) there was no such redress except that embodied in the costly procedure of the Joint Stock Companies Act of 1844, which excluded associations with fewer than twenty-five members and permitted transfer of shares, and the consequent possibility of one man's gaining control of an association. Further legislation, endowing co-operators with corporate personalities, able to hold property, borrow money and invest freely, was imperative to create the conditions of freedom in which co-operative associations could take root and thrive.

Slaney secured his committee, and the barrister members of the group testified before it. Hughes, in his evidence in May 1850, stressed the need of empowering the associations both to receive loans and to invest their surplus funds in their own trade organisations, instead of for such specific objects as were prescribed by the existing law. The committee reported in 1850 in favour of these recommendations, but nothing more was done, partly owing to its division of opinion over limited liability, partly to parliamentary fear of trade unions participating in co-operative movements. In the following year Slaney again secured the appointment of a committee, which again reported along the same lines. This time, Hughes, with Neale and Ludlow, organised a deputation to the Home Secretary to press for legislation, and when they received no redress, organised another in February 1852. But they were told that the unfavourable political climate (the engineers were then locked out) made it very difficult. In the spring, however, a Tory government, not so wedded to *laissez-faire*, and wanting a sedative for labour unrest, came to power. Hughes and the two barristers went to work again and with such effect that the bill which they had drafted was read a second time on 21 April, and on 30 June became law as the Industrial and Provident Societies Act (15 and 16 Vict. C. 31). During its passage through the House from its introduction on 19 March, Hughes had worked hard, with Neale and Ludlow, to secure its comprehension, appearing on 27 May before the committee after the second reading to explain certain clauses. The associations themselves, unaware that without legislation in their favour they would be ruined as soon as they were worth ruining, refused to show, as Hughes regretfully remarked, that they cared a straw about the matter.[34]

The result of his efforts was a real charter for the co-operative movement. Canon Raven has described it 'as in some respects the most important piece of social legislation of the century'.[35] For under its clauses the co-operative societies found real shelter. They were freed from the onerous requirements of previous legislation (an Act of 1844), obliging them to register as joint-stock companies if they numbered more than twenty-five members in a society. They were recognised as corporate entities before the law; free to accept loans from their members up to four times the amount of their subscribed capital; able to accept from individuals amounts up to £100 in share capital; and safeguarded in their tenure of such shares (or 'subscriptions', as they were called) by a provision which required subscribers either to sell them back to the society or secure the assent of the society before transferring them to anyone else.

Three months after it became law, the Society for Promoting Working Men's Associations published a set of model rules, approved by Tidd Pratt, the official registrar, to guide co-operative societies throughout the country.

Meanwhile, the society had furnished for themselves a hall for meetings in the building of their first association, the Working Tailors. This, a month after the Act became law, they had opened with a National Co-operative Congress, where Hughes explained the provisions of Slaney's Act to co-operative delegates from all over the country. This was followed by further activity on the part of Neale in establishing the Co-operative League, whose *Transactions* ventilated the practical problems of establishing co-operative societies and suggested solutions. A Co-operative Investment Society was mooted, whereby a reservoir of capital could be accumulated to encourage further co-operative experiments, and the National Association of United Trades for the Protection of Labour promised their support.

9

The climax of the Christian Socialist movement was reached in the summer of 1852.

In the following year, 1853, a further conference was held at Manchester in which the northern societies (mostly consumers) played the leading part. The Christian Socialist Society for Promoting Working Men's Associations changed its name to the Society for Promoting Industrial and Provident Societies, and withdrew from the centre to the periphery of the movement. When the next Co-operative Congress met in Leeds in 1854, they had been displaced, and disappeared as an organised society.

This loss of influence in the movement was a severe blow to the enthusiastic group which had started out with such hopes in 1850. Moreover, in the meantime, among the promoters themselves centrifugal forces were operating. Kingsley's wife Frances, seven years older than he was, worried herself into a nervous breakdown over his activities, and they migrated to Torquay. There Kingsley was fired with enthusiasm for a new crusade: to defend the white Rajah of Borneo against the head-hunting Dyaks. Sir James Brooke, the rajah, was standing trial in London for his anti-Dyak activities, and Kingsley felt impelled to champion this son of Devon against the hostility of public opinion. Ludlow urged him to concentrate on English working men, but Kingsley refused, telling Hughes that Ludlow was becoming 'censorious' and 'infallible in his own eyes'.[36] By 1855 he could even write to Hughes:

'If I have held back from the Socialist movement, it has been because I have seen that the world was not going to be set right in any such rose-pink way, excellent as it is, and that there are heavy arrears of destruction to be made up before construction can even begin, and I wanted to see what those arrears were.' [37]

Ludlow, for his part, was more than ever convinced that the movement which he had done so much to initiate should become more selective if it was to retain its Christian character. This brought him into collision with Neale, who, as the realist financier of the movement, was prepared to broaden the movement to include the secularist legatees of Robert Owen—men like G. J. Holyoake, who he saw had a moral fervour which would sustain the cause of co-operative production and help it to take root in the north. An index of this fission was the separation, in June 1852, of the Wholesale Society which his money had created (the Central Co-operative Agency), and the Society for Promoting Working Men's Associations, which, since the former's inauguration the year before, had shared a common headquarters at 76 Charlotte Street. Now the Society moved to the building of the Working Tailors in Castle Street, where a hall was furnished. Neale's Agency remained for a time in Charlotte Street, and then moved to 356 Oxford Street in the spring of 1853.

Moreover, Neale's practical scheme, which might have fused both producers and consumers into a very workable anticipation of the modern C.W.S., was further jeopardised by the secession of the jelly-like Frenchman, from whom the suggestion had originally come. For, just at this very moment of weakness, in December 1852, St. André chose to break with the movement and secede to found a rival organisation known as the 'Universal Provider'. This rival organisation drew off much custom, including that of the Rochdale Pioneers, from the parent body. Though its existence was short (some three years), it proved long enough to wreck Neale's Agency.

And what of the original prophet of the movement—Frederick Denison Maurice? When he had inspired his followers with the words 'the Kingdom of Heaven is to me the great existing reality which is to renew the earth and make it a habitation for blessed spirits instead of for demons', there was no hint of failure. No cunning working men had impounded funds, no great strikes like that of the engineers in 1852 had threatened the foundations of society, no rifts had appeared in his small and obedient congregation.

But now other sounds were heard from him: sounds which perplexed such Liberals as Jowett, who, after hearing him preach a university sermon, said with a shrug of his shoulders, 'Well, all I can make out is that today was yesterday and this world the same as the next'. Some of these sounds echoed an anti-democratic bias that had always lurked in Maurice's thinking:

'Reconstitute Society upon the democratic basis—treat the sovereign and the aristocracy as not intended to rule and guide the land, as only holding their commissions from us—and I anticipate nothing but a most accursed sacerdotal rule or a military despotism with the great body of the population in either case morally, politically, physically serfs, more than they are at present or have ever been.' [38]

Maurice's shying away from action taxed all Tom Hughes' resources, till he admitted, 'It was awful work having to fix him up again against his will in one post or another which he thought he might slip out of'.[39] Each fresh exfoliation of the society brought a renewed protest from Maurice. The climax came in 1852, when Hughes, in his capacity as editor, accepted a pamphlet by Lord Goderich on *The Duty of the Age* for inclusion in the series of tracts. It was duly printed in Maurice's absence. The 'duty' which Goderich outlined was universal suffrage, and when Maurice read it he was furious. Hughes received 'a precious wigging (the only one I ever had) with orders to suppress the whole edition'. Loyally, Hughes obeyed. Characteristically, Maurice also suspended publication of any further tracts.[40]

For some time Maurice had been in trouble with the authorities at King's College, where he had held the chair of English Literature and History since 1840. In 1851 he had been called upon by the Principal to clear himself of the charge of heterodoxy advanced by the *Quarterly Review*, and had been cleared by a committee of inquiry in the following year. But when his *Theological Essays* were published in 1853 he was formally asked to resign.

With Maurice's resignation the active members of the group rallied to sympathise. On 27 December 1853, at a meeting of working men in the Hall of Association in Castle Street, he was presented with an address, and one member hoped 'that he might not find it a fall to cease to be a professor at King's College and to become the Principal of a Working Men's College'.

The Christian Socialists were turning upon another tack.

10

In the meantime their beloved associations were falling to pieces, and it was recognition of this fact that really brought the Christian Socialist movement to an end. The bankruptcy in 1854 of the Mile End Engineering Association, followed shortly by that of the Atlas Works, in which Neale lost thousands of pounds, was a clear sign of impending disaster. These failures, wrote Hughes many years later, were a grievous disappointment.

'We had thought now, when the pick of the artisans of England had come into association, we should have great examples to hold up to our tailors and cobblers, who seemed never able to get through a month without a crisis. We found the engineers at least as jealous of each other, as difficult to manage, as ready to shirk work, as their humbler brethren in comparatively unskilled trades.' [41]

A general collapse was only a matter of time.

Throughout the 'fifties one association after another either failed or became a private concern, and the final blows came in 1860, when the excellent North London Builders finally gave up, and the Working Tailors which, Hughes told Goderich, cost him £1,000 and 'kept me a poor man for years',[42] split in two. Of the fifteen associations represented at the conference of 1852 only the Hatters survived to 1869. To top it all, the Central Co-operative Agency, unable to sustain the expense of moving in 1853, was transformed in 1857 into an ordinary business as Woodin, Jones & Company. Whatever might be the future of co-operative production, conditions were not ripe nor the workers morally ready for it in 1852. London, with its lack of local camaraderie, was perhaps the worst place to begin. Yet it is noteworthy that producers' associations started by northern consumer societies, such as the Rochdale Co-operative Manufacturing Society, fared no better. In 1862 the shareholders of the Rochdale Society objected to sharing with workers, and the society became a joint-stock company.

Though Hughes never regretted a penny of the money he had lost, nor retreated even for a moment from his basic convictions —in 1855 he accused Kingsley of being a regenade to socialism[43]— he was for the first time in his life temporarily deeply discouraged. 'If the faith was all that we held it to be,' he wrote Lord Goderich in October 1855, 'not even our clumsy proclaiming of it and our astonishing differences in general beliefs could have made such a hash as we did of a good deal of our work.' Was *the* right thing for that time (he spoke of the years 1849–1850) the proclaiming of working associations

'as the practical Christianity to be got about before all other things? ... I doubt. I don't doubt that Christian Socialism was, is and forever shall be *the* thing to preach, but our application of it for that time? ... However none of us were men in authority so perhaps we couldn't have done otherwise than we did.' [44]

Writing to Kingsley in the spring of 1856, Hughes even insisted, somewhat bitterly, that he had seen the 'weak places' in the movement and had warned his colleagues against them, which drew from Kingsley the comment, 'You are an old darling, and who says no, I'd kick him, if it wasn't for my cloth; but you are green in cottoning to me about our '48 mess.' [45]

In the same year Hughes sent Lord Goderich a piece of legislation he had concocted, asking:

'Is the enclosed chewed small enough to suit the limited intellects of the Peers of the Realm, or must I swallow it and bring it up again before they can understand?' [46]

NOTES

[1] Letters, Tom Hughes to Fanny Ford, 6 Nov., Dec. 1946.

[2] F. Maurice, *Life of Frederick Denison Maurice* (New York, 1884), i, 427.

[3] Ripon Papers, B.M. Add. MSS. 43,511, Hughes to Ripon, 6 Jan. 1858.

[4] C. F. G. Masterman, *Frederick Denison Maurice* (London, 1907), 143.

[5] Mounstuart Grant Duff, *Notes from a Diary, 1851–1877* (London, 1897), i, 78–79.

[6] C. E. Raven, *Christian Socialism, 1848–1854* (London, 1920), 93.

[7] *Co-operative News*, 28 March 1896, 313.

[8] Una Pope-Hennessy, *Canon Charles Kingsley* (London, 1948), 77.

[9] *Economic Review* (1896), vi, 299; Raven, *op. cit.*, 131.

[10] Letter, Hughes to Ludlow, Berg Collection, New York Public Library.

[11] Hughes, *Memoir of a Brother*, 113; Charles Kingsley, *Alton Locke, with a prefatory Memoir by Thomas Hughes* (London, 1876), xxiv.

[12] F. J. Furnivall was the scholar, Lord Goderich (later Lord Ripon) the politician; Charles Robert Walsh the doctor; Archibald Mansfield Campbell (introduced by Mansfield) the architect; Francis Cranmer Penrose the astronomer; the Rev. John Sherren Brewer the clergyman; Cuthbert Edward Ellison (according to Ludlow the original of *Pendennis*) the swell; A. H. Clough the poet; David Masson the critic; and Daniel and Alexander Macmillan the publishers. The last-named brought in undergraduates from Cambridge like Fenton J. A. Hort, Llewellyn Davies and Westlake.

[13] Kingsley, *Alton Locke*, xxx; (Mrs. Charles Kingsley), *Charles Kingsley: His Letters and Memories of His Life* (London, 1883), 2 vols., i, 218; ii, 45.

[14] *Proceedings of the 25th Annual Co-operative Congress* (1893), 111; *Economic Review* (1893), iii, 40 ff.

[15] L. Wolf, *Life of the First Marquess of Ripon*, i, 150, 162, 285, 347; Ripon Papers B.M. Add. MSS. 43,514, letter, 10 Aug. 1862.

[16] F. Maurice, *op. cit.*, i, 549; letter of Hughes, *circa* 1870.

[17] An amusing picture of Hansard in later years was drawn in 1862 by a Miss Eden in a letter to Hughes' sister Jane. 'I have got a domestic Chaplain for my Sunday Services of the most magnificent nature—(I really like him very much

if I don't look at him). He frightens me and Stokley out of the few wits we possess—his manner and appearance are utterly disagreeable and odious—I dare say *you* hate him! He *says* he is one of your brother's great friends??—(Hansard his name is). He really is something *too* hideous to look at—like a toad in beard and spectacles and he is so frightfully vain and conceited and boastful it is quite absurd—why don't men knock him down I wonder—I sh'd in a minute if I could—but yet the odd thing is, I like him (to *work* with) 10,000 times better than *your* pet old Clark—he is so much more sincere, and behind all his snarls and growls and snappishness and *rudeness* even he does work like a dray horse, and never fails one—He will give up every engagement to come and help, and the navvies literally worship him—(beard and all)—As a man in private life I think Clark too charming, 'Septimus' *quite disgusting* but as a fellow labourer I think Clark a bitter disappointment and *a sham* altogether,—and Hansard a real treasure—a sincerely good, useful, sensible, excellent worthy creature, and *such* a socialist!—why are *they* all (I don't know your brother remember, perhaps is he not) so vain and foolish *outside*, and so really good *inside*. Not that I think Septimus a devout man *internally*, at least he does not talk as if he was, but in public, oh! my goodness he is all fancy painted a *perfect preacher* and I daresay also, parish priest as well but this I have only *his own* word for, wh—I sh'd think had better go for nothing—or he ought to be made Saint Septimus Bishop and Martyr on the spot.'

[18] *Economic Review*, i. (1891), 209.

[19] F. Maurice, *Life of Frederick Denison Maurice*, ii. 10.

[20] G. J. Holyoake, *Bygones Worth Remembering* (London, 1905), i, 88–89.

[21] J. McCabe, *Life and Letters of G. J. Holyoake* (London, 1908), i, 191.

[22] Brown, *True Manliness*, xvi.

[23] Hughes, *Memoir of a Brother*, 109, 111.

[24] *Economic Review* (1893), iii, 189.

[25] Kingsley, *Alton Locke*, xxxvi.

[26] Brown, *True Manliness*, xviii.

[27] T. Wemyss Reid, *Life of W. E. Forster* (London, 1888), i, 279.

[28] V. A. Huber, *Reisebriefe . . . im Sommer 1854* (Hamburg, 1855), ii, 40–47.

[29] *Macmillan's Magazine*, March 1877, 33 ff.

[30] *Christian Socialist*, i, 93.

[31] Maurice, *Life of F. D. Maurice*, ii, 75; *Economic Review* (1893), iii, 42; (1896), vi, 302.

[32] *Journal of Association*, 9, 11, 17, 31, 57–58.

[33] The contact seems to have been made through H. R. Vaughan Johnson, who collected evidence for Slaney: *Economic Review* (1896), vi, 300. J. J. Dent, J. M. *Ludlow* (Manchester, 1921), says that Hughes 'secured' Robert Slaney, 'who was willing to be the promoter' to act as a parliamentary mouthpiece.

[34] *Journal of Association*, 3 Jan. 1852.

[35] C. E. Raven, *Christian Socialism*, 333; G. D. H. Cole, *A Century of Co-operation* (Manchester, 1944), 97 ff.

[36] Una Pope-Hennessy, *op. cit.*, 125–126.

[37] Guy Kendall, *Charles Kingsley and His Ideas* (London, 1947), 73. M. B. Reckitt, *Maurice to Temple* (London, 1947), 219.

[38] H. G. Wood, *F. D. Maurice* (Cambridge, 1950), 160.

[39] Maurice, *Life of F. D. Maurice*, ii, 172–173.

[40] Maurice, *Life of F. D. Maurice*, ii, 126.

[41] *Economic Review* (1893), iii, 46.

[42] Ripon Papers, B.M. Add. MSS. 43,515, letter, Hughes to Ripon, 26 Jan. 1856.

[43] (Mrs. Charles Kingsley), *op. cit.*, ii, 335.

[44] Ripon Papers, B.M. Add. MSS. 43,510, letter, Hughes to Ripon, 28 Oct. 1855.

[45] Kingsley, *Alton Locke*, iv–v.

[46] Ripon Papers, B.M. Add. MSS. 34,511, letter, Hughes to Ripon, 23 May 1856.

CHAPTER FIVE

New Men and New Talent, 1854–1857

I

THE first social activity of the Christian Socialists had been the Little Ormond Yard school. There, in a spot where even police dared not venture when night had fallen, the slow process of enlightenment had continued. In the manifesto of the Society for Promoting Working Men's Associations, one of their aims was categorically stated as 'establishing among all the Associations admitted into the Union, institutions for the common benefit of the members, as Friendly Societies, Model Lodging Houses, Schools etc.'

As the Associations grew, the Central Board began to discuss ways and means of establishing these, and in the *Christian Socialist* for 1 November 1851 regulations for a library were printed. In the following July, when the Society moved into the premises of the Working Tailors in Castle Street East, one of its members, F. C. Penrose (who later built the entrance gate at Magdalene and a wing of St. John's College, Cambridge), re-designed the upper floor as a 'Hall of Association'. This was immediately utilised for lectures and classes as well as business meetings, and a winter programme was elaborated. Penrose himself, who had just been appointed deputy surveyor of St. Paul's Cathedral (a post in which he accomplished much necessary restoration), lectured on 'Architecture and its Influence, especially with reference to the Working Classes'. The rest of the original members also gave classes: Maurice (Shakespeare), Cooper (Burns), Lord Goderich (entomology), Hansard (astronomy), and William Johnson (rivers). University teachers like John Hullah (music) and R. C. Trench of King's College (proverbs), and N. S. Maskelyne of Oxford (photography) also came to add variety to the programme.[1]

Another series of lectures was started for evening sessions. In this Tom Hughes and A. A. Vansittart (Neale's cousin) directed classes in English Grammar, while such subjects as book-keeping, singing, drawing, political economy, and history were projected. This was in accordance with Ludlow's article in the first number of the *Christian Socialist*:

'We shall all probably agree that our Universities must be universal in fact as well as in name; must cease to be monopolised for the benefit of one or two privileged classes; we may differ as to the means by which that monopoly is to be broken up, that universality attained, whether by lowering the benefits of University education to the reach of the many, or by drawing up to them the pre-eminent few of every class.' [2]

2

Much the same language had been used earlier in the decade by a fervent young Congregational minister of Sheffield, R. S. Bayley. Bayley had been so impressed by the educational activities of the Chartists, and so disgusted by the barren pasture afforded by the mechanics' institutes, that he had formed a People's College in Sheffield, which soon enrolled 300 students. Bayley was fighting against two redoubtable adversaries, both of whom made a strong appeal to the working classes of the north. One, G. J. Harney, was the first English Marxist; the other, G. J. Holyoake, was the apostle of secularism in the West Riding. Against the class doctrines of these two, Bayley put forward a more palatable doctrine, that salvation could only be achieved by those who were educated up to their responsibilities—a doctrine which Kingsley was to echo six years later. When Bayley left the town in 1848, his students continued the work, and constituted themselves as a self-governing body.[3]

So successful was the People's College, that Lloyd Jones, on his missionary journeys for the Christian Socialists, brought it to the notice of the Council of Promoters. It stirred many of them, Charles Mansfield in particular. When Maurice was dismissed from his chair at King's College, London, the idea of emulating the Sheffield experiment took root. Neale wrote to the secretary of the People's College, and communicated the reply to a meeting of the Promoters of Industrial and Provident Societies (as the group were now called) held on 11 January.

After Neale's report, Tom Hughes made a formal proposal:

'That it be referred to the Committee of Teaching and Publication to frame, and—so far as they think fit—to carry out, a plan for the establishment of a People's College in connection with the Metropolitan Associations.'

He was seconded by Lloyd Jones. The committee accordingly met, and requested Maurice to lay his plan before them. To air the debate, Maurice also gave a series of lectures on his plan in June and July of that year. The proposals were favourably received: On 30 October, Maurice, as principal, was able to deliver an inaugural address at St. Martin's Hall. Three days later the Working Men's College began to function at 31 Red Lion Square.

Its object was twofold. On the one hand, the wealthy were to be influenced by giving them contact with the poor; on the other, workers were to be trained to share the life of the nation, and so reform it from within. In a day when university settlements were unknown, when university extension was a pious sentiment delivered before the Universities Commission then sitting,[4] when mechanics' institutes reached only the prosperous working classes, and then only to pander to their desire for the merely utilitarian, the Working Men's College was something new. It offered, not a commercial or narrowly technical education, but a broad liberal pasture, where metropolitan workers could crop. Wisdom, character, and *esprit de corps*, were cultivated through knowledge. The aim of the promoters was to produce, not only good citizens, but also good Christians. All classes were in the evening between eight and ten. Maurice taught the Gospel, politics in English literature, and Shakespeare; Ludlow lectured on partnerships for association members; Furnivall taught grammar to shoemakers. Later famous outsiders came also to teach: Rossetti, G. Lowes Dickinson, and, above all, Ruskin, who taught drawing and had his 'Nature of Gothic' separately printed for the use of the students.

It was probably here—he taught until 1860—that Ruskin got his first impulse towards sociology. But he never became intimate with any of the Christian Socialist leaders or—judging from a fascinating unpublished letter in 1868—learned to overcome his almost pathological humility even before Tom Hughes, the least formidable of men. Ruskin's cousin had been made very happy, Ruskin wrote Hughes,

'most of all by the kind things you said of me. Do you know, I always fancied that you didn't like me! That, while you were glad to see what I was trying to do—and sympathized with me in many feelings and aims, you would never care for me at all, myself—

'I thought you must know so many cheerful, nice people—and in all truth—and in no self-deprecation—I always feel myself heavy and stupid in society, and think that I only bore people. That is mainly why I come out so little. But Joanna says you said you really would both like to come and see me—and so now—please come as soon as you can—and I shall be so very happy—there are millions of things I want to chat about—and I should have come long before now to see you—only I thought you must always have people about you better worth your time. I won't teaze—I say this again—only remember, it is the fact.'[5]

When Hughes' wife started reading *Fors Clavigera* in 1874 Hughes commented gaily:

'I am rather maliciously amused at thinking of you dipping every now and then into Fors Clavigera and getting very angry at it—however there really are gems scattered about in the midst of all the crazy stuff . . . I should advise you darling to read it by the Index—that is to say look first at the index and select your subject and don't plunge into the chaos without a clue.' [6]

3

Hughes' role at the Working Men's College was a characteristic one. As he says himself, he had trouble finding a mission at the College. At the beginning he examined students for matriculation; he also proposed to lecture on sanitary legislation, but there were no students; for two terms he instructed workers on the laws of combination and association, but got only eight or ten students. For all other subjects that he was competent to give there were, he modestly believed, better-qualified men, and, except for a number of Bible-classes in the 'seventies, he did very little further teaching.

But he soon found a congenial field: sparring. 'Round shoulders, narrow chests, stiff limbs, were, I submitted, as bad as defective grammar and arithmetic.' Maurice was somewhat taken aback at the idea, but allowed Hughes to start exercises on the parallel bars and boxing classes in the cellar. Profiting by his Rugby training, where the big boys made the little ones fight until they lost their tempers, and by his Oxford experience ('at last it became clear to me, that all my Oxford time spent in such matters had not been thrown away'), Hughes made a science of his work. Everyone had to box with Hughes, who met them in trousers and flannel shirt with sleeves rolled up, and soon convinced even the broad-shouldered joiner Hantler that strength and indifference to punishment were not enough. It was 'a pretty sight', wrote Furnivall, 'to see him, with his lithe well-built form and cheery smile, as, vigorous and alert, he met the onslaught of rougher assailants and boxed gracefully and smartly with those who were more scientific in the use of the gloves.' Though these classes were, as Ludlow said, a 'school of good humour', one had to be careful. 'Mind you don't hit Hughes on the nose by accident,' warned Jim Donovan, Hughes' best pupil. 'If you do, you'll catch it.' [7]

From these boxing classes grew informal social gatherings, pleasing to all, which helped break down shyness and reserve. There were tea and coffee, and sometimes political discussions and sometimes singing, but no set speeches. Once Hawthorne, then American Consul at Liverpool, came, and, according to Hughes, quite lost his shyness. Later Hughes organised a cricket and rowing club—from these clubs he later organised the College Corps of Volunteers, made up of many who did not go to the College— and country excursions. All in all, he thought what he accomplished the best social work he ever did. He certainly enjoyed himself more and probably performed a more useful function than he did later as president of the College.[8]

Hughes later extended his interests in workers' education beyond the Working Men's College to the Working Men's Club and Institute Union, founded in 1862, on whose Council he served and which he helped in its setting up of Working Men's Institutes. Hughes spoke before these institutes at various times, and in the 'sixties also did some boxing at one of them. He suffered a disaster there that no one has reported as having occurred to him at the Working Men's College: a burley 'dokker' 'pummelled him so unmercifully that "time" had to be called!' [9]

For one as energetic as Tom Hughes neither sparring classes nor legal work were, however, enough to provide full employment. Co-operation offered no immediate outlet, and for the moment he could not do much to help Maurice in the project nearest to his heart: reforming the Anglican Church and orienting its outlook to contemporary social problems. At loose ends, Hughes resorted almost inadvertently to an interest that was suddenly to make him famous and to precipitate him into the arena of public life.

4

In 1853 the North London Working Builders' Association had built for Hughes and Ludlow a communal house on the Ridgeway at Wimbledon, overlooking the Surrey hills to the south. F. C. Penrose designed 'The Firs' with the same care as he had devoted to the Hall of Association. Here, as the Working Men's College took shape, the two families moved in the spring of 1854.

The new home was soon the scene of lively parties for the College, when Kingsley would talk on botany, Lord Goderich would show his wonderful cases of butterflies, and Hughes himself would draw the company into games of cricket, or even leap-frog. Mrs. Gaskell, who, like the Christian Socialists, had come under the lash of William Rathbone Greg for her novel *Mary Barton* (1848) and *Lizzie Leigh* (1855), would visit them. So would George Grote, friend of the French Liberals and campaigner for the secret ballot, and Alexander Macmillan, then embarking on the publication of Kingsley's *Westward Ho*.[10]

Hughes' family was increasing rapidly. Maurice, the eldest, and Evie were already out of their cradles. Jim was on the way, and before the decade was over, Caroline was to make a fourth. Another five were to follow. With the Ludlows in the 'common library' there was little chance for quietness, and the constant flow of visitors and acquaintances (who found the room 'the subject of much chaff and fun')[11] made complete relaxation difficult.

5

Perhaps for this reason, the Hughes left Wimbledon for the Long Vacations of 1855 and 1856. In the summer of 1855 they visited Tom's brother John at Longcot Rectory, some three miles from White Horse Hill.

'We are making a famous beginning to our vacation', he wrote Lord Goderich, 'interrupted only by a miserable client of mine, for whom I am preparing the elaborate will of a rich gent whose brain is softening; I wish you would bring in a Bill to make it unlawful for parties to let their brains soften in the long vacation.'

Describing their visit to White Horse Hill, he continued:

'We proceeded along crossroads, which have never improved (or, rather, have grown much worse) since Alfred's time; the cart had nothing but a cross board for seat with no back; however, as Fanny declared that she was much less jolted than she has been in your wife's brougham in Pall Mall, there was nothing much to complain of. We arrived at the foot of the hill, up which nothing four-legged short of a dragon could drag anything, and then he would have his tail to help him, and then Fanny and the children got out and we scrambled up, the wind, which is always fresh there, having taken Evie clean off her legs once; it is delicious to see how children take in good dragon stories when they have been well brought up, and if we had had a spade and pick I should have been quite ready myself to have dug for the dragon's bones, as Maurice proposed. We left Fanny on the plaid there, and John and I, with a child apiece, scrambled up to the White Horse, another 150 feet, and down again; the children tried the expedient of sliding down, but soon came on their legs again by reason of what Evie called "those beastly flowers," meaning the thistles.

'We then shambled home through Uffington, where at the East End of a magnificent Early English church the bones of many generations of my illustrious progenitors rest, and we went about the village visiting old servants, one who was maid to my great-grandmother, and partaking of all sorts of refreshments from the strongest ale to hard-bake and barley sugar, of which last the children have store enough to kill a second dragon. Altogether, I think Fanny must have scrambled and walked three miles and is only healthily tired, so I look towards great improvements in the health line. We leave this middle-age neighbourhood on Monday, with great regret, for the sophistications of Torquay.' [12]

The following summer Hughes left his family behind. Kingsley in a hundred lines of rhyme, urged him to

'Leave to Robert Browning,
Beggars, fleas and vines;
Leave to mournful Ruskin
Popish Apennines,
Dirty stones of Venice,
And his Gas-lamps seven—
We've the stones of Snowdon
And the lamps of Heaven.'

Since Tom Taylor, Liberal wit and dramatist, was to make a third, Hughes complied, leaving London in August for Snowdonia. Here they spent days by loch and river, searched, drenched, and drilled by a rain which stung them like 'minie bullets'.[13] They never even caught a salmon, only small trout and par, 'all of which we should have thrown in again in civilised streams'.

Yet 'we certainly enjoyed ourselves famously', as Hughes wrote Lord Goderich at the time. They stayed at a 'small public kept by the best of Welshmen and his wife' at the top of 'the highest watershed in these parts', from which ran three valleys and above which towered Snowdon. When it rained too hard to go out they amused themselves by trying to put some learning into the heads of the wild Welsh children of their landlord, Henry Owen. On other days they climbed Snowdon, where Kingsley left his boy's knife, lent him for the tour, on Glyddn Vawr, 'a huge mass of syenite and trap and other volcanic rock, the wildest hill I ever was on', coming home at night to dream of 'knocking about the Pyramids and doing many stranger things' in this 'wonderfullest place for dreams that ever was'.

What really made the trip memorable, however, was the company. Hughes' description of their appearance, penned to Lord Goderich, gives the spirit of the occasion:

'Pen-y-Gwryd N.W. Aust 20/56

Scene—Pot-house parlour, looking on wild bogs and mountainous mountains, Dramatis Personæ—Tom Taylor, in a great beard and barnacles and a feu d'enfer, his English breeches, patched across behind with a piece of Welsh red-and-blue flannel (cut, I believe, from our hostess's petticoat), the patch having been necessitated by reason of the series of muckers gone by him in yesterday's scramble over precipitous precipices. Parson Lot stealing everybody's paper to dry plants in, and jogging of the table in an unchristian manner so that parties can't write a bit; his neck half-broken by a rock in the stream where we bathed this morning, and otherwise much knocked about by wind and weather, but struggling still into respectability by reason of the common domestic linen collar and a clean shave. I, with battered hands and knees, in the poor mangled remains of my wardrobe, to wit, a flannel shirt, do. trousers very dirty and in considerable rags, and an old boating coat.'

Tom Taylor interrupted Hughes a paragraph or so later to comment on Hughes' punctuation ('which is on a radically erroneous principle and past emendation') and to complain about his predicament:

'I am abandoned to two wild men—mountain-climbers, salmon-seekers, plant-pickers, rock-renders—and if I come back with whole bones it will be a crowning mercy. I write cheerful letters home, not to alarm my wife, but, in truth, I go in fear of my life between this Socialist lawyer and this Socialist parson—two unnatural varieties of the genus professional man, each caring more for his neighbour than himself or his cloth, and thus departing from the wholesome rules of his craft.'

After Taylor finished, Kingsley contributed a few lines, calling Goderich by his title, which drew from Hughes the comment that Kingsley didn't really believe in brotherhood, since he didn't know how to practise it with those above him. 'The Parson has all the prophecy knocked out of him,' Hughes added, 'and can only talk slang, which is very refreshing.' [14]

Hughes, Taylor, and Kingsley all penned verses on various subjects, ranging from food and drink to patched pants as mementoes of their trip. Kingsley later quoted some modest lines that Hughes contributed to the visitors' book:

'I came to Pen-y-gwryd a larking with my betters
A mad wag and a mad poet, both of them men of letters;
Which two ungrateful parties after all the care I've took
Of them, make me write verses in Henry Owen's book.' [15]

It was characteristic of Hughes that he should have written these lines at the very moment that he was planning, and had perhaps actually written some of the book that was to make him a famous man of letters. But neither he nor anyone else foresaw this outcome of his labours—labours which he kept very much for himself. 'God forgive me,' wrote Ludlow when the book appeared, 'but . . . I had in no wise realised his literary power': sentiments which Kingsley echoed. For in 1856 it looked as if Hughes, his youthful fling over, was settling down into the comfortable obscurity of the rest of his family.[16]

NOTES

[1] J. M. Ludlow, 'The Origin of the College', in *The Working Men's College, 1854–1904* (London, 1904), ed. J. Llewelyn Davies, 14–21.

[2] W. H. G. Armytage, 'The Sheffield People's College' in *Sheffield University Gazette* (1950), vii, 2–3.

[3] For the general movement for University reform at this time see 'James Heywood's Resolution: Prelude and Finale' in *Universities Review* (Bristol, 1950), xxii, 139–152.

[4] Lionel James, *A Forgotten Genius, Sewell of St. Columba's and Radley* (London, 1945), 253, 258.

[5] Letter, Ruskin to Hughes, 30 June 1868.

[6] Letter, Hughes to his wife, 6 Dec. 1874.

[7] Llewelyn Davies, *op. cit.*, 60.

[8] Brown, *True Manliness*, xviii; *Cornhill Magazine*, lviii, 'Fragment of an Autobiography'.

[9] *The Times*, 26 March 1896, 5. In 1872 Hughes took over the presidency of the Working Men's College, a task that he might have found rewarding had he not taken up the reins dropped by Maurice 'much against my will' merely because the 'council would have it so'. As it was, he gave 'scarcely any time to the College', contenting himself with lecturing there on occasion and chairing important functions, when his warmth and story-telling ability made him popular and drew people together in a good fellowship too seldom seen at such times. Once he told how he and others had put a bankrupt brushmaker back on his feet, and how the latter in gratitude had made them brushes with hard bristles. Lowell, who was present on the occasion, eyed Hughes' shiny bald head and 'in stately and measured tones expressed hope that all the students of the college did their work so thoroughly and effectively as the brushmaker had done his'.

Of actual administering or educational planning Hughes did very little. Hughes delegated authority to R. B. Litchfield, vice-principal from 1872 to 1875, and his assistant, George Tansley, who completely reorganized the college and were loyally supported in doing so by Hughes, despite protests from Ludlow and others. In 1872 old teachers were gone, classes languished, finances bad and administration inefficient. Litchfield replaced the unwieldy council of sixty by a smaller one, which he trained to administer the college after he left, and placed finances under a corporation with Hughes as chairman. A decade later the college was out of debt, and had twenty-four teachers, thirty-nine classes and 607 students. Hughes was able to retire from an institution that was flourishing as it had not been for a generation. [Hughes] *Early Memories for the Children*, 67; *Cornhill Magazine*, New Series, xli, 421.

[10] *Working Men's College Journal*, May 1896, 69; Davies, *The Working Men's College*, 60 ff.; Ripon Papers in British Museum, Add. MSS. 43,511; letter, Hughes to Ripon, 1 Sept. 1856; Lowell Papers at Harvard (Mrs. Rantoul Collection), letter, Hughes to Lowell, 25 April 1891.

[11] Brown, *True Manliness*, xviii.

[12] Wolf, *The Life of the First Marquess of Ripon*, i, 151, letter, Hughes to Ripon, 25 Aug. 1855.

[13] *Macmillan's Magazine*, Aug. 1880, 298–301. For Kingsley's rhymed invitation see his works x, iv.

[14] Wolf, *The Life of the First Marquess of Ripon*, i, 153–156, letter, Hughes to Ripon, 20 Aug. 1856; also i, 160, undated letter, Hughes to Ripon.

[15] (Mrs. Charles Kingsley), *Charles Kingsley: His Letters and Memories of his Life*, i, 25.

[16] *Economic Review*, iv, 1896, 506; *Working Men's College Journal*, May 1896, 80. Tom's sister Jane or Jeannie Senior was the most interesting of his brothers and sisters, having inherited a good deal of her father's talent and her grandmother's energy. Artistically inclined, she studied music under Manuel Garcia, and later corresponded with and won the admiration of Jenny Lind, with whom she was asked to sing in public. Millais made her the central figure of 'The Rescue' and Watts painted her portrait. Later in life she worked with Octavia Hill (cleaning up tenements), with George Eliot and with Florence Nightingale; from Jan. 1873 to Dec. 1874 she was inspector of schools for girls.

George, Tom's idol, was a disappointment to everyone but Tom, even Lowell averring, when Tom's *Memoir of a Brother* appeared, that he wished George 'had done more'. After giving up his law practice to live abroad, he returned and dabbled in farming, amateur theatricals, home soldiering and magistrate's work, haunted for years by his failure to hold a regular position. Hastings, a business man in the sherry trade, involved himself and Tom in financial difficulties in the 'seventies.

John lived forty years in obscurity as vicar of Longcot in Berkshire.

Arthur, completing the round of the professions typical of the gentry, went into the army and died in India in 1867.

Scott's godson, Walter, had been in the army before he died of fever on a fishing trip in British Guiana in 1846.

Henry, of whom Leslie Stephen was fond, died of an accident in 1862 before achieving anything.

CHAPTER SIX

'Tom Brown's Schooldays', 1857–1858

I

In that long vacation Tom was preoccupied with the question of his son, then eight years old. 'Thinking over what I should like to say to him before he went to school,' wrote Hughes, 'I took to writing a story, as the easiest way of bringing out what I wanted.' It was done mainly in the long vacation of 1856.[1]

In a letter written to Lord Goderich from Deal (where Tom had joined his family after coming down from Snowdonia), Tom reveals this pre-occupation with his son:

'We are in the most ridiculously small house here you ever saw. There is no room for Maurice and me to wash, so we turn out to the beach every morning at 7 to bathe, a source of danger just now as it is very rough with a great under-tow, delicious swimming, but as you come ashore the waves cut you over and mingle you with the pebbles in a surprising manner, and as I am obliged to spend most of my time among them (i.e. the breakers) holding on to Maurice who can't swim, I am having rare practice in picking myself up; I am delighted to find how plucky he is, and if not carried out to sea in the next few mornings he will make a rare young water dog.' [2]

As the book progressed, however—Hughes didn't mention it to Goderich, though he dilated on Kingsley's forthcoming work and Taylor's articles for *Punch*—a purely artistic motive was added to the practical one. Returned to Wimbledon, Hughes was sitting with Ludlow in the library one day when, as Ludlow wrote:

'The talk fell on children's books, and Hughes said he had often thought that good might be done by a real novel for boys—not didactic, like *Sandford and Merton*—written in a right spirit, but distinctly aiming at being interesting. I agreed with him. He then went on to say that he had tried his hand on the thing but did not know whether it was worth publishing. Sometimes he thought it was, and sometimes that it wasn't. Would I mind looking at what he had written? I said that I should be glad; and either that night or the next, I forget now which, he put into my hands a portion of Tom Brown.'

In neither account, be it noted, does Tom say he wrote the book, as some have claimed, as a memorial to Arnold.

Ludlow read the manuscript, he owned, with amazement, and found that he 'was reading a work of absorbing interest which would place its writer on the front rank in contemporary literature. As I handed it back to him, I said, "Tom, this *must* be published." ' [3]

The logical place to turn was Macmillan and Company. Alexander Macmillan and his brother Daniel, who had entered the publishing field in 1844 chiefly as purveyors of books on religious liberalism and social reform, were admirers of Carlyle and of Coleridge, Dr. Arnold, Stanley, and other liberal churchmen. They had actively supported the Christian Socialist movement: Alexander wrote for the *Christian Socialist* under the name of Amos Yates. They had already published a book by Maurice and one by Kingsley. So on 25 September Hughes sat down and wrote Alexander Macmillan one of his characteristically exuberant letters:

'My chief reason for writing is that, as I always told you, I'm going to make your fortune, and you'll be happy to hear that the feat is almost or at least more than half done. I've been and gone and written or got in my head a one vol. novel, a novel for boys, to wit Rugby in Arnold's time. Ludlow is the only one besides my wife who has seen a word of it (and mind if you take it or don't I can't afford to have it known) and he thought it would particular do, and urged me to go on with it which I have this vacation, and only want the kick on the breach that some cove's saying he would publish would give me to finish it. Shall I send you 3 or 4 chapters as specimens or will you meet me in town next Wednesday, Thursday, Friday or Saturday? Do come up and we'll have a dinner and nox together with baccy.' [4]

Macmillan quickly responded to the invitation. He was instantly taken with the book, and readily agreed to publish it. Indeed, Hughes never had to turn elsewhere for a publisher. Macmillan acquired such a taste for Hughes' work that he was extremely annoyed with his Glasgow friends who 'could not share his admiration for all the works of Tom Hughes'.[5] The two men became fast friends, Hughes asserting in old age that there were few people 'whom I have known longer or been on more intimate terms with'.[6] When, in the 'eighties, Alexander wanted a memoir written of his brother Daniel, it was natural for him to turn to Hughes.

Before the end of November Macmillan had produced a format for *Tom Brown's Schooldays*. Some proofs were pulled, which drew from Hughes the following gay remonstrance:

'Woe unto them that make the homar small and the ephah great (something or other, I've forgot it and spelling be blowed. You'll find what I mean somewhere in Amos, or some other jolly old hard-mouthed prophet) that they may sell the refuse of the wheat? Ours ain't refuse, at least we hope not, so why make your page so small and margin so *huge* as in the proofs you sent me? I hate short measure. What's the use of it here? I'll write any amount of nonsense which you'll publish, so why stint folk of it? With the present size of type and margin folk will only get about 30 short lines in a page, and it will be too much to see one's schoolboy stories covering such huge lots of paper. Reconsider this point if it can be done without expense. I've corrected the proof and followed all your suggestions, putting the Latin in notes and dropping some of my familiarity, but if I'm to write at all it must be as I think and talk which is always in the vernacular and chawbacon way of my native country. I never yet was on stilts, moral, intellectual or physical (no, I lie, on physical I have been) and please God don't ever mean to get there . . . I am going for a day or two to Rugby next week to freshen my memory.' [7]

While Hughes was worrying about the format and the style, Ludlow was worrying about sales. Ludlow was afraid they would not be commensurate with the book's worth because Hughes was a new author, so he suggested that if the book were first serialised in a magazine it would no longer be new when published.[8] But Macmillan did not take kindly to the suggestion, and there was no serial publication. For a while, indeed, it looked as if there would be no book. On 3 December Tom Hughes lost his eldest daughter Evie of scarlet fever. Maurice got it first, and then Evie and Jim and Caroline and Fanny; even Tom had a touch. But Evie was apparently getting better when, without any warning except a certain lightheadedness, she died in Tom's arms 'in 5 minutes'. For forty-eight hours afterwards Fanny had no 'more life in her than just enough to keep the body from stiffening'.[9] Tom rallied marvellously, but he hadn't the heart to go on with the book, and took his wife down into Devon and then to Brighton. Ludlow was even for publishing it as a fragment, or getting Hansard, another 'Arnoldian', to finish it. Fortunately this was not necessary, as Hughes took up his task again early in 1857. If the later parts of the book are 'graver and deeper' than the earlier, Ludlow is surely right in attributing this to Hughes' loss, as much as to the nature of the material, which has to do with Arthur's character and the influence of Arnold.

3

When Kingsley saw the finished book in the middle of February he was overcome with excitement:

'If you do not push that book of Tom Hughes's,' he wrote Daniel Macmillan, 'why then I shall set you down for no Scot. For why? It will be a very great hit. It is an extraordinary book. Take it all in all, you won't see such smart writing, such knowledge of slang and all manner of odds and ends, combined with the actual knowledge of boys, and with the really lofty tone of religion and the broad humanity, in any living writer.' 'I have laughed and cried over the book to my heart's content. Funny bits of it are worthy of Lever; and serious bits of it are worthy of —— I can't say whom.' 'Beside, it is the only book of its kind. I should have been proud to have written that book, word for word as it stands. . . . As sure as eggs are eggs, the book will pay both of you well.' [10]

Even Kingsley, however, was not prepared for what happened when the book appeared in print on 24 April:

'I have often been minded to write to you about "Tom Brown",' he told Hughes. 'I have puffed it everywhere I went, but I soon found how true the adage is that good wine needs no bush, for everyone had read it already, and from everyone, from the fine lady on her throne, to the red-coat on his cock-horse, and the schoolboy on his forrum (as our Irish brethren call it), I have heard but one word, and that is, that it is the jolliest book they ever read.' [11]

That Kingsley was not exaggerating is evident from a letter of Hughes' to his wife on 24 June: 'I met [Leslie] Stephen on my way up who turned and walked up here [his office] with me, he is almost the most enthusiastic party about Tom Brown whom I have met—It is certainly very odd how it suits so many different folk.' [12] Though the book appeared anonymously under the pseudonym 'An Old Boy', it 'made such a hit', Hughes wrote later, 'that the publishers soon betrayed the secret, and I became famous'. [13]

The professional reviewers were as enthusiastic as the general public. There were occasional complaints about the book's sentimentality and some of its moral and religious views; a few reviewers even tended to treat it, as Ludlow asserted hotly, as merely a child's book. But from the southern American *DeBow's Review* and the New England *Brownson's Quarterly*, to the serious Irish and English magazines like the *Dublin University Magazine*, the *Eclectic Review*, the *North British Review*, and the *New Quarterly*, there was unanimous agreement as to the book's merits, even the *Christian Observer*, which on religious grounds thought the book ought to be kept out of the hands of boys, stating its opinion with regret. Nobody, indeed, would, as Hughes himself wished, 'really set about and criticise it as severely as possible'. Richard Ford in the *Quarterly*, Kingsley in the *Saturday Review*, and Fitzjames Stephen (who had severe strictures about the book's ideas) in the *Edinburgh Review* could none of them find praise 'too high for it'. In October *The Times*, in a two-and-a-half-column review, put its official imprimatur on what it called the 'truest, liveliest, and most sympathising description of an unique phase of English life that has yet been given to the public'. [14]

In terms of modern best-seller sales the success of *Tom Brown's Schooldays* is hardly impressive, but for its day it had an amazing vogue. July saw a second edition, September a third, October a fourth, and November a fifth. In these seven months Hughes received £1,250. On 23 December Alexander Macmillan wrote gleefully that they had sold nearly the ninth thousand; by early January Macmillan had broken into the eleventh thousand and talked 'of another 5,000 edition, which,' wrote Hughes, 'if he gets through half of it even, will give me much tin at Midsummer'. [15] This new sixth edition came in February, and contained a preface by Hughes on bullying. The book went on selling, and has continued to do so both in America and in England down to our own day. Parrish lists nearly fifty editions or reprints in England alone down to 1890. Twenty-nine editions are listed in the catalogue of books in print in 1928. The book has been translated and discussed abroad (the French title was *Les Annés d'Ecole de Tom Brown*), most notably by Emile Montégut in France in his series of 'Ecrivains Modernes'. It was translated into German in 1866 as part of the 'special duties' of the translator, 'the education of a young German prince'.

4

The huge success of *Tom Brown's Schooldays* was owing in large part to its genuine literary merits. It has weathered great changes in literary taste as well as marked transformations in the educational *milieu*—many of which Hughes himself helped bring about. Though it belonged definitely to a particular time and place, it has survived the complete disappearance of the world of which it was a part. Signs that its long reign may be coming to an end are belied by even fresh editions; and many of those who read it neither in youth nor as adults have recently seen it as a successful film. Hughes' achievement was a great one. His was literally the first work of fiction to present a real world of boys in the setting of a real English public school. And it is still, despite the many recent novels on the subject, the most vigorous, the most convincing, and the most deeply moving of all.

That Hughes, who so typically was a follower, not an innovator, should single-handed have created a new literary genre, is not the least of the mysteries surrounding *Tom Brown's Schooldays*. It merely begs the question to say, though it is the only explanation available, that he had no choice but to be an originator once he had decided to write about his schooldays. There had been books written specifically to amuse and edify the young ever since John Newbery wrote *A Little Pretty Pocket Book* in 1744. Prior to that the young had simply appropriated (and who shall say they were not better off?) such books as *Pilgrim's Progress*, *Gulliver's Travels*, and *Robinson Crusoe*. The most notable of these children's books—the works of Maria Edgeworth and her father, and Thomas Day's *Sandford and Merton*, mentioned by Hughes to Ludlow—were still popular in Hughes' day and had been read by him as a boy. But neither they nor their many followers offered him much help. Though sometimes gifted as story-tellers and not entirely ignorant of the nature of the young, these writers had very little sense of the individuality of boys and girls, and were wedded to the belief that their prime function was to teach facts and moral lessons, to be served up in an odious atmosphere of sin and tears. Moreover, they rarely wrote about schools and never, except for two brief tales by Maria Edgeworth —'Eton Montem' and 'The Barring Out',[16] which inevitably viewed their subjects from the outside—about public schools. Hughes also had available to him the account of Mr. Creakle's school in *David Copperfield* and of other so-called places of instruction in Dickens's work and of Lowwood in *Jane Eyre*. But these accounts, so far above Hughes' powers, were brief, and neither Dickens nor Charlotte Brontë nor any of the top-flight writers, except Thackeray in a casual way, touched on public schools. The uninspired *Recollections of Rugby* (1848) was the nearest to a model Hughes possessed. He became perforce the inventor of a new form.

To the greater mystery of Hughes' immense achievement in his chosen form there are some suggestive clues, though perhaps no ultimate answers. None of Hughes' early writings shows any extraordinary talent, neither his letters, nor his journal, nor his verses [17] (only one of these, 'Milton and the Swedish Lord', found its way into print, in *Ainsworth's Magazine* in 1842, probably through his father's friendship with Ainsworth) nor his copious writings for Christian Socialism. But they do reveal a hard grasp of fact, a concentration on concrete detail, a pervasive humour, gusto, and even eloquence, and occasionally a pungency and power of visualising a scene that belong to the writer of fiction. Given the proper occasion, Tom Hughes might well surpass himself. And in his schooldays and in his love for Arnold—the most vivid realities of his life—he found such an occasion. They were an elixir that fused and strengthened his gifts, giving a magic power to his talents that they had never possessed before and were never to possess again, not even, except at moments, in the very readable *Tom Brown at Oxford*.

If it is the expression of Hughes' love of Arnold that gives *Tom Brown's Schooldays* its ultimate power to move us, it is his love of his boyhood that endows the book with its extraordinary kind of reality. Hughes loved his schooldays so much that he remained to some extent a boy all his life. He was thus able to see and to let us see the universe through the eyes of the young themselves, a point of view rarely achieved by adult writers. There is nothing in Hughes of a Canon Farrar, whose *Eric* and other improving books gave Hughes' generation what an adult thinks a child ought to see and feel; and there is even less in him of our own A. A. Milne, with his coy and sophisticated Christopher Robin books. Hughes lived in a boy's world, and can therefore make us live there with him. We experience Tom's schooldays as Tom experienced them, from the first shy entrance on the coach and the gruff beginning of friendship with East, through the years of carefree amorality to the final parting by Arnold's grave. Hughes still knew in his blood, and can therefore make us know in the same way, how Tom and East felt about feasts and football and fagging and Hare and Hounds and friendship and heroes; and he still shared their joys in athletic victory and their devotion to their heroes, whether they be old Brooke or Arnold. *Tom Brown's Schooldays* has about it the zest and joy of happy memory, the love of frosty mornings and endurance, and the eager anticipation of life.

As an instrument of Hughes' vision his very defects become

virtues. His lack of subtlety, his penchant for melodramatics, his slangy colloquialisms, his Kingsleyan heartiness, and his occasional staccato Carlylisms are all perfectly appropriate to the world he is creating, are, indeed, an essential aid in conveying the atmosphere of that world. For whatever else they may be, boys are not sober and subtle realists, and to describe the melodramatised and over-simplified world of their dreams in such terms would be to misrepresent it. Tom Hughes' imagination and his talents were in perfect accord with his subject.

Not, however, in such perfect accord that creator and creation became indistinguishable. *Tom Brown's Schooldays* is a work of art, not a social document. Like the far greater works in its field— *David Copperfield* and *Huckleberry Finn*—*Tom Brown's Schooldays* has double vision. It is a boy's dream of school; and it is a true picture of the dreamer and a recognisable sketch of his actual world. There is, it is true, no trace in *Tom Brown's Schooldays* of the modern searching realism of a *High Wind in Jamaica*, with its penetration—for the benefit of a strictly adult audience—into the terrifying abysses in the mind of a ten-year-old girl. But Hughes was enough removed from his protagonist to see him without illusions—not as he saw himself, but as he was—and to view his life with some objectivity and in a larger context.

5

Hughes' aim as an artist, indeed, was not to tell his own story, but to picture Rugby life in general, to give his readers an understanding of the system of public-school education through embodying it in individuals. There is even the pretence that Tom Brown is not Tom Hughes, but the 'commonest type of English boy of the upper middle class', not too clever, but with a good training in Church catechism, 'which wouldn't let him be an idle loafer, though he might look on the masters as "the other side" in the education game'. He therefore named his hero Brown, 'first of the trio of Brown, Jones, and Robinson, which has come to be synonymous with the middle class, and prefixed it with Tom, a more English name than John, as seen in tom-boy, tom-fool'. When Hughes was asked in 1895 whether Tom Brown was a real boy, he answered that he was and is 'at least 20 boys, for I knew at least that number of T. B.s at Rugby'.[18] Hughes never actually convinced anyone that he had drawn other than himself as his hero, though Tom Brown's life is more coherent and meaningful than that of his *alter ego*. But he did better with the other characters, none of whom, except Arnold and Cotton, is a recognisable portrait, though various suggestions have been made. Arthur is supposedly a composite of Theodore Walrond, W. P. Adam, and August Orlebar; East is chiefly W. P. Adam, for years the Liberal Whip in the House of Commons; the two Brookes are Tom and his brother George, and the two Walronds, Henry and Theodore with some of Charles Penrose, Dr. Arnold's nephew, in the elder Brooke; Crab Jones is Edmund Smyth, and the 'Slogger' had his original in Buckley O. Jones, later Chancellor of St. Asaph and Warden of Ruthin. Each of them, from the eccentric Martin to the saintly Arthur, is a created individual, and each one represents a different version of the genus boy to be found at an English public school. Hughes the man as distinct from Hughes the boy saw Rugby life from a middle distance, and he made a largely successful attempt to comprehend it as a whole.

6

The modern reader is inclined to feel, indeed, that perhaps Hughes tried rather too hard to 'comprehend'. Not content to tell his story and draw his picture, he was constantly interpreting, commenting, perorating, and even, despite his professed dislike of didacticism, preaching. As William Dean Howells wrote, he was 'always putting his hands under its [the story's] arms and helping it, or his arms across its shoulder and caressing it'.[19] He was quite shameless about it. For he was not content to be the artist creating form and reality: it was to him but a doorway to what ought to be.

'My whole object in writing at all', he said in the preface to the sixth edition of the book, 'was to get the chance of preaching. When a man comes to my time of life and has his bread to make and very little time to spare, is it likely that he will spend almost the whole of his yearly vacation in writing a story just to amuse people?'[20]

Hughes' conception of literature was Carlyle's prophetic one: he cared for no book without 'some definite witness to the Living God in it'. That was why he preferred Lowell to Byron.

However much it may offend the modern reader, Hughes' didacticism did not disturb his Victorian audience. As G. G.

Bradley said in writing to Hughes about his preface, 'It is only a very few I take it who kick at the preaching of the book'.[21] On the contrary, Hughes' earnest partisanship, his efforts to extract lessons, sometimes by main force, from the world he had created, were as welcome as the creative power which made that world. The *Spectator*, indeed, in the most interesting of contemporary analyses of Hughes' writing, found his superiority to lie in just this ability to combine the 'ethical instincts of a genuine writer', happier in struggle than in 'tranquil observation or sympathy', with the passivity that permitted images to be reflected accurately. Hughes' sketches were 'as clear and vivid as the hills in a bright autumn sunlight, when the mists have risen, and the landscape seems cut in crystal'; at the same time, the 'healthy firmness of his moral convictions' did not melt away into a mere desire to study people objectively.[22] *The Times* in its review of *Tom Brown's Schooldays* laid special favourable emphasis on the vast 'amount of good' the book would do because of its 'very noble and successful attempt to Christianize the society of our youth'. And Kingsley wrote Hughes with glee, not long after the book was published, that it was already justifying its existence by working such good.

'Among a knot of red-coats at the cover-side, some very fast fellow said, 'If I had such a book in my boyhood, I should have been a better man now!' and more than one capped his sentiment frankly. Now isn't it a comfort to your old bones to have written such a book, and a comfort to see that fellows are in a humour to take it in?' [23]

No, except for the few who objected to the particular lessons taught, criticism of *Tom Brown's Schooldays* was more likely to be on the score of Hughes' outspokenness than of his didacticism. Before the book was published, Kingsley wrote to Macmillan, 'I only wish a few "damns" had been left out. Folks are mealy-mouthed hypocrites at best.' [24] That Kingsley knew what he was talking about was soon made plain by the letters and articles that began to appear, objecting to the strong language and the slang, which was considered untrue to life and some of it 'too vulgar to be printed'. As late as 1888 Ginn & Company omitted the word 'nasty', some references to bottled beer, and an allusion to taking maggots out of a cow's back and sides, from its editions of the book. Even so, the *New York Evening Post* was not satisfied, wanting some of the pugilism abated. Ginn & Company's action so infuriated Hughes that he tore up the publisher's letters, but then, 'on second thoughts', collected the pieces and sent them to Macmillan to find out if they couldn't stop publication of his book in this 'garbled form' to suit Ginn's 'fanatic teetotal customers. It is bad enough that they can publish at all without my or your consent, but "wus" if they can garble to toady fanatics.' [25]

7

The main lesson of *Tom Brown's Schooldays*, inculcated through emotional stressing, interpretation, and the mere way the story is told, as well as through direct preaching, is a very simple one. Be straightforward, honest, and self-reliant, and use your strength and power under God in the service of others. Life is an eternal war between good and evil, and the true Christian is the one who manfully devotes his life to co-operating with others in waging this war on the side of right. Since Hughes had himself for nearly a decade been exemplifying this thesis in his own life, it came from his pen with a warmth and sincerity that make it impressive despite its obviousness.

As an interpretation of what Arnold was trying to do at Rugby no less than as a programme for the conduct of life it has, however, its limitations. Whether for good or ill, Dr. Arnold was much more than a strong, fearless, and just captain who led his lieutenants to war against petty selfishness and cruelty. He had great intellectual powers, which he tried, as we have seen, to pass on to his best students; and he was possessed by a spiritual demon which often, as Fitzjames Stephen wrote, made him consider what was mere fun 'awful wickedness', and which caused him to try to turn his favourite boys prematurely into a 'sacerdotal fraternity' of over-earnest men.[26] Hughes had had little experience of this side of Arnold's nature, and he tended to deny its existence. In his novel he made a point of stressing Arnold's downrightness and exuberance and kindness, and underplaying the awesome or subtle or fanatical. His was a more earthly and useful but a barer and less interesting concept of both Arnold's personality and teaching than the reality.

Of Arnold's concern for the mind there is not a trace in Hughes, whose attitude is almost pointedly anti-intellectual. Hughes vigorously denied any such imputation on several occasions, was as upset as G. G. Bradley by what the latter called 'Rugby thoughtlessness', and certainly exhibited in his own life no hostility to ideas. Yet even in later years Hughes wondered whether Rugbeians 'would make half as good Englishmen even if they had learned to turn out good "longs and shorts" or Greek Alcaics before they left school'; as for studying the English language, 'when the boys have all learned to write like Julius Hare or Matt. Arnold or Goldwin Smith, I doubt if they will make or play a better hand for the old country than our lot did who only learnt our English by haphazard'.[27] In *Tom Brown's Schooldays* the belief that knowledge and the cultivation of ideas are of minor importance is no mere youthful predilection of Tom's. Tom's father has no concern that his son learn 'Greek particles' or be anything but 'a brave, helpful, truth-telling Englishman, and a gentleman, and a Christian'; and Tom's hero, old Brooke, would 'sooner win two schoolhouse matches running than get the Balliol Scholarship any day'. The eccentrics who care about ideas may be likeable—the humorous and slightly mad naturalist Martin is a case in point—and they certainly ought to be protected from their coarser companions. But nowhere in *Tom Brown's Schooldays* is there a suggestion that a public school would be a better place if a large number of its boys felt the spur to disinterested intellectual endeavour or cared to win scholarships (Gray, the winner of the Balliol, is, as *The Times* says, a silent character in the book) or admired the paintings of Titian or the poems of Shelley.

8

On the moral side the chief weakness of Hughes' position is its over-emphasis of simple manliness—or, as Hughes defines manliness later on, high spirits, self-reliance, and courage at the service of good works—as the basic and virtually sole Christian virtue. This attitude, which Hughes shared with or derived from Kingsley rather than from Dr. Arnold, had its origin, as Fitzjames Stephen put it, in 'the utter detestation which these excellent writers [Kingsley and Hughes] feel for the practical Manichæism which would check every natural impulse, and stigmatise the strongest feelings of human nature as marks of corruption'.[28] 'Pietists of all ages (George Fox, my dear friend, among the worst),' Kingsley wrote to Hughes, 'never made a greater mistake than in fancying that by keeping down manly θυμός, which Plato saith is the root of all virtue, they would keep down sensuality.' On the contrary, the pietists and the middle classes that followed them were the sensualists because they were effeminate. Pietism, fortunately, was gone, and 'Tom Brown' is a heavy stone in its grave. ' "Him no get up again after that", as the niggers say of a buried obi-man.' [29]

The trouble with this exaltation of manliness, which Hughes' contemporaries nicknamed 'muscular Christianity', was that it impoverished religion by under-estimating gentleness and charity, and led to an identification of Christianity with pugnacity. The orthodox of Hughes' own day had far harsher criticisms than this. *Tom Brown's Schooldays*, they felt, was a vicious influence because it left out revelation and a 'sense of sin as an offence against God'. It would produce 'sensual, careless, bookhating men,—low in morals, lower in religion, and destitute of all those qualities which fit men, not merely for the occupation of heaven, but for the higher offices and duties of life.' [30] Since Hughes had learned from Dr. Arnold to identify whatever seemed to him important with eternal right and wrong, he, too, readily came to believe, as *The Times* said, that there was some great moral meaning in the mere occurrence of a fist-fight. Hughes had loved fighting from his earliest days at backswording matches. 'After all, what would life be without fighting, I should like to know,' he said in *Tom Brown's Schooldays*. 'From the cradle to the grave, fighting, rightly understood, is the business, the real, highest, honest business of every son of man.' [31] (Though Hughes glorified fighting with fists, he always loathed professional prize-fighting. 'Fighting in cold blood for money', he wrote in 1874, 'is under any conditions as brutal and degrading a custom as any nation can tolerate.') [32] Courage and self-reliance were key virtues, to be inculcated in "milk sops" by the rough-and-tumble of a public school (bullying to be excluded) even at the cost of much pain. The ultimate end, service in the good cause, too easily got lost in concentration on the means.

This was particularly so because of Hughes' emphasis on games as a prime educational instrument. Games, like warfare, were a training-ground for courage; they taught co-operation; and they were the basis for local—and ultimately national—patriotism, of the feeling that this is 'the dear old school-house—the best house of the best school in England'. Hughes wanted games spread over England. Unless the old country sports, now gone, were replaced by something to try men's muscles and endurance of heart,

England was doomed. The trouble with games is that they teach nothing about the ends for which the virtues they stress are to be used. Though he may have had no thought of Hughes in mind, it is interesting to note, as does S. M. Ellis, that George Alfred Lawrence's *Guy Livingstone* gives an account of Rugby that embodies a legitimate outcome of Hughes' muscular doctrine. Lawrence's hero had the muscularity without the Christianity, and is thus both harder and morally weaker than Tom Brown; he not only flirts with the headmaster's wife—Mrs. Tait, whose husband succeeded Dr. Arnold in 1842, a year after Lawrence came to Rugby—but carries off a flower as a gage.[33]

9

Hughes propounded in *Tom Brown's Schooldays* a social creed that was to thread all his later books. Compounded of his father's and Scott's Tory paternalism and his own sentimental memories of country life, with a dash of Kingsleyan jingoism, Carlylean anti-intellectualism, and Maurician glorification of the Church, it hymned the virtues of the small squires, his own ancestors, as the backbone of England, who fought her wars, ploughed her fields, knew and preserved her ancient traditions, and were the repositories of true patriotism and true democracy. Unlike the modern generation of cosmopolitan city-bred folk, who knew science, language, and art, but not the land, or modern farmer's daughters, who preferred 'bad foreign music' to 'good English cheeses', these wonderful squires mingled freely with the poor at the great Church festivals and valued men for themselves, not for the externals of rank and fortune. They knew none of what Hughes calls, in his best Carlylese, the 'philanthropic intellectualism' of snobs, with its pretence of democracy, which produced mere 'priggism' and 'Pharisaism'. Unless England could revive or find a substitute for the ancient squirearchy, the Church, and ancient custom, commercialism, and over-civilisation would effect a permanent separation of classes.

Hughes thus allied himself in his thinking with his greatest enemy, Disraeli, and with a whole host of romantics lost in an industrial age who, from Scott and Coleridge to Carlyle and Newman, tried to turn back the clock to unite the Church and the squirearchy with the lower classes against middle-class democracy. That such medieval paternalism, which has its echoes in the anti-rationalism of our own day and its grim perversions in the doctrines of Hitler and Mussolini, was inconsistent with Hughes' own belief in democratic socialism never bothered Tom Hughes. As Emile Montégut said, writing of Hughes, if political prejudice were able to kill a nation, the English would long ago be dead.[34] Hughes wanted to find a place for his own class in the new world a-coming, to foster class reconciliation and not a realignment of classes, 'So down . . . went', as one commentator put it, his picture of the squires—'sometimes soldiers, or sailors, clergymen, lawyers or merchants, but always gentlemen'—fighting as private soldiers alongside of yeomen 'without much thought of its historic truth'. It had 'a nice Democratic flavour'.[35]

10

The book had far-reaching effects. It influenced to some extent all later fiction about public schools. *Blackwood's* asserted in 1861 that Hughes had made a hero of the schoolboy, considered before his day an unlovable bore, and that dozens of novelists were already trying their hands at school fiction with virtuous protagonists.[36] But most of these writers, *Blackwood's* found, produced poor imitations of the original. It was not until the beginning of the new century that anyone wrote a public-school novel that could, like *Tom Brown's Schooldays*, be read with pleasure by adults as well as by boys. And these books—*Stalky & Co.*, the *Harrovians*, and the *Loom of Youth*—bear only a remote resemblance to *Tom Brown's Schooldays*. Yet Hughes' book was in the memory of all later writers and set the general pattern for school fiction.[37]

Much more important was Hughes' influence on the schools themselves. It is no exaggeration to say that *Tom Brown's Schooldays* made the modern public school. Dr. Arnold had done the work of reform, bringing the eighteenth-century school into conformity with middle-class ideas of morality, humanity, discipline, and learning. But Hughes' novel, through its immense popularity, spread Arnold's fame abroad in a way that neither Arnold nor Stanley could spread it. And it brought Arnold's often radical and lofty ideas down to a level that made them vastly appealing to the public. The middle-class public, indifferent or hostile to Arnold's intense spirituality, his almost heretical religious and social views, and his deep respect for learning, responded readily to the more mundane idea of a group of self-

TOM'S VISIT TO THE TOMB OF DR. ARNOLD
BY ARTHUR HUGHES

FROM THE FIRST ILLUSTRATED EDITION OF
TOM BROWN'S SCHOOLDAYS (1869)

reliant, manly boys tamed into submission to Christian principles. Perhaps life never really copies art. But the public schools, which since 1857 have spread in an ever-widening net-work over the land, have most of them tried to be as much as possible like the Rugby of Hughes' dream.

They have not, however, really succeeded in being so. The forms have been there, but seldom the spirit. The late nineteenth-century public schools had games, prefect systems, and improved relationships between master and boy; they emphasised self-reliance and service to others. But self-reliance, under the pressure of preparation for the business world, tended to degenerate into the competitive spirit. This in turn was accentuated by the games Hughes so much loved, which tended to become semi-professional combats leading to success in school and—hopefully—in after-life. And service to others but infrequently meant voluntary service, and even less frequently service to the poor and weak in accordance with Christian teaching. With the decline of the re-ligious and social liberalism that had inspired both Arnold and Hughes, and the rise of the new imperialism, what was wanted were not knights in shining armour, but honest, patriotic, un-thinking young men to man Britain's outposts around the world. The better discipline and *esprit de corps* that Arnold had helped establish in order to effect liberal moral ends, became fetters bind-ing the average public-school boy to that worst of idols, 'good form': a reverence for things established.

II

But in 1858, such developments were unforeseen. The middle-class Englishman who read the papers could see how the Rugby spirit was saving the sum of things, even on the boundaries of the empire. For William Hodson, Tom's contemporary, who had captured a king, and gave his name to 'Hodson's Horse'—a famous Indian regiment—was shot at Lucknow in action in this very year.

His death, fittingly mourned by Tom Hughes himself in *Frazer's Magazine*, provoked young Fitzjames Stephen to write in the *Edinburgh Review*:

'Take a man of this order at random, throw him into strange circumstances, repose confidence in him, subject him to responsibility, and Major Hodson is the result.'

And the clergy, the lawyers, the small squires, and the gentlemen who made up the mid-Victorian equivalent of a professional class were all Hodsons in their own lights, especially if they were Arnoldians.

NOTES

[1] Brown, *True Manliness*, xviii.

[2] Wolf, *The Life of the First Marquess of Ripon*, i, 161–162. undated letter, Hughes to Ripon.

[3] *Economic Review*, vi, 1896, 306.

[4] Graves, Charles L., *Life and Letters of Alexander Macmillan* (London, 1910), 90.

[5] *ibid.*, 396, 408.

[6] Letter, Hughes to George Macmillan in possession Macmillan & Co., 26 Dec. 1892.

[7] Graves, *Life and Letters of Alexander Macmillan*, 91, letter, Hughes to Alexander Macmillan, 22 Nov. 1856.

[8] *ibid.*

[9] Ripon Papers in the British Museum, Add. MSS. 43,516, letter, Hughes to Ripon, 8 Dec. 1856.

[10] Graves, *Life and Letters of Alexander Macmillan*, 94.

[11] (Mrs. Charles Kingsley) *Charles Kingsley: His Letters and Memories of his Life*, ii, 54.

[12] Letter, Hughes to Fanny Hughes, 24 June 1857.

[13] Brown, *True Manliness*, xviii.

[14] *The Times*, 9 Oct. 1857, 10.

[15] Ripon Papers in the British Museum, Add. MSS. 43,511, letter, Hughes to Ripon, 6 Jan. 1858.

[16] 'Eton Montem' partly contrasts two types of Eton Boy, the honest independent, and the extravagant snobbish. 'The Barring Out', rather a good story, tells of a rebellion in a small school led by a boy who has learned ambition and party strife at a public school.

[17] Parrish has in his collection of Hughes' first editions some words for songs written to music by Henry F. Shroeder in 1856 and 1857 which he attributes to Hughes. But the Thomas Hughes who wrote those words was surely not the author of *Tom Brown's Schooldays*. They are signed in a different hand from Hughes' and dated Windsor, where Hughes never lived. Parrish also attributes, incidentally, a book called *Notes for Boys* written in 1885 by 'An Old Boy' to Hughes. The fact that the author never mentions Lowell in his recommendations on books is alone enough to stamp the book as not being by Hughes. The author was apparently one Edward Bellasis.

[18] (T. Hughes), *Tom Brown at Oxford*, Preface; letter of Hughes 3 Nov. 1895 in the Berg Collection of the New York Public Library.

[19] (T. Hughes), *Tom Brown's Schooldays*, Harper's 1911 edition, Introduction.

[20] (T. Hughes), *Tom Brown's Schooldays*, xvii.

[21] Letter, G. G. Bradley to Hughes, 2 Feb. 1858.

[22] *Spectator*, 23 Nov. 1861. 1288 (in a review of *Tom Brown at Oxford*).

[23] (Mrs. Charles Kingsley) *Charles Kingsley: His Letters and Memories of his Life*, ii, 27.

[24] Graves, *Life and Letters of Alexander Macmillan*, 94.

[25] Letter, Hughes to Craik, 25 June 1888, in possession of Macmillan & Co. See also *The Times*, 29 June 1889, 14; 6 Sept. 1889, 6; *The Critic*, 30 July 1889, 34.

[26] *Edinburgh Review*, Jan. 1858, 85.

[27] Letter of Hughes, 3 Nov. 1895, in the Berg Collection of the New York Public Library; Graves, *Life and Letters of Alexander Macmillan*, 384.

[28] *Saturday Review*, 5 Nov. 1889, 540.

[29] (Mrs. Charles Kingsley) *Charles Kingsley: His Letters and Memories of his Life*, ii, 54.

[30] *Christian Observer*, June 1858, 491.

[31] (T. Hughes), *Tom Brown's Schooldays*, 242.

[32] Letter of Hughes, 25 March 1864, in the Manuscript Room of the New York Public Library.

[33] S. M. Ellis, *Wilkie Collins, Le Fanu and Others*, 197.

[34] Montégut, Emile, *Ecrivains Modernes De L'Angleterre*, Troisième Serie (Paris, 1892), 248.

[35] *Standard*, 24 March 1896.

[36] *Blackwood's Magazine*, Feb. 1861, 131.

[37] For a detailed discussion of modern public school fiction see Edward C. Mack, *Public Schools and British Opinion 1860–1939* (New York, 1941).

CHAPTER SEVEN

Pen in Park Street, 1859–1865

IT was bitter reward for the success of *Tom Brown's Schooldays* that his eldest son, Maurice, for whom Hughes had written it, should die in 1859.[1] This, following on the death of his daughter Evie in 1856 and his father in 1857, prostrated his wife Fanny. He consoled her that the 'terrible affliction' was a 'lesson we were meant to learn'. Fanny began to ail and feel herself inadequate as a wife. Hughes rallied to assure her: 'There is no single thing in you which for my sake I should wish to have changed.' When money came, Fanny developed scruples about spending it, but Hughes urged her to treat herself 'to a brougham and the necessary number of new drapes'.[2]

Through it all, Hughes refused to introspect, to grub 'about in my bowels to find what's there', as he told Lord Goderich. 'Every change', he believed, 'is a transformation to something higher'. He continued:

'I have got myself into the habit of looking on all visible things and all accidents which can affect (except insofar as right and wrong are involved therein) as not of the slightest importance. . . . It does not seem the least strange to me, but inexpressibly real and joyful and soothing, to have a little golden-haired angel daughter whom I cannot see, but who is far more with us all than ever she was on earth, and whom I shall never have to look sternly at for not learning her lessons.'[3]

His cheerful optimism was buoyed by such serene faith, and cushioned by such emotional stability, that he acted as a tonic upon all who came into contact with him. 'I must have a good effect on their lives', he wrote his wife after an evening of charades at Maurice's, 'for I made them laugh till they cried. . . . I don't think I ever saw the dear old prophet so tickled.'[4]

I

Such good spirits, which he shared with his sister Jeannie, made Tom Hughes a welcome guest in London. And he began more and more to utilise that welcome, particularly after he moved in

1859 from 'The Firs' at Wimbledon to a house of his own in Park Street—between Hyde Park and Grosvenor Square. In this delectable quarter of Mayfair, first at number 113, then at 33, then at 80, he was to spend the next twenty-three years.

We catch a glimpse of him in 1858 dining with Tom Taylor, that prolific humorist, leader-writer, and wit, who had staged a play in the West End every year since 1848 and was then engaged on *Our American Cousin*. Taylor had invited the Misses Thackeray and Hughes to dine. 'Old Thack', as Hughes called him, could not come, 'for he is driven for time with his number and had been nearly seven hours at work and had only written one page! That beats me all to fits in my most crabbed times', Hughes remarked.[5]

The following year, 1859, we catch a further glimpse of him at the house of the beautiful and witty Mrs. Norton, who, despite her love affair with Lord Melbourne and unhappy life with her husband, had earned a reputation as a champion of female rights. Hughes confessed that she 'soon bored' him, 'for though I like and sympathise with Mrs. Norton, she does not fascinate me as she seems to do so many people'.[6]

At other times he appears at Lady Stanley's, or at an 'artistic swarry' at Lowes Dickenson's or at the famous tea-parties at Little Holland House, home of the Prinseps. There he introduced Grant-Duff,[7] and mixed with Tennyson, Browning, Gladstone, Disraeli, and the strange and moody G. F. Watts, then the 'Signor' of the Prinsep household. Indeed, Jeannie, Hughes' sister, was at this time Watts' moral support in a black and bilious world: a support which he acknowledged by sketching her portrait,[8] as well as painting Tom's.

But 'the pleasantest place in Great Babylon'[9] for Hughes was the Cosmopolitan Club, near his home in Mayfair. There was many a 'queer little talk and smoke' with the oscillating energy of the sociable Monckton Milnes, Lord Houghton, to animate the discussions.

Though fundamentally a quiet person, with no social ambitions, Hughes found himself saddled with more calls and acquaintances than he knew what to do with. Even in the autumn, 'that comfortable, jog-trot' time when the reception-rooms of the great folk were closed, 'you might dine out every night if you did not carefully guard yourself against the commencement of hostilities in any new quarter'. Hughes solved that problem by accepting invitations from the great and near great to visit their country-houses. Here, among people who were not addicted to horse-racing, Hughes enjoyed himself thoroughly, shooting, fishing, and playing cricket during the day, and talking over cigars and sherry in the evening. Fanny found diversion too: croquet and gossip in the mornings, riding and driving in the afternoon, and, when the men had returned from their smoking, cards and dancing in the evening. Tom often lamented the luxury of such establishments, with their armies of servants, among whom his own maid was a guest and did not work. But he salved his misgivings by the reflection that, after all, it was a step towards democracy, since parsons' daughters could here mix with those who would have rigidly excluded them from town houses.[10]

Hughes' own house was simple both for the family and visitors. Motley, the great American historian, dined there in the late 'sixties 'quite en famille', the only other guest being Kennedy of Baltimore:

'It being Sunday, the dinner was cold . . . perfectly good in every way, and I liked the plucky way in which all pretence of a small banquet was avoided. Some of the children, the oldest boy and two girls, dined with us, and I am sure that Susie would have been in raptures if she could have seen little May. She sat at my side and took me under her especial protection. The servant girl had been sent out of the room, and the two little girls helped us help each other at the table. Little May was perpetually getting up and changing my plate and bringing me an immense salad bowl, bigger than herself, and insisting on my gorging myself. . . . The Hugheses are, what they always were, genuine, kind-hearted and delightful, full of warmest inquires for you all.' [11]

2

Of all Hughes' social engagements, the one to which he looked forward most was the 'Tobacco Parliament' which Alexander Macmillan initiated in the firm's new London branch at 23 Henrietta Street, Covent Garden. Daniel Macmillan had died in 1857 (Hughes later wrote his biography), and Alexander, anxious to extend the family interests, would come up every Thursday from Cambridge to meet the assembled company.[12]

At Hughes' suggestion, the Working Men's College made a round table especially to be used on these occasions. On its bevelled edge can still be seen the signatures of those who attended. There was David Masson, the first volume of whose memorable *Life of Milton* was published at this time; F. T. Palgrave, then an examiner in the Education Department at Whitehall, soon to publish his *Golden Treasury*; Richard Garnett, then in his early thirties, who had just become an assistant in the library of the British Museum; Alfred Ainger, an old student of Maurice's, also, like Palgrave, a friend of Tennyson's. There was Tennyson himself, grave, solid, and sober, before whom even Tom Hughes subdued his high spirits.[13] There was the pre-Raphaelite Thomas Woolner, contributor, with Coventry Patmore, to *The Germ*. Woolner had just executed his bust of Tennyson, and was settling down after his brief and unfortunate experience of emigrating to Australia, while Coventry Patmore had yet to lose his first wife, and could still enjoy the pleasures of protestant polemic before the rich darkness of his conversion encompassed him.

To these eager and artistic imaginations was sometimes added the abrasive intellect of Herbert Spencer, then planning his ambitious 'synthetic philosophy' to merge the boundaries of ethics with these new intellectual continents revealed by biology and psychology; and the powerful solvent of T. H. Huxley's agnosticism revealed in *The Theory of the Vertebrate Skull*, delivered before the Royal Society in that year.

On 16 March 1858 (nearly three months before Alexander Macmillan confided in his Glasgow associate MacLehose) Hughes wrote to Fanny:

'Macmillan has just been here about a new quarterly which Davies and the Prophet [Kingsley and W. E. Forster were also involved, he added six weeks later] are hatching and which is to speak the truth to this wretched old dead state of things—Everyone to sign his name and no flippancy or abuse allowed.' [14]

In May he expanded to Layard, the excavator of Nineveh, who had just lost his parliamentary seat at Aylesbury:

'Many men can't get heard in the present quarterlies because their opinions are unpopular, the editor is afraid, or for one reason or another equally fertile. Our first number will come out towards the end of the year, and will be a very strong one: no man need be ashamed of his companionship at any rate.' [15]

It was originally intended that Hughes should sit in the editorial chair:

'He is an honest free man, tied to no notions and theories about books,' wrote Maurice, 'able to judge what is worthy to go forth whether he agrees with it or not; one who will fearlessly admonish a contributor, and never dictate or be squeamish. . . . He says he wishes to preach, and he ought to have a pulpit if one can be found for him.' [16]

But he must be urged to undertake such a task, Maurice told Kingsley, for he would need convincing, since he was a humble man.

Nothing came of the idea of a quarterly, partly because Kingsley was 'half-hearted' in the matter, and partly because Richard Bentley, publisher of the 'Young England' newspaper thirteen years before, was projecting his own quarterly Review, which appeared in 1859. George Smith of 65 Cornhill, London, who was rising to greatness as a publisher on the sales of Charlotte Brontë, John Ruskin, and Thackerary, offered Hughes the editorship of what was to be a new line in journalism—a shilling monthly.[17] Hughes, however, felt morally bound to his own publisher, Alexander Macmillan, so the editorship of the *Cornhill* passed to Thackeray.[18]

By the spring of 1859 the original idea of a quarterly had been abandoned, and a monthly was well launched, on Hughes' suggestion. For it he promised to write a continuation of *Tom Brown's Schooldays*, or 'a new story illustrating the contrast of rural and city life'. By July he and Ludlow had managed to persuade David Masson to undertake the editorship. On 6 October, Macmillan could exult that besides *Tom Brown at Oxford*, 'which opens brilliantly—quite Tom Brown himself', Hughes and Masson were writing a series to be called *Colloquies of the Round Table*: 'Hughes has a capital song in No. 1', he added, 'and the whole thing looks promising'.[19]

Macmillan's Magazine, born at the Round Table (after which it was to have been called), was launched by an inaugural dinner on 1 November that year. It appeared two months before George Smith's *Cornhill* and was destined to outlast the century. From the first number it maintained the principles which Hughes had outlined: signed articles, no abuse, a high moral tone, and a religious outlook. It served as a useful platform for liberal writers, and an effective counterpoint to the wayward brilliance of the *Saturday Review*, whose two lights, A. J. Beresford-Hope and J. D. Cook, were apt to lead their readers on retrogressive paths.[20]

Hughes was very concerned with the magazine in its early years. He invested money in it, and watched over its progress with fatherly interest. He also wrote much for it, including an account of the adventures of a club like the 'tobacco parliament', which the *Saturday Review* derided out of print.[18] By 8 March

1861 he could write gleefully to his wife that, despite the jibes of *Saturday Reviewers*, the magazine was a success.[21]

3

In the meantime Hughes had been busy writing novels that were to capitalise on the success of *Tom Brown's Schooldays*. His sister Jeannie, indeed, advised him in her vehement manner 'to give up law altogether and take to literature'. 'Very likely,' Hughes answered. But he was sorely tempted. 'I had managed to get over and live down Christian Socialism,' he wrote, 'but who on earth would bring business to a successful author?'[22] If only, he wrote some years later, Macmillan knew of 'any party desirous of presenting, say, £1,500 a year, to a deserving pater-familias'.[23]

Six months after the publication of *Tom Brown's Schooldays*, he was hard at work on a novel describing the adventures of a country clerk who witnesses the great festival of the Scouring of the White Horse of Uffington. His father drew the frontispiece, and Dicky Doyle, who had executed similar services for Ruskin and Thackeray, agreed to do the illustrations. Alexander Macmillan, anxious to repeat the success of Hughes' first book, was very enthusiastic.[24]

But by January 1858 the story was hanging fire. He went down to Berkshire

'to see if my bodily presence wouldn't have more effect on squires and yeomen than my letter, and help me to the last materials necessary before I can hand it over to D—— They gave me turkeys game and good cheer enough to bury myself in, also information on every point except those I was at fault about, so I come back pretty well as wise as when I went and shall now wind up the best I can and get quit of the concern anyhow.'[25]

Then silence for nine months till 27 October, when Macmillan finally wrote that Dicky Doyle, 'that dilatoriest of men', had at last sent in his illustrations, so that the book would 'assuredly be out' by 20 November. He continued:

'We are going to press with 5,000 copies, and from all I can judge, from what is ordered and the kind of anxiety with which the book is looked for, we will probably sell the larger part of the edition before Christmas. Hughes has spent a good deal of the Long Vacation in recasting a considerable portion of it by making the clerk Richard tell everything. This gives the book more unity than it had when the 'Editor' stepped in and took up the narrative—like a showman dancing among his puppets. He was urged to make this change by some literary friends whose judgement on this point was of great value.'

The Scouring of the White Horse appeared as scheduled. Six thousand copies were sold in a fortnight, and at the end of December Macmillan was confident that he would exhaust the second edition.[26]

Hughes' friends were enchanted, especially Kingsley, who wrote to the publisher:

'I have read it through with great pleasure. . . . I think it as a work of art an improvement on Tom Brown. It abounds meanwhile, with those little touches of Dutch painting which are peculiar to him, and which, in their unexpected quaintness are to me most pathetic, even when on unpathetic matters. I know not why that man's writing has a power of calling tears into my eyes which nought else but an old ballad has. I suppose it is the undefinable thing called genius—what this is God wot, not I.' [27]

Similarly Benjamin Moran found it fresh, hearty, and excellent to read: full of pictures of English life.[28]

But others were not so enthusiastic, and Alexander Macmillan heard such unfavourable reports that he wrote rather tartly to MacLehose:

'I really regret that your Glasgow literary folks can't see merit except after their own ideas of how it should demean itself. Surely a great historical event and an immemorial English custom affording outcome for all manner of "humours" ought to be looked as worth representing. The fact is the book is "queer", and cannot be put under any category by your literary pedants. Never mind; let them read and learn.' [29]

The reviewers, while not on the whole unfavourable, all expressed or implied disappointment. The *Saturday Review*, though it was reminded of Thackeray's 'Great Hoggarty Diamond' by the liveliness and gaiety of this 'prettiest' of 'idyls', found the book more an evidence than a fulfilment of talent: the material was thin and the didactic part wrong-headed. *The Times*, in a two-column review, made only one comment of any kind: the story was a mere thread on which to hang legends, most of them lies, about the past.[30] The public agreed with the reviewers: no third edition appeared until 1889, when the book was reprinted for the last time.

There seems little call to reverse the contemporary verdict. *The Scouring* is wordy and pretentious, and has less than no narrative or human interest. All the people—the clerk, the country lad Joe, the parson, the squire, and the girl Lucy, with whom the clerk has a tepid flirtation—are mere cardboard figures, awkwardly invented as vehicles for describing the customs or for illustrating a type. And they are all so hopelessly good. Here are no flesh-and-blood Easts, not even any nightmarish Flashmans. Hughes did not live with these people; he constructed them synthetically. And once having done so, he couldn't let them alone, but must talk at them and through them. The lesson of *Tom Brown* is convincing because it grows mainly out of the characters and the story. But here all is as artificial as a stuffed doll, and the preaching is dreary and bloodless.

The social philosophy of *Tom Brown's Schooldays*, elaborated on here, hardly improves on closer inspection. No one will quarrel with the idea of overcoming the prejudices of an urban white-collar worker against rural life. Hughes' hero is industrious (here there is a good word put in for the Working Men's College) and independent (he knows he well earns his money or the boss wouldn't keep him), but he has no conception of anything except 'getting on'. He is impatient of anyone who is proud of his family's never having moved. He thinks all squires and parsons are tyrannical snobs. Hughes takes him to watch the Scouring of the White Horse in Berkshire, to learn to love 'our own quiet corner of the land of our birth', to awaken his memories of the great deeds of the past, and to bring to life in him 'the feeling that we are a family, bound together to work out God's purpose in this little island'.

But Hughes is not content to stop there. He must draw the parson as a paragon of humanity and democratic feeling, and the squire as an ideal democratic leader, manly, frank, and cheery, who 'looked you so straight in the face' that when you looked back you 'were twice as good a man at once yourself while you were talking to him'. And he must inflate his admiration for his rural neighbours' staunchness, naturalness, goodness, and common sense into a preference for women with no pretence to cleverness or learning and for men whose blind faith in God's power made them scorn the modern practice of fighting with the biggest battalions on their side. Infusing the whole story is Hughes' nostalgia for the good old days, when an unpaid magistracy and a powerful Church united the people in fellowship before God.

4

The Scouring of the White Horse had not even been published when Hughes began to write *Tom Brown at Oxford*. 'By this time my clients had become case-hardened and finding no particularly ill effects from my previous escapades, I gave in in a weak moment, to a tempting offer of Macmillan's.'[31] The original intention was to publish it in monthly numbers. In October 1858 Macmillan was hoping that Tom Hughes could let him begin the first number by March of the following year:

'We think of making it a serial,' he wrote, 'say twenty shilling numbers. We think of printing it like Tom Brown, giving three sheets—or forty eight pages with two illustrations to each—so making when completed a guinea book. I think we might pretty safely calculate on a sale of 10,000 copies per month. The portions that I have already seen are quite equal—if not better—than the best parts of T.B., and he is daily acquiring more command of his pen.' [32]

But it was over a year before *Tom Brown at Oxford* appeared. In the meantime *Macmillan's Magazine* had been launched, and Hughes' novel began to appear there with the first number in November 1859. At the same time Ticknor and Fields published seventeen monthly numbers for Americans at 12 cents apiece.[33] Even then Tom Hughes hadn't finished writing it. As late as 12 March 1861, when nearly two-thirds had already been printed, Tom was only approaching the end of the last chapter, and wondering whether he was right in having Mary's father not invite Tom Brown to the house, so that Tom, when he called, was only able to shake hands with the heroine on the stairs. He consulted his wife. She ought to have known! It was finally completed and published in book form four months later in America. The English edition appeared in November, and was pounced upon by the *Saturday Review* as a failure which got 'more dull, purposeless and depressing as it proceeds'.[34]

The public were quick to see what was obviously true: *Tom Brown at Oxford* came from the head, not from the heart. Though there were twelve printings of the English second edition during the century, it never had the lusty life of its predecessor—*Tom Brown's Schooldays*. In *Tom Brown's Schooldays* the living memory of scene and person came first, the meaning afterwards. In *Tom Brown at Oxford*, which records less emotionally important experience, deliberate objective description and prosaic analysis have taken the place of vivid recall. It is a colder book. And it is a weaker one. For Hughes—like so many one-book novelists of our day—lacked the power to give reality to a world not intimately associated with himself; and he had not the sure grasp of fact or meaning that might have compensated in part for lack of imaginative penetration.

Yet *Tom Brown at Oxford* is still very readable, and it is immensely valuable as a picture of Oxford and an interpretation of English life in the early 'forties. Hughes' work does not equal *Pendennis*, or even perhaps Disraeli's *Coningsby*, Kingsley's *Yeast*, or Henry Kingsley's *Ravenshoe* at their best; and the spiritual worlds of Froude's *Shadows of the Clouds* and *Nemesis of Faith* and Newman's *Loss and Gain* are closed to Hughes. But *Tom Brown at Oxford* covers more territory and has infinitely more interest and variety than any of the four full-length books on Oxford written by Hughes' contemporaries, the Rev. Joseph Hewlett's *Peter Priggins*, Cuthbert Bede's *The Adventures of Mr. Verdant Green*, Robert Plumer Ward's *De Clifford* and Lockhart's *Reginald Dalton*, the first of the Oxford novels, published in 1823. *Peter Priggins* and *The Adventures of Mr. Verdant Green* are less serious studies than slapstick caricatures. Both books have a certain dash and some vivid disconnected episodes and descriptions; and *Peter Priggins*, which Hughes had read, satirises bootlicking authorities and snobbish idlers. But one seldom mistakes the Augustus Noodledoodle Nincompoops and the Viscount Drypurses of those books for reality; nor does one really believe that this world of juvenile tricksters and aristocrats afraid to fish because fishing might spoil their complexions, is the whole of Oxford. *De Clifford* and *Reginald Dalton* are more complete and more serious, and the former manages in the course of recounting the troubles of a poor, shy exhibitioner at Queen's to present one or two devastating pictures of the egotistic, lawless, and immoral aristocrats of the day; but both books are long-winded, awkwardly written, melodramatic, and dull.[35]

Hughes, on the other hand, did make a real attempt to show the many-sidedness of Oxford life; to display the evil, the queer, and the ordinary as well as the good. *Tom Brown at Oxford* is a veritable portrait-gallery of Oriel types: the aristocratic commoner Drysdale; the competitive Blake, a talented person who cannot enjoy work for its own sake because he is constantly struggling

H

to 'keep up' financially and intellectually; and the blossoming Christian Socialist, Hardy. And it is full of details of Oxford custom and life; from the dons and gentlemen commoners at the high table in velvet caps and silk gowns, to bawdy fishing-trips, Oxford Movement wine-parties, town and gown riots, boat races, and examinations. Hughes has not made either people or scenes come completely alive, but he has managed to convey a sense of the quality of Oxford life, both in its lighter and its more serious side, and of the snobbish prejudices and high thoughts that lived side by side in Oxford's all-embracing walls.

As in *Tom Brown's Schooldays*, the only plot is the hero's moral and intellectual progress, though Hughes has seen fit to 'enliven' his story with love complications and a certain amount of melodrama. *Tom Brown at Oxford* takes, however, a very different course from the earlier book. For here is no simple society being reformed by a Dr. Arnold, but a complex, confused world in which the only guide and mentor, the young Maurice-like Hardy, is nearly as disturbed as Tom Brown. There can thus be no straightforward and inspiring story of internal and external change. In compensation Hughes has given us a close and illuminating account of his hero's struggles, and has applied his maturest thinking to an analysis of Oxford's plight and of her and her son's and the world's road to salvation.

The basic trouble with the Oriel of 1843 was, according to Hughes, the golden calf, which had tainted an institution that could once boast of learning and gentlemanly conduct. The College was peopled more and more by the rich, and studies, no less than athletics, were neglected by the authorities and the student body alike. As a consequence, idleness sapped the moral fibre both of the rich and of the few quiet, studious fellows, who were appointed in reaction to the current worship of wealth. The rich inevitably spent their time sowing wild oats, which ought to be burnt, not sown, and ended up as avaricious, hard, suspicious old men. The studious, excluded from the company of the rich, were bitter and lonely, and, with little to keep them busy, since their work was easy, were driven to fruitless introspection in an effort to 'keep some living faith . . . that the world, Oxford, and all, isn't a respectable piece of machinery set going some centuries back'.

As in *Tom Brown's Schooldays*, more attention to games was a partial solution. The boating crowd were at least busy at a useful and healthful occupation, and had learned the Carlylean lesson that intellect is not enough and that introspection is evil. Hughes was happy to reach 'the right hand of fellowship . . . from these pages' to his boating companions of yore, who were 'surely none the worse Christians and citizens'—Hughes had read the reviews of *Tom Brown's Schooldays*—for their 'involuntary failing of muscularity'. '*Cæteris paribus*' a man who could lift a hundredweight around his head with his little finger was better than one who 'can expound the doctrine of "contradictory inconceivables".' [36] But even the muscle men must have a cause to serve: the ultimate solution for boaters, no less than for students and gentlemen, was to discipline themselves in the service of a faith. And this meant the cultivation of intelligence, since only through thought could one find the good cause, know it was the good cause, and then fight off 'godless' self-assertion in order to serve it.

The social faith that Tom Brown learned to follow, after a searching exploration, was not as specific or as radical, perhaps, as it might have been had Hughes written the book in 1849 instead of in 1859. Though there is little here of the sentimental paternalism of *Tom Brown's Schooldays* or of *The Scouring*, there is also less concern for self-help and democracy, less baiting of the upper classes, and more emphasis on the harmony of classes and on upper-class assistance to the lower than was typical of Hughes in his Christian Socialist days. Tom Brown has not only gone through a period of radicalism that antedated Hughes' own flirting with Chartism, but has come out on the other side even of the early phase of Hughes' Christian Socialism.

The change, however, was more in the times than in Tom Hughes. Tom was still a democrat: 'Gentleman's flesh and blood', he has Captain Jervis say, 'are just the same, and no better than another man's.' Give poor men a chance—as Tom Brown and East tried to give the skilled workman Harry Winburn—'and they will tread on his heels soon enough'. Moreover, Hughes was just as bitter towards the upper classes of 1848 as he had been at the time, both towards squires who resisted traditional claims to independence and equality and towards manufacturers who fought trade unions, which were 'defensive organisations' that masters, by being fair, could have handled. But by 1859 England had, Hughes believed, learned its lesson.

5

For the social cohesion of which Hughes had dreamed in these two novels had been apparently, if only temporarily, secured by the threats of Napoleon III. The volunteer movement, which began in 1859, just as Hughes was immersed in these literary projects, was fostered by the belligerent Lord Palmerston (who became Prime Minister in June of that year) and blessed by the Queen and Prince Albert, who, as Bright remarked, reversed the normal habits of royalty to inspect troops and watch shooting-matches. The Queen actually opened a shooting-match by firing a rifle specially laid to hit the bull's-eye of a target.

Hughes was one of the first forty or fifty to join the movement at its very beginning.[37] He raised a corps of two companies from the Working Men's College, which in time became one of the well-known volunteer corps of London, pictured with its own distinctive uniform side by side with the H.A.C., the Inns of Court, the Kensingtons, and other famous regiments.[38] By 23 June 1860, when the Queen reviewed two divisions of volunteers at Hyde Park, Hughes commanded the Working Men's Corps (now the 19th Middlesex), which marched at the very rear of the fourth brigade under Lord Elcho. *The Illustrated London News* wrote that they were 'especially noticeable', since 'their step was as regular and their front as accurate as if it had been ruled by a line'. Though last in the cavalcade of the 1st Division, which took forty minutes to march past the Queen, they were among the first for bearing and deportment.

He endured more than the fatigues of marching and adminis-tration. His horse disliked rifle-fire. He had to attend concerts where the music bored him. Yet even as he sat in court waiting for his opponent to finish a case, Hughes would be found writing articles for the *Volunteer Service Gazette* (founded and edited by Jack Templer, one of the Masters of the Court of Exchequer). He defended the movement in *Macmillan's* as the saviour of the home, the spreader of freedom, and the solvent of class antagonisms.[39]

In a letter to Lord Goderich (who lent him a mare for the occasion) he wrote an account of a field day which took place in 1862. The manœuvres were complicated, covering four or five square miles with four lines successively in action, 'and all within sight of the grandstand (to please the lady spectators, which the old chief insisted on doing, as he said that part of the success was quite as important as the military business)'. 'Every regiment, I am sure, must have had a full dose of soldiering'. Except that 'one regular brigadier . . . broke down *completely*' and a divisional general 'instead of bringing a proper staff, had two young boys for aides . . . who couldn't carry messages', everything went well: 'I certainly never saw troops change front or deploy quicker or to all appearances more steadily than the greater part of those here yesterday did, but of course my experience is small.' Hughes felt that soon the volunteers would be mature enough for a military staff of their own, though on this occasion when one volunteer 'mounted a cocked hat' it was 'provocative of mirth' though it 'gained him great respect from railway officials'.[40]

In July 1861 Earl de Grey (as Goderich must now be called) became under-secretary at the War Office (a post he had previously held in 1859), advancing in April 1863 (on the death of Sir G. Cornewall Lewis) to cabinet rank as Secretary for War. He recognised Hughes' enthusiasm, and commissioned him to revise military regulations. This appointment was very distasteful to certain Conservatives, and one of them wrote to a friend in Australia:

'Well, Sir, this said Hughes is a man to me most objectionable. He frequents Chartist platforms and is a Radical of the deepest dye. The result of this is his appointment to the post of 'Reviser of Military Regulations' by Earl de Grey—Ripon. His next book may possibly be called *Tom Brown's Sinecure*.

His appointment is perhaps more immediately the result of his threatening to contest Halifax in the Radical interest against that Solon, Sir Charles Wood. The post has been created for him, and is as neat a piece of Whig jobbery as I have known. To qualify him for this post, it is but fair to state that Mr. Hughes has seen considerable military service—in the neighbourhood of Primrose Hill, being Lieut. Col. of the Bloomsbury Rifles !!' [41]

6

Hughes' militancy was taking on religious overtones, as can be seen from a hymn which he wrote called *O God of Truth*.[42] It is a stirring call to war against sin, couched in battle imagery like the more famous *Onward, Christian Soldiers*. Phrases like 'blood-stained vesture' and 'fiery rain' show the direction in which his imagination was leading him.

He was also becoming—and for good reason—militant about his religion. These were most trying and difficult times for the old Church which Hughes loved so dearly, which the Wattses had graced for a century or more, and into whose service he would have entered had he felt more worthy. As he told his wife, 'panic-stricken folk' were of the belief that 'the Church of England is going suddenly to blow up and disappear'.[43] Such panic was well justified, for from many quarters attacks converged during the years 1859–1861.

From the first quarter was mounted the direct assault of Darwin, whose *Origin of Species* appeared in 1859. Instead of rallying to meet this, the Church had to suffer, at the same time, internal defections, both from the liberal churchmen and from the legatees of the Tractarians. The Tractarians Hughes had disliked from his Oxford days, and he retained little sympathy for the parish-clergyman who employed their furniture and vestments to impress working-class congregations. Such practices, however, were on the increase. The Rev. John Purchas of Brighton published in 1858 a book entitled *Directorium Anglicanum*, in which full and elaborate instructions for such rites were outlined. Bishops, as far as possible, turned a blind eye where a church incumbent was doing good pastoral work, but on other occasions were forced to act by the pressure of public opinion.[44]

The most flagrant case now occurred near the London Docks. There, in the parish of St. George's-in-the-East, among the stews and degradation which at that time marked all dock areas, in a region infested with land-sharks, prostitutes, and publicans, the Rev. Bryan King held a cure of 38,000 souls. For fourteen years he had drifted up the tide of rubrical exactness, his congregation diminishing at each step, till in 1856 he adopted full Eucharistic vestments. Disturbances broke out, which increased in violence when King circulated a catechism stating that the first in honour among bishops was the bishop of Rome, Patriarch of the West; that confession was a Church commandment; and that the bread and wine of the Communion was the actual transubstantiated body and blood of Christ. So bad did affairs become that in 1859 the Bishop licensed a strong Evangelical who had been chosen by an indignant vestry. Pandemonium followed. Bryan King insisted on holding his own services after those of the Evangelical, whose congregation remained behind, ostensibly to pray, actually to hurl hassocks and books at the altar and furniture. King, in a pamphlet *Sacrilege and its Encouragement*, claimed to have been 'spat upon, hustled and kicked within the church for several Sundays past'. Someone aptly compared the clash of the two congregations to that of a 'handful of singing mice in a cage surrounded by an army of starved cats'.[45]

Police were stationed at the doors. The Bishop ordered the offending furniture to be removed, but the riots still continued till they came to a head on 29 January 1860. On that day 3,000 people were in the church, and as the rector read the service they roared obscene responses in reply. At this point the Bishop found opportune assistance from Hughes and A. P. Stanley. Hughes, playing the role of lay assessor, persuaded his old friend Septimus Hansard to accept the curacy of St. George's and brave it out before an empty church. He and his friends gave Hansard their whole support. King was persuaded to retire to Bruges.[46]

Hughes could not understand why 'the Established Church on its trial could trifle with all this millinery business', which only served to give 'a little fanciful importance' to 'young idiots in large towns who have little brains or character of their own'.[47] Nor, even more important, could he support the tendency for the Church to identify itself with the established order, and prostrate itself before wealth and worldly position. Remarking on the deferential pealing of bells in Manchester, which always greeted the appearance of Lady Stamford, who, according to Hughes, was 'married from the streets', he wrote:

'Poor old Mother Panther: She must indeed be founded on a rock if eucharistic vestments of the Pan Anglicans, and the eternal damnation of the Calvinists and the serenading of prostitutes and unworthy magnates, such as this reprobate Stamford, doesn't bring her about our ears before long . . . However, I am forced to add that of all her dangers I count this of the bowing down to rank and wealth, of which perhaps the Archbishop of York may be taken as the highly respectable leader, as by far the greatest.'[48]

Just when the St. George's case was settled, the Church was thrown into an even more widespread paroxysm by the appearance, in the spring of 1860, of seven papers in a modest little book named *Essays and Reviews*. Rugby, in the persons of Hughes, Stanley, and Hansard, might save the side in London's dockland, but in the person of Frederick Temple, author of one of the *Essays*, it was letting it down. So thought many of the episcopal bench, who rallied to demand synodical action against these heretical questioners of the sacredness of parts of Scripture. For

Temple and his six coadjutors they entertained much the same feelings as the Thebans had done towards the seven against them.

Hughes deplored the witch hunt. In a letter to his wife, he declared, 'The Bishops, London included, have behaved as badly and foolishly as men could'. He met A. P. Stanley 'coming away from Convocation in a dazed state at the folly of mankind, above all of Bishops and members of Convocation'.[49] Like Stanley, he was anxious that the essayists should be permitted the freest expression of their views. But, like Maurice, he felt that such destructive criticism could never confirm faith. To inspire the main body of opinion, he maintained that there should be a positive assertion to which 'men of all parties in the Church with any living faith in them and not fearfully clinging on to the letter and disregarding the spirit' could agree.

To that end, on 11 March 1861, he declared that he and Ludlow had 'settled on a good proposal'.[50] Two weeks later he dined with Maurice 'to read him what is done of my essay and get last words on it'. This essay, a statement of his basic beliefs, he called *Religio Laici*, and it was published as the first of a series called *Tracts for Priests and People* which he and Llewelyn Davies edited under the inspiration of Maurice.[51]

The *Religio Laici* states with great simplicity what to Hughes was the basic truth that once Christ has been found by the worshipping mind to be the ideal man, He immediately becomes the Son of God, because no man can render complete loyalty to anyone who is not both God and man. Even the freedom of God over natural laws thus becomes tenable, so long as the miracles are what 'a loving Father educating sons who had strayed from or rebelled against Him would . . . have done'.

The *Religio* made no pretence of being anything but Maurice's theology passed through what Llewelyn Davies calls Hughes' simple and devout mind. As Hughes himself said, he was neither divine, scholar, nor critic, and had no interest in the intricacies of theology, or 'multitudinism, or evidential views, or cosmogonies'. But neither had the 'men and women occupied with the common work of life—who are earning their bread in the sweat of their brows, and marrying, and bringing up children, and struggling, and sinning and repenting'. And it was to these that Hughes, acting in his characteristic role of catalyst, wanted to pass on the word of hope and faith that he had learned from his master.

It is doubtful whether he reached many of them. They did not perhaps mind—though the *Westminster* and the *National Review* did—his 'good-natured free and easy' logic, which first discarded everything but the 'idea of Jesus, as a beautiful and noble mythical personage', a name to 'float down on the stream of time, to have such effects on the hearts and wills of men, as all beautiful and noble ideas will have, and no more', and then rebuilt the whole Anglican creed, even to miracles, merely by assuming the 'worshipful nature of man', which was above, and therefore defied, the dead laws of the universe. But they were too torn between the science that was making for agnosticism and the sects whose warfare bred extremism to listen to Hughes' attempt to compromise between free thought and revelation, individualism and the Church. Views similar to Hughes' were subscribed to by so many intellectuals—Coleridge, Arnold, George Eliot, Meredith, Ruskin, Kingsley, Browning, Tennyson and Thackeray —that they seem characteristically Victorian. But they had few followers among the masses. It has always been more difficult in England to get a hearing for meliorism in religion than in politics or economics.

Yet Hughes' little essay is very moving, both in its sincere attempt to put itself 'honestly at . . . the point of view' of ordinary folk, and in its clear and direct expression of a deeply held faith. Hughes' was, as he said, a faith to 'live and die in':

'It has had to carry me through years of anxious toil, and small means, through the long sickness of those dearer to me than my own life, through death amongst them both sudden and lingering. Few men of my age have had more failures of all kinds; *no* man has deserved them more, by the commission of all kinds of blunders and errors, by evil tempers, and want of faith, hope and love.'

Yet Christ had always carried him through, giving him peace within and the certitude of a more perfect communion with God after death. One feels these things when reading the *Religio Laici*.

7

Neither surplices nor uniforms could long distract the working classes from their legitimate grievances. Seventy-year-old Lord Brougham, who had spent a long part of his political career in enabling these classes to become articulate, was so well aware of this that he helped to establish, in these years, an association for promoting the study of social science. The annual conferences of this association soon turned their attention to the problem of strikes, and in 1858 invited Hughes to serve as secretary to a committee charged with the responsibility of investigating trade unions.

For this committee Hughes wrote a good account of the lock-out in the engineering trade, of which he had such bitter experience in 1852. In this account he tried, in spite of the masters' refusal to give information, to present a fair case for both sides, concluding with the following general statement:

'After years of watching these Societies [i.e. trade unions] and disliking many of their doctrines and doings as much as any man, I am most firmly convinced that we are only mischievously shutting our eyes to the truth when we go on declaring that they have not the confidence of the body of the mechanics and artisans of the nation . . . that they are got up and led, not by good workmen, but by designing and idle men for their own purposes . . . that they exercise an unpopular tyranny and surveillance over the trades'.[52]

This opinion, and the report, Hughes defended with great spirit before the Congress of the Association at Glasgow on 27 September 1860. The report generally endorsed Hughes' views, and Hughes warned such of the employers as heard him that the mistake of treating labour as a commodity had brought about the French Revolution and produced slavery in America. Trade unions, made legal and treated intelligently, he asserted, tended to stop strikes, which could also be reduced in number by arbitrative tribunals.

More important for Hughes' future relations with the labour movement was the part he took in the strike of Master Builders called in 1860 [53] to secure a nine-hour day and to fight against payment by the hour. Through intervening in this strike Hughes and a number of other young barristers came for the first time in contact with William Allan and Robert Applegarth, who were soon to head the Junta, an organisation of trade unions led by the new Amalgamated Society of Carpenters and the London Trades Council, and aiming at securing legal recognition for trade unions. Hughes and his friends liked these new conservative labour leaders, who opposed strikes and advocated parliamentary action to gain their ends. From 'this time forth' they 'became the trusted legal experts and political advisers of the leaders of the Trade Union Movement'.

With respect to the strike, Hughes was very sure where he stood: 'I will go into the strike business with you when I get down', he wrote his wife, 'you depend on it, I am *right*.' [54] He served on a committee with Ludlow, R. H. Hutton, editor of the *Spectator*, his Rugby friend Godfrey Lushington, and E. S. Beesly and Frederic Harrison, the positivists, to meet the union leaders and inquire into the strike. He was also one of eight to sign the two letters urging fairness in *The Times* in July and September 1861, that helped produce a compromise.[55] As a result of this, though the ten-hour day remained, piece-work was ended, and a half-holiday on Saturday was secured.

Hughes also wrote two articles for *Macmillan's* in August and October 1861, which made his position about labour public in a way that it never had been before. They showed, above all, what the next step should be now free trade had been granted. Its great protagonist, Cobden, to whom Hughes addressed his first article, might smugly proclaim that since the triumph of free trade there were no longer any real issues. But, asked Hughes, was not 'this open state of war—almost chronic now—between the employers of labour and the men . . . a big enough question for every English statesman and every Englishman to spend his whole force upon?' It was as much a civil war as the one in America, though 'thank God, the weapons are not the same'. Workers, Hughes insisted, were not against the accumulation of capital; they merely didn't think a few men should have it all. And these few men were becoming fewer as the large fish 'ate up all the little fish of their own species'. 'Our eggs are getting into too few baskets', and there was no compensatory increase in wages or in the quality of goods produced. As a result, workers clung together for safety in trade unions, in spite of the harangues of *laissez-faire* economists about the iron law of wages. Unions spelt independence and strength, for which ducal and episcopal charity was no substitute. Hughes feared, indeed, nothing so much as the defeat of the workers in this strike. Even tyrannical, rude, and immoral victors were preferable to defeated workers such as could be seen in the East London tailoring shops, where the trade either killed men or 'grinds them into dangerous slaves'. The true solution, however, was compromise by arbitration, which would reconcile differences and lead to a partnership of the warring factions. If unions were legalised, made responsible, and given the right to know the financial condition of the business that employed them, workers would begin to feel that their interests coincided with those of their masters, and England would be at peace.[56]

Hughes was immediately and viciously attacked by the *Saturday Review* in two articles which, except for their literary flavour, might have been written by a current spokesman for the National Association of Manufacturers. Concentrating their attention on the violence encouraged by George Potter, leader of the Amalgamated Bricklayers and an opponent of the Junta, the *Saturday Review*ers accused Hughes and his friends—genial socialists, they called them—of being literary apologists for murder. Mr. Hughes, whose fervid imagination, kindly heart, and 'perfect obtuseness to argument' endowed him with the 'requisite amount of credulity and inconsequence which is necessary in the advocates of Mr. Potter', evidently preferred prosperity with crime to poverty without it: 'Of course there is no disputing about tastes, but this is really carrying geniality rather far.' Would Mr. Hughes, who justified threats, bombings, and tyranny, also defend adultery? A wilful optimist, he gave 'good names to the worst deeds upon the plea of sympathy' and sought to 'cure evil by sentimentality'. Yet all such coercive attempts to prevent masters from hiring other workers would fail in the face of the inexorable laws of supply and demand, though workers might temporarily destroy liberty. As for making trade unions legal, that would simply allow them to 'hold by law what they now only possess by usurpation' and further the prevalent 'inclination towards despotism'.[57]

In the face of such response it is little wonder that Hughes' optimism momentarily deserted him. Symbolically, he stopped his sparring classes at the Working Men's College. But Kingsley cheered him, telling him not to be discouraged, that his work was doing spiritual good,[58] and Hughes rallied, as he was to do from far worse depressions. Within a few years he was to have the opportunity to help create, in the teeth of the *Saturday Review* and its allies, the laws about trade unions that lay so near his heart.

8

He was soon off in full campaign on another front. At the beginning of 1863 a new weekly, *The Reader*, was launched, commanding the services of distinguished writers in every branch of literature and science, in an attempt to review all contemporary progress in the march of human endeavour. This ambitious essay in cultural synthesis was at first piloted by J. M. Ludlow, with the old brigade of Christian Socialists stocking the columns: Llewelyn Davies, Lowes Dickinson, Furnivall, Kingsley, Maurice, Neale, Westlake, and, of course, Hughes. It was issued from 112 Fleet Street, and its promoters proudly asserted that they were 'totally unconnected with any publishing firm'.

In the days when Ludlow and Hughes had lived together at Wimbledon, one of their neighbours had been a young amateur astronomer, then a clerk at the War Office, called Norman Lockyer. The three of them used to travel up to town on the train together, often with Tom Taylor. Lockyer had a capacity for popularising scientific discoveries and had in 1862 managed to become a contributor to *The Spectator*. When Ludlow was succeeded as general editor of *The Reader* by David Masson, Lockyer wrote scientific articles for it too, extending and enlarging its scope in that direction.[59]

By November 1864 it was decided to turn *The Reader* into a limited liability company, and Tom Hughes was the active spirit of the committee of management. On the 22nd of the month he wrote to Huxley from 78 Grand Parade, Brighton:

'I have just been writing to Galton to ask him to name time and place for meeting of the Reader Committee next Tuesday or Wednesday. Earlier I can give no time except in Lincoln's Inn in the daytime, which would not suit you I take it. On either of those days I can give any requisite time.

'My strong belief is that at present Lockyer can do all the general editing and will be the best man for us. He knows the machinery having been there from the first, has been in constant relations with such men as Ludlow & etc. who must be had for writers on general subjects not yet occupied, has the science already in the right grooves, and is not above taking advice, is a real good worker and above all has his heart in the business.

'He will do the work too gladly at a lower figure than any other competent man, a consideration to be regarded at the present until we get our capital and know where we are. We have bought a pig in a poke and shall want careful management, and above all plenty of give and take and pulling together to pull our pig out of the poke and make him a comely grunter fit to run alone. With care the Reader may be made a first class paper and a good property, but a little bolting and jibbing will have us all in the ditch amidst the jubilations of newspapers'.[60]

Huxley agreed, and three days later wrote to Lockyer asking him to superintend scientific matters in *The Reader's* office. Things went along happily enough for nine months or so, but there was great reluctance to take shares in the venture. Finances deteriorated. An attempt was made to enlarge the circulation by lowering the price from fourpence to twopence, but that proved a failure. Ultimately, to Huxley's regret, the paper was sold in August 1865 to thirty-eight-year-old Thomas Bendyshe, Fellow of King's College, Cambridge, and a barrister of the Inner Temple, who had in the previous month been expelled from the Conservative Club on the grounds that he had voted for John Stuart Mill at the Westminster Election of 12 July. Bendyshe edited it for a year, writing a serial entitled *Letters of a Suicide*, which did nothing to enhance his own or the paper's reputation.[61]

Yet *The Reader* did not exist in vain. Long-range forerunner as it was of the more ambitious 'digests' of our own day, it also had an immediate successor which has become world-famous. For Lockyer, the editor whom Hughes sponsored, went on to broach to Alexander Macmillan the idea of publishing a general scientific periodical. Alexander Macmillan responded with warmth, and the result was *Nature*, the first number of which came out on 4 November 1869. To this day, *Nature* retains the format, and even the very type, of those stirring days.

NOTES

[1] To Lord Goderich (who in this year succeeded his father as Earl of Ripon and his uncle as Earl de Grey) Hughes wrote on 25 July 1859 that Maurice's death made him feel old for the first time in his life, which was, he avowed 'a very good thing for me' ; Ripon Papers B.M. Add. MSS. 43,512.

[2] Conversely, when they were down on their luck, he would console her by announcing that money was 'just the measure by which the *value* of *nothing* can be tested'. Better to be themselves, he continued, than that 'old knave Morrison just dead, worth four million' who 'fancies that he lived on 1s. a day which his gardener used to have to pay him for weeding'; 8 and 10 March 1861 and one undated letter: Hughes to Fanny Hughes.

[3] Hughes to Ripon Feb. 1859, B.M. Add. MSS. 43,511; Hughes to Ripon, 12 Dec. 1856; Wolf, *Life of the First Marquess of Ripon*, i, 148.

[4] Letter, Hughes to Fanny Hughes, 26 Feb. 1861.

[5] Letters, Hughes to Fanny Hughes, 17, 18 March 1858.

[6] Letter, Hughes to Fanny Hughes, 24 Feb. 1859.

[7] To little Holland House, under the wing of T. Hughes. 'Little Holland House . . . was a great place of resort with a certain set about this time, the presiding genius of the place being Mr. Watts, who was always spoken of as

"the Maestro".' M. E. Grant Duff, *Notes from a Diary*, 1851–1877 (London, 1897), i, 141.

[8] Ronald Chapman, *The Laurel and the Thorn* (London, 1945), 60, 77. The gooseberry wine made by Hughes' mother seems to have been a welcome present. For the sketch of Jeannie Senior, see Mrs. Russell Barrington, *G. F. Watts, Reminiscences* (London, 1905), 5.

[9] Lowell Papers at Harvard, Letters, Hughes to Lowell, 2 June 1860, 29 June 1884.

[10] *New York Tribune*, 6, 13 Sept., 9, 29 Nov. 1866.

[11] G. W. Curtis (ed.), *Complete Works of John Lothrop Motley* (New York, 1910), xvi, 6; xvii, 157.

[12] Charles Morgan, *The House of Macmillan*, 1843–1943 (1943), 50–53.

[13] Graves, *Life and Letters of Alexander Macmillan*, 115, 147; Letter, Hughes to Fanny Hughes, 8 March 1861. These gatherings lasted till 1866.

[14] Letter, Hughes to Fanny Hughes, 18 March 1858.

[15] A. S. Layard papers in the British Museum Add. MSS. 38,986; letter, Hughes to Layard, 7 May 1858.

[16] Maurice, *Life of F. D. Maurice*, ii, 321–323.

[17] Lewis Melville, *William Makepeace Thackeray* (London, 1910), ii, 31. The name 'had a jollity and abundance about it' that would have pleased Hughes.

[18] Lionel Stevenson, *The Showman of Vanity Fair* (New York, 1947), 35.

[19] Graves, *Life and Letters of Alexander Macmillan*, 130, 133.

[20] A. J. Beresford Hope (1820–1887) was educated at Harrow and Trinity, sat as M.P. for Maidstone 1841–1852, and 1857–1865, transferring to Stoke, which he contested in 1865–1868. He was a generous friend of the Church, buying St. Augustine's Abbey, Canterbury, as a college for missionary priests in 1844, and five years later building All Saints', Margaret Street. With J. D. Cook (1811–1868), a reporter for *The Times*, and editor of the *Morning Chronicle* from 1852 to 1855 he became the joint owner and editor of the *Saturday Review*, the first number appearing on 3 Nov. 1855. Beresford-Hope wrote *A Popular View of the American Civil War*, published in 1861, which ran to three editions in twelve months. See James Grant, *The Saturday Review, Its Origin and Progress* (London, 1873).

[21] *Macmillan's Magazine*, Nov. and Dec. 1859, 78 and 48; *Saturday Review*, 12 Nov. 1859, 572. Hughes wrote a jaunty song about the fate of some modern but sinful knights of the round table, such as

> 'Choleric Bishop Brozier
> Of Barleymow Abbey the chief;
> Who banged his monks with a crozier,
> And pelted beggars with beef

and

> 'Fat Sir Gorbuduc Griskin
> Who would eat and call for more;
> He swore with grief that a baron of beef,
> Was woundy short commons for four'.

[22] Brown, *True Manliness*, xviii.

[23] Letter, Hughes to Fanny Hughes, 30 Oct. 1857, letter, Hughes to Alexander Macmillan, Christmas Eve, 1863.

[24] Letter, Hughes to Fanny Hughes, 30 Oct. 1857.

[25] Ripon Papers B.M. Add. MSS. 43,511; Hughes to Goderich, 6 Jan. 1858.

[26] Graves, *Life and Letters of Alexander Macmillan*, 124.

[27] *ibid.*

[28] *Journal of Benjamin Moran, 1857–1865* (Chicago, 1948), 2 Dec. 1858, i, 474.

[29] Graves, *op. cit.* 124.

[30] *Saturday Review*, 11 Dec. 1858, 589; *The Times*, 27 Dec. 1858.

[31] Brown, *True Manliness*, xix.

[32] Graves, *op. cit.*, 120.

[33] In 1860 Harper's published a pirated and incomplete version, but the following year the Ticknor and Fields edition appeared with a dedication to Lowell. It was to boost the sales of this that James T. Fields projected an article in the *Atlantic Monthly* on Hughes, and Macmillan suggested that Ludlow was the best man to write it. But he warned Fields 'Hughes is essentially a private, domestic sort of man, about whom there could be no gossip that would not savour of intrusion on the sanctities of private life'. This injunction, incidentally, was always scrupulously followed by Hughes himself in his biographies of other men, though he did object to Fanny Kingsley's excessive reticence about her husband. *Macmillan's Magazine*, March 1877, 337 ff. and Graves, *op. cit.*, 178.

[34] *Saturday Review*, 14 Dec. 1861, 611; see also *Blackwood's*, Feb. 1861, 131.

[35] *Reginald Dalton, A Story of English University Life* (1823) was the work of John Gibson Lockhart, Scott's son-in-law and biographer, at the age of twenty-nine.

De Clifford; or, The Constant Man (1841) was the last of three society novels written by the lawyer and politician, Robert Plumer Ward, when he was seventy-six. After the second of these novels, *De Vere; or, The Man of Independence*, Canning is reputed to have said that Ward's law-books were as pleasant as novels, and his novels as dull as law-books: a remark due probably to the fact that Canning himself was identified as De Vere.

Peter Priggins, The College Scout (1841) was the work of Joseph Thomas James Hewlett, a forty-one-year-old clergyman, illustrated by Phiz and edited by Theodore Hook.

The Adventures of Mr. Verdant Green, an Oxford Freshman . . . with numerous illustrations by the author (1853), the first of a trilogy which included *The Further Adventures of Mr. Verdant Green* (1854) and *Mr. Verdant Green Married and Done For* (1857) was the work of Edward Bradley, a graduate of University College, Durham, who, at the age of eighteen, in December 1845, is credited with the design of the first Christmas card. He took the *nom de plume* of Cuthbert Bede for his contributions to *Bentley's Magazine*, which began in 1846, and he used it for other work in *Notes and Queries* from 1852 until 1886. Bradley had a happy gift of illustration: he drew for *Punch* from 1847 until 1856, among his cartoons being the first four caricatures of photographers in 1853; and for the *Illustrated London News*, in which the first twenty-five plates for *The Adventures of Mr. Verdant Green* first appeared on 13 Dec. 1851 and 17 Jan. 1852. His talents extended to puzzle-making and song-writing: he claimed to have introduced the double acrostic into England, conducting a column called 'Acrostic Charades' in the *Illustrated London News* from 30 Aug. 1856; and was responsible for the famous comic song *The Ratcatcher's Daughter*, sung with such success in the provinces and in London during the years 1855–1863 by Sam Cowell. *The Adventures of Mr. Verdant Green*, together with its two successors, have been republished four times in the twentieth century: by J. Nisbet (1900), H. Young and Sons (1909), Nelsons (1911), and Herbert Jenkins (1921).

[36] (T. Hughes), *Tom Brown at Oxford*, 29, 98, 131.

[37] Brown, *True Manliness*, xxi.

[38] *The Illustrated London News* published a large double-page coloured picture of the metropolitan rifle corps uniforms, and the Working Men's College (on the extreme left!) is given equal prominence with the others. In the Hyde Park Review, the metropolitan corps provided 13,226 of the 18,450 troops on parade.

[39] *Spectator*, 14 Sept. 1860, 667; *Macmillan's Magazine*, March 1861. Letters, Hughes to Fanny Hughes, 2, 6, 8, 11 March 1861. It is remarkable that so many of the Liberals who were to figure prominently in the politics of the next two decades took a prominent part in this movement, e.g. Reid, *Life of W. E. Forster*, i, 320; Wolf, *Life of Ripon*, i, 151; Armytage, *A. J. Mundella: The Liberal Background of the Labour Movement* (London, 1951), 29–30.

[40] Wolf, *Life of Ripon*, i, 186.

[41] S. M. Ellis, *The Letters and Memories of Sir William Hardman, 1863–1865* (London, 1925), 243.

[42] For which see *Hymns Ancient and Modern* (No. 440), or *The English Hymnal* (No. 449), or C. G. de M. Rutherford, *Lays of the Sanctuary and other Poems* (London, 1861).

[43] Letter, Hughes to Fanny Hughes, 11 March 1861.

[44] F. Warre Cornish, *A History of the English Church in the Nineteenth Century* (London, 1910), ii, 16–24.

[45] R. E. Prothero and G. G. Bradley, *Life and Correspondence of A. P. Stanley* (London, 1894), ii, 27–28.

[46] *Harper's New Monthly Magazine*, Nov. 1881, 911.

[47] Letter, Hughes to Fanny Hughes, undated.

[48] Letter, Hughes to Fanny Hughes, 24 Sept. 1867.

[49] Letter, Hughes to Fanny Hughes, 27 Feb. 1861.

[50] Letter, Hughes to Fanny Hughes, 11 March, 1861.

[51] It was reprinted by Macmillan's in 1868 as *A Layman's Faith*. It should not be confused (as easily it might be) with the anonymous *A Layman's Faith* published by Trübner in 1866, the author of which was apparently Thomas Crowther Brown. The views expressed in both pamphlets are much the same, only T. C. Brown appears to be more learned than Hughes.

[52] *Trade Societies and Strikes* (London, 1860), 187. The Webbs, *History of Trade Unionism* (London, 1920), 227, n. 2. wrote, 'This inquiry . . . resulted in . . . the best collection of Trade Union material and the most impartial account of Trade Union action that has ever been issued. As a source of history and economic illustration this report is far superior to the Parliamentary Blue Books of 1824, 1825, 1838 and 1867–8.'

[53] Webbs, *op. cit.*, 215.

[54] Letter, Hughes to Fanny Hughes, 30 July 1861.

[55] D. O. Wagner, *The Church of England and Social Reform since 1854* (New York, 1930), 130; *The Times*, 15 July and 22 Sept. 1861.

[56] *Macmillan's Magazine*, Aug. 1861, 329–335, Oct. 1861, 494–498. Hughes' disregard of his personal reputation at this time can be seen in his attack on 'Anonymous Journalism' published a month later. A defence of the proclaimed policy of the magazine, it permitted Hughes to tilt with his two chief journalistic foes, 'Leviathan'—the *Times*—and the *Saturday Reviews*. Both used anonymity as a mask, the latter to hide behind after making scurrilous attacks on its enemies, the former to justify, under the plea of 'impersonality', its refusal to lead public opinion. 'When the Ethiopian can change his skin', Hughes wrote a few years later, 'and is able to hold his own without help from anyone the *Times* will come out for him—not a moment sooner.' It prefers to be the 'great stalwart leader at the head of a mob, who shoulders you from the wall and if you remonstrate, kicks you into the gutter.' By putting into words the idea that is 'just coming to maturity' in John Bull's brain, it keeps John Bull 'in the best humour with himself,' and nurses 'his already sufficiently strong belief that he is quite the freest and finest Bull on the earth's pastures'. Hughes followed his own principles all his life and led the ways towards what has, in the democracies at any rate, become common practice. But in his own day his plea for men to have the courage of their convictions fell on deaf ears, the dominant view being, as voiced by the fiery Jacob Omnium (M. L. Higgins) to Hughes, that anonymity permitted greater independence. *New York Tribune*, 2 September 1866, 1; *Macmillan's Magazine*, December, 1861, 167–168.

[57] *Saturday Review*, 5 Oct. 1861, 350–351; 12 Dec. 1861, 63.

[58] (Mrs. Charles Kingsley), *Charles Kingsley, Letters and Memories*, ii, 124.

[59] T. M. Lockyer and others, *Life and Work of Sir Norman Lockyer* (London, 1928), 15–31.

[60] Huxley Papers in Imperial College of Science and Technology, London.

[61] T. H. S. Escott, *Platform, Press, Politics and Play* (Bristol, 1895), 238–241.

CHAPTER EIGHT

John Bull and Jonathan, 1861–1865

ONE day in 1850, Ludlow rushed into 3 Old Lincoln's Inn waving the *Morning Chronicle*. It contained, not a favourable report of a Christian Socialist meeting, but a book review by young Henry Maine, called to the Bar in that very year. It was not so much the review which excited the two young barristers, as the book reviewed: the *Biglow Papers*, from which Maine had quoted a few lines.

Beaming with delight, Ludlow proceeded to read. The very first verse

> 'Thrash away, you'll hev to rattle
> On them kettle drums o' yourn'

took 'a hold on me', Hughes confessed. And as Ludlow read on, Hughes in listening to him 'felt at once that a new star had risen above the literary horizon . . . at any rate for me'. So, in the midst of all the work he was doing for the cause, he set himself to learn all he could about the author, whose name he didn't even know. He found that it was James Russell Lowell.[1]

When 'The Firs' opened its hospitable doors three years later, some Americans found their way to the parties which Hughes and Ludlow jointly staged. One of them was J. L. Motley, a handsome incarnation of Boston culture, fresh from communion with the great collections of European archives. The manuscript of his *Rise of the Dutch Republic* was published in England in 1856 and sold 17,000 copies in that year. 'If ten people in the world would hate despotism a little more and love civil and religious liberty a little better in consequence of what I have written,' he said, 'I shall be satisfied.' And at 'The Firs' he had a sympathetic audience. So did a less worthy fellow-countryman of his, one Hurlbert, who, by pretending an intimacy with Lowell, wormed his way into that audience and proved hard to shake off. He travelled abroad with Hughes in 1859, and fastened himself on Lord Goderich, whose plaid he stole in Lucerne. At first, however, the unsuspecting Hughes thought him 'the jolliest Yankee I ever met', a man with 'righteous faiths on the subject of property', and a great capacity for mixing a sherry cobbler. Hurlbert did Hughes one service in return for all this hospitality, for on 12 July 1858 he brought to Wimbledon the secretary of the United States Legation in London, Benjamin Moran, who was later to secure for Hughes the position of honorary equity counsel to the United States. Moran declared that his day at 'The Firs' was one of 'perfect abandonment to enjoyment': he thoroughly enjoyed the view, the large and friendly company, the talk of dogs, horses, guns, fishing, hunting, and racing: but he was particularly enchanted with his host, whose sandy—though fast-thinning—hair, blue eyes, strong limbs, deep chest, and cheery kindness, exactly fitted his preconceptions.[2]

I

Nicholas Trübner, '*un bouche d'or*', as Louis Blanc called him, was a publisher who developed the English book trade with America. He issued, among other things, *A Bibliographical Guide to American Literature* in 1855. In four years this expanded to five times its original size. In 1859 he invited Hughes to edit the first English edition of the *Biglow Papers*. That he did so was a tribute to Hughes' position in the world of letters, for Trübner numbered among his numerous literary friends men of the calibre of G. H. Lewes, W. R. Greg, Douglas Jerrold, and Bret Harte.

'I eagerly consented', Hughes said, 'as it gave me the chance of writing to the author, which I had long wished to do, but for which, till then, I had had no excuse.'[3] He need not have hesitated. For Lowell, in reply to Hughes' first letter, confessed to a similar admiration for Hughes, writing:

'Just behind me is the portrait of some fine oaks painted for me by an artist friend of mine [W. J. Stillman]. He wanted a human figure as a standard of size and so put me in as I lay in the shade reading.

'So long as the canvas lasts I shall lie there with the book in my hand, and the book is *Tom Brown*. A man cannot read a book out of doors that he does not love.'[4]

This first exchange of letters contained more than just mutual admiration for each other's brain-children, for both had lost their own flesh-and-blood sons. They became 'friends at once' and for life. A correspondence sprang up which was to last for more than thirty years. For Hughes at least it was to be an 'unfailing source of joy and strength'; he showed this by dedicating to Lowell the American edition of *Tom Brown at Oxford*, published in 1861, and thirty years later he edited Lowell's collected works as a labour of love. Lowell, in return, wrote an admiring preface for an anthology of Hughes' work published in 1880.[4]

From the very beginning, Hughes' admiration was open and unashamed. For him Lowell stood 'quite alone amongst Americans', the only poet 'beyond question entitled to take his place in the first rank, by the side of the great political satirists of ancient and modern Europe'. Hawthorne's power, according to him, was vitiated by morbidity and bad taste, and Emerson was a counterfeit genius—Hughes was quickly to regret this judgment —who seduced men by his wit and the 'singular metallic glitter of his style'. Only Lowell possessed the 'unmistakable genius' that 'knocks a man down at a blow for sheer admiration, and then makes him rush into the arms of the knocker down and swear eternal friendship with him for sheer delight'. Lowell for his part was so delighted that he could hardly wait to show Hughes' words to his wife, and refused to let any but his intimates see them.[5]

Lowell was the last of Hughes' gods: the peer of Arnold and Maurice. His works stood beside theirs in a 'small prophetic bookcase' to which Hughes would admit little else except some of Kingsley, Carlyle, and Emerson. To this 'small prophetic bookcase' Hughes would go

'back and back again and again whenever I have half an hour or so to do what I really like in. . . . I get *strength* out of them as well as pleasure, and of how many vols. in the whole library of the careful old world can one say that?'[6]

From them he would read aloud to his friends, to his children, or to anyone he wished to convert to his faith.

For in that faith Hosea Biglow stood strong. 'Conciliate! that jest means be kicked!', 'You got to get up early if you want to take in God': these, and many other maxims of the rhyming rustic clung to Hughes' lips on public platforms and in private conversation. He openly admitted Lowell's failings as a craftsman, a minor matter, however, to one who believed with Carlyle in the primacy of the poet's prophetic role. Lowell's greatness lay in his power of speaking as the conscience of the time:

'Of the poets of our time', declared Hughes, 'he is the one in whom the spiritual discouragement and disappointment so characteristic of the last half of the century . . . the yearning for a faith which seems to have vanished past the hope of recall . . . has taken the lightest hold.' [7]

His 'strong noble Christian purpose' and 'scorn for all that is false and base' were tempered, to Hughes' delight, by a fine humour, neither cynical nor morbid.

Lowell was wedded to the same political beliefs. He loved liberty, but was suspicious of complete democracy. He was firmly convinced, as he told Hughes in 1859, that it was the destiny of the English race to occupy the Continent, and 'to display there that practical understanding in matters of government and colonisation which no other race has given such proof of possessing since the Romans'. When the volunteer scare began in England, he prophesied that Napoleon would be taught

'a severer lesson than his uncle learned on sea and land half a century ago. Though you English (most of you) insist on misunderstanding us Yankees, you must not think that we forget what blood runs in our veins'.[8]

2

That Hughes felt the same blood affiliation with the American was evident in the following year, when the Southern States seceded from the Union and chose Jefferson Davis as their president. 'You cannot know', he told Lowell in July 1861, 'how deeply all that is soundest and noblest in England is sympathising with you in your great struggle.' [9] 'If the North is beaten', he wrote two months later in *Macmillan's*, 'it will be a misfortune such as has not come upon the world since Christendom arose.' So strongly did Hughes feel about the cause that he once harangued a man for twenty minutes before taking breath, only to discover that the man had agreed with him in the first place.[10]

From the very beginning the cause of the North was a straight moral issue as far as Hughes was concerned. Jefferson Davis became Flashman, and the issue was never in doubt, for God meant, by using the North as His agent, to make an end of 'the most degrading and hateful slavery that has been before the world for thousands of years'. 'One of the lessons', he wrote, 'which stand out in letters of sunlight on the face of History is, that He is against all such compromises [as the Missouri Compromise] . . . that He will allow no system of wrong or robbery to be fixed on any part of His earth!' [11]

By 14 September 1861 the *Saturday Review* had singled out
Hughes as the leading English advocate of the obnoxious idea of
freeing the slaves immediately. This was partly due to the long
letter which Hughes had written to *Macmillan's* while on holiday
at Cromer. Dated 12 August, it was a stinging attack on the
English worship of success, which undoubtedly accounted for
much of the popularity of the South after their victory at Manassas
Junction. After a spirited defence of Harriet Beecher Stowe's
insistence that emancipation was the true aim of the North,
Hughes turned to lecture at the Working Men's College in
November 1861 on the significance of the struggle in Kansas:

'My deepest sympathies', he told his audience in an address which was subsequently printed, 'are with those who are struggling for freedom all over the
world . . . of the body, of the intellect, of the spirit . . . I believe it to be the
will of God that all men should be free, and that Christ came into the world
to do God's will, and to break every yoke. That was His work, and that is the
work of every true follower of Him. Therefore, I do not pretend that I am
not a partisan in this struggle in Kansas. I think that the free-soilers were as
much in the right, and the pro-slavery party as much in the wrong, as parties
composed of human beings are ever likely to be.' 12

3

Other calls on his energies had made a rest and change of scene
imperative, so he went on an extended sight-seeing tour of
Europe. Having no money to finance the trip, he inquired of
R. H. Hutton of the *Spectator* if they would take such letters as he
wrote 'at the usual tariff for articles'. Hutton agreed to do so,
and Hughes set off for Bonn in August on a three-months' trip
that was to take him as far afield as Constantinople and Athens.

His letters, signed Vacuus Viator (from Juvenal's '*cantabit vacuus
coram latrone viator*', freely translated by Hughes as 'the hard up
globe trotter will whistle at the highwayman'), breathe the spirit
and prejudices with which we are by now familiar. He thought
Germans ought to learn about English 'eight-oar' races, frowned
on the Hungarians for enslaving the Slavs, disliked the snobbery
of Austrian social life, and came home feeling that London was
'unmistakably the very heart of the old world'. But London
looked dingy, unkempt, and seedy, in contrast to Continental
cities; there was more order, independence, and religious feeling
in Austria; and Belgian seaside prosperity exposed the sorry state
of English towns.

'When', he cried, 'will an Englishman be able again to look on a fête-day in Belgium, or Switzerland, or Germany, or France, without a troubled conscience and a pain in his heart, as he thinks of the contrast at home, and the bitter satire in the old, worn-out name of "Merry England"?'

Perhaps Hughes' views about the Turks are the most startling. He found them more honest and trustworthy than the Greeks or the Armenians, with an able, vigorous government that might educate them into modernity. He regarded them as the anti-Russian buffer on the Bosphorus, to be maintained as such against the Greeks, Serbs, and Bulgarians. As regards their religion, Hughes 'had no sort of doubt whatever that sooner or later they will become Christians'.

The holiday refreshed him, for, as he said, 'I had never been so far and so long away from England'.[13]

4

On the day before he returned, Gladstone made a speech which seemed to promise recognition of the South:

'There is no doubt that Jefferson Davis and other leaders of the South have made an army; they are making, it appears, a navy; and they have made, which is more than either—they have made a nation. . . . We may anticipate with certainty the success of the Southern States as far as their separation from the North is concerned.'

That was 7 October 1862. Just over a month later the London Emancipation Society was organised by sixty-year-old George Thompson, whose lifelong zeal for the abolition of slavery had once made it necessary for him to escape from Boston in an open boat. Assisting him in this was his son-in-law, F. W. Chesson, a journalist on the *Morning Star*, a young man half his age. Manchester followed suit with a Union and Emancipation Society which met for the first time on New Year's Eve to congratulate Lincoln on his Emancipation Proclamation. In the next six months the two societies disseminated two and a quarter million pages of information, and organised 150 meetings throughout the country.[14]

Their major demonstration was staged in the Exeter Hall on 29 January 1863 before 10,000 people, who overflowed into the street, blocking the Strand. Hughes was a star speaker, evoking such cheers that according to Henry Adams he had to stop and beg for silence. Flanked by such virtuosos of the emotions as sixty-five-year-old Baptist Noel,[15] Hughes did well enough to evoke supercilious sneers from the *Saturday Review*:

'And so the British nation has pronounced—at least Mr. Baptist Noel, and Mr. Newman Hall and Mr. Taylor M.P. and Mr. Hughes have pronounced—and in the eyes of Exeter Hall it is all the same thing. One warning we must venture to give to Mr. Lincoln and his friends. If they imagine that this sort of trash, and all the volubility of Exeter Hall, and all its vast cheering, howling horde of men, women, and dissenting preachers, is the expression of English sentiment, they will commit the very same blunder which Russia made in mistaking the Peace Society and the Manchester clique for the same people.' [16]

Hughes was modest enough about it all. 'You may judge of the difficulty of getting our public men of note to take active sides with the North', he wrote, or to go 'to public meetings and speak against secession and slavery' 'by the fact that I was about the most prominent speaker at the first great public meeting which was held in London' and 'was (unwillingly) pushed a good deal to the front'.[17] It was not surprising that his speech, reprinted by the Emancipation Society and circulated as a pamphlet, should contain the words of James Russell Lowell:

> 'We know we've got a cause, John,
> That's honest, right, and true;
> We thought 'twould win applause, John,
> If nowhere else, from you.
> The South cry poor men down, John,
> And all men up, cry we,
> Black, yellow, white and brown, John,
> Now which is your idee?' [18]

Though he later wrote that he took no pleasure 'in gabble of any kind and only really cared about doing what work I can for causes I really believed in',[19] he travelled as far afield as Liverpool, Birmingham, Leeds, Bristol, and Manchester to speak at similar meetings. Resolutions at these provincial meetings were transmitted by the American Minister to his Secretary of State, and though *The Times* sneered at such meetings as composed of nobodies, yet the minister observed:

'They are just those nobodies who formerly forced their most exalted countrymen to denounce the prosecution of the slave trade. . . . If they become once fully aroused to a sense of the importance of this struggle as a purely moral question, I feel safe in saying there will be an end of all effective sympathy in Great Britain with the rebellion.' [20]

5

Agitation for the Northern cause was a golden opportunity for working-class politicians in England. The presence of that veteran agitator G. J. Holyoake on the platform with Hughes was indication enough of that. When Adams, who witnessed the gathering at Exeter Hall, thought it was 'likely to create a revolution',[21] he was really thinking of the vast springs of working-class sentiment which such meetings could tap throughout the country. And they did: for of the eighty-two public meetings held for the Northern cause in 1863, fifty-six of them were almost exclusively working-class in origin and sentiment. One of the most successful of these took place in St. James's Hall, London, on 26 March 1863, when trade union leaders like George Odger, Randall Cremer, and George Howell, all proposed and carried propositions 'that the success of free institutions in America was a political question of deep consequence in England and that they would not tolerate any interference unfavourable to the North'.[22] John Bright swayed the vast audience by his moral strength, and ensured by his presence that the meeting was reported in the newspapers.

Henry Adams, whose report on this meeting was enclosed by his father, C. F. Adams, the American minister in London, in an official dispatch to Seward, maintained that

'the meeting was a demonstration of democratic strength and no concealment of the fact was made. If it did not have a direct political bearing on internal politics in England it needed little of doing so. There was not even a profession of faith in the government of England as at present constituted.' [23]

Well might the perceptive Matthew Arnold, another old Rugbeian, observe that the rule of the aristocracy was already passing, and bend his thought to the task of discovering 'some influence which may help us to prevent the English people from becoming, with the growth of democracy, *Americanised*'.[24]

Hughes rode on this tide of labour sentiment by his pro-Northern activities. How threatening this tide was becoming by the middle of the year can be seen from the formation of a Southern Independence Association under the chairmanship of the editor of the *Saturday Review*, Beresford Hope. This attempted to strike back by organising counter-demonstrations, but was exposed by Goldwin Smith in a *Letter to a Whig Member of the*

Southern Independent Association. Hughes, by public speeches, also contributed to expose the true roots of pro-Southern sentiment: fear of democracy, love of false gentility, apprehension of a further cotton famine, and jealousy of the power of a really united America.[25]

Hughes' other public gestures on behalf of the North, like the dispatch of his autograph to be used by the New York Metropolitan Fair, his introductions of Englishmen to prominent Americans, and his reception of such Americans as Henry Adams, increased his stature with liberal elements on both sides of the Atlantic.

When Henry Adams came to England as secretary to his father, he naturally looked to Hughes to introduce him to what he called the literary and progressive set.[26] And when William Evarts, in England on a mission from Lincoln about the Southern steam rams, wanted to give a breakfast to cement Anglo-American relations, it was natural that Hughes should be one of the six or eight Englishmen, 'good men and true', whom he would invite. It was equally to be expected that Hughes would accept, and would enjoy the 'delicious broiled salmon and such like delicacies' especially because 'at that hour of the forenoon' he ought 'to have been ensconced in my dingy corner of Lincoln's Inn, and absorbed in the preparation of a Bill of Complaint in her Majesty's High Court of Chancery'.[27]

After the war Hughes put a finishing touch to his labours with an article for *Macmillan's* called 'Peace on Earth' (reprinted as *Young Heroes of the Civil War*), to show his countrymen the 'heroism of the men of gentle birth and nurture' who, scorning to send substitutes as they were accused of doing, gave their lives for the Northern cause. Lowell's family headed the list of those who suffered casualties with a loss of eight men under thirty, including Lowell's nephew, Charles Russell Lowell, but Motley, Longfellow, Holmes, and the other great men of New England were not far behind in the sacrifices demanded of them. The Second Massachusetts Infantry, to which many belonged, lost five-sixths of its officers and 850 of 1,000 men.

'Conceive a struggle', Hughes concluded, 'which should bring one in every five of the men who have taken degrees at Oxford and Cambridge under fire, and which should call on us, besides our regular army, to keep on foot and recruit for three years a volunteer army five times as large as our present one.'[28]

Hughes became one of the foremost protagonists of 'a really intimate alliance' between England and America; an alliance which, by including the 'Cape and Australias', would bind the world 'round by a chain of free English-speaking nations which would have little trouble making their will respected and keeping the world's peace for the rest of time, or till Armageddon at any rate'.

Though he had seen too many of his 'millenniums miscarry for the real article in our time', Hughes did everything he could in the 'sixties to prepare for the day when such an alliance would no longer be an impossible dream. So long as the English treated America, in Lowell's words, 'as if we had been a penal colony' (Longfellow overheard two English girls excusing American girls' manners on the ground that Americans were descended from convicts and labouring men), and assumed 'that England had a point of honour to maintain, and all along implied that this was something of which we naturally had no conception', there was no hope even of friendship. On the other hand, as Hughes said after Sumner had talked the Senate into turning down a treaty over the *Alabama* claims negotiated in 1869 by the unpopular American minister, Reverdy Johnson, 'the signs of feeling on your side, the blindness to at least half the case' were equally disheartening. Feeling, as he told a hostile Parliament, that he had 'taken more trouble to understand America than most Gentlemen in that House', Hughes worked tirelessly to overcome prejudices on both sides.[29]

To influence his own countrymen, Hughes spoke vigorously in parliament and out of it in favour of arbitrating the *Alabama* claims, lest America come to believe that only force counted with England and that Lord Derby really meant to imply that laying the Atlantic cable gave England dominion of the seas. To help cement ties with America, Hughes laboured hard for the Freedman's Bureau, acted without retainer as honorary equity counsel to the United States, and umpired a race between an Oxford and a Harvard crew on the Thames. To reach an audience in America, where, as he wrote to the *Tribune*, 'there is as much misunderstanding about England as we have here about you', Hughes had become in September 1866 Special London Correspondent of

Greeley's *New York Tribune*, to which he contributed weekly and at length for four months.[30] Hughes had wanted some such connection in 1865, and was disappointed that Lowell had not pushed the idea. The *Tribune* was the most satisfactory medium. He would naturally not write for either the *World* or *Herald*, which he felt to be scurrilous sheets with Southern sympathies. For *The Times* he 'probably could not', he said, write 'if I would, and certainly would not if I could'.[31]

Hughes' *Tribune* letters—chatty, opinionated, and unabashedly hortatory, as one would expect—were as mildly conciliatory as an Englishman's writings could possibly be. Not only did Hughes 'rub' his 'hands and chuckle gently' over the American crew victory at Cherbourg—a victory of the old unbeatable 'English-speaking stock'—but avowed that he was perfectly content to see the United States surpass England in power, wealth, and numbers in a generation. In commenting on English affairs, his one desire, apart from giving Americans the liberal view on such issues as the Governor Eyre case, the Colenso fight within the Church, and Reform Bill agitation, was to present pictures of English life—of 'driving grouse', of feasting on Lord Mayor's Day, of 'the business of dining out'—that would familiarise Americans with English customs, and thus make them more friendly to the old country. Yet so bitter was the feeling towards England that Hughes was forced to stop his articles in January 1867: 'I received so many letters', he wrote, 'from the many persons who differed from my views that this course became necessary.' Though Hughes still occasionally wrote innocuous pieces for Greeley, not until December 1869, when he was moved to write in disapproval of American demands for an apology because England had let the *Alabama* escape, did he again venture to speak on Anglo-American affairs in the *Tribune*.[32]

Hughes' Anglo-American sentiments were yet further nourished by his widening circle of American friends. John Forbes, the railway magnate and banker, whom Hughes called the oldest of these, later became the father-in-law of Tom's brother Hastings.[33] When prominent Americans came over to England bringing letters of introduction, it was invariably to Hughes that such letters were addressed: young Oliver Wendell Holmes brought two from Motley and Sumner in 1866. In 1867 Hughes received William Lloyd Garrison, for whom he helped organise a great

breakfast at St. James's Hall,[34] and Abram Hewitt, who later induced Hughes to write a biography of Peter Cooper, Hewitt's
father-in-law.

Soon he was to meet these friends in their own homes.

NOTES

[1] *The Poetical Works of James Russell Lowell*, with an introduction by Thomas
Hughes, Q.C. (London, 1891), v–vi.

[2] Letter, Hughes to Lowell, 25 April 1891; *Journal of Benjamin Moran, 1857–
1865* (Chicago, 1948), i, 370–372.

[3] *Poetical Works of Lowell*, vi.

[4] C. E. Norton (ed.), *Letters of James Russell Lowell* (New York, 1894), i.
297.

[5] *Poetical Works of Lowell*, vi; M. L. Parrish and Barbara Kelsey Mann,
*Charles Kingsley and Thomas Hughes First Editions (with a few exceptions) in the
Library at Dormy House, Pine Valley, New Jersey, described with notes* (London,
1936).

[6] *The Biglow Papers* (ed. T. Hughes) (London, 1859), xiii–xiv. In 1870 he
insisted that 'Sir Launfal' was superior to 'The Holy Grail' and that if 'as trustee
for the English-speaking people' he had to choose between Lowell and Tennyson,
he would choose Lowell. In 1889 he asserted that Lowell's 'Christmas Carol
was the best English hymn carol or poem on the glorious topic, bar none—yes
bar none!' Lowell Papers at Harvard, letters, Hughes to Lowell, 3 Jan. 1870,
26 Dec. 1889.

[7] Lowell Papers at Harvard, Hughes to Lowell, 21 Nov. 1867; *Working
Men's College Journal*, May 1896, 80.

[8] *The Biglow Papers* (ed. T. Hughes), vii, xv; *Poetical Works of Lowell*, xvi–xxxi.

[9] Norton, *Letters of James Russell Lowell*, i, 299.

[10] Dedication to the American edition of *Tom Brown at Oxford* (Boston,1861);
Macmillan's Magazine, Sept. 1861. 414 ff; *The Times*, 25 March 1876, 8.

[11] T. Hughes, *The Cause of Freedom: Which is its Champion in America, The
North or the South*, speech delivered 29 Jan. 1863 in Exeter Hall.

[12] Notes for speeches in Hughes Papers; *The Struggle for Kansas*, in Ludlow's
A Sketch of the History of the United States (Cambridge, 1862); *Macmillan's
Magazine*, Sept. 1861, 414 ff.; *Saturday Review*, 14 Sept. 1861, 262.

[13] T. Hughes, *Vacation Rambles* (London, 1896), 1–60.

[14] For their work see E. D. Adams, *Great Britain and the American Civil War*
(London, 1925), ii, 106 ff. and 224 ff.; D. Jordan and E. Pratt, *Europe and the
American Civil War* (Oxford, 1931), 141 ff.

[15] Baptist Noel, youngest son of Sir Gerard Noel-Noel, was a Church of
England clergyman who, fourteen years before, had been publicly re-baptised
by immersion in a Baptist chapel before being received as a minister in the
Baptist Church. The *Saturday Review* sneered at him as 'good and prosy'.

[16] *Saturday Review*, 31 Jan, 1863, 132.

[17] Letter, Hughes to Fanny Hughes, 18 July 1862; Brown, *True Manliness*,
xix–xx.

[18] T. Hughes, *The Cause of Freedom*, speech delivered 29 Jan. 1863 in Exeter Hall.

[19] Letter, Hughes to Fanny Hughes, 3 Oct. 1866.

[20] Adams to Seward, 22 Jan. 1863, quoted E. D. Adams, *op. cit.*, ii, 108. Two months later he transmitted resolutions passed by similar meetings at Sheffield, Chesterfield, Crophills, Salford, Cobham, Weybridge, Bradford, Stroud, Glasgow, South London, Bath, Bromley, Middleton, Edinburgh, Aberdare, Oldham, Merthyr Tydfil, Paisley, Carlisle, Bury, Pendleton, Bolton, Newcastle-on-Tyne, Huddersfield, Ashford, Ashton-under-Lyne, Mossley, Southampton, Newark, and York.

[21] W. C. Ford, *A Cycle of Adams Letters, 1861–1865* (Boston, 1920), ii, 251.

[22] Karl Marx is credited with the idea of organising this meeting, 'the most important of all . . . held in England during the American Civil War'. Three thousand picked representatives of the trade unions attended. E. D. Adams, *op. cit.*, ii, 132–133, 134, 291–293. John Bright was the main speaker.

[23] E. D. Adams, *op. cit.*, 302.

[24] Matthew Arnold, *Mixed Essays*. For a fuller discussion see W. F. Connell, *The Educational Thought and Influence of Matthew Arnold* (London, 1950), 68 ff.

[25] Joseph H. Park, 'Thomas Hughes and Slavery', *Journal of Negro History*, xii, 590–608.

[26] W. C. Ford (ed.), *Letters of Henry Adams, 1858–1891* (Boston, 1930), i, 95, 97.

[27] N. F. Adkins, 'Thomas Hughes and the American Civil War', *Journal of Negro History*, xviii, 322.

[28] T. Hughes, *Young Heroes of the Civil War*, Old South Leaflets, No. 181 (Boston, N.D.).

[29] Lowell Papers at Harvard, letters, Hughes to Lowell, 25 Sept. 1865, 1 Dec. 1867, 20 May 1869; Norton (ed.), *Letters of James Russell Lowell*, ii, 40; *Hansard* (3rd Ser.), 181: 1053.

[30] Letter, Hughes to Benjamin H. Moran, 7 Feb. 1868. In Parrish Collection at Princeton; Lowell Papers at Harvard, letter of Hughes to Lowell, 31 Jan. 1870; Norton (ed.), *Letters of James Russell Lowell*, ii, 40; *The Times*, 20 Nov. 1866; *Hansard*, 181, 1053.

[31] Lowell Papers at Harvard (Mrs. Rantoul Collection), letter of Hughes to Lowell, 25 Sept. 1865; New York Public Library, letter of Hughes, 25 March 1864; *New York Tribune*, 6 Sept. 1866.

[32] Morgan Library, letter of Hughes, 3 Jan. 1867; *New York Tribune*, 9 and 29 March, 15 Oct., 10 and 31 Dec. 1866, 11 Sept., 25 Dec. 1869, 15 Jan. 1870.

[33] Lowell Papers at Harvard, letter, Hughes to Lowell, 5 July 1885; S. F. Forbes (ed.) *John Murray Forbes, Letters and Recollections* (Boston, 1899), ii, 38.

[34] *William Lloyd Garrison, The Story of His Life* told by his Children (Boston, 1894), iv, 196.

CHAPTER NINE

Rising Radical, 1865–1868

As early as 1862 Hughes had toyed with the idea of standing
for Parliament: he was then, as he told Lord Ripon,
'sufficiently before the world . . . professionally and otherwise, to risk it'.[1] At first Finsbury seemed a possible seat, till
Holyoake suggested another:

> 'For more than 20 years no man (if we except Molesworth, Layard and
> Fawcett) has offered himself for a metropolitan borough for which any man
> would care. The Kingdom would care for you and it and London would be
> proud to see you in Parliament. The school of thought and action you represent
> ought to have, and is expected to have, members in Parliament. Decline to
> pay anything but hustings expenses. Lambeth has a right spirit as well as
> Finsbury. It ought not to be left to the foxes to invoke it.' [2]

The mention of Molesworth and Layard was a shrewd appeal to
any ambitious strain in Hughes' nature, for Molesworth had been
Colonial Secretary, while Layard was still Under-secretary for
Foreign Affairs. Both were aggressive John Bulls: Molesworth
having been expelled from Cambridge for challenging his tutor
to a duel; Layard being a knight of the Macmillan round table.
Nor was young Henry Fawcett any less so, for though blinded
soon after he became a student at Lincoln's Inn, he was already
such an authority on electoral reform that the following year he
was to be elected to the professorship of Political Economy at
Cambridge.

I

But in 1862 Hughes followed neither his own promptings nor
rose to Holyoake's bait. He felt, as he told his wife, that the
invitation would be repeated, and 'if questions come up on home
politics on which I feel strongly . . . I should probably want to go
in'.[3]

And it was. In 1865 Holyoake again suggested him to the
radicals of Lambeth 'as a good fighting candidate, who has sympathy with working people, and who, being honest, could be

trusted in what he promised, and, being an athlete could, like Feargus O'Connor, be depended upon on a turbulent platform'. Nor did Holyoake stop at this; but introduced him to members of the electoral committee; overcame Hughes' reluctance to issue his address on a Sunday in order to get it written immediately; insisted that the address be rushed to the printers in a cab; and turned his house into a polemic arsenal for the issue of handbills.[4]

Just how much Hughes leaned on this industrious secularist is revealed from a letter he wrote just before the election:

'I am waiting in some anxiety for news from you. When shall I go on the stump? or shall I meet any persons, when and where? . . . I am game for any-thing except going in for the public-house and cab line. I shall tell the electors this plainly from the first . . . if the whole thing has collapsed, never mind. I shall find the right place some day, and if not the world will slide all the same.'[5]

Far from collapsing, Hughes' candidature drew national atten-tion. Even the *Saturday Review* remarked that it was 'highly desirable that the working class should be represented in the House of Commons, and if the people of Lambeth return Mr. Hughes they will have furnished one argument in favour of large constituencies of humble station'. There seems to be little ground for the complaint in Holyoake's autobiography that Hughes for-got to whom he really owed his election, since the working-class electorate were behind him to a man, and from a committee room in a back street over 200 volunteer canvassers went forth to solicit votes.[6]

Canvassers were needed, for the two sitting members, Frederick Doulton [7] and James Clark Lawrence,[8] employed much labour on the south bank: Doulton in his earthenware factory, and Lawrence at his big building works at Pitfield Wharf. In the days of open balloting, to vote against the boss might mean loss of employ-ment. Doulton was subject to apoplexy, and Lawrence, a leading Unitarian, was a sheriff of the City, and an alderman who com-manded respect among the shopkeepers from Westminster Bridge to Poplar. The *Saturday Review* put the case between the chal-lenger and the two occupants by remarking that 'Mr. Hughes has devoted himself to the advocacy of the rights or pretensions of working men', while 'Mr. Doulton and Mr. Lawrence are local employers of labour', and concluded: 'It will not be surprising if business relations prevail over philanthropic claims'.[9]

Cynics and pessimists generally subscribed to the view voiced

K

by the correspondent of the Radical *Sheffield Independent*, who wrote, 'I fear Tom Brown is not destined to enter the new Parliament through the constituency of Lambeth'.[10] But cynics and pessimists could not appreciate the tide of feeling which Hughes' part in the events of the previous five years had aroused. Behind Hughes, behind even Holyoake, there was the formidable machinery of the Reform League,[11] and the tractive power of the London Trades Council,[12] both in the hands of those very labour leaders who had passed the resolutions at the pro-Northern meeting on 26 March 1863. George Howell [13] held the strings of both in his capable hands, and paid Hughes' election expenses, some £634 19s. 9d. The artisans and mechanics rallied, responding to the appeals of 200 canvassers and to Hughes' own manly presence, with the result that the poll on 12 July read:

HUGHES	6,143	ELECTED
DOULTON	5,897	
Lawrence	4,272	
Haig	455	

The last-named, an otherwise unknown Conservative, never expected to be elected, but drove up to the poll in a carriage and four to win laughs by saying ruefully that his supporters had walked out after getting him to spend £1,000.[14] Another Conservative marvelled at the fact that Hughes did not have to spend a penny:

'All his efforts fail to obtain his bills from his committee; they tell him the expenses of the election are *their* affair not *his*. I understand the sum required will be mainly raised by a shilling subscription among the working men. This is something to be *proud* of. Hughes has the art of ingratiating himself into the favour of the artisans . . . A leader of the people he undoubtedly is'.[15]

2

When Tom Hughes led blind Henry Fawcett to his new place in the House of Commons on the afternoon of 1 February 1866, he symbolised his adhesion to the new party of intellectual radicalism. Their unofficial leader was John Stuart Mill, now the member for Westminster. Indeed, the *Economist* professed to find in the return of three such forthright independents a justification for retaining the existing franchise. Extending it would not discover any greater friends of the working man. And it would certainly effect no advance in standard. Hughes, from the very beginning, declared that he would not be led by the wishes of his constituents. He had, before his election, refused to sponsor the secret ballot, regarding it as unmanly. Nor did he accept it as any part of his task to flatter his hearers, preferring to 'elevate' them both morally and socially. He also refused to give his constituency more than sympathy and an accounting of his stewardship.[16]

This quartz-like independence relieved the uniformity of many a conference and congress. In the days before the wire-pullers and the manipulators of disciplined majorities had perfected their techniques, when the exhausting procedure of discussion in open congress was often deliberately preferred to the informed deliberations of a select committee, when few professional administrators had appeared on the scene to play the tune, men like Tom Hughes could command attention and respect, although their opinions might run counter to those of every person present.

A typical case occurred three months after he was elected to Parliament. Announced to open the discussion of the Sheffield Congress of the Social Science Asociation, he did not appear until later in the day. The local paper called his non-appearance 'one of the "misfortunes" ' of the meeting. When he did appear, it was to attack compulsory arbitration between masters and workmen in spite of the fact that a bill had been introduced for that purpose in this very year: a project dear to unionists, who had just been troubled with a macerating strike in the file trade of the town. In the same evening he went to a working-men's meeting in the Alexandra Meeting Hall and humorously rated his audience for sporting beards and moustaches in a town famous for its razors. In the course of an extended pæan on the necessity of mechanising industry against the wishes of the trade unionists, he roundly accused the Sheffield trade unionists of screening the authors of the many outrages which had made the town a byword for labour troubles. The following day he expanded this theme, denouncing the Sheffield unionists as disloyal to the cause of labour. These words were not lost upon the national papers, and the *London Telegraph* reported:

'Mr. Thomas Hughes, instead of complimenting the men of Sheffield, has been reading them a lecture which it must have exercised the moral courage of the speaker to utter, and the patience of his auditors to hear.' [17]

So hardly did the Sheffield labour leaders take Hughes' condemnation of the dishonourable, crooked, and unchristian manner in which they pursued their ends, that William Dronfield and Robert Applegarth waited on him with an explanatory memorandum in which they denied that they screened the authors of any outrages, and put into his hands certificated proofs that they had done all in their power to prevent their recurrence, as well as to discover the perpetrators of such outrages.[18]

Hughes reserved judgment.

3

'Our trial, our day of the Lord, is upon us. Can we meet it, or must the Scepter pass from us? I hope your readers will not think me profane or mad. I speak the words of sober conviction which has been coming on me during twenty years of earnest watching and waiting here.'

So Hughes summed up for the readers of the *New York Tribune* the feelings which animated his actions during his first parliamentary year. For the challenges were indeed coming in from every side. Anglo-American amity, so strong in the 'fifties, had now disappeared; tyrannies were arising in Germany and Russia; more deadly military weapons were being discovered every minute; at home the poor 'were never ceasing from the land'. 'Blockheadedism and scoundrelism were walking up and down the face of the poor old world' and all Hughes could hear was talk of 'enlightened self-interest and laws of supply and demand'.[19]

Certainly the swelling clamour of the town artisans was the most immediate challenge for Hughes to accept. He urged their very great need of dwellings which building societies did not supply. 'Many parts of London', he told the House, 'are frightfully overcrowded.' He accordingly supported a proposal for Government grants-in-aid for building such houses, although a fellow-radical, W. E. Ayrton, M.P. for Tower Hamlets, described such a scheme as 'a system of communism the end of which could not be foreseen'.[20]

Hughes also drew the attention of the Commons to the alarming exodus of industrial talent, and suggested a remedy.

'From one part of Wales, ninety families of skilled artisans had sailed for America. That is not a solitary instance, and I fear that unless Parliament meet the people fairly and give them a direct share in the representation of the country—make them what were called 'full citizens'—before long we might find the skilled artisans estranged from the country.

'Unless we do this, their minds will get more and more unsettled; we shall find that they no longer hold on to England with the same feelings as their fathers; they will continue to leave us more and more while we should feel we could spare them less and less; and we shall at last lose the pith and marrow of the working class who contribute so largely to the wealth and prosperity of the country.' [21]

This speech, interrupted by frequent cries of 'Question?' and denounced when finished as irrelevant, was the expression of a powerful pressure group which was gathering strength in the country. Eight days earlier, on 11 April 1866, Hughes had participated in a great meeting of the Reform League, when Edmond Beales took the chair in St. Martin's Hall. Beales, twenty years older than Hughes, was a veteran of such demonstrations. He had opposed the Southern Confederate States Aid Association, helped to organise the Polish Exiles Friends Society, the Circassian Committee, the Emancipation Society, and the Garibaldi Committee, all of which were shadow organisations for political reform in England. An equity draftsman and conveyancer like Hughes, he failed to keep this meeting quiet when Lord Elcho, who opposed the extension of the franchise, appeared on the platform to state his case. It was left to Hughes to emerge from the general body on the platform and appeal successfully for order.

The Liberal Reform Bill fell to pieces in the trembling hands of the Liberal ministers. Some, thinking that America afforded a poor example of the workings of a democracy, lost faith; others, like Robert Lowe and Lord Grosvenor, never had it. So they gave way to the Conservatives who kissed hands in June 1867. Meanwhile the Reform League prepared to stage a demonstration so gigantic that no hall could contain it. The venue selected for this massing of force was to be Hyde Park, the day, the 23 July. But on that day, the Home Secretary, on legal advice, decided to close the park gates. The demonstration was held as planned, outside the gates, and so great was the crowd that the railings of the park collapsed under pressure; nearly a mile of them disappearing underfoot.[22]

Hughes' friends urged him to resign from such a troublesome body, but he refused, though he had opposed both the meeting and the ban. Taunted in the House of Commons by Sir Charles Russell, a holder of the Victoria Cross and Conservative member for Hughes' own native Berkshire, Hughes replied 'that, having denied the requests of my friends to resign it is not likely that now I should reconsider the question [i.e. of his membership] upon the pressure of the hon. baronet and of the gentlemen who think with him, for whose judgement I have not a high respect and whose good opinion I am not anxious to obtain'.[23]

But privately he told Howell that he did not intend to speak at further meetings:

'I have considered the matter as carefully as I can and have come to the conclusion that I shall serve the cause of Reform better by not speaking at the meeting at Islington on Monday. As this is so I had better not be there. A man can only act according to his honest convictions.' [24]

But his public adhesion to the cause of the Reform League in this time of their trial drew from Henry Kingsley, Charles's industrious novelist brother, a tribute.

'Bright, Gladstone and Russell are behaving very badly,' he wrote to Alexander Macmillan. 'How nobly our dear Tom is behaving. There is a *man* for you, though he and you are inclined to go a bit further than I. I'd go for universal suffrage in Scotland or America, but the uneducated swarming masses of England are not fit for it.' [25]

Such manliness was acknowledged, too, by Leech, in a cartoon called *Gladiators Preparing for the Arena*, published by *Punch* just before the opening of the Parliamentary session in February 1867. It showed Hughes as a boxer, flexing his biceps in the centre of a distinguished group: before him was Disraeli, sharpening a sword on a grindstone turned by Lord Derby; beside him John Bright, punching a bag marked 'aristocracy', and John Stuart Mill holding a cup marked 'logic'.

Both Hughes and Mill, realising that they were spokesmen for a hitherto unrepresented class, contemplated a little book which, in Mill's words, would 'hoist the flag of a future party of practical reformers, in anticipation of the time for following Parliamentary reform to its consequences'.[26] 'Labour is here at the door', wrote Hughes in the *New York Tribune*, 'asking respectfully that it may be opened.' The middle class, he mused, had better not bang the door in labour's face, lest it be kicked down. So he was perfectly willing to stand by and see the Conservatives pass the Reform Bill in 1867, though he deplored the shameless opportunism of their bid.[27]

Nor was English labour the only trouble-maker. The cruelty displayed by Governor Eyre towards Jamaican Negroes roused

GLADIATORS PREPARING FOR THE ARENA.

WALPOLE, ROEBUCK, HARTINGTON, STANLEY, HUGHES, LOWE, CRANBORNE,
RUSSELL, PAKINGTON, GLADSTONE, DERBY, DISRAELI, BRIGHT, MILL

Hughes to demand Eyre's trial. England, with her vast mandate for two million coloured people, could not be too careful in her stewardship before God. With John Stuart Mill and T. H. Huxley he took his stand in demanding that Eyre should be punished, even though it meant opposing his old friend Kingsley and most of the literary men of the day. Carlyle had no patience with such views, and described Eyre as a just, humane, and valiant man, and his opponents as 'a lot of nigger philanthropists'. And Hughes was consistent. Three years later he was to protest about the cession of Gambia to France on the grounds that 'it was quite time that we should recognise no distinctions of colour in free citizens'.[28] Similar encouragement to his friend Lord Ripon, when Viceroy of India, was to come in the future.

4

Hughes' gaze was raised above the ballot-box by the unexpected materialisation of his dominant dream. Henry Briggs, chairman of the Employers' Association of South Yorkshire, and owner of the Whitwood and Methley Collieries near Normanton, decided to institute a system of industrial partnership and profit-sharing at his works as from 1 July 1865. The circumstances that led him to this decision were unhappily characteristic of most mining districts in the 'sixties; severe strikes, totalling on an average one year out of seven, inflammatory remarks by the miners—'all coal masters is devils, and Briggs is the prince of the devils'—and an equal determination by Briggs to crush the South Yorkshire Miners' Federation, had led to a complete deadlock. From 1 July, not only were the employees to be admitted to share-ownership, but they were also to enjoy a share of such profits as would remain after the normal running expenses of the mine had been met and a 10 per cent dividend issued to the normal shareholders. A committee of the workmen was called together to discuss proposals for improving the process of mining, and a public accountant was chosen to verify the accounts at the end of each year.[29]

After the first twelve months the scheme was a complete success. The number of worker-participants rose from 30 to 80 per cent of the entire staff. Old Henry Briggs himself went to the Social Science Congress in 1866 to dilate on its advantages, and his two sons, Henry Currier and Archibald, seconded their father's efforts.

John Stuart Mill, and his friend W. T. Thornton, Henry Fawcett (to whom Henry Currier Briggs ascribed the original idea), Louis Blanc, and G. J. Holyoake, were fired by similar enthusiasm, while Dr. Engel, the director of the Royal Bureau of Statistics in Prussia, and the Comte de Paris (whose book Hughes was to introduce to an English public) were prepared to recommend the experiment as a decisive solution of the class war.

Hughes visited the Briggs Collieries on 2 October 1866, and wrote to his wife with infectious enthusiasm. He was the centre of a great social gathering:

'40 lbs of tea in a great boiler, and the colliery folk all coming and going and eating and drinking, and congratulating each other and everybody on the day, the decorations of the wagon shed, the bonus, the end of strikes, and I know not what other great matters, and the boys letting off crackers in the background. . . .

'Three batches of tea, 600 or 700 sitting down each time followed . . . all the people sung before beginning the grace of four lines usual in these parts, the effect to my mind was most magnificent. . . .

'We, (the platform) tea'd with the middle batch . . . the speaking came off soon after 8 lasting till 10.15 and was very satisfactory. We (the company) besides paying 13% on capital have divided £2,700 in hard cash amongst the people besides paying them high wages, and have put by a large reserve fund, so you see dearest this corner of the new Jerusalem is flourishing as to cash success. What is far better, the whole tone of the neighbourhood is raised as two or three parsons testified, and there on the platform were 2 of the leading hands who could not find words to express their thankfulness at and hope in the new state of things, who *that very day* four years back had been arrested in these same collieries as ringleaders in a great strike against the then firm of Briggs. Now they are *pillars* of the church and believe in the Briggs father sons and friends as nobody has been believed in I should think since St. Paul's time.'

The next day he went to a part of the pit christened the 'Hughes' End' and 'exploded a mine', coming away feeling 'there is a fine simple honesty and purpose about them [the Briggs] which is very attractive to me, and they have done a great work and no mistake'.

The Social Science Congress held at Manchester, at which Henry Briggs gave such a favourable account of his co-partnership experiment, was also the occasion for the floating of another experiment in which Hughes was a shareholder and director. The mill which had originally belonged to Richard Cobden (who died in 1865) at Sabden, near Blackburn, had been silent ever since the cotton famine. The owner, Nicholas Heald, arranged with E. O. Greening to purchase the property through a co-operative association. Members of the association planned a 'co-operative fête' on 6 October to open the mills. Trains full of co-operators, social scientists, and holiday-makers, came from as far afield as Manchester, Bolton, and Darwen. The mill was to be fitted with 400 looms and 27,360 spindles. It began work in September of the following year, and in three months showed a small profit. Other companies soon followed suit: Fox and Head (iron), Greening's own South Buckley Coal and Fire Brick Company, Crossley's (carpets), Goodall's (printing) and Lloyd and Summerfield (glass) showed that the co-partnership, profit-sharing gospel was spreading through the industrial areas of Lancashire and Yorkshire. Hughes had already become a share-holder in a further venture of Greening's—a co-operative wire-work factory, which distributed all profits over $7\frac{1}{2}$ per cent to its workers as bonuses.[30]

In the meantime in London a new co-operative producers' association raised its head, reviving in a more literal form Hughes' ideas of 1849. In 1867 Hughes became a director of the newly reconstituted Framemakers' and Gilders' Society of Red Lion Square, originally begun by Robert Newton in 1858 after he had heard a talk by Hughes at the Working Men's College. Started with a capital of £8, it was employing, by the time Hughes became a director, forty men and doing nearly £10,000 worth of business annually. For many years it wandered, as Beatrice Webb wrote, 'like Joseph among the Egyptians in the unconquered land of private enterprise and held aloft the standard of self-employment'.[31]

One more venture of Hughes' was to have great consequences. In discussions with Greening at Manchester, they had both agreed that the working man needed a reliable source of seeds and nursery goods.[32] Hughes was much impressed with Greening's arguments in favour of agricultural co-operative enterprise, and invited him to London. There five others—E. V. Neale, W. Morrison, James Beale (leader of a movement which ultimately resulted in the establishment of the L.C.C.), Cowper-Temple (the late Lord Palmerston's son-in-law), and F. Pennington (an East India merchant)—set up the Agricultural and Horticultural Association —a name, said Holyoake, which would sink any ship. But they didn't sink. On the contrary, within four years they were doing business at a rate of £1,000 a week, and were the object of interested enquiries from both the Prussian and Austrian Ministries of Agriculture.

5

In these years of promise, Hughes, ignited with enthusiasm, was spending his money with great willingness. At the celebration of the first half-year of Greening and Company he spent most of the time praising his host. He was perfectly willing to lose money in such enterprises, for, as he told them,

'every man must have some way of spending his spare cash. Some men like moors in Scotland, some like keeping hounds and horses, and for many years I have had a taste for co-operation.' [33]

In 1867 he attended a festival at Greening and Company, where he was presented with a testimonial, a 'graceful and prettily painted piece of wire work, supporting 9 nice pots', which Tom was sure his wife would be able to use outside the dining-room window. Describing the scene to her, he wrote:

'All the men came to tea (heavy) at the house at 5.30. They were almost all very early and sat round and squeezed together and were excessively solemn and subdued, only answering monosyllabically in general and looking very uncomfortable. The other directors however came in and went to tea which warmed them up more or less, and I felt very convivial and I know imparted much of my feeling to the table. I could see what a fine set of fellows they were and that they only wanted to be sure that we shouldn't bite to enjoy themselves thoroughly.'

After the stiffness had gone and all the speeches had been made, everybody sang and ate apples, pears, and grapes, until 11.30—

'all of them deeply vowing to make G. & C. no end successful—and I am inclined to think they will too for it is an excellent manufactory for work and they are all in earnest about getting a good bonus.' [34]

This festival at Greening & Company was the climax of a week's trip which had also given Hughes his second look at Briggs & Company, and which was to take him to Rochdale, to a conference and public meeting at Manchester (a city about which he always had mixed feelings, liking its vigour and the relative absence of the 'profligate vices' of London, but hating its atmosphere of money-making, 'which envelopes you like a cloud'), to the Cobden Mills and to Bolton. At the Cobden Mills, where he stayed with young Heald, the manager, who after leaving Rugby had gone into the factory to learn to work 'with his own hands', he was pleased to learn from the parson that there had been improvement in the parish since the mills were started. At Bolton he stayed with Harwood, a manufacturer who had 'joined us as a Director of the Cobden Mills. . . . His wife is scarcely a lady but apparently a good soul.' His second son was 'vigorous, intelligent, full of Carlyle and Tennyson', and his friends were, like himself, 'full of interest on the deepest subjects and eager for new ideas and new truth, and far more ready to talk on such subjects than the ordinary youngster of the upper classes'. Here Hughes saw deputations of men at the 'leading factories', who loaded him with 'beautiful specimens of cotton work', and attended a bumper meeting where he discoursed an 'hour and a half to a platform of parsons and manufacturers and a hall full of operatives'. 'So you see,' he told his wife, 'my side of the movement goes right everywhere whether we make our fortunes by trying to do justice or not.' 'Really with a little wisdom and care poor old England may yet be made a good place for poor folk to live in.' [35]

Hughes' friend Ludlow violently disagreed with Hughes about the virtues of industrial partnership, claiming that a paper read by Archibald Briggs to the Co-operative Congress showed that the scheme ran 'exactly counter to the most vital points of Co-operation'. According to Ludlow, the plan had as its purpose 'to extract from the worker the largest possible amount of labour for the smallest bribe in the way of bonus', since he got but one half the excess profits 'created by his own exertions' and no participation in management at all. H. C. Briggs admitted with disarming candour to the Trade Union Commission that he had instituted profit-sharing to avoid strikes, that it 'infinitely' strengthened the hands of employers, and that the addition to wages was more 'apparent than real'. In the light of these confessions, Wagner in his *Church of England and Social Reform since 1854* finds Hughes' 'estimate of profit-sharing . . . a little disheartening', an inexplicable 'aberration' resulting from 'good humour, lack of comprehension, or disillusionment'.[36]

Though it is hard not to agree with Wagner that Hughes was somewhat naïve, as he so often was, in the faith that he placed in this latest of his panaceas, his behaviour was far from being inexplicable or inexcusable, or even inconsistent with his previous beliefs. For years Hughes had been trying to reconcile three ideas:

his love of the common man; his feeling that perhaps workers were not quite ready to handle their own affairs; and his desire to save his own class from being considered useless or pernicious. So, along with his work for Christian Socialism, the American North, and labour unions, he had flirted with thoughts of a revived squirearchy. When an idea like industrial partnership appeared, with twin promises of better conditions and more dignity for workers, together with an opportunity for business men to play the educative and paternal role of Squire Brown, Hughes was bound to find it irresistible. It was not Socialism or even Co-operation. But it seemed to provide a heaven-sent chance to end strikes (that was why Briggs's statement didn't bother him) and effect a reconciliation of classes on the basis of Christian brotherhood. 'The employer', he said, 'has at last found his place in the association for production'; indeed, the war between capital and labour was perhaps over. Moreover, unlike all the producers' associations Hughes had known, industrial partnerships were likely to make money, since they had business brains at the control, and therefore avoided the managerial problems of the associations. This consideration weighed more heavily with Hughes than it did with Ludlow, about whom Hughes wrote with understandable amusement to his wife:

'Greening is receiving critical letters from old Gruff, who is beginning of course to object to our proceedings now they are turning out so profitable. . . . You know it all, I chuckle, as G has to answer them and not I.' [37]

The crucial point for Hughes was the direction the movement was likely to take, and this depended on the spirit of the participants. Hughes felt he had every reason to be confident. Briggs' workers had not perhaps received all they were entitled to, but £2,700 in the first year was £2,700 more than they had ever received before. Even *The Times* was impressed when Greening & Company paid a bonus, though it deplored any attempt to draw ethical meaning from the event.[38] Workers, Hughes saw with his own eyes, were no longer disgruntled slaves tied by the Carlylean 'cash nexus', but were being trusted with at least the details of management. They voluntarily took a wage reduction at Greening & Company when business was bad in 1869, and Hughes saw no reason why in the future industrial co-partnerships should not be able to win the same loyalty that unions had won, particularly if wage funds were established to tide workers over the brief depression that might occur. Greening and the Briggs family, who invariably treated Hughes and Fanny as if they were of the aristocracy, inspired him with confidence that if that class were awakened to its responsibilities, all might not yet be lost.

6

Any immediate realisation of such hopes had been shattered by the explosion of a can of gunpowder in the cellar of a saw-grinder's house in Sheffield on 8 October 1866.[39] It was not so much the explosion which caused the trouble as the reaction against it. The employers of the town, animated by the editor of the local Conservative newspaper, pressed for the appointment of a Royal Commission to investigate the powers of the intimidating trade unions of the town; for the saw-grinder had twice deserted his union and was, at the time his house blew up, working as a blackleg for a firm whose workers were on strike.

The Sheffield Association of Organised Trades acted swiftly. Inspired by their secretary, who, with Applegarth, had made representations to Hughes when he had attacked them the year before, they appealed to him. That appeal was not in vain, for on 26 October, just as public indignation was reaching a further height, Hughes appeared in print to defend the unionists from a charge of complicity in the case. In the course of a letter to the *Spectator* of 26 October he made public four important facts: first, that the Sheffield Association of Organised Trades not only never countenanced the crime, but had done all they could to prevent it; secondly, that hitherto they had been largely successful in such efforts; thirdly, that the joint committee of masters and men which had been set up after a similar outrage six years previously had collapsed because of the masters' refusal to attend; and lastly, that the previous outrage which had called forth public indignation in 1861 had not been the work of a unionist at all.

The Government were also perturbed: the Queen's Speech on the opening of Parliament on 5 February 1867 admitted that 'it cannot be denied that the old relations between masters and men are things of the past'. They decided to appoint a Royal Commission, and four days later the Home Secretary announced that he had received a petition from the London working men asking for the appointment of either Goldwin Smith, Ludlow, G. Lushington, or Professor Beesly to the Commission.

Hughes protested against the clauses in the bill establishing the Trade Union Commission which offered indemnity to the perpetrators of violence if they turned King's Evidence, but his objections were overruled.[40] However, he, together with the young positivist barrister, Frederic Harrison, was made a member of the Commission, charged with the duty of investigating the effect of trade unions on employers, workers, and trade in general. This was a preliminary to the amendment of the existing Combination Acts, which, by failing to define the term conspiracy, had made it impossible to tell whether or not a combination was lawful.

This problem was even more aggravated by a decision in the Court of Queen's Bench which, in 1867, 'completely shattered' the legal security of unions as such, leaving their hardly-massed funds at the mercy of any branch secretary who might choose to abscond with them. For the decision gave to magistrates the right to decide whether a society was in restraint of trade, and thus to exclude them from the benefits of the Friendly Societies Act of 1855. If unions made any show of violence whatever, they could be condemned as restraining trade.

In this crisis, Hughes and the three positivists, E. S. Beesly, Frederic Harrison, and Henry Crompton, did all that lay in their power to help the unions. In a generous tribute, all the more remarkable in view of her animosity against Hughes' co-operative views, Beatrice Webb and her husband wrote:

'Applegarth's minutes show how frequently all four were ready to spend hours in private conference at the Engineers Office in Stamford Street, and how unreservedly they, in this crisis, placed their professional skill at the disposal of the Trade Union Leaders. It would be difficult to exaggerate the zeal and patient devotion of these friends of Trade Unionism, or the service which they rendered to the cause in its hour of trial.' [41]

But there was little they could do at the moment. Hughes' and Neate's 'Association of Workmen Bill', introduced on 10 April 1867 to restore trade union rights temporarily—rights that unions could not exist without and that they had thought they had—was quashed by the Attorney-General's decision against provisionally sanctioning illegality.[42]

The new Commission did not appear to offer much help to labour. Charged with finding out if unions by their very nature contributed to such things as the Sheffield outrage, it seemed more like an inquisitory body than an impartial investigating agent. Its composition accentuated this feeling: employers were represented by two of the ten members—not considered enough by some—and the workers by no one. Though Hughes, the workers' 'principle spokesman in the House', according to Frederic Harrison, could be counted on to take the workers' side, yet he felt that 'single handed he could do little for his friends', so Harrison and William Matthews were added, at his suggestion.[43] To have actual workers sitting on the Commission was considered prejudicial to impartiality, a notion which gave substance to Gladstone's concern for labour's freedom if the Commission were appointed and to the reluctance of Liberals like Neate and Goschen to have the general problems of unions treated together with the Sheffield outrages. Ludlow and Lloyd Jones, writing not long after the appointment of the Commission, warned that 'the air-gun and the powder-can of the Sheffield unionist no more prove that all trade combinations should be suppressed than the dagger of Ravaillac proves that all religious organisations should be put down'.[44]

So it is little wonder that Hughes wrote to Lowell on 1 December 1867:

'We are going to have a very trying winter here such as we have not known since the corn laws were repealed; and may probably see a state of things which to outsiders it will all pass and I do hope will leave us in better fettle than we have been since Palmerston got over Johnny's head and became (heaven help the mark) leader of the *Liberal* party, so called. The old reverence for law has had a shake from his devil may care leadership. . . . But Providence 'wu'nt set down' and in spite of all her meannesses and stupidities the old country has a great stroke of work to do yet.'[45]

7

Hughes and Harrison conducted the trade union case before the Commission in consultation with Applegarth, whom the Junta deputed to attend meetings. Though Hughes was, according to Harrison, 'too busy with many things in Parliament and outside to give regular work to the Commission, which he was very willing to leave to me', no man could have been a 'more loyal or more genial comrade than he proved to be throughout'. Through the nearly two years that the Commission was collecting data and formulating its views, the two men acted, as Harrison urged that they should, as one man. Harrison's positivism bothered Tom Hughes as little as did Lord Ripon's later Catholicism or Holyoake's agnosticism, so long as there was agreement on the issues at hand. Fortunately, Hughes had been dead for fourteen years when Harrison wrote of Maurice: 'A more utterly muddleheaded and impotent mind I have never known.' [46]

The Liberal Opposition needed all the strength it could muster. In its original form, the final report made workers virtually bondsmen to employers. As an interesting unpublished letter of Harrison's to Hughes, written just before the election of 1868, indicates, the majority were for retaining the combination laws, with severe punishments against workers for a 'combined effort to coerce the will of another in the free exercise of that in which the public have an interest'. How could Liberals, Harrison asked bitterly, stand for legislation that 'by sweeping phrases which include everything down to a cough or a chuckle', penalised workers for doing what landlords and merchants did automatically? 'This is as bad as Warsaw', he exclaimed, asking whether Hughes couldn't work into his speech something on the lines of his election declaration, which had quite acted 'on the tone of the country'. Harrison suggested a tentative resolution that he would vote for a Bill to suppress intimidation by workers when he saw a dozen landlords and a dozen M.P.s imprisoned for 'putting on the screw'. Hughes was sympathetic and told his wife that he refused to 'have stringent work with the poor illiterate uneducated while we swallow infinite camels amongst the rich and strong'.[47]

When the Commission met in December 1868, Hughes and Harrison fought the report, Harrison wrote,

'line by line, and succeeded in deleting about nineteen out of every twenty clauses—mainly, I must say, by the vigour and good feeling of two Peers who were the only truly impartial members of the Commission. Lord Elcho's ability and Lord Lichfield's sense of justice [in 1892 Hughes also paid tribute to these two Peers] with occasional help from the cool intellect of [Herman] Merivale, bore down the majority; and the Chairman's weakness, coupled with his natural desire to get some report agreed on, led to clause after clause being thrown overboard, to the rage and scorn of John Roebuck.' [48]

Even so, Hughes and Harrison, who were joined by Lord Lichfield, refused to sign the principal report on the basis that, though it advocated the legality of combining even in restraint of trade, it carefully said nothing about a union's right to sue, urged separation of strike funds from others, and did not soften the provisions against coercion and picketing, thus failing to end the distinction between crimes committed by labour and other crimes.[49] The three men embodied their ideas, as Harrison had the previous year urged that they should, in a separate report that could be the 'armoury of the opposition on the Liberal side' and that would continue to have an effect till 'our side' won. Hughes and Harrison (Lord Lichfield did not sign this) also published a long appendix to the minority report justifying their position. These documents, according to the hostile *Edinburgh*, were the most effective *apologia* unions had ever found or were likely to find. They became, Harrison and Ludlow averred, 'the foundation of all subsequent debates in Parliament' and thus 'of all subsequent legislation on the subject'.[50]

Unions were, according to Hughes' and Harrison's appendix, both desired by the workers and on the whole beneficent, particularly the large new non-militant ones. The higher wages, the safety, and the reduction of hours, no less than the collateral benefits like sick pay and help to emigration that unions secured, were in the interests of the community, whose aim should be the welfare of the people, not mere multiplication of goods at cheaper prices. It had yet to be proved that unions were responsible for any falling off in trade that occurred, and if they kept wages from dropping to meet foreign competition, that was good. In general, unions were a necessary corollary of a capitalist society.

'Under a system which professes the right or rather the duty of all men peacefully to pursue their own interests for themselves, unionism appears to us the exact correlative of competition. The stronger prefer to pursue their ends by means of competition, the weaker by means of combination. But for the capitalist to deny the workman unlimited freedom to combine, is for the stronger to object to the weaker pursuing his interests by the most obvious resource in his reach.'

If the capitalist 'cannot find workmen to fill' the places of workers on strike, 'his position may be highly inconvenient, but this is no ground for his calling upon the State to coerce his workmen to work for him on terms which they decline'. The State was not there to enforce morality or punish unsocial conduct that was not criminal. In line with these thoughts the minority report recommended that laws making combinations illegal and possibly punishable conspiracies 'should be broadly and unequivocally rescinded'. Abrogating it partially or in words while keeping it in force by a series of intricate provisos would be to add 'fresh uncertainties to a very difficult branch of law, and to involve the associations in latent liabilities without any compensating public good'. Special laws relating to labour were wrong and dangerous, especially when they condemned such vague practices as 'intimidation', 'molestation', and 'obstruction'. By simple registration unions should be entitled to the protection of their property so long as no criminal charge was proved against them; in return, unions should give full publicity to their finances, and be willing to submit disputes—as capitalists should be too—to voluntary boards of arbitration.[51]

NOTES

[1] Ripon Papers, B.M. Add. MSS. 43,515, Hughes to Ripon, 23 Dec. 1862.

[2] Letter, Hughes to Holyoake.

[3] Letter, Hughes to Fanny Hughes, 23 April 1862.

[4] Holyoake, in his *Bygones Worth Remembering*, ii, 106–109, which also gives samples of these handbills:

> 'Hughes for Lambeth'.
> Vote for 'Tom Brown'.
> Vote for a gentleman who is a friend of the People.
> Vote for a Churchman who will do justice to Dissenters.
> Vote for a tried Politician who will support just measures and can give sensible reasons for them.
> Vote for a distinguished writer and raise the character of metropolitan constituencies.
> Vote for a candidate who can defend your cause in the Press as well as in Parliament.
> Vote for a man known to be honest and who has long worked for the industrious classes.
> Electors of Lambeth, vote for Tom Hughes.

[5] J. McCabe, *Life and Letters of G. J. Holyoake* (London, 1908), ii, 18–19.

[6] *Sheffield Independent*, 12 July 1865.

[7] Frederick Doulton was born in Lambeth in 1824, and in 1856 became a member of the Metropolitan Board of Works. He first contested Reigate in 1858. He won Lambeth on 5 May 1862, and held it till 11 November 1868, dying of apoplexy at Tunbridge Wells on 21 May 1872. See G. Hill, *Electoral History of the Borough of Lambeth* (London, 1879).

[8] James Clark Lawrence was born in 1820, and became in 1860 an alderman for Walbrook Ward. Two years later he became the Sheriff of London and Middlesex, and on 9 May 1865 was elected M.P. for Lambeth—holding the seat for only two months before the General Election. Though defeated by

Hughes, he was elected in 1868 and held the seat till 18 Nov. 1885. He was later Lord Mayor of London, and died in 1897.

[9] *Saturday Review*, 3 June 1865.

[10] *Sheffield Independent*, 8 July 1865.

[11] For which see S. Maccoby, *English Radicalism, 1853–1886* (London, 1938), 84–94.

[12] *The London Trades Council, 1860–1950* (with a preface by Julius Jacobs) (London, 1950), 1–36.

[13] His letters are at present in the Bishopsgate Institute, London.

[14] F. E. Gillespie, *Labor and Politics in England, 1850–1867* (Durham, 1927), 247; letter, Hughes to Fanny Hughes (undated); Brown, *True Manliness*, xiv; *The Times*, 30 May, 1 June, and 12 July 1865.

[15] S. M. Ellis, *The Hardman Papers, 1865–1868* (London, 1930), 34.

[16] Leslie Stephen, *Life of Henry Fawcett* (London, 1885), 221; *Economist*, 19 July 1865; *The Times*, 20 Nov. 1866.

[17] For report of the proceedings and commentary, see *Sheffield Independent*, 11 Oct. 1865.

[18] *Notes and Queries* (London, 1948), 145–148.

[19] *New York Tribune*, 1 Sept. 1866, 7 Jan. 1867.

[20] *Hansard*, clxxxi, 1792, 22 March 1866.

[21] *Hansard*, clxxxii, 1700 ff., 19 April 1866.

[22] For another old Rugbeian's view of this affair see Matthew Arnold, *Culture and Anarchy*, first published in 1869, who writes of 'Barbarian Secretaries of State' who allow the park railings to be broken down by 'London roughs'.

[23] *Hansard*, clxxxvi, 1935, 1868.

[24] Howell Papers, Bishopsgate Institute, Hughes to Howell, 9 Feb. 1867.

[25] S. M. Ellis, *Henry Kingsley* (London, 1930), 158.

[26] *Punch*, 2 Feb. 1867, 46–47; letter, Mill to Hughes.

[27] *The Times*, 20 Nov. 1866; *New York Tribune*, 31 Dec. 1866.

[28] *Hansard*, clxxxiv (183), ccii (366), ccxii (825).

The Times, 20 Nov. 1866.

A. Haultain, *Reminiscences of Goldwin Smith*. 361–362.

That Hughes not only had a heart instinctively on the Liberal side but could be fair and objective is illustrated by his behaviour in another less famous case involving discipline a few years earlier. A certain Colonel Crawley of the 6th Dragoons in India had in 1861 court-martialled his paymaster Smales and three non-commissioned officers in an effort to secure discipline. One of the officers, Sergeant-Major Lilley, died in prison, a howl went up from the Liberal press in England, and after many long months Crawley was brought to England in 1863, and tried on the grounds of inhumanity. Just before the trial, Jacob Omnium wrote an account in the *Cornhill* of the Indian court-martial, which he claimed had white-washed Crawley, and asked Hughes to comment on it in the *Spectator*. Hughes wrote the article, but not in the way Jacob wished. For after studying the case, Hughes decided that Jacob's article had been a brief for the prosecution before trial, not a fair account. He therefore wrote not to plead for Crawley, but to see that fair play was done: the weak was in this case being persecuted by the Press. Unfortunately Hughes did not tell Jacob what he intended to do, and the latter never forgave him. Hughes' dreams were for some reason haunted by the incident a quarter of a century later.

A. G. Gardiner, *The Life of Sir William Harcourt* (London, 1923), i, 157; *Spectator*, 31 Oct. 1863; Wolf, *Life of Ripon*, i, 193–194; (T. Hughes) *Early Memories for the Children* by the author of 'Tom Brown's Schooldays' (London, 1899).

[29] N. P. Gilman, *Profit-sharing between Employer and Employee* (London, 1889), 243–277, for full account and bibliography of the Briggs scheme.

[30] In his speech at the Manchester Town Hall to mark the first half-year's working reported in the *Liverpool Mercury* on 21 May 1866, and in the *Sheffield Independent* on 22 May 1866, he called it 'the first of the new industrial societies under the New Friendly Societies Act' and 'the very first society' in which workers were admitted to co-partnership. Benjamin Jones, *Co-operative Production* (Oxford, 1894), ii, 444, wrote, however, that at the end of 1865 the firm of Greening and Company wire-netting makers, Manchester, was turned into a limited liability company, and Mr. Thomas Hughes became a shareholder as he said 'from a desire to help on the movement', although the business of the company 'was on a small scale'.

[31] B. Potter, *The Co-operative Movement in Great Britain* (London, 1910), 134.

[32] T. Crimes, *E. O. Greening* (Manchester, 1923).

[33] *The Co-operator*, 1 June 1866; *The Times*, 22 May 1866.

[34] Letter, Hughes to Fanny Hughes, 25 Sept. 1867.

[35] Letter, Hughes to Fanny Hughes, 23, 24, 26, 27 Sept. 1867.

[36] Wagner, *The Church of England and Social Reform since 1854*, 128–129.

[37] Letter, Hughes to Fanny Hughes, no date.

[38] *The Times*, 22 May 1866; *Spectator*, 26 May 1866.

[39] For the Fearneyhough affair see *Notes and Queries* (London, 1948), cxciii, 145–148.

[40] Hughes protested when the scope of the Commission was extended beyond Sheffield, *Hansard* 118, 1406.

[41] S. and B. Webb, *The History of Trade Unionism* (London, 1920), 265.

[42] *Parliament, Sessional Papers, Bills, Public*, 1867, i, 129. Tall, gaunt Charles Neate (1806–1879) was a fellow of Oriel, and called to the bar at Lincoln's Inn. He sat for Oxford from 1863 to 1868, and partnered Hughes in presenting this bill.

[43] Webb, *op. cit.*, 248.

[44] J. M. Ludlow and Lloyd Jones, *Progress of the Working Class, 1832–1867* (London, 1867), xiii. This attempt to write the history of the nineteenth century in terms of the labour movement is significant at this time, and can be compared to Bishop Sprat's history of the Royal Society, written two centuries before, for the same propagandist reasons.

[45] Lowell Papers at Harvard, letter, Hughes to Lowell, 1 Dec. 1867.

[46] F. Harrison, *Autobiographic Memoirs*, i, 149; ii, 70.

[47] Letters, Harrison to Hughes, no date; Hughes to Fanny Hughes, 8 Jan. 1869.

[48] Harrison, *op. cit.*, ii, 70.

[49] *Parliament, Sessional Papers, Reports of Commissioners, 1868–1869*, xxxi, 235 ff.

[50] *Edinburgh Review*, Oct. 1869, 396; Harrison, *Autobiographic Memoirs*, ii, 70; *Economic Review* (1896), vi, 309.

[51] *Reports of Commissioners, 1868–1869*, xxxi, 263, 275 ff.

CHAPTER TEN

Honeymoon with Labour, 1868–1870

LAMBETH soon became an uncomfortable seat for Hughes. From his first entering Parliament he had persistently worked for legislation against false weights and measures, and, in an access of strangely puritanical zeal, had been a staunch advocate of early closing laws for public-houses and of a ban on Sunday trading.

The numerous publicans and small retailers of his constituency were not inclined to tolerate such fads from one who was also known to favour co-operative trading. As they grew restive, Hughes grew tired, wearying of the corruption that flourished freely, yet determined not to add to it from his own slender resources.

I

These resources were more stretched as his family increased. Time was so mortgaged that Motley found him 'working himself half to death'.[1] In 1866 he had succeeded Sir Joseph Paxton as chairman of the Crystal Palace Company after it had suffered a disastrous fire in the north transept. This vast conservatory he now helped to revive to something of its old splendour, encouraging exhibitions, shows, and festivities within the grounds at Sydenham. On 26 June 1867 the Prince of Wales was present at a grand concert held to raise funds, and eight months later the restored north wing was reopened. On 25 June 1868 the first aeronautical exhibition was held, and in January 1872 the Great Aquarium was opened. Further splendours followed, culminating in the completion of the great clock in November 1876.

Three times between 1864 and 1866 Hughes had been forced to reject tempting literary offers, including an invitation to write for a projected magazine of Trollope's because he had 'no time whatever to spare for new undertakings'.[2] But need pressed, so in June 1869, just after being appointed a Queen's Counsel, he wrote to Macmillan:

'I shall have my fees to the Clerk of the Crown etc. to pay in a few days amounting to £100 or thereabouts, and as a professional man with 7 children doesn't keep large balances shall be glad of whatever may be coming.'

He referred to the new illustrated edition of *Tom Brown's Schooldays*, and went on to offer himself for any literary chores that might occur to Macmillan. Even when he attended a party of nineteen old Rugbeians (Stanley and the two Arnolds among them), he covered his expenses by 'taking notes' for the *Pall Mall Gazette*.[3]

2

So when the general election came late in 1868 he thankfully changed his seat at Lambeth for the 'quieter and more distant' one of Frome, a market town in Somerset with a few small factories as its only industrial element. His election, and the subsequent Gladstonian administration, led him to look for further employment from his friend Lord Ripon, now Lord President of the Council. He wrote to Ripon on 1 June 1869 asking to be considered as a Government arbitrator in any cases which might occur. Ripon did not forget, and Hughes was given several small strikes to settle.[4]

The increased leisure which followed both his change of seat and his appointment as a Q.C. enabled him to turn to his pen once more; so that by the end of the year a further book was emerging from the Press. In this he tried to weave a pattern of his own social creed into the fabric of a historical study. Alfred the Great was the leader who created a society based not on a cash nexus but on mutual responsibility. This society had been afflicted by God with the Danish invasions because it sought individual gain at the expense of the common good. But Alfred changed all that. His people, the 'grand, tough, much-enduring old English stock', knew about Socialism in spite of their 'imperviousness to ideas', their 'obdurate, nay pig-headed . . . adherence to old ways'.[5]

Alfred the Great released Hughes' cry for the great need of his own times—a need felt by the old Saxons before Alfred became king.

'In an inarticulate way the confession rises from the mass of our people, that they too feel on every side of them the need for wise and strong government—or a will to which their will may loyally submit—before all other needs.'

But at this point Hughes stopped short, afraid of the conclusion he must draw. For if, as Carlyle said, the great need was 'kingship',

who was to be king? [6] Hughes was ready to welcome the dominance of labour—providing labour had been educated by the best
and ablest. Till that was so, Hughes called for the dictatorship
of God. But his political actions in these two years showed
how far he was prepared to go to enable labour to assume that
dominance.[7]

3

His first and greatest service was to the trade unions, still hover-
ing in the shades of uncertainty as to the security of their funds and
doubtful of the legality of their existence. His brother-in-law,
Nassau John Senior, translated into English what was to be the
first objective study of the place of trade unions in the national
economy.[8] Hughes himself edited the book, and called attention
to the fact that it was being published at the very time when, after
a lapse of half a century, Parliament was again considering the
position of unions. Being the original work of a foreigner, and a
nobleman at that, the book had little in common with the general
run of partisan literature.

This editorial task was finished on 19 June 1869. At that very
time a Bill, drafted by Frederic Harrison and sponsored by
Hughes and A. J. Mundella, was lying on the table of the House,
with the object of securing parliamentary recognition for the
minority report of the Trade Union Commission. The Bill was
meeting strong opposition. The employers denounced it, and one
of their number, Edmund Potter, M.P. for Carlisle, had published
their views in *Observations upon the Law of Combinations and
Trades Unions.*[9]

The accumulated pressure of the labour leaders, exerted steadily
behind similar bills sponsored in the past by Charles Neate in 1867
and Sir T. Fowell Buxton in 1868, could not be ignored. So the
Government hurriedly drafted a temporary bill to secure the funds
of the unions until the end of 1870. This Bill, introduced on 13
July, was read a second time a week later, and received the Royal
Assent on 9 August.[10]

So for a time the problem was shelved.

4

In fighting to safeguard trade union funds, Hughes was hoping
to be able to divert them to co-operative production. Like the

Comte de Paris, he envisaged a time when trade unions would be active nuclei of producer co-operatives, new elements of productive power, and guarantors of social peace. Hughes never visualised a vast industrial labour army, disciplined in divisions and squadrons, fighting for purely secular ends, but a harmonious federation of interrelated groups, embracing co-operators, trade unionists, and consumers alike.

His hopes were all the more sanguine in that at this very time the Co-operative Movement was more prosperous than it had ever been before. Thanks to the industry of E. V. Neale, an Act had been passed in 1862 which, by allowing co-operators to be incorporated as limited liability companies and to accept loans from other co-operative bodies, provided the necessary legal framework upon which a co-operative wholesale society could grow.[11] This project, it will be remembered, was one of the cardinal aims of Hughes and Neale when they were trying to find an outlet for the products of their early producer co-operatives ten years before. Moreover, in the administrative hierarchy of this new wholesale society their old associate William Cooper stood high: being secretary of the society from its inception in 1863 till his own death in 1868. The Co-operative Wholesale Society stretched its tendrils as far as Tipperary, where within three years of its establishment it had a depot for collecting butter.

In fostering this growth Hughes had himself played no small part. In 1867 he successfully piloted a Bill through the House of Commons to remove the limit of £200 capital which one society could invest in another. So, from 1867, further reservoirs of capital from the numerous consumer societies springing up throughout the country were now made available to irrigate the growth of the Co-operative Wholesale Society. By 1869 that Society could claim a yearly sales record of half a million pounds, and, confident as to future expansion, could build a large headquarters in Balloon Street, Manchester, which was opened on 15 May. Hughes wrote to Abraham Greenwood,[12] the president, rejoicing in the Society's success, and hoping for 'great things' in the future.

5

Those 'great things' were more specifically outlined in an anonymous article published by the *Spectator* a fortnight later.[13] Written to publicise the deliberations of the Co-operative Congress convened in London by Hughes, Greening, and W. Pare, the article hoped that the delegates would consider how trade unions could be utilised for co-operative purposes, how co-operative societies could be made mutually helpful in the spheres of banking, labour-exchange, and horticulture, how profits in partnerships of industry could be best divided between capital and labour, and how knowledge of the principles of co-operation could best be diffused. The article commented on the existence of

'a vast organisation of the working class, engaged in painfully heaping up capital, but only to spend it again without profit to itself; in possession of large funds, but unable to apply them to any reproductive purpose. Meanwhile, little groups of men here and there are endeavouring, too often under every disadvantage, to devise and apply some system which shall bear in reference to production the like results as those already recognised in reference to consumption',

and asked:

'Why cannot all these isolated forces be brought to unite? Why must co-operative consumption be throwing away capital whilst co-operative production has to be established and made successful? Why must trade societies be doing nothing with a large portion of their accumulated funds, instead of applying them to reproductive purposes?'

Hughes was anxious to explain the provisions of the Act he had successfully carried to the statute book two years previously, and in doing so to explain his scheme for directing the flow of such co-operative capital to productive enterprise.

6

Such was Hughes' objective in promoting the Co-operative Congress held from 31 May to 3 June in the rooms of the Agricultural and Horticultural Association at 29 Parliament Street. No setting was better suited for his purpose, for the Agricultural and Horticultural Association was the latest of his co-operative enterprises, and Greening, from whose fertile brain the idea originated, took a leading part in the Congress.

Hughes, as chairman of the convening committee, made the opening speech on 31 May. He called attention to the last national congress in London—that held in the Working Tailors' Hall seventeen years before—and pointed out that of the fifteen producer co-operatives represented at that conference, only one—the Hatters—survived. He pointed out that the great advantages conferred upon them by the Industrial and Provident Societies Act of 1867, which now enabled every retail society to hold any amount of capital in any other registered society, and cited the example of the Halifax Co-operative Society, which had taken out £10,000 worth of shares in the co-partnership of Henry Briggs.

He cited three producer co-operatives which would welcome similar assistance—the Framemakers' and Gilders' of Red Lion Square, the Perseverance Boilermakers of Deptford, and the Cabinetmakers of East London—all of whom required capital to meet their bills.

He looked forward to the day when a Co-operative Bank would be established to facilitate such a flow of capital to languishing producers. It would also save, he told the Congress ruefully, 'the burning of fingers which he himself had experienced in such investments'.

To challenge the response of the retail societies still further, he spoke at the social evening, and took the chair at a public meeting. The delegates were then conducted to 337 The Strand, where an exhibition of the products of twenty-five producer co-operatives was displayed—from the wire-fencing of Greening to the coal of the Briggs co-partnership.

He reminded them that he was a cautious optimist, characteristically quoting Lowell:

> 'Not as I'm one as much expec'
> Millennium by express tomorrow,
> They will miscarry, I recollec'
> Too many on 'em—to my sorrow.' [14]

7

Had he been freed from the trammels of party parliamentary claims he might have fostered the amalgamation of retail and producer societies. But Hughes could never keep one iron in the fire at a time: he had to have, as his old law tutor said, seven times more than anyone else and heat them seven times as much.[15] On each one his generous expenditure of time and thought was spent to little apparent purpose.

Most of these causes were essentially social and undramatic, serving only to irritate vested interests and eliciting little sympathy from the Government. On four different occasions—on the last one he felt as if he were 'striking a feather bed'—he pressed vainly for legislation enforcing standard weights and measures. He crusaded for a reorganisation of the government of the City of London, following up action in Parliament by an article in *Macmillan's Magazine* for 1870 on 'The Anarchy of London'. He twice advocated legislation to secure life insurances for the poor. He twice protested against the indiscriminate enclosure of public lands, which deprived cities of their lungs and the poor of their playgrounds. He sponsored Bills having as their object the creation of parish councils where laymen and clergy might meet to the mutual advantage of each. He protested against public schools becoming preserves of the Established Church, and strove to allay Nonconformist suspicion. Suggested laws against racing two-year-olds, for Sunday closing of public-houses and shops, served merely to irritate members of his own party, till both Gladstone and Sir William Vernon Harcourt thought he was raising tempests in teapots.[16]

So when the second Co-operative Congress was convened in Manchester at the Memorial Hall in Albert Square, Hughes was absent, attending to his parliamentary obligations. He wrote a letter to the delegates:

'I still fear we are in great danger of being carried away by the commercial success of the movement and of forgetting the principles which should leaven our whole action and life as Co-operators. I think the Congress should appoint a small committee of two or three members and give them power to act for the whole body . . . with a view to obtaining as soon as possible the passing of an Act which will give co-operative societies a distinct and independent position, instead of keeping them (as at present) under Acts which are intended for quite another kind of society.'

But the letter did not reach the secretary until after the Congress had broken up.[17]

NOTES

[1] Curtis (ed.), *Works of Motley*, xvii, 171.

[2] Macmillan & Co., letter of Hughes to Alexander Macmillan, 18 Dec. 1866; New York Public Library, Berg Collection, letter of Hughes, 15 May 1865; letter, Hughes to Fanny Hughes, 18 June 1866.

[3] Macmillan & Co., letters of Hughes to Alexander Macmillan, 27 May, 1868, 1 June 1869; G. W. E. Russell, *Letters of Matthew Arnold, 1848-1888* (London, 1895), ii, 24-25.

[4] Ripon Papers, B.M. Add. MSS. 43,520, Hughes to Ripon, 1 June 1869. In 1870 Hughes acted as arbitrator in the northern iron trade, but strikes broke out soon afterwards because prices rose immediately. *The Times*, 18 Oct. 1871; *New York Tribune*, 21 July 1871.

[5] The reviewers were very kind, though they resented such flights into the present, and the use of Alfred as a 'peg for spasmodic discourses'. Even the *Saturday Review* (30 April, 1870) praised his narrative skill, knowledge of history, and sensitivity to local colour. Nine printings were sold in thirty years, and the book was republished as late as 1930. Alfred emerges from the welter of sermons as a bright, sensitive, and reverent Y.M.C.A. leader, deeply imbued with 'patience, humility and utter forgetfulness of self'.

[6] Dean Stanley, in thanking Hughes for a copy of the book, regretted the 'frequent sense' he experienced of the 'Ghost of Carlyle', and the *Spectator* (5 Feb. 1870) found the book 'infected' with Carlyle's 'rhetorical mannerisms'.

[7] *Alfred the Great* (London, 1901), 134, affords one of many examples of his refrain that God's laws will work out as surely as the laws of gravitation. 'In due course! perhaps, but what if this due course means life times, centuries? Alas! This is indeed the cry which has been going up from the poor earth these thousands of years. . . . How long, O Lord, How long? The precise times and seasons man shall never know on this earth. These the Lord has kept in his own power. But courage, my brother! Can we not see, the blindest of us, that the mills are working swiftly, at least in our day? This is no age in which shams or untruths, whether old or new, are likely to have a quiet time or a long life of it. In all departments of human affairs . . . religious, political, social . . . we are travelling fast, in England and elsewhere, and under the hand and guidance, to be sure, of Him who made the world, and is able and willing to take care of it'.

[8] M. Le Comte de Paris, *The Trade Unions of England*, translated by N. J. Senior and edited by Thomas Hughes, M.P. (London, 1869).

[9] It was originally intended that A. J. Mundella, recently elected M.P. for Sheffield, should introduce the Bill, but Mundella demurred, owing to Hughes' longer experience of the House and its customs. Harrison disagreed, but Mundella was adamant, see W. H. G. Armytage, *A. J. Mundella: The Liberal Background of the Labour Movement* (London, 1951), 68. For Hughes' speeches see *Hansard* cxcvii (1344), cxcix (767), and *Parliament, Sessional Papers, Bills, Public*, v, 323.

[10] G. Howell, *Labour Legislation, Labour Movements and Labour Leaders* (London, 1902), 175–179. Hughes also introduced young Thomas Brassey, son of the great railway contractor, to Howell. Brassey was then engaged in his monumental *Work and Wages*.

[11] The Bill was originally to have been introduced by R. A. Slaney, but on his illness J. Southeron Estcourt took over. P. Redfern, *The Story of the C.W.S., 1863-1913* (Manchester, 1913), 25–28.

[12] Abraham Greenwood had been the chairman of the original Pioneers Wholesale Committee at Rochdale.

[13] *Spectator*, 29 May 1869.

[14] *Proceedings of the Co-operative Congress held in London*, 31 May, 1, 2, 3 June 1869.

[15] *Economic Review*, 1896, vi, 303.

16 *Hansard*, 3rd ser. cxcv, 554; cxciii, 1924; cci, 1508; ccv, 1163; cc, 1379; *Parliament, Sessional Papers, Bills, Public* (1867), iv, 267, 447; iii, 207, 419; (1870), iii, 601; (1871), ii, 431; (1873, iv, 159; *Macmillan's Magazine*, Jan. 1870, 273). Hughes was no prohibitionist, believing that 'John [Bull] is an obstinate old sinner, a stickler for all his rights (so called) including that of making a beast of himself by means of strong drink if so minded'. He attacked Sir Vernon Harcourt as the champion of drunkards (*Hansard*, cxc, 1865; ccxiii, 650; *Parliament Sessional Papers, Bills, Public* (1871), ii, 599, 603; (1872), ii, 203; *New York Tribune*, 2 June 1871). But his crusade against Sunday trading, against which he brought a Bill with wearisome regularity every five years, merely exacerbated the Sabbatarians, as well as those who did not believe that the poor could be made religious by Act of Parliament (*Hansard*, clxxxvii, 576; cxciv, 551; cxcv, 799 ff. *Parliament, Sessional Papers, Bills, Public* (1867), vi, 371; (1869), v, 251; (1871), vi, 217).

17 *Report of the Second Co-operative Congress.*

CHAPTER ELEVEN

John to Jonathan, 1870–1872

A T forty-eight, Tom Hughes was at the zenith of fame and fortune; not only as an author, but as a politician, business man, and national figure. His views on the necessity of legalising the trade unions had been recognised by Parliament; his services to the cause of co-operation by election to the chairmanship of the first congress of the movement; his practical outlook by an invitation to preside over the affairs of the great Crystal Palace at Sydenham. He was a Queen's Counsel, and in May 1870 he became a bencher of his Inn. G. F. Watts had painted his portrait. As the very model of what a Labour M.P. should be, J. E. Ritchie had included him in a gallery of leading British senators.[1]

I

One experience still eluded him—a meeting with Lowell. All through the period of the Civil War he had dreamed of making a trip to America 'before we loafers have got too grey in the autumn world'. A chance had offered itself in 1867, when he was to have crossed to examine witnesses in a big legal case, but 'the parties (drat them) compromised, thereby saving themselves a lot of money (like mean cusses)'. So Hughes was left to envy Dickens from afar, and to vent his frustration by doubting whether Mr. Pickwick was '*man* enough for what I fancy the staple of the Adirondack Club for instance, of which Stillman used to rack on to me till my mouth watered'.

As his family grew up around him, the prospect receded, and Hughes saw little chance of one day 'walking in' on Lowell 'with a carpet bag' to spend a 'quiet week in the place which has more associations after all for an Englishman than any other corner of the earth out of his own island'. It but added to his impatience that Mabel Lowell should cross to England with J. T. Fields and whet his appetite by descriptions of Boston. Strolling with her through Green Park, the Mall, and St. James's Palace, or taking tea with her on the terrace of the House of Commons, Hughes dilated on the historic associations of his island.[2]

Suddenly, in June 1870, the impossible trip materialised. 'Come early and come often, as they say to the voters in New York', urged Lowell: the elms were at their best, and he had secured an invitation to Newport for Hughes. So Hughes took advantage of the parliamentary vacation to book a passage on the *Peruvian* to Quebec, and travel down to Boston to be at Lowell's command.[3]

The welcome he received in America was one of the most sincere that any Englishman has ever received.

'There was love in it, you beloved old boy,' wrote Lowell, 'and no man ever earns that for nothing—unless now and then from a woman. . . . I would rather have the kind of welcome that met you in this country than all the shouts of all the crowds on the "Via Sacra" of Fame.' [4]

Hughes himself confessed:

'Certainly I never saw, heard of, or could imagine anything like the hospitality . . . it is no doubt in some degree and in individual cases, owing to the part I took during the war in England, but Democrats as well as Republicans have been amongst our warmest hosts; in fact, I am fairly puzzled, and allow the tide at last to carry me along, floating down it and enjoying everything as well as I can.' [5]

By the end of his trip he felt

'almost glad to get away, for I feel awestricken and humiliated beyond expression at the sort of greeting I get from all people in this country—one ought to get in one's shell and think it all over with God—that's the real fact—and I shall hope to be able to do this on shipboard'.[6]

2

Sailing as planned from Liverpool—noted, Hughes told his wife,[7] for its particularly 'faithful set of worshippers' of Mammon —Hughes immediately relaxed into his 'vacation' frame of mind, refusing to compete even for a seat at the saloon table. His bright eye observed the absence of 'anything very attractive in the shape of good looks on board' and censured 'the sort of indifferent airs which youngsters give themselves now'. He deplored the way two strapping daughters allowed a young stranger to take care of their sick old mother.

But what interested him most were 500 immigrants in the

steerage, a third of whom were being brought to Canada by a parson and a philanthropist. Hughes gave stamps to these 'respectable, sweet, serious people', the only passengers to attend the church services on board, took one sea-sick couple into his cabin, and in general exercised what was considered by his shipmates his 'remarkable talent for making folk agree and pull together'. He also, characteristically, made a little speech, advising hard work, mutual help, and avoidance of the liquor bottle as the sure road to independence, and urged the immigrants never to forget that they were members, 'however humble, of the nation which has spread free speech and free thought round the world, which was the first to declare that her flag never should fly over a slave'.[8]

The trip up the St. Lawrence was punctuated by news of the French defeat at Prussian hands. Hughes had always had mixed feelings about France, particularly under Napoleon III. At the World's Fair of 1867 he had been enchanted by French artistry, and impressed by the clean streets, the absence of beggars and shocking clothes, and the 'improving fever' in 'New Paris'—he said nothing about the trains running on time. (He had also had his first taste of America at the Fair: 'an ambrosial drink called American Soda, a beverage in all respects worthy of the land of Lincoln—a mixture of mashed ice, soda-water, some suspicion of alcohol, and cream, flavoured delicately with pineapple, all exquisitely blended, and resulting in a compound such as one had hitherto only encountered in dreams'.) On the other hand, Hughes was well aware of the evils of Napoleon's dictatorship, and could never forget his threats against England. Paris and the French were not naturally to Hughes' liking. After ten days in Paris, 'I get mad to smash some of the mirrors on the boulevards and to punch the heads of some of the little coxcombs who sit sipping and smoking all along the Cafe fronts'. So Hughes at first welcomed Napoleon's defeat as a hopeful augury, marking the end of a regime that for eighteen years had pandered to the worst tendencies of France. Not long afterwards, however, sick about the agony of the French exodus, he regretted these sentiments, wishing 'Bismarck, Moltke and the King Kaiser [sent] to their appointed places'.[9]

Hughes landed in Montreal on 17 August, and the first whiff of American air, 'the most wonderful one ever tasted, or dreamt of', dispelled all thoughts of Europe. After staying briefly in Montreal with the manufacturer George Stephens, who introduced him to politicians, merchants, and 'other big folk', Hughes made straight for Boston via the Connecticut River, noting en route only that the coaches on the train were 'democratic' and that the people, whom he had expected to find voluble on every subject from 'Adam's fall to Huldy's bonnet', were remarkably silent. 'Whatever else goes by the board (and much that I had ideas about must)' the visit with Lowell 'mustn't.'[10]

3

On the train Hughes suddenly began worrying 'whether a most precious illusion might not be about to vanish'. He had lived so much in Lowell's work for so many years that 'I almost trembled as I drove up . . . in the Boston hack through Cambridge'. For a few seconds after his arrival—until the Irish maid told him and his companion, a young Oxonian named Rawlins, 'to sit right down' —his premonitions seemed about to be borne out. Lowell was not expecting him, having evidently not received his letter from Montreal telling of his change of plans, or even of his arrival. But 'all doubt vanished' when Hughes looked into Lowell's eyes. He was 'sitting on his verandah smoking a long clay pipe and talking with John Holmes, the brother of "the Autocrat",' and 'this peculiar beauty of the eyes was the first thing that struck me. . . . They made you feel at home at once, and in love with their owner'. It was long past the hour for food

'in primitive [SIC] Cambridge, and, though we had not dined, we were too eager to get to talk, and to give no trouble, to accept any of his hospitable offers except a glass of Sherry and a biscuit. These he brought out triumphantly after a short search, excusing the slight delay as Mrs. Lowell was out. The Sherry was in a large stone jar, and looked rather light in colour as he poured us out bumpers. The first mouthful was trying to thirsty souls after a hot fourteen hours journey. It was fine old whiskey, and he hurried off to change the jar, explaining that the only alcohol in the house was in these jars, and he used it so seldom that he did not well know them apart. And so we sat on in the moonlight, falling through the "English elms" of which he was so proud, till late into the night, when I went to bed as happy as the Queen of Sheba when she found that the realized Solomon was far better and bigger than all the accounts she had heard of him in her own land.' [11]

In the week or more that Hughes spent with Lowell—the first week's visit was interrupted by a trip to Naushon, 27 to 30 August, but Hughes returned to Boston later—this impression was but strengthened.

'I need hardly say', Hughes wrote on the eve of his final departure, 'that the dearest memory of my sojourn in America will cling round Elmwood—I carry away much treasure laid up for the rest of my life which is beyond the reach of moth or rust—I only wish you had kept my old "duster", in fact I shall send it back, as the thought of you sitting in it o' summer nights, with the Katydids serenading, on the balcony before the study window in the moonlight, when the sweet moment for the whiff of bacchy comes (if the cussed thing will only wash which I doubt) will fill my soul with quiet pleasure in great Babylon, and the Palaver House.' 12

Lowell was equally enthusiastic about Hughes, whom he found

'as charming as man can be—so simple, hearty, and affectionate. . . . We liked him better and better. His only fault is that he *will* keep quoting the "Biglow Papers", which he knows vastly better than I. I was astonished to find what a heap of wisdom was accumulated in these admirable volumes. I was really saddened to part with him—it was saying good-bye to sunshine.'

To Hughes himself Lowell wrote after his departure:

'As I took my solitary whiff o' baccy, after I got home, my study looked bare, and my old cronies on the shelves could not make up to me for my new loss. I sat with my book on my knees and mused with a queer feeling about my eye-lids now and then. And yet you have left so much behind that is precious, too, that by and by I know that my room will have a virtue in it never there before, because of your presence.' 13

During his first stay in Boston, Hughes was kept in a continual whirl of entertainment and sight-seeing, all of which he took in his stride. He climbed Bunker Hill (it was Lowell's first, and was, he was sure, to be his last ascent); drove to Concord along the road taken by the retreating English, and dined at Judge Hoar's, where he 'enjoyed the dinner and smoke afterwards immensely'; met Emerson and Longfellow; visited Hawthorne's house and Thoreau's wood; and saw 'young' Howells, then editor of the *Atlantic Monthly*, and 'young' Holmes, whom he had already met in England.

'We did the University of Cambridge, Lowell's "Open Sesame" even gaining us admission to the very wholesome mysteries of the students at a meeting of the Φ.B.K. Society.'

In Boston he 'called on the Autocrat of the Breakfast Table, who is one of the best talkers I ever met, and quite worthy to be the Colonel's father'. Above all, he dined at the famous Saturday Club in the place of honour between Sumner (the chairman) and Boutwell, the Secretary of the Treasury. (As he later remembers the scene Emerson, not Boutwell, was on his left.) Despite the honour of his position, he was rather envious of Rawlins, who sat between Lowell and Holmes at the foot of the table, from which 'echoes of the fast and furious mirth rolled faintly up to our dignified end of the table'.[14]

Story's statue of Everett displeased Hughes, and a Methodist meeting he attended while visiting Forbes on Naushon was too full of heresy and positivism to edify him; but those were Hughes' only unfavourable impressions. He quickly decided, in fact, that next to living in England he would like to settle down in a house bordering the Common, a house like Lowell's, homely and cultivated but with 'no pretence' to 'neatness and finish'. Nevertheless, on 2 September he set off for Newport and New York, and a swarm of new impressions. His progress was, as he describes it, royal: at each station the principal citizens met him, lodged him in the best rooms, introduced him to the best people and showed him the sights: they even made a point of keeping the servants out of the way when he left, so he wouldn't have to tip.

Hughes arrived in New York, preceded or accompanied by a letter of introduction from Emerson to Ward, who, Emerson hoped, would 'temper our puritanism by the freedom of New York', and acquaint Hughes with others besides those most 'rabid Americans, Judge Hoar, Lowell, and John Forbes'. He stayed with Abram Hewitt and his father-in-law, Peter Cooper. Cooper Union Hughes found the best Working Men's College he had ever seen, and Cooper 'the simplest most utterly guileless of old men who ever made a big fortune in this world or any other I should think'. Hughes hoped that he had brought together his hosts and John Roebuck, who with five other men from the Working Men's College was in New York longing to be in England. Roebuck, for whom Hughes had written an introduction to America in 1864 (being sure that Americans would not confuse him with the 'unspeakable M.P. for Sheffield'), would, he felt, 'put some good W. M. College notions into the New Yorkers'.

He was much impressed, as well he might be, by breakfast at Cooper's, which started with

'a huge slice of melon and glass of iced water following with grapes, pears, and peaches as we liked; then a cup of coffee to wash down broiled chicken, soft crab, sweet potatoes, and chops; then a form of hominy and cream, to conclude with a saucer full of peaches and cream'.

Hughes was lavishly entertained at the Manhattan, Union League, and Century Clubs. Yet New York, symbol of modern America, was not the place for Hughes; as he told Lowell many years later, 'I never could feel the least drawn to it.' [15]

He was soon off to West Point, where he stayed at Garrison's Landing with William H. Osborn, the ex-president of the Illinois Central Railroad, and then to Niagara Falls, which made him long for his wife and vow to bring his whole family over when his wife could stand the passage. He and Rawlins solaced themselves by showing two girls the cataract, Hughes handing the 'pretty' and 'simple' one over to Rawlins and giving 'my arm to the English one (who was also nice and decent looking)'. Americans in general, Hughes wrote, 'continue to be the most silent and reserved of any race I have ever been amongst'. While in Niagara, Hughes took the boat across to Toronto, whose prosperity pleased him, though he was annoyed at having to be convivial with a couple of M.P.s whom he met: 'the pick me up is decidedly one of the most loathesome inventions of a decrepit civilization'.[16]

4

From Niagara Falls Hughes started on 11 or 12 September for an exciting whirlwind tour of the West. Forbes had already given him passes on all railways. Now Osborn was to take him in his private car on a special train to the farthest railway outposts along the Missouri. The first leg of the trip was by train across Canada, by ferry to Detroit, then by sleeping-car to Chicago. Hughes was a bit squeamish about undressing in an upper berth with a lady across the way, was concerned lest the Pullman cars, which seemed too heavy for the tracks to carry, would break down, and was amused to watch the train come into Chicago on piles in the lake. Rolling west from Chicago on the luxurious two-car special, he saw a house being moved, enjoyed that fine American dish, tomatoes sliced with oil and vinegar, found himself disappointed with a prairie, and marvelled that thirty-six tons of strawberries were brought to Chicago in a day. He and Osborn and Douglass, the president of the road, discussed the future of the country, railway competition, land grants to the roads, which sold land to their future customers, and the uncertainty of everything as evidenced by the failure of Galena, Illinois, ever to become a big city. Crossing the Missouri, they saw half-built Dubuque, Fort Dodge, and Storm Lake, where 1,400 miles from the Atlantic land was already $10 an acre, and reached the ugly and capricious Missouri at Sioux City, 100 miles into the open prairie. In Sioux City—a rowdy, loafing, vagabond city—there were four gambling-houses and sixty-three (in another place Hughes says seventy-three) saloons for 4,000 people:

'The Editor of the *Sioux Tribune*, an Irish Yankee of queer morals and extraordinary go, took us into one of the sixty saloons stood drinks round and expounded the ingenious games by which the settlers and officers of the Indian fort up the stream are cleared of their money.'

The party then moved on to Council Bluffs and Omaha, and were back in Chicago by the 16 or 17 September. Hughes hoped he had been good company, as 'when one is treated like the Grand Turk or the Emperor of Roopia, the least one can do is to be pleasant'.[17]

Having been royally welcomed to Chicago by Lincoln's son, Robert, and given a testimonial reception by the graduates of American universities, he was off to St. Louis, Cincinnati (which he regretted to find had an entirely secular programme of education, the only one in the United States), and Philadelphia, where he stayed with John Field, the banker, a 'famous, frank, good-looking, John Bullish man of the world', the 'heartiest cheeriest tenderest vehementist openmindedist of Americans (bar Yankees)'. Field entertained him at the Union League Club, and took him to a normal school, where the plain dresses 'rejoiced' his 'democratic soul' and where he listened to a class on the revolutionary war 'without turning a hair'. Field and Rosengarten, General Reynold's aide-de-camp, then carried him off to Gettysburg, a place whose deep symbolism was enhanced for Hughes by witnessing the Aurora Borealis there. Baltimore and Washington, where the Secretary of State and others overwhelmed him with attention, were his final stops before he once again, on 5 October, nosed round 'to dear Cambridge, the highest ground still in all this vast land though there are a sight of tall places in it, *I tell you*'.[18]

5

In Boston he was greeted by a full-page engraving of himself in *Every Saturday*, a renewed round of festivities, and many requests to visit and speak. 'You know how hard it is to me', he wrote his wife the day of his arrival, 'to refuse anyone anything when gratifying them can be done simply at my own inconvenience.' He lunched with Longfellow, whom he found 'genial and modest as a big man should be', went to Lowell's Harvard lecture and met the 'able and pleasant' staff, and helped lay the cornerstone of a hall to those who died in the war, in company with 'Mr. Adams' and his sons, Henry and the 'Colonel', Emerson, Dana, 'Colonel Holmes', and the 'autocrat', young Forbes, and General Meade in uniform. On Sunday 9 October he visited St. Mark's School, run as a sort of American Rugby without fagging or monitorial responsibility by Lowell's brother, a high-church non-ritualist. Though Hughes was pleased with the religious atmosphere, which he found unusual in America, where the people he met seemed to 'have very little real feeling or any crave for worship', he decided that he would try the public schools first before sending a boy to St. Mark's. And this in spite of criticisms he heard to the effect that the high schools were 'not liberal enough in the direction of the humanities, so that the boys get trained more into competitive money making machines than into thinking cultivated men', and that 'a large class of children of Irish and other recent arrivals go there whose language and manners make them dangerous classmates' for the children of upper-class New Englanders. On Monday Hughes spoke by request to 500 Harvard undergraduates, and on Tuesday climaxed his stay with a speech at the Boston Music Hall.[19]

Hughes' trip was now almost over, but he was still to go to Syracuse, where he rejoiced that the Germans spoke English and thus spited Bismarck,[20] and to Ithaca with Goldwin Smith. Just before coming to America, Hughes had written a eulogy of the new Cornell University [21] for its audacious combining of the practical and the cultural on an equal basis, for its riding rough-shod over England's religious difficulties by being Christian but not sectarian, for its admitting all but the 'idle and the vicious', and for its self-government, on a military basis. In a changing world, in which commerce, engineering, and emigration offered the best outlets, Oxford and Cambridge, whose graduates of Hughes' generation were in 'utter ignorance of the first principles of mechanics' and incapacitated 'for handling any tools but the gun, a fishing-rod, or a cricket bat', had better follow Cornell's example, Hughes felt, or they were doomed. Whether Cornell lived up to Hughes' expectations we do not know, since he was too near the end of his trip to write another letter home. From Ithaca Hughes returned to New York, where he went with Peter Cooper to the opening of the City College and spoke briefly to the boys, and where on 31 October he made a farewell speech at Cooper Union under the auspices of the Mercantile Library Association before as 'intelligent and representative an audience as ever assembled within its walls'. The next day he sailed for England on the *City of Brooklyn*.[22]

Hughes certainly covered as much ground and saw as many people as could possibly be crammed into a two months' stay. Evidently he was unable to accept Bayard Taylor's invitation of September to visit the Pennsylvania Quakers; William Lloyd Garrison was too ill to hear Hughes' Boston lecture, and Agassiz to be seen at all; and a final trip to see Emerson at Concord had to be abandoned. But Hughes missed few other sights or celebrities. Tom Hughes and the United States had met, and with mutual satisfaction.

6

In his role as expositor of the ways of John to Jonathan, Hughes tried to allay the hard feelings evoked by the English attitude during the Civil War. Much of his propaganda was deliberately directed toward such influential figures as Judge Hoar, Osborn, Forbes, and Field. Talking to them, as he told his wife:

'I am obliged to give up poor old Pam, the mercantile community of England and the majority of the aristocracy, but when I have made a Jonah of these I always succeed in bringing these good simple candid impulsive fellows to admit that we did them no bad turn in their troubles. . . .

'With a very little tact and judicious handling on our side . . . international relations may easily be made all we can wish for as far as New England is concerned.'[23]

In addition to his individual contacts, Hughes made a number of public speeches for the cause, despite his peremptory refusal to rise to the bait of $500 a night for lecturing and Lowell's assurance that this was a legitimate way of earning an honest penny: 'Heaven forbid,' he wrote Lowell before his arrival in America; 'I have written that I can't lecture, hate lecturing, shall have no time etc. . . . I can't think there is any need for me to go on the stump?'[24] Hughes defended England before Harvard undergraduates, Normal School students, and audiences at the Philadelphia Union League Club, at New York's Cooper Union, and above all at the Boston Music Hall—Hughes remembered it as Fanueil Hall—on the night of 11 October.

This music-hall speech, given as the first of the Parker Fraternity lectures—'so you see the class of things at once', Hughes wrote home—was the climax of Hughes' stay in America. Since, as he told his wife, he was 'in for it much against my will', the forum of Sumner, Wendell Phillips, and Emerson provided an ideal opportunity for him to have his say before the best people.[25] They were certainly all there, including the Governor of Massachusetts, two ex-governors—Senators Sumner and Wilson—Longfellow, Hoar, Richard H. Dana Jr., Lowell, Peabody, and Eliot of Harvard, Josiah Quincy, Oliver Wendell Holmes, Wendell Phillips, 'and 3000 of the brainiest men in Massachusetts'. The *Boston Journal* said there had been no parallel since Dickens's visit.[26] Realising that he was no orator, Hughes determined to talk to this distinguished gathering in a simple, straightforward way, trying both to salve the wounded pride of the 'over-sensitive' Yankees, whom he loved 'too well to say anything that will really hurt them', and to be absolutely honest, trusting that his position as a spoilt child, who could get away with anything, would prevent him from being misunderstood.[27] Above all, he made it clear at the start of his speech—which he called 'John to Jonathan' in response to Lowell's well-known 'Jonathan to John' —that he was not an American and hoped he hadn't been treated so well because people thought of him as one. 'I am before all things an Englishman—a John Bull, if you will—loving old England and feeling proud of her', and that meant, as he had said in Philadelphia, that he would not let Americans 'separate' even the aristocracy, whom he fought at home, 'from the nation'. The rest of his talk was an attempt to answer charges that England was haughty and imperious, given to subsidising and hectoring friends, holding foes down with a brutal and heavy hand and interfering everywhere. Actually, England was much divided and 'deeply stirred' over the Civil War.

'The dress suit, and the stomach and digestive apparatus, of England were hostile to you, and you have taken them for the nation: the brain and heart and muscle of England were on your side, and those you have ignored and forgotten.'

On the whole, England's conduct—over neutrality, recognition of the South, rebel cruisers—had been above reproach. Now was the time, Hughes concluded, to forget old hatreds and work together to solve the problems of the future, 'which go right down amongst the roots of things'.

Lowell had been so worried about the audience's reaction that he had 'disposed batches of his Harvard pupils about the room' to ensure applause. The precaution was unnecessary. Though there was general agreement that as a speaker Hughes was somewhat hesitant and possessed little magnetism, the response to his words was all anyone could wish. The occasion was, Hughes himself wrote, a 'brilliant success' from the first moment when the organ pealed 'God Save the Queen' to the end of the speech, which held the attention of the audience for an hour, drew cheers from everyone, was printed verbatim in the papers, and brought Hughes 250 unasked-for dollars and thousands of offers to lecture. Though no speech could make America abandon her position on the *Alabama* claims, the *Tribune* asserted editorially, words such as Hughes' could move her to generosity and to the valuing of English friendship. America trusted Hughes, with whom she could speak 'more freely than with any Englishman who has ever been here'. The *Tribune* reporter professed himself especially moved by Hughes' last words, as are we who have seen his prophecy borne out to the full.

'In a choking voice, a voice that fills the house', wrote the reporter, 'the "noble Tom Brown" expressed the belief that if someday the old islander should want a name on the back of one of her bills of indebtedness, America will sign it.' [28]

7

The deepening of his friendship with Lowell followed. Of this, Hughes wrote movingly on Christmas Eve 1870, sitting in his London study surrounded by his new treasures—the complete Emerson that Lowell had given him, Lowell's 'blessed little Green Vol.', and Field's facsimile of the Declaration of Independence. In midsummer 1872, Lowell 'came to England with his wife', and Hughes did his best to 'repay him', but found it at first difficult. Hughes got him lodgings in Chester and then in London, had his name put on the distinguished guest list at the Athenæum, and asked those who liked his writings to meet him: but, though gentle and courteous, Lowell 'was somewhat reserved and silent'.

'On the other hand, he joyfully went with me to the Working Men's College, where he was quite himself, and made one of the most genial and witty speeches at a students' supper that even he ever gave utterance to.'

The coolness, indeed, soon wore off, and later visits were more successful. In 1873 Hughes 'laid rope' for Lowell's Doctor's degree at Oxford, writing to a schoolfellow of his on the Hebdomadal board who was to propose Lowell's name. Like a fussy nurse, Hughes warned Lowell that he must come himself and must buy, not hire, a scarlet gown with velvet sleeves. The ceremony would be enlivened, Hughes hoped, by Bryce's attempt to allude to 'Bird o' freedom' in Latin. From 1873 on, and particularly after Lowell became ambassador at Madrid in 1877, Hughes saw him nearly every year. When Lowell came to England as ambassador in March 1880, Hughes acted as his chaperon, seeing that he met the right people and acted in the proper manner. He must, Hughes told him, meet Lady Galloway, who regretted not seeing him to 'speak to'; he should make Lord Carlingford, who had lost his wife, 'feel good'; he ought to 'develop' Lord Compton's inclination 'towards liberal $X^t y$'; he owed it to himself to join Hughes at Lady Granville's salon, as he might there make himself an 'opening' with 'G', who would probably be Prime Minister soon. Hughes' friendship, indeed, did much to compensate Lowell for the America that he sorely missed.[29] In their declining years, when the two men were again separated for long intervals, their correspondence grew more garrulous and if anything more personal and intimate, as other friends dropped by the wayside and the relationships that were left came increasingly to be relied on to keep life fresh and interesting.

Typical of their friendship was a charming nonsense verse written by Lowell in Paris 2 June 1873 for Hughes' daughter May:

'Copy of verses addressed to a young lady by the late Mr. Pope, Anno Dom: 1698, aet. 10, when as is well known, he "lisped in numbers".

> May ith the month that poeth love,
> Her apron full of leavth and floweth,
> Her thkith thoft breathted ath a dove
> Her momenth loitering hourth.

The prethage of a name like yourth
May nothing ever croth or thtain
And if a cloud your thky obscurth
Be it more full of thun than rain

_____

Whether ath maiden or ath wife,
May the Thoul's thpringtime light your way
And may May Huytheth happy life
Be ever thteeped in heuth of May!

It was conjectured by the celebrated Dr. Bentley that there was an obscure allusion in the last stanza to a lady named Hughes'.[30]

Other literary friendships made in America, particularly with Holmes and Emerson, must have been nearly as gratifying to Hughes. Before he met Holmes, Hughes had read his 'Guardian Angel' with great delight and had begun, as he told Lowell, 'to feel to *him* Holmes as I used to do to you, and have the advantage too of knowing that fine young fellow his son which ripens ones friendship with an unseen friend'. The meeting confirmed the friendship, but Holmes did not endure for Hughes as a poet as did Lowell. Re-reading him in 1891, Hughes found that he repeated himself like the Whitechapel actor who, when he forgot his cue, always told the same laugh-provoking story in order to give him time to 'stagger to the prompting box'. And 'then the moment he touches the deeper waters and comes to "eternal life" I feel that our dear Doctor is rather out of his depth'. Emerson, on the other hand, improved with re-reading.

'I soaked myself in him on the voyage home, and repented in dust and ashes of some hasty criticism of mine in the introduction to the edition of Biglow which I wrote for Trübner—I had only a smattering then of here and there one and another of his lighter work—never had taken a "steady drink" at him.'

Now he knew his real greatness, 'his self prized independence and fearlessness and the debth of his stroke—Why I have found the root in him of about half the best thought I have ever come at'. Hughes' one regret was that he had not been able to spend that second day in Concord with Emerson.

'It would have been worth sacrificing my week in the west for—However, it can't be helped now, but do tell him how penitent and grateful a cove is sitting in this roaring Babylon in the last hours of the terrible year of 1870, and thinking of and thanking him.' [31]

Hughes was always closer to these American poets than he was to his great English contemporaries, and admired them with less qualification. He often discussed them with Lowell: Browning, Hughes told Lowell, he didn't know well enough to write someone an introduction to, though he was sure that 'that burly and genial poet' would welcome any 'finely appreciating students of his enigmas'. Tennyson he knew better from *Macmillan's Magazine* days, and had been one of an adoring circle who had heard the poet read *Maud* at Little Holland House in 1865. But his praise of him, especially as a person, was qualified. 'I am as fond of the dear old man', he wrote Lowell in 1890, 'as anyone in spite of his vanity, which is so open and superficial as to be quite inoffensive.' 'Matt' Arnold Hughes knew best, but he never expressed any opinion about him or his poetry.[32]

8

From his trip to America Hughes also acquired a working knowledge of the country, which he put to good use in the next three years. For audiences at the Working Men's College, the Working Men's Club and Institute Union, and the Camberwell Institute he drew enthusiastic pictures of the roar of New York, the beauty of Boston (the 'seed-plot of American thought'), student life at Harvard and Cornell, and American economic and political conditions, and hymned the great opportunities for immigration offered by the American West, with its caste-free system and high wages. A *New York Tribune* reporter who attended the Working Men's Club talk on 10 June 1871 was amused to see Hughes tracing his travels with a pointer on a large glaring map which hung on the 'dingy' wall, and which showed Concord as big as Boston, Syracuse bigger than Buffalo, and Chicago—of which Hughes' audience had never heard—bigger than St. Louis.[33] Hughes also wrote a long 'chatty business, interspersed with stories' about his 'Week in the West' for *Macmillan's* beginning in August 1871, and a short article on his impressions of Harvard for *Every Saturday* in March of that year.[34] This latter piece understandably annoyed the Harvard undergraduates, who resented Hughes calling their chapel ugly, their library both ugly and pretentious, their clubs hopelessly non-intellectual, their educational system productive of 'respectable mediocrity', and their games inadequate. (There was no swimming, cricket, football, tennis, fives, or rackets—only baseball, a good enough game but dangerous, since the ball was thrown so hard, and without 'a tithe of the skill or variety of cricket'.) All this might have been forgiven had Hughes not insisted, by way of compliment, that the 'one thing' Harvard could 'no more manage than Thor could manage to lift the world serpent' was to 'de-anglicanise herself'.

9

Hughes was naturally even more concerned with Anglo-American relations after having been in America than he had been before. And matters were approaching a climax in the early months of 1871. At the end of January a Joint High Commission was appointed to meet in Washington and make a final settlement of differences between the two countries. Hughes was elated, and wrote to Lord Ripon the day before he sailed for America as one of the commissioners: 'It is the biggest bit of work going for England.' [35] Hughes also wrote immediately to Whitelaw Reid of the *Tribune*, pointing out to him that Lord Ripon was the most liberal peer in the Government except the Duke of Argyle, and had been a good abolitionist in 1861, though he hadn't been able to speak out. Reid printed Hughes' remarks, but disguised the authorship by mentioning Hughes in the remarks, and promptly wrote to tell him that his words were the cause of great gratification in Washington, where he had mentioned them 'to the President, and to several members of the Cabinet'.[36]

Hughes inevitably felt the need to play some public role during these stirring times. In December 1870 he had formed an Anglo-American Association for, as Lowell put it, 'mutual enlightenment', and during 1871 he busied himself receiving, giving advice to, and getting hearings for prominent Americans like Robert Lincoln and Chief Justice Chase, and gaining introductions for them to members of the Government, especially to Lord Granville, to whom Hughes had previously given his views on America.[37] The Association lasted into 1872, but it virtually came to an end in the autumn of 1871 owing, ironically enough, to Hughes' praiseworthy attempt to collect for fire-demolished Chicago a new library composed of books donated by living authors and the families of dead ones.[38]

Hughes also began once more writing London reports for the *Tribune*, his first piece appearing on 27 February 1871, four days after the arrival of the Joint High Commission in Washington. Though he now wrote only as an 'Occasional Correspondent,' and clung, except for a long and amusing account of the famous Tichborne trial,[39] to straight political reporting of major events, he contributed fairly regularly every two to four weeks until 13 September, when he went on a two months' vacation, and apparently gave up newspaper reporting for good. As in 1866 Hughes was careful, just because he felt so strongly about the subject, not to use the *Tribune* as a forum for special pleading about Anglo-American relations, and did not sign what is obviously his piece assessing the work of the Joint High Commission.

Despite the Anglophobes and their English counterparts, the Commissioners came to an agreement, called the Treaty of Washington, in May, which referred outstanding grievances to a Geneva Board of arbitrators. Hughes was delighted, and wrote to Lowell that the 'sound part of the nation' was overjoyed at what the 'high joints' had done, though, of course,

'the Saturday Review, the quidnuncs of Pall Mall, and a sprinkling of truculent Lords and sich are howling that England is humiliated, that we have given up every point, have owned up that we are sorry if not ashamed, and have turned not only the other cheek but a less respected portion of the national person to the Yankee smiter'.[40]

In the *Tribune* he also expressed himself as satisfied, though a trifle worried over the clause forbidding neutrals to use their ports for arms to belligerents (as he thought Bismarck might demand indemnity) and sorry America had not granted Canada a reciprocity treaty:

'While you had grievances against us, and the sense of wrong was still rankling, we expected that you would continue to put the screw on us in the way we should feel it most—by punishing us through the Canadians.'

But—

'we had assumed . . . that, now that the mother country had agreed to bow her proud old head, and express her sorrow for what happened in your war, you would act generously to her younger daughter'. [41]

The Treaty of Washington was not, unfortunately, the last hurdle. When, in January 1872, arbitration before the Geneva Board was about to begin, the English suddenly discovered, to their apparent amazement, that the Americans had no intention of waiving indirect claims for damages—that is, expenditure on the pursuit of the *Alabama*, extra war insurance, transfer of

American merchant marine to a British flag, and the cost of prolonging the war. The English refused even to allow such matters to be arbitrated, an *impasse* resulted, and there was actually talk of war. Seeing all his efforts and hopes going by the board, Hughes tried to enlist the help of Cyrus Field, detained in England by illness, urging him either to give testimony on the English side or to state publicly that 'Americans had never waived indirect damages, since such a statement from such a source would induce most public men who were strong unionists to submit'. (Field replied immediately by sending Hughes a copy of a long letter he had written to Vice-President Colfax, which Hughes sent to *The Times*.) On 26 January Hughes himself wrote a long public letter, which the *Tribune* printed on its first page, though the letter proved nothing, it felt, except that even a man as 'free from the influence of national prejudice' as Tom Hughes couldn't judge his own case.

'You have obtained an expression of regret from England', Hughes wrote with unusual bitterness, 'and a modification of the rules of International Law, expressly agreed to by us for the purpose of bringing the case of the Alabama within the cognizance of the Tribunal of arbitration, and you have given absolutely nothing in return.'

If England were forced to withdraw from arbitration, it would be 'the most deplorable political event of this untoward time'; after so much sacrifice of pride and prejudice it would be criminal to let 'reckless pleading' for claims (that even American jurists did not believe could be seriously maintained) wreck the peace.[42]

The *Tribune*, which maintained that the Treaty of Washington was less a settlement than an admission that the two countries couldn't alone settle their grievances, had a great deal of fun chaffing Hughes for his refusal to let England's case be tried by arbitrators none of whom was English and one of whom was a Republican:

'We cannot help reminding Mr. Hughes that they probably speak American worse than they do English, and that two of them are monarchists.'

Fortunately, however, the *Tribune's* main contention was denied. Though negotiations several times almost broke down, in June the Geneva Board threw out the indirect claims, which were not popular even in America, and a settlement was finally reached.

Tom Hughes must have felt that here at last was one victory to set against defeats that were to pile up in the 'seventies.

10

Canada, which Hughes had visited briefly while in America, came to interest him in the 'seventies almost as much as did the United States. Here was a country possessed of all the advantages of the United States, plus the ties to England that meant so much to Hughes. And these ties, Hughes believed, as he wrote in the preface to a *Guide Book to the Canadian Dominion* in 1871, were unlikely to be broken. If she were given the freedom she deserved —the right to make treaties and to control her own finances and legislation, rights denied by the British North America Act of 1867—Canada would voluntarily retain a connection with the mother country:

'Apart from and below all question of the commercial advantages to them of forming part of the Empire, there is a strong appreciation of the sentimental value of British citizenship, which, whatever clever writers of articles and essays may say in its disparagement, is not a possession to be lightly cast aside. As for the prevalent belief that the United States would forcibly annex Canada,' that was 'one of the wildest notions which has ever found serious advocates at Home, or in the Colony.'

Brother Jonathan was not fool enough to desire to have a conquered country at his back door ready to make common cause with the South. Peaceful annexation, on the other hand, might come: 'The best men in the country', the New England upper classes, wanted 'a make-weight and counterpoise to the vast un-English and anti-English emigration, which they are receiving so fast.' Nor would it be a disaster, Hughes was broad-minded enough to grant, especially if Canada proved unable to stand alone: 'the sight of a whole continent confederated under one Government, but needing very little government of any kind, will be an excellent lesson to the old world'. Yet Hughes did not, as some Canadian papers misquoted him as saying, advocate union with the United States. Union was good, but not when it meant the 'lion swallowing the lamb'. An alliance of the three English-speaking Powers with their free institutions but differing traditions was far better than 'colourless uniformity'.

Whatever happened politically, Canada's future was, Hughes felt, assured. She had good soil, forest, water power, and a 'brave, hard-working, simple-living folk, contact with whom freshens up and braces the spirit of the wanderer from the old world, as the superb climate does his body'. A good mechanic could reap 'rewards' enough to give his daughters large dowries and to buy farms for his sons. There were no bad times in Canada 'except for wastrels'.[43]

Indeed, emigration to Canada seemed to Hughes in the early 'seventies the best compromise that one could make between the sentiment for England, which made Hughes regret that the rising generation, disgusted with the learned professions, was leaving home, and the realistic perception that England was overcrowded. Thus, though he himself would never emigrate, if only because 'middle aged folks shouldn't leave their own country', Hughes made a point, while in America, of laying the foundations for his oldest son Jim's career in Canada.[44] Jim became the first Hughes to desert the mother country for America. He did not, however, stay in Canada, but moved across the border into Colorado in 1874 and then into Texas, where he went to work as a cattle-ranger with a Marylander, named Dave McCormick.[45] And a few years later Tom himself threw over his own compromise and became a passionate advocate of English colonisation in the United States. His reception, the contacts he had made, and the influence of the country itself drew Hughes into closer touch with America than he realised. Though he died at home and his son Jim returned to England to wed a relative of the Duke of Buckingham, his mother and youngest son and several of his brother Hastings' children went to the United States to live and die. Today the only direct descendants of Tom Hughes in the second generation are Americans.

NOTES

[1] J. Ewing Ritchie, *British Senators* (London, 1869), 151.

[2] Lowell Papers at Harvard, letter, Hughes to Lowell, 20 May, 26 July, 1869. Lowell Papers at Harvard, letters, Hughes to Lowell, 21 Nov., 1 Dec. 1867, 26 July 1869, 3 Jan. and 26 July 1870; Mrs. Rantoul Collection, 25 Sept. 1865.

[3] Norton (ed.), *Letters of James Russell Lowell*, ii, 58–59.

[4] T. Hughes, *Vacation Rambles* (London, 1895), 135.

[5] Lowell Papers at Harvard, letter, Hughes to Lowell, 19 Oct. 1870.

[6] Norton (ed.) *op. cit.*, Lowell to Hughes, 18 Oct. 1870, ii, 67.

[7] In the following account of his trip to America, it has been better to adhere to the original letters where available, rather than to the printed versions in the

Spectator and *Vacation Rambles*, since they occasionally contain material of a more personal nature.

[8] Letter, Hughes to Fanny Hughes, undated; Hughes, *Vacation Rambles*, 106–109.

[9] Lowell Papers at Harvard; letters, Hughes to Lowell, 31 Dec. 1870, 13 March 1873.

[10] ibid., letter, Hughes to Lowell, 17 Aug. 1870.

[11] Norton (ed.), *Letters of James Russell Lowell*, ii, 61; Lowell Papers at Harvard, letter, Hughes to Lowell, 19 Oct. 1870. *The Poetical Works of James Russell Lowell*, Introduction, viii.

[12] Lowell Papers at Harvard, letter, Hughes to Lowell, 19 Oct. 1870.

[13] Norton (ed.), *Letters of James Russell Lowell*, ii, 61–67.

[14] *The Poetical Works of James Russell Lowell*, vii; Hughes, *Vacation Rambles*, 135.

[15] Letters, Hughes to Fanny Hughes, 31 Aug., 9 Sept., 5 and 7 Oct. 1870; Lowell Papers at Harvard, letter, Hughes to Lowell, 30 Jan. 1887; letter of Hughes, 25 March 1864, in New York Public Library.

[16] Letter, Hughes to Fanny Hughes, 11 Sept. 1870; *Macmillan's Magazine*, Nov. 1871, 1 ff., Dec. 1871, 150 ff. 'A Week in the West', by Thomas Hughes.

[17] *Macmillan's Magazine*, Nov, 1871, 1 ff.; Dec. 1871, 150 ff.; letters, Hughes to Fanny Hughes, 9, 15 Sept. 1870.

[18] Lowell Papers at Harvard, letter, Hughes to Lowell, 30 Sept. 1870; letter, Hughes to Fanny Hughes, 23 Sept. 1870.

[19] Letters, Hughes to Fanny Hughes, 27 Sept., 5 and 9 Oct. 1870; *New York Tribune*, 30 Dec. 1870, 5; typescript at Harvard of Hughes, Thomas, 'Recollections of American Universities', printed in *Every Saturday*, 25 March 1871, 286.

[20] *New York Tribune*, 30 Dec. 1870, 5.

[21] *Macmillan's Magazine*, July 1870, 161. 'The Youngest Anglo-Saxon University', by Thomas Hughes.

[22] *New York Tribune*, 22 Oct. 1870, 1.

[23] *Vacation Rambles*, 135; Letter, Hughes to Fanny Hughes, 9 Sept. 1870. He pointed out that though Americans could teach Englishmen how to spend money in that they founded Cornell's and Cooper Unions, they could with profit learn from the English public-school spirit as a corrective to their own professionalist attitude, and profit from the exemplary manner in which labour disputes were settled in England. Letter, Hughes to Fanny Hughes, 11 Sept., 9 Oct. 1870; *New York Tribune*, 22 Oct. 1870.

[24] Lowell Papers at Harvard, letter, Hughes to Lowell, 26 July 1870; Norton (ed.), *Letters of James Russell Lowell*, ii, 61.

[25] Letter, Hughes to Fanny Hughes, 16 Oct. 1870.

[26] *Grand Army Journal*, 22 Oct. 1870.

[27] Hughes, *Vacation Rambles*, 169 ff.

[28] Hinton, *English Radical Leaders*, 105 ff.; *New York Tribune*, 12, 13 Oct. 1870.

[29] Scudder, Horace Elisha, *James Russell Lowell* (Boston, 1901), ii, 15, 183; Lowell Papers at Harvard (Mrs. Rantoul Collection), letter, Hughes to Lowell, 24 Nov. 1888; Lowell Papers at Harvard, letters, Hughes to Lowell, 13 and 22 March 1873, and several undated letters assuredly belonging to 1880–1881.

[30] Hughes Papers.

[31] Lowell Papers at Harvard, letters, Hughes to Lowell, 1 Dec. 1867, 31 Dec. 1870, 25 April 1891 (Mrs. Rantoul Collection).

[32] Lowell Papers at Harvard, letters, Hughes to Lowell, 2 Jan. 1870, 29 June 1884, 26 Dec. 1889, 20 June 1890.

[33] New York Tribune, 30 Dec. 1870, 5; 28 June 1871, 2; The Times, 12 June 1871; 7 Nov. 1873, 7.

[34] Typescript at Harvard, of 'Recollections of American Universities', by Hughes; Lowell Papers at Harvard, letter, Hughes to Lowell, 15 May 1871.

[35] Wolf, Life of the First Marquess of Ripon, i, 240.

[36] Letter, Reid to Hughes, 12 March 1871; New York Tribune, 2 March 1871, 4.

[37] Norton (ed.), Letters of James Russell Lowell, ii, 69; Lowell Papers at Harvard, letters, Hughes to Lowell, 31 Dec. 1870, 18 and 23 June 1871.

[38] New York Tribune, 28 Nov. 1871, 2; The Times, 6 Dec. 1871, 6.

[39] New York Tribune, 2 June, 21 June 1871.

[40] Lowell Papers at Harvard, letter, Hughes to Lowell, 15 May 1871.

[41] New York Tribune, 8 June 1871, 1.

[42] Letter, Hughes to Field, 1 March 1872 in Morgan Library; The Times, 4 March 1872, 12. New York Tribune, 13 Feb. 1872, 1. For a tribute to the power of Hughes' articles in America at this very time see The Political Correspondence of Mr. Gladstone and Lord Granville 1868–1876 ed. Agatha Ramm, Camden Soc. Publications 3rd Ser., lxxxii (1952) ii, 314.

[43] Philpot, Harvey J., Guide Book to the Canadian Dominion, with a preface by Thomas Hughes, Esq., M.P., London, 1871, xvii–xxxii.

[44] Letter, Hughes to Fanny Hughes, 11 Sept. 1870.

[45] Letter, Hughes to George Stephen, 29 Nov. 1875; Lowell Papers at Harvard, letters, Hughes to Lowell, 25 Dec. 1871, 17 May, 28 June 1874.

CHAPTER TWELVE

Divorce from Labour, 1870–1874

H UGHES returned from his triumphal American tour to parliamentary duties that were becoming increasingly uncongenial and unrewarding. In the 'seventies Parliament broke his heart. Ignored, laughed down, shouted at, Hughes had few of the talents which could turn such situations to his own advantage. Like the very angular Saxon he professed to be, he found it impossible to reply in kind to the treatment he received.[1] His friend Llewelyn Davies ascribed his difficulties to 'decidedly moderate' abilities as an orator. Tom Hughes would charge, head downwards, into the centre of affairs, attacking minor and major issues alike with the same gusto, and almost bovine determination. Though there were many eccentrics, intellectuals and idealists like himself in Parliament, few were so quixotic as to consistently offend every recognised pressure group. Too often for his own good he was identified with his creation Tom Brown and treated like a boy who had never grown up. In such a highly sophisticated political world this was inevitable. Hughes himself shrank from having to work with men who openly professed a complete lack of principle, and, as he told Lord Ripon, 'what is almost worse . . . no shame whatever at avowing the springs of their action'.[2]

Ludlow's keen insight predicted Hughes' difficulties when he commented on Leech's cartoon which caricatured Hughes feeling his muscles among a crowd of leading politicians:

'This, I think, exactly hits off his position. He had many qualities which tended to fit him for the championship, but had he quite muscle enough?'[3]

It was in the years 1870–1874 that Hughes was to lose whatever claims he had previously earned to be considered as a possible champion.

I

Immediately Hughes had returned from America, he was solicited by the Labour leaders to fight a ministerial Bill, drafted to make provision for the financial and legal status of the unions, once more uncertain now that the temporary Act, passed in 1869, had lapsed at the end of 1870. Though this projected measure was a considerable advance on its predecessor—it proposed to endow the unions with the same rights as those enjoyed by joint-stock companies—it did not please the Labour leaders. For the third clause carried the stringent penalty of three years' imprisonment for anyone found guilty of 'intimidation and molestation': words which covered such apparently harmless activities as following a blackleg from place to place.

George Odger rallied the union leaders to a meeting in the Sussex Hall, Bouverie Street, on 1 March 1871, and a hurried congress was summoned to meet five days later. With A. J. Mundella, Hughes agreed to fight the obnoxious clause,[4] and so far at least were they successful that the proposals were withdrawn and split into two Bills. The first, endowing the unions with a legal personality as states within the State, became law three months later. The second, rechristened the Criminal Law Amendment Act, consisted of the obnoxious clause three. It too passed into law, and remained for the rest of Hughes' time in Parliament as a thorn in the side of the Labour leaders.

But to Hughes it was no thorn. He was convinced that enough had been done for the unions, and strongly disapproved of the forthright language of the union leaders as expressed in their manifesto of 7 October, which described the Act as more unjust and one-sided than the Bill it superseded. He also deprecated their belligerent attitude at the Trade Union Congress held at Nottingham from 8 to 13 January the following year. Writing to his parliamentary ally A. J. Mundella, he expressed his sorrow that

'the Trade Union Congress ran amok at the Criminal Law Amendment Act—I warned them not to do it, and only to go for a modification of subsection three of clause 1. I, for one, won't go in for total repeal, and have so written to the *Co-operative News*.'[5]

Readers of the *Co-operative News* were also informed of further tensions between Hughes and the workers in the North of England Iron Trade, where he was an arbitrator. After one of his awards, reported the *Co-operative News* on 21 October 1871, he 'met a most ungracious reception'. Hughes was quick to rebuke the men.

'You ought to be ashamed of yourself,' he told them. 'Since I have been your arbitrator, in two years your wages have advanced 15 per cent, and now you won't listen to a man who wishes to give his reasons for one adverse decision. You come here like spoiled children, and won't listen to me because I have only given you an advance of 5 per cent when you ask for 10 per cent.'

The tone of his public speeches began to alter. More of his time seemed to be spent in opening working-men's clubs, where he would divert the attention of his labour audience to the desirability of emigration, and the greater opportunities offered to working men on the other side of the Atlantic. Thus, speaking at the Working Men's Institute at Denmark Hill, Camberwell, on 6 November 1873, he pointed out the greater facilities offered by the United States to would-be purchasers of land, and referred to the Western States as forming an invaluable outlet for the surplus population of the European Kingdoms. He sketched the attractive future awaiting would-be emigrants: a farm and homestead of their own, common schools for their children, and a higher standard of living.

'English artisans', he concluded, 'should understand that there is a wide field and opening for them, one which affords the prospect of bringing their children up in a manner very much better than they could in this country.' [6]

This attitude, involving as it did an overt rejection of the possibility that a better future could be obtained in England by labour action, revealed Hughes' displacement from his former position as a leading advocate of labour's claims in the House of Commons. His place was taken by the brass-lunged black-bearded A. J. Mundella, an industrialist who sat for Sheffield. In the inner councils of the unions, such assistance as he had formerly given was now freely offered by two positivists, Frederic Harrison and Henry Crompton: both of whom spared no pains to draft Bills along the lines desired by the labour leaders. That positivists should gain ascendancy in the councils of the labour movement was all the more prejudicial to Hughes' own social programme, in that they were also leading the attack on an institution to which his loyalties now drew him—the Established Church.[7]

2

The splenetic nature of the attack on the Established Church after 1870 owed much to the Education Act of W. E. Forster passed in that year, which had allowed the Church to maintain, and even strengthen, its hold on the elementary schools of the country. Hughes had supported Forster against the Nonconformists, and had joined the National Educational Union (a body composed mainly of Churchmen) as opposed to the National Education League (a body composed mainly of Dissenters and Secularists). The successful passage of Forster's Act precipitated the Nonconformists into the arms of the Secularists, and had so exacerbated their feelings that they rallied for a direct parliamentary assault on the Church itself.

Hughes was well aware of this, and in 1870 had joined Llewelyn Davies and others in founding the Church Reform Union. He realised that to meet this assault, the Church would need to be purged of the abuses which made it such an easy target for the slings and arrows of Dissenters, Positivists, and Ritualists. The last-named were to Hughes almost as dangerous as the other two, since they wantonly provoked scenes of pandemonium in churches which should be fulfilling a necessary social function. So on 15 February 1872 Hughes participated in a large demonstration by the Church Reform Union in St. James's Hall. This meeting pressed for the admission of a lay element in the deliberations of the Established Church by means of parish councils and discussion of rubrical changes in Parliament, the relaxation of the rubric demanding the recitation of the Athanasian Creed, and the reform of patronage.[8]

This new interest brought Hughes into strange company for an avowed Liberal. Associated with him in the presentation of a bill for securing parish councils in the previous year was Lord Sandon, son of the Earl of Harrowby, and one of the main pillars of the National Society. When Hughes travelled round the country to speak for the Church Reform Union, he found himself flanked by Conservative M.P.s, and subjected to heckling by Liberal elements in his audience. Such an occasion occurred on 12 May 1873, when he spoke at Norwich for the Defence Association with Clare Read, a Conservative M.P. who had been a strong parliamentary opponent of Mundella and Fawcett, on the platform. His working-class audience kept shouting that they would rather allow landlords to possess the endowments, and that freedom was better than unity. The meeting was very noisy, and the partisan spirit was sustained by an energetic heckler named Scurll, who made it necessary for Hughes to break the thread of his argument and plead for order.[9] Five months later, on 9 October, Hughes spoke at a working-men's meeting at Bath, where he had travelled to attend a meeting of the Church Congress—the first to which he had been invited. He took the occasion to point out the faults of trade unions, lamenting that

'work is not the same as it had been twenty years ago. You do not put the same honest vigour into it, nor do you have the same delight in it, nor do you turn it out as well as you possibly can'.

'These assertions', reported *The Times*, 'provoked loud cries of discontent.'[10] One voice shouted 'coals two shillings a hundredweight!' and when Hughes asked them how they invested their savings, another cried, 'We've got no savings; look at the price of food.' But Hughes went on to plead that working men should not destroy the best and greatest inheritance they had received, but should hold fast to the Church and hand it down to their descendants. Such a direct appeal was due to the menacing language used by a young Birmingham politician in the *Fortnightly Review*, that the workmen would side with the Nonconformists in attacking that Church.[11]

3

Like his teachers, Arnold, Maurice, and Stanley, Hughes was a passionate believer in the Church's social mission. 'Neither utilitarianism nor the worship of humanity', he asserted, could 'fill the vacuum which would be created in men's hearts if it were disestablished.' All men who looked in their hearts knew that 'man was not an automaton', despite 'twaddly materialistic talk founded on the propagation of reptiles and the like'.[12] And only the Church, as the established embodiment of such religious feeling, could 'raise and purify trade, and show a materialistic and demoralised generation that the principles of the Gospel will have to be applied to the trade intercourse of men'.[13] It was 'the nation organised for spiritual purposes', and even in its imperfect state it offered help to the poor, prevented intolerance, endowed a host of scholars, and could shame 'the legislature and the country again and again till the national conscience is tender enough to put God's laws above men's self-seeking and cunning'.[14] So highly did Hughes estimate the call of a clergyman that he wished—vainly, as it turned out—to see his sons Arthur and George 'both parsons' in this time of trial when the Church needed 'the best blood the nation can give it'. His daughter Lily—later to be drowned in the *Titanic*—married a clergyman in 1889, and Hughes wrote at the time: 'I hold a parson's work done as it should be done to be just the noblest given to the sons of men, so rejoice in the match which most folks would call a very poor one.' [15]

Hughes declared himself prepared to fight to the death against disestablishment 'with comrades of any party'. But he was also genuinely anxious to bring the Nonconformists back into the fold, to make the Church truly national. And he did not shrink from the reforms that this entailed: changes in the Thirty-nine Articles, repeal of the Act of Uniformity, removal of the Athanasian Creed. He followed the disestablishment motions of Edward Miall in the House of Commons with reasoned pleas for the relaxation of the rubrical difficulties and patronage abuses which so effectively prevented the Nonconformists from re-entering the Church.[16] He supported the abolition of tests and the opening of endowed schools to Nonconformist influences. To those of the Church who shrank from such reforms he retorted that 'men who can make matters of conscience of such trivialities as the shape and colour of vestments, the burning of candles and incense, the position of tables and the like' were not fit to be 'trusted with the spiritual guidance of any portion of our people'.[17]

Such remarks antagonised conservative churchmen. And considering that the High-Church movement was in the ascendant in industrial towns, and that the Church itself was convulsed with debates on the recommendations of the Ritual Commission, Hughes was not only burning his fingers, but also his political boats. Lord Shaftesbury, whom Hughes so strangely resembled in outlook, had written sorrowfully in his diary after similar activities only four years before, 'Never again will I interfere in Church matters. All establishments are doomed, and perhaps wisely.' [18] As to Hughes' Liberal friends, they gave him very little support. His former associate in trade union matters confided to a friend:

'I am very anxious about Tom Hughes. He is poor and has a large young family and his earnings are dependent on his health';

and then added:

'I walked out when Hughes' motion was put. I am sick of the attempts at Church Reform; they all come to nothing.' [19]

4

Crushed as he was between the right and left wings of both labour and religious pressure groups, Hughes escaped to salvage his hopes by an even more intense devotion to the work of co-operation. Here at least there lay hopes of establishing the new Jerusalem.

To hasten this, Hughes threw himself into removing the restrictions which hampered co-operative expansion. Generous as Estcourt's Act had been in allowing co-operative societies to register as limited liability companies and to accept loans from other bodies, it had specifically prevented such societies from undertaking in mining operations, from holding land, and from embarking as bankers. The first of these restrictions—mining—Hughes had removed by his own Bill which reached the statute book in 1869. The second he succeeded in lifting two years later, when it became legally possible for co-operative societies to make advances to members on the security of real or personal property.[20] This was a great boon to societies needing short-term capital and encouraged the Co-operative Wholesale Society to undertake, on its own initiative, a tentative evasion of the third restriction by starting a regular banking department to receive deposits from, and make advances to, member societies.

Here was the beginning of the mighty reservoir which Hughes fondly hoped would infuse capital into the languishing producer co-operatives, and, by great good fortune, Hughes was chairman of the Co-operative Congress which met at Bolton on 1, 2 and 3 April 1872 to discuss, among other matters, the operations of the bank. Though rain fell continuously throughout the proceedings, it could not damp Hughes' spirits. His presidential address contained a ringing reassertion of Christian Socialist teaching, made all the more memorable since the shadow of Maurice's death hovered over him:

'We cannot repudiate the name "Socialist" in so far as it implies belief that human society is intended to be organised, and will not be in its true condition until it is organised, from the top to the bottom; but we have never looked to the state to do this for us, we have only asked that state to stand aside, and give us breathing room and elbow room to do it for ourselves.' [21]

'Doing it for ourselves' was the pregnant phrase, for the Congress heard of the establishment of a co-operative engineering works at Ouseburn, near Newcastle.

This extension of co-operation into one of the basic industries arose from the great strike of engineers at Newcastle in the preceding year. The Rev. Dr. Rutherford, of Bath Lane Chapel, had invited working men to meet him in the Bath Lane Schoolroom on 12 June 1871, and within a fortnight the articles of association had been drawn up and signed for a co-operative works with a capital of £100,000. Nearby co-operative retail stores rallied to support it at a meeting on 8 July. Blaydon, Halifax, Heckmondwike, West Cramlington, Mossley, Seaton Delaval, and Chester-le-Street took £6,750 worth of shares and loans, and each worker contributed. By the end of August 130 men were employed, and on 7 September the first pair of cylinders was cast. By September the firm had orders worth £65,000 and arrangements were made to put the works on a double shift and employ 800. Its engines gave great satisfaction, and were 'admitted by engineers on the Tyne to be inferior to none'.[22]

At the next Co-operative Congress, held, appropriately enough, at Newcastle on 12, 14, 15 and 16 April 1873, a breakfast was given to the delegates at the Ouseburn Engine Works. Dr. Rutherford told the delegates that the works was making twenty engines, but that unfortunately they had accepted them at such a low price that the firm was £25,000 worse off than it should be. Hughes promptly proposed that the co-operatives should take this up, and his motion was passed without a dissentient. Halifax increased its investments to £10,000, Heckmondwike to £3,000, while the Co-operative Wholesale Society lent £5,000 on debenture bonds.

The banking activity was watched by the interested parties in the House of Commons with a greater interest than had hitherto been evoked by co-operative activities. Hughes had tabled a Bill during the 1872 session for the formal legalisation of co-operative banking. It was a small two-clause affair, which merely proposed to repeal the existing clause in Estcourt's Act. He and Walter Morrison, as promoters of this Bill, saw Winterbotham at the Home Office, and persuaded him that it was harmless enough. But, as Hughes told the Newcastle Congress,

'a day or two later we got a number of messages from different members asking what we were about, and stating that they thought the Bill was a very dangerous one, that the second reading had been taken quite unexpectedly, and that lots of people had great exception to it. A motion on the subject was then put on the table by a member, a very able attorney, who had only just got into Parliament. He was a Tory. . . . I believe the bankers of the country do not understand the Bill.' 23

He advised them to go home and put pressure on their M.P.s to secure support for its passage.

5

But pressure, as Hughes well knew, was being exerted against himself. Early in 1870 a pressure group of aggrieved retailers was formed as the Tradesmen's Protection Association, which was, by 1872, bestirring itself with vigour. Marshalled by Arthur à Beckett as secretary from headquarters in 10 Duke Street, St. James, this body offered an active and determined opposition to the activities of the co-operators, who they suspected would drive them out of business. Various trade journals took up the cry, notably the *Grocer* and the *Drapers' Trade Journal*.

Their emissaries were at hand to hamper Hughes, who ruefully confessed:

'I find at every political meeting that one of the greatest and almost the only objection to me is that I am "backing up those Co-op fellows who are going to upset the world".' 24

He was soon to pay the penalty of being neither a bona-fide Conservative nor an effective Radical. *Vanity Fair*, under a caricature of him published on 8 June, printed a typical assessment. On the one hand, it declared, Hughes was too much 'like a grown-up schoolboy in a large playground', and not enough 'like a middle-aged gentleman working for his own interests by the ordinary methods'. On the other, he was too benevolent, too strictly practical, and too superficial to slay the monsters of abuse: 'precisely the kind of Englishman that Rugby, Oxford, and a summary view of surface principles would produce, acting upon an intelligence somewhat above the average'. His popularity, it concluded, was among those 'who think that the great will be terrified when they see the small led away captive in ropes of sand'.25

To the outsider, Hughes' politics were ambivalent. On the one hand, he was completely at home in the aristocratic world—he loved London society, and had no intention, as he told his wife in 1874, after four dinners in ten days, of dropping out of the

THOMAS HUGHES
AS SEEN BY THE CARTOONIST 'SPY' IN 1872

'London groove'.[26] On the other, he was a co-operator and a socialist. And to make matters worse he was possessed of a native independence that asserted itself against his supporters on both sides.

Particularly disastrous were his continuing attacks on labour. Though he still accepted trade unions as necessary, and supported not only the dock workers in their strike but the efforts of the agricultural labourers to form a union, yet he was sharply critical of the unions for demanding too much. He declared that labour wanted 'someone to represent their narrowness with more fidelity'. He told working men that they were no more concerned with economic justice than were the employers; and that the question was 'no longer whether John O' the Smith shall get his right, but whether he will leave any for other folk'.[27]

6

His parliamentary record in these last four years was not such as would encourage even the reflective element among the Frome electorate to vote for him. Having made relatively little effort to push Bills in which he was interested, he had frittered away his time over matters either of no importance or else of such magnitude that he was unqualified to deal with them.[28] A typical instance was his attitude to the House of Lords. Though he felt convinced of the necessity of its reform he did not attend a meeting called to urge reform of that body.

So it is little wonder that in the winter of 1872 he had a 'smart differ' with his constituents. He had predicted trouble in August, and in October a group of rowdies, presumably hired by the publicans, had broken up one of his meetings so badly that he had decided 'probably not to go back there'.[29] But, as he wrote to Lowell in 1873, he was 'not going out of Parliament (if I can help it)', though he had made two bids for appointments which would remove him from that assembly: the first, for the Chief Commissionership of Police in 1869, and the second, for the Judge Advocateship in 1870.[30]

So in 1874 he turned to Marylebone. There, to face the hostility of the tradesmen, he believed himself to be assured of the support of the professional and working classes. In his address, as a concession to tradesmen, he declared that he would support the abolition of the Income Tax if it was accompanied by 'a corresponding remission of taxes on articles of common consumption'. He even roundly condemned the Civil Service Supply Association as a joint-stock company masquerading as a co-operative.[31]

His election campaign generated much bitterness. Peter Graham, the chairman of the local Liberal Party, decided that Hughes could not possibly win, and at a closed meeting of the Liberal Party, held on 28 January 1874, Daniel Grant was chosen in his place to run as second Liberal candidate by a vote of 55 to 8.

Hughes had jumped from the frying-pan into the fire. Though the vicar of Marylebone, the Rev. W. Fremantle, was an associate of his in the founding of the Church Reform Union, and the curate, the Rev. S. Barnett, was like-minded, there lived in the parish another old friend whose zeal on his behalf became a liability rather than an asset. This was Miss Octavia Hill, who had recently so exacerbated the majority of the Marylebone Vestry by her condemnation of some of the houses under her care that one member fervently hoped they 'would hear no more of her and her houses'. Nor was this all, for by advocating a more disinterested management of a particularly odious public-house in the parish and opposing the renewal of its licence, she provoked a public rebuke from the local J.P.[32]

Octavia Hill, however, was a born crusader, a true granddaughter of Southwood Smith. Believing Hughes to be both a good and a great man, she organised an army of canvassers which sallied forth from 14 Nottingham Place with election circulars. But, knowing her character, a number of influential voters did not attribute this to friendship for Hughes, but to a fervent desire for female suffrage.

In addition to these embarrassing handicaps, Hughes also had to face the fact that the first Liberal candidate was Sir Thomas Chambers, a near Tory, Deputy Recorder of the City, Common Sergeant, and soon to be president of the National Chamber of Trade: the sworn foe of co-operators.[33] Though Hughes might campaign vigorously, this fission of opinion prevented his obtaining the undoubted help which a running partner could give him—help which was already being accorded to Daniel Grant.

So Hughes' friends, led by Anthony Trollope, put the case to higher authority. Henry James, Gladstone's Attorney-General, arbitrated on 2 February at the hour before midnight. The question was battled out by Trollope and Hughes against Grant and his supporters till one-thirty the following morning. James, who declared that he would stay all night if necessary, finally decided that Hughes had least chance of winning and declared against him. The Tories were jubilant and the Liberals mortified. For Hughes had already alienated the publicans and tradesmen of the constituency before his late withdrawal. Smalley of the *Tribune* probably diagnosed the affair correctly when he said that the real decision was left by Henry James to Sir Thomas Chambers, who chose Grant because he feared for his own seat.[34]

The decision of Henry James was made in the light of popular hostility to the Liberal licensing policy. Since Disraeli in his Bath letter had encouraged the publicans to hope that, by returning him, the Government would cease to 'harass every trade, worry every profession, and assail or menace every class, institution, and species of property in the country',[35] every beerhouse and gin-palace in the metropolis blossomed with blue posters.[36] In Marylebone, as in Finsbury, Lambeth, Towers Hamlets, and Westminster, these were the resorts of a number of voters not usually classified as artisan. Against such intoxicating enthusiasm, Hughes, in common with many other Liberal M.P.s who had pressed for stricter licensing regulations, were borne down, as their great leader declared 'in a torrent of gin and beer'.

Hughes was completely drowned. When the poll was declared early in February, Chambers was elected as junior colleague of a Conservative, who polled 9,849 votes to Chambers' 8,251. Grant, who was running as the official Liberal second string, followed with 7,882 votes. Hughes received only 294. Few parliamentary defeats could be more discouraging.

NOTES

[1] *Macmillan's Magazine*, May 1896, 77–80.

[2] B.M. Add. MSS. 43,519, Hughes to Ripon, 10 May 1867.

[3] *Economic Review*, vi, 1896, 311.

[4] Odger said, 'If we picked the House of Commons through, we could not find two more earnest men with regard to trade unions than Mr. Mundella and Mr. Hughes. They are prepared to attend our meetings, to consult with us and to learn our opinions, to understand our especial considerations, and

to arrive at conclusions which they believe would be calculated to benefit the future conditions of our societies.' W. H. G. Armytage, *A. J. Mundella*, p. 96.

[5] Sheffield University Library, *Mundella Correspondence*, Hughes to Mundella, 20 Jan. 1872.

[6] *The Times*, 7 Nov. 1873.

[7] Frederic Harrison's article in the *Fortnightly Review* of November 1872 was a typical example of his attempts to 'divert the stream of faith from the channels in which it had previously been flowing to his own carefully prepared dykes'. *The Spectator*, 9 Nov. 1872, called him 'superior of the order of positive jesuits ... whose positive cynicism [was] but a new faith travelling incognito'. For an attack on Harrison by another old Rugbeian see M. Arnold, *Culture and Anarchy*.

[8] *The Times*, 16 Feb. 1872.

[9] He reprinted his speech in his *The Old Church. What Shall We Do With It?* (London, 1878).

[10] *The Times*, 10 Oct. 1873.

[11] Joseph Chamberlain's agitation against the clerical dominance in education stressed this theme. See his article in *Fortnightly Review*, Sept. 1873. Hughes even ventured to speak in Birmingham against him.

[12] Letter, Hughes to Fanny Hughes, 9 Oct. 1874; Notes for Speeches.

[13] Letter, Hughes to Fanny Hughes, 2 Sept. 1874, 27 Feb. 1877; Notes for Speeches.

[14] Speech at Norfolk, 12 May 1873; letter, Hughes to Fanny Hughes, 27 Feb. 1877.

[15] Lowell Papers at Harvard, letter, Hughes to Lowell, 26 Dec. 1889; letter, Hughes to Fanny Hughes, 27 Feb. 1877; Notes for Speeches.

[16] See *Hansard*'s reports on the debates on Miall's motions of 9 May 1871 and 16 May 1873.

[17] *The Old Church. What Shall We Do With It?* (London, 1878), 95. The High-Church party were much excited at this time by the decision of the Judicial Committee of the Privy Council given on 23 Feb. 1871 in the case of *Hebbert v. Purchas*, in which the eastward position and vestments were declared illegal. On 5 May 1873 the Archbishops received at Lambeth a deputation representing 60,000 people, which demanded the entire suppression of 'ceremonies and practices adjudged to be illegal'.

[18] Quoted by F. W. Cornish, *The English Church in the Nineteenth Century* (London, 1920), ii, 181.

[19] Sheffield University Library, Leader Correspondence, A. J. Mundella to R. Leader, 12 Aug. 1871 and 4 July 1872.

[20] *Parliament, Sessional Papers, Bills, Public*, 1867, iv, 201; 1871, ii, 431; 1872, ii, 135; 1873, i, 149.

[21] *Report of Co-operative Congress held at Bolton*, 1, 2, and 3 April 1872.

[22] Benjamin Jones, *Co-operative Production* (Oxford, 1894), ii, 447–450.

[23] *Report of Co-operative Congress held at Newcastle*, 12, 14, 15, and 16 April, 1873.

[24] *ibid.*; J. A. Rees, *The Grocery Trade* (London, 1910), ii, 300–302, points out that in the year 1873 not only was the Manchester Grocers' Association re-established ('since which date it has been in the forefront of the grocers of

the Kingdom'), but the Birmingham and Midland Counties Grocers Protection and Benevolent Association was also formed.

Hughes published his enthusiasm for Co-operation. He wrote a long letter to the *Spectator* (which was reprinted in the *Co-operative News* of 21 Oct. 1871) describing the system of industrial partnership adopted by Brewster & Company, Carriage Builders of New York, and lectured before the Social Science Association in the same year on 'The Present Position of Co-operation'.

[25] *Vanity Fair*, 8 June 1872, 183.

[26] His social circle included such people as Lord Granville, The Marquess of Northampton, Col. and Lady Romilly, Lady Colville, Lord Coleridge, Lady Eastlake, Lady Alwyne Compton, Lord Carlingford, Lady Galloway, and Lady Waldegrave. Letters, Hughes to Fanny Hughes, 8 Dec. 1874 and several undated.

[27] *The Times*, 23 Nov. 1871; *Church Congress, Official Report*, 1873, 222; *Macmillan's Magazine*, May 1873, 84–96; May 1896, 78–80. T. Hughes, T. Brassey, E. A. Freeman, Judge Cooley, and others. *The Labor Question and other vital questions* (New York, N.D.), 1 ff.

[28] e.g. Plimsoll's Bill to protect seamen, the trial of the ex-Nawab of Tark, the hours of women working in the textile trade. Bills he co-sponsored included ones to prevent Sunday trading and betting on races, to curtail liquor licences. Motions he seconded included one to stop the Chinese coolie trade.

[29] Ripon Papers, B.M. Add. MSS. 43,528, Hughes to Ripon, 17 Aug. 1872; Lowell Papers at Harvard, Hughes to Lowell, 13 March 1873; *New York Tribune*, 12 Oct. 1872.

[30] Ripon Papers, B.M. Add. MSS. 43,522, Hughes to Ripon, 7 Nov. 1870; *New York Tribune*, 26 Dec. 1871; Lowell Papers at Harvard, letter, Hughes to Lowell, 13 March 1873.

[31] Notes for a Speech in Hughes' papers; *The Times*, 31 Jan. 1874.

[32] C. E. Maurice, *Life of Octavia Hill* (London, 1913), 260–262.

[33] Sir Thomas Chambers, 1814–1891, was a lawyer who sat for Hereford from 1852 to 1857 before being elected for Marylebone on 12 July 1865, which he continued to represent until 15 Nov. 1885. He was knighted on 14 March 1872. F. Boase, *Modern English Biography* (Truro, 1908), iv, 634.

[34] *The Times*, 30, 31 Jan., 2, 3, 4, and 14 Feb. 1874; Brown, *True Manliness*, xix ; *New York Tribune*, 23 Feb., 14 March 1874.

[35] Written with prophetic relevance to Lord Grey de Wilton on 3 Oct. 1873 in support of Forsythe, the Conservative candidate for Bath at the by-election fought as Hughes was attending his first Church Congress, held in the town at that time.

[36] The London Correspondent of the *Sheffield Independent*, 7 Feb. 1874.

CHAPTER THIRTEEN

Outrageous Fortune, 1874–1881

'THE old world', Hughes admitted before his political defeat, 'is a tough subject to keep straight at the best of times, and I begin to doubt if ours is the best.' [1] His fiftieth year had crept up and passed; no longer could he 'run down in the morning to a northern town to lecture and run back again by night to work in the morning without feeling the strain'.[2] Shorn of his political commitments, he might have hoped to salvage some of his other irons from the fire. This was not to be. For disasters gathered thick and fast around him.

I

He made one more attempt to play Androcles to the labour lion. The Criminal Law Amendment Act (which had invested picketing with the criminal penalty of three years' imprisonment) had been a thorn in the union's path since the first year of the decade. This thorn the Conservatives, with their majority of 51, announced that they were determined to remove by appointing a Royal Commission to review the existing laws against combinations of labour. The trade union leaders were furiously angry. Meeting on 17 March 1874, two days before the Queen's Speech announcing this, the Parliamentary Committee of the Trades Union Congress passed a unanimous resolution 'deprecating' the reference of the picketing restrictions to a commission, and recording their opinion that 'the time has come for immediate legislation'.[3]

Hughes was not only present at this meeting, but, in the view of one observer, actually strengthened the wording of the protest which was drawn up. Yet two days later, when invited to the Home Office, he actually agreed to serve as a member of the Royal Commission. The announcement of his adhesion (together with that of Alexander MacDonald, the chairman of the Parliamentary Committee of the T.U.C.) aroused 'great disappointment and caused much bitterness of expression' among the labour leaders.

Meeting once more at 37 Villiers Street, off the Strand, their criticisms were so strong that MacDonald resigned his chairmanship. Hughes fared badly in explaining his conduct: 'his defence', wrote an observer, 'was his worst accusation'.[4]

Yet it was hard to blame him for doing what the chairman of the Trades Union Congress had done. Both admitted they had been deceived.

'The way the whole thing was managed was singularly ingenious and crafty . . . and as good as a play. Hughes was put in one room at the Home Office, Burt in another; one was played off against the other and both against Mac-Donald till two had given their assent.' [5]

But, trick though it may have been, bad feeling lingered on in the councils of the trade union movement. When Hughes, as a commissioner, wrote a week later to ask the secretary of the Parliamentary Committee of the T.U.C. for such evidence as he might give that would shorten the inquiry, he said:

'I don't ask the Parliamentary Committee to recognise the Commission in any way, but merely to give me at my request documents of public interest which they are desirous to circulate or at any rate not afraid to circulate.
'If you can let me have these it will save me labour, and help on the chance of speedy legislation without in the least compromising your position. You do not recognise the Commission or me as Commissioner, but, for old acquaintance sake, or out of courtesy, give me copies of documents which you would not refuse probably to any decent stranger.' [6]

Such language reveals that hard words had passed between the two men.

Nor did Hughes take the opportunity to justify his conduct by attending the Trades Union Congress held at Liverpool in January 1875, when the propriety of his and MacDonald's actions were again brought under scrutiny, replying:

'I am in the agonies of settling this reform—which will take all my spare time and force for some time, and in any case I could scarcely come till the Commission is defunct. I was away when your note came and am sorry it has been overlooked till this moment.' [7]

The Commission duly reported in the following month—February 1875. Though divided on the question, they recommended retaining the gaol sentence for breach of contract in the Master and Servant Act, applauded the majority report of the 1867 Commission, which maintained that a law of conspiracy was necessary, and found no fault with the anti-picketing provisions of the Criminal Law Amendment Act, which had been the original cause of their sitting.[8]

From these inconclusive and conservative findings, Hughes demurred in a memorandum attached to the report. In this he condemned the approval with which his colleagues regarded the provisions of the anti-picketing laws. But he signed the report: an action involving approval of the very opinions from which he had so emphatically dissented eight years before, when, with Frederic Harrison, he signed the minority report of the 1867 Commission. Moreover, he signed it with enthusiasm:

'I think we shall do real good by the report of this Commission', he told his wife, 'which is always a satisfaction when one has done work at anything . . . [it] may take the wind out of the sails of some of the noisy and mischievous advisers of the working men.' [9]

Even Disraeli's Ministry, however, found such recommendations hard to welcome with approval. Having already been denounced for appointing the Commission as a device to avoid legislation, they could scarcely adopt a report which virtually endorsed that accusation. To Hughes' amazement, the Ministry now proceeded to erase from the statute book the very laws which had caused all the trouble. The Criminal Law Amendment Act of 1871 was repealed, as also was the Master and Servant Act of 1867. Two new Acts replaced them. The first, the Conspiracy and Protection of Property Act, set reasonable limits to the application of the law of conspiracy in trade disputes; the second, the Employers and Workman Act, put servants on a parity with masters before the law where breach of contract was concerned, abolished imprisonment of workmen for such breach of contract. Peaceful picketing was now permitted. The words 'molest' and 'coerce' were now eliminated from the law. Labourers were no longer the victims of special treatment under a draconian code, but, like masters, were to be tried by the normal processes of criminal law for offences which incurred such trials.[10]

The trade union leaders were duly grateful to the Ministry, and acknowledged their gratitude. But at the same time they passed a vote of thanks to Hughes to show him that they appreciated his past activities. Hughes replied with a letter which reveals the misgivings he entertained of the secular course steered by the unions:

'As to such work as I was able to do in past years, it was done, I trust, with no eye to reward of any kind, except the consciousness of helping a just cause to the best of one's power. This I shall always retain, while acknowledging how full of error and weakness one's best efforts have been. The present position and prospects of the labour position in England, though full of difficulty, are to my mind, also full of hope.

'At any rate, their future is practically in the hands of the workpeople themselves (as I have always worked and striven that it should be), and it is for them to show that they can rise to the new situation and prove themselves patriotic and true Englishmen who can put their country before their class. It is quite natural that a new generation should turn to new admirers, and I certainly am neither sad nor sorry that it should be so. If they should ever want help or advice from me, it will always be very readily given, and in any case I shall always watch their efforts with the deepest interest, tempered I am bound to add (in view of much that has happened of late) with no little anxiety.' [11]

His anxiety was well-founded. The unions, by participating in political agitation, had set in motion machinery which was quite alien to the personal, humane association of co-operators which Hughes had hoped to establish. Their militant class attitude estranged him, and his eyes turned elsewhere for the New Jerusalem.

2

He was displaced, too, in the hierarchy of co-operation. At the Co-operative Congress held at Halifax in April 1874 it was Thomas Brassey who endorsed co-operative partnerships and profit-sharing, while Hughes was called away to arbitrate in a cutlers' dispute at Sheffield. But he returned in time to warn a meeting held on Saturday evening at Heckmondwike, with Goldwin Smith in the chair:

'The stone has been rolled up the hill and it seems likely to go down on the other side. I must say I feel rather troubled as to what the future may be. Where there is a carcase there are sure to be eagles and there is no want of eagles to pick the carcase of co-operation. . . .
'I sometimes tremble at the idea that you are in danger of over-organisation, and of trusting in a great system.' [12]

His forebodings were confirmed a month later when the Co-operative Wholesale Society elected J. T. W. Mitchell as president. Mitchell, son of a servant-girl's chance love-affair, rose from a cellar to dominate the C.W.S. meetings. Big and hearty, he was in every sense a product of the consumers' movement, keeping it rigidly to the path of consumer co-operation, never allowing the more aerial schemes of Hughes and the advocates of producer co-operation to deflect him.[13]

Mitchell's homespun heartiness appealed to the canny co-operators who had begun to venture into ownership of factories to supply their needs and it would have appealed to Hughes had Mitchell's intrusion into co-operative ownership of productive enterprises been balanced by a corresponding extension of the basic principles of co-operative enterprise: profit-sharing and workers' contracts.[14]

Such a gesture on Mitchell's part would have been all the more welcome in view of the fact that in 1875 the Co-operative Congress established relations with a Co-operative Trading Company in the Mississippi Valley. Here was an Anglo-American channel along which co-operative ideas could flow to the mutual refreshment of both countries. Moreover, since this Congress was the first to receive delegates from the T.U.C., and to send corresponding delegates to the T.U.C. in exchange, the flow of co-operative feeling to that now unregenerately secular body might have worked a great change. But co-operators had no intention either of giving independence to the productive enterprises they initiated nor of sharing profits with their workers. Thus not only did Hughes experience the defeat of his schemes for winning the Congress over to producer co-operation but was forced to witness the triumph of the very principles against which he was struggling. Neither at the Congress of 1876 (at Glasgow) nor that of 1877 (at Leicester) was Hughes able to present his point of view.

It was bitter irony that at the very time of these reverses all the experiments in co-partnership in which Hughes had invested so much time and money crashed about his ears in the economic winter of 1875.

The numerous coal-mining co-operatives started in the boom of the previous years—to one of which Hughes 'had lent a considerable sum on mortgage . . . and was like to lose it all'—were the first to collapse.[15] The co-partnership of Briggs and Company, which had bought a mine, voted to end profit-sharing entirely in February 1875, after some bitter experiences of strikes and demonstrations. Hughes was so fair-minded that he actually sided with the workers for their selflessness in jeopardising £50,000 in bonuses through going on strike.[16]

Other ventures were still-born before they could begin proper operations. The London Company of Builders, formed in June 1872 'in great measure at the instance of Mr. Hughes', never even started business.[17] The Cobden Mills, from which the directors declined all remuneration, witnessed their shares fall to half their value and pass to William Nuttall, who promptly made the mill pay by abandoning the manufacture of pure cloth. This was a most bitter pill for Hughes to swallow, for Nuttall became one of his most persistent opponents at subsequent co-operative congresses; taunting him with the jibe,

'The Cobden Mills began to make profits when it ceased to make pure cloth. That was the difference between the theorist (Mr. Hughes) and the practical man (myself).' [13]

Greening & Company had already closed its doors, and in the same decade Hughes' beloved Framemakers' and Gilders' Association collapsed after a desperate effort to obtain capital, with a total loss to all shareholders and a payment to loan holders of two shillings and sixpence in the pound.[19]

3

Personal losses and sorrows followed. In 1875 Kingsley died—three years after Hughes had lost both his brother George and his friend Maurice. Moreover, his ailing wife, Fanny, whom he always buoyed with false hopes, became particularly ill: her left lung needed treatment, and she went away for two months, 'sadly ill', to Littlehampton. In the summer of 1875 Tom himself was laid so low by inflammatory rheumatism that Jeannie had been moved to talk of the consolation of friends gone before and the superiority of death to life. By the following March, Hughes was not yet recovered, and had to rent a house in the country for his health, since he could not take the complete rest which the *New York Tribune* thought 'would probably be the best medicine for him'.[20]

On this distressed family scene impinged the financial disasters of that winter. Apart from Tom's own losses in the many and various enterprises, his brother Hastings went bankrupt. Eight years before he had been in trouble, but help from the family had put him on his feet again, and Tom hoped that, having been once frightened, he would now conduct his business properly. But the winter of 1875 swept the ground from under Hastings' feet: his mine shares suffered with the rest, and a paper in which he had been concerned brought disaster upon him in December 1875. Jeannie had to move from the great family mansion Elm House, and send Hastings' children and Tom's mother to the Isle of Wight. Things were so bad that Tom thought he would have to give up co-operation. The thought that this might happen bothered Jeannie even more than her brother's losses. Tom was inclined to blame Hastings for the disaster, but Jeannie persuaded him that the losses were caused by 'trusting and believing in the goodness and honesty of your fellow-creatures'—a fault which Tom could easily forgive.[21]

Loyally, Tom rushed into print to secure the reputations of his dead friends. For Maurice, 'the best and wisest Englishman I have ever known! . . . who had done more than any other man to widen and deepen English thought,' he wrote a preface to his *Friendship of Books* in 1874. In this, Hughes pointed out how superior Maurice was to Matthew Arnold, the best part of whose *Literature and Dogma* was what Maurice had said; how infinitely superior to the positivists, to Morley, to revolutionists who did not see that revolution was not enough, and to Mill, whose *Autobiography* then published had so depreciated Maurice and the church he served so well. 'Maurice', declared Hughes, 'had scattered more mists and slain more hobgoblins than all his contemporaries put together.' [22]

For Kingsley, Hughes did the same. Both by a preface to *Alton Locke*, and in a review of Mrs. Kingsley's life of her husband, he tried to refute the dual accusation that Kingsley had waved too red a flag in 1848 and then deserted the cause entirely in 1854. Even Jeannie thought the latter charge was true, and declared that Kingsley had done many unforgivable things, like attacking Newman unfairly, taking the side of the South in the American Civil War, loving royalty too much, and neglecting Maurice. But Tom would not have it. Kingsley was consistently good.[23]

For George Hughes, Tom planned an even more ambitious work, which would bring the virtues of this 'private domestic man' living a 'true life' before a wider public. George, Tom felt, offered a timely example of the 'quiet lives that would come to the front in England in a time of stress', and such men ought not to be forgotten. Tom found the memoir, however, 'cruelly hard to do'. George had achieved very little worth recording and some things that definitely ought not to be: he had been guilty of 'little' faults, such as reading while visitors were calling, had shirked trouble and been indolent about money matters—he had refused to pay his keeper, Tom's one-time idol Henry New, because he claimed New had cheated him, and now New's family were starving. Jeannie was at first shocked by the idea of printing George's letters at all, and begged Tom to make no 'allusion to my father's state of religious depression'.[24] The *Memoir of a Brother* skirts all these dangers, but at the cost of inevitable thinness. The ever-faithful Lowell 'sat up (like a naughty boy) till half-past one and read every word of it'. He 'quite fell in love with your father', from whom Tom had got, he discovered, 'a great deal of what I love in you', was touched by the 'affection and unity of your household', and felt that the book would do 'a great deal of good and add to the number of honest men in the world'. The reviewers and the public, which bought six printings in a year, were kindly.[25] Yet the modern reader, unless he is looking for biographical fact about Tom Hughes, is more likely to agree with the dissenting opinion of the *Dublin Review*, which averred that George was neither remarkable nor ideal, that what interested Hughes' family was 'mere twaddle' to the world at large, and that the book's acceptance 'by a particular set must not make a reviewer shrink from condemning the patent folly' of publishing it at all.[26] Read today, the *Memoir* has little interest except as a characteristic product of Victorian reverence, like solemn funerals and black-bordered letters.

Perhaps the greatest personal loss of all was that of his sister Jeannie. 'I have never lost so many in all previous years as in the last, including my only sister', he wrote to Lowell in 1877.[27] It was made no easier by the fact that the Co-operative Congress was being held at that very time in Leicester. Hughes could not attend, but wrote from Ethelbert Terrace, Margate, on 1 April a letter to Neale which displayed the gloom he felt:

'I do trust this Congress will take a strong line against the demoralising influences under which the movement has been suffering of late. I have heard numerous expressions of astonishment and regret that we get no such recruits now as we used to get. My wonder is rather that we hold together at all. It was one thing when our co-operation was declared to be an attempt to apply Christianity to trade, and quite another now, that it is an attempt to combine all our consumption so as to save another 6d. in the pound. I don't think you, I or any of our old friends would have bothered our heads about the latter prospect. If we will only go back to our old aims and principles, I believe we shall soon pick good new blood. I am anxious about this Congress; and very sorry to be absent, but I feel (apart from all conventional notions of propriety, which I would gladly have disregarded as my dear sister, an ardent co-operator, would have been the first to wish me to do,) that I could not have faced it to any good purpose.' [23]

But his Christian faith reasserted itself, and six months later he was back facing another set of enemies, the intransigent majority at the Church Congress. Against A. Beresford Hope, his old opponent of the previous decade, he asserted that it was mainly owing to the attitude of the clergy that strained relations existed between the Established Church and Nonconformity. He warned his listeners that they were separating themselves too much from the nation in general, and especially from their Dissenting brothers. He was howled down when he suggested that the title 'Reverend' was a national title, and angry cries of 'No! no!' greeted his suggestion that the Church should not refuse interment in a church burial-ground to a Nonconformist. *The Times* deplored the words of dissentients, regretting 'this growing spirit of distrust on the part of the clergy towards their more experienced leaders', and added 'the Clergy, as represented at this Congress, seem to have entrenched themselves in the graveyards as obstinately as the Turks at Plevna, and to be resolved that they will only be dislodged by force'.[29]

4

It was this faith which led Hughes to give a course of lectures at the Working Men's College during the year 1876 on Jesus, which he republished three years later as *The Manliness of Christ*. As a layman, he knew that most people would shy from priests, with their mediational claims, and in these lectures he preached the effective gospel of the so-called Broad Church party. It was an answer not only to those who had scoffed at his 'muscular Christianity', but also to those who sneered that Christianity appealed to the element of fear in men's nature.

He tells the story of a simple, courageous, selfless Man, loyal to the truth at the cost of friendships, popularity, and life; Who fought doggedly for the right against dead formulæ and powerful

THOMAS HUGHES

FROM THE PORTRAIT BY LOWES DICKINSON PAINTED FOR
THE WORKING MEN'S COLLEGE

men. In writing it Hughes was writing autobiography, as he so frequently did, and was finding surcease for all his personal troubles. And, like his other work, it was read. The *Spectator* declared it the best book for telling the 'intelligent masses' about Christianity, and by 1880, as Lowell declared, it was appearing in four forms in America.[30]

Inspired by his theme, Hughes was soon back in the arena, tilting at the selfishness of the C.W.S. He saw that the urgent need of the movement was to wrest control of the bank from the C.W.S. and use it as a great labour bank. So in 1877 he participated in the deliberations of a co-operative committee which embodied these ideas in a report which was submitted to the Co-operative Congress the following year. The speeches he made showed that he had now quite recovered his old form. Pointing to the fear which industrial association excited in the breasts of politicians of all creeds, he laughed, 'They clothe it with all sorts of dreadful attributes, give it names like "big bad democracy", "communism", "socialism", "the revolution" and so on.' But Hughes warned his listeners that the name then being applied to their fellows—the masses—aptly described their condition: 'a floating mass of atoms without coherence or order, and therefore, without power'. The power he urged them to grasp was that which could only come from association in the field of productive enterprise. He closed with a fine quotation:

> 'Surely the wiser time shall come
> When this fine overplus of might
> No longer sullen, slow, and dumb
> Shall leap to music and to light.
> In that new childhood of the earth
> Life of itself shall dance and play;
> New blood in times shrunk veins make mirth
> And labour meet delight half way.' [31]

But the co-operators had no time for prophets. They preferred the profits which came from consumer co-operation, which in the year 1877 reached some £36,979 on total net sales of £2,697,366.[32]

But Hughes kept steadily on his course. In 1877 he wrote two papers: one on banking and one on labour in co-operative workshops. Hard work, honest trading, and wise spending were his watchwords:

'The let-alone system of unimpeded individual activity and equal individual rights . . . is no more adequate for its purpose, than a similar system, applied to rivers and brooks, would be sufficient to secure the distribution of natural waters in the way adapted to produce the maximum growth of the plants useful to man.'

Only the principle of free association would enable the processes of production and distribution to serve the masses, and at the same time save England from the Nihilism of Russia, the Socialism of Germany, the Communism of France, and the violence predicted by Karl Marx. To compare English co-operators with Continental Socialists, Hughes declared, was to identify those who blew up a house full of people with those who blew up a rock that impeded progress. His eyes were fixed not on a State which should be the sole landowner, capitalist, and employer of labour, but on a congeries of free associative enterprises, in which the labour parliament (or co-operative congress) would take an important part. It was an anticipation of syndicalism and guild socialism of the type that Orage and Penty were to expound with greater clarity and intellectual force.[33]

By 1878 he was the moving spirit in a new co-operative propaganda organisation—the Guild of Co-operation, 'established to investigate the principles and to promote the practice of Co-operation'. Taking the chair at the initial meeting on 22 June 1878, Hughes enrolled such members of the older generation as Daniel Guile, and of the new as J. J. Dent and the Rev. Stewart D. Headlam. They used to meet monthly, but subsequently decided to meet four times a year. Their principal sphere of activity was the south of England, where by determined effort and publicity they succeeded in extending co-operative enterprise—especially in the metropolis itself.

5

So there was much to draw him back into politics. The American elections of 1876 elicited a preference for Hayes, who had driven him through Central Park in 1870, and whose hand he hoped would be as light on men as it was on horses. He was moved to express strong aversion for Disraeli, 'that mischievous plotter and dreamer who has managed to get astride the Tory party here, and is driving poor old John Bull's coach along the Devil's highway'.[34] Then, too, there was Harcourt, 'the Big

Man', as Hughes called him, who had swaggered into power by endorsing popular policies—friendship with the North, legality for the trade unions—at the last possible moment.

'Surely', mused Hughes, 'he *must* come to be prime minister No. 2 of the Disraeli type as the culmination of such a history—the two men are wonderfully alike in type tho' very unlike superficially. Fortunately for us all, thank God, England is much too great a country to be hurt seriously by any individual men, but a series of Dizzy's big men appealing only to men's weaknesses and meanness, and swaggering into the enjoyment of other men's work, and so offering the worst example of the successful game, may Heaven deliver us from.' [35]

Harcourt's equivocation on the question which was inflaming the country during the years 1876–1878, together with Disraeli's 'Asiatic instincts', drew Hughes to a public platform in St. James's Hall on 7 May 1877 to protest against Turkish tyranny in the Balkans and any thought that England might go to war with Russia. He described Disraeli as a premier 'who had never understood or sympathised with any but the mean side of this nation', and the Turks as doomed. For Hughes the issues were as crystal clear as when he spoke on behalf of the North. Only now his was but one of many voices lifted up on the side of right.[36]

Stimulated by such forays, he essayed an entry to the House of Commons. In June 1878 he had spoken at Salisbury, conceding, in an effort to mollify the provincial Anti-Co-operative Society, whose secretary had written Hughes that the society would prevent his election anywhere, that possibly co-operation was not necessary where, as at Salisbury, tradesmen acted on co-operative principles, and asserting that he favoured opening museums and galleries on Sunday. In December he had made another visit to the town, evidently, the *Tribune's* correspondent asserted, to meet his future constituents, though he had spoken on the politically neutral topic of the *Song of Roland*. During 1879 he made several trips, one of which his wife, whose brilliant political tactics the *Tribune* praised, said 'has been very useful' since it 'has made Tom much more known and I feel hopeful'. At the last minute, however, the 'Trades Protective people permitted the party organisation to throw me over', and on 1 March Hughes retired: the tradesmen of the town were against him, he told the Co-operative Congress of 1880, and he didn't want the Liberals to lose. The opposition of Ralph Dutton, chairman of the South-western Railway—'a hard man to fight', Fanny Hughes told Alexander Macmillan—

plus the strongly Tory traditions of this cathedral town were too much for Hughes.[37]

Even had he been able to return to Parliament after 1880 it is doubtful whether, despite a hankering that never quite left him, Hughes would really have wanted to. He had never taken to party politics, he told Lowell, the personal caucus being to him the 'unswallowable bolus'. And now with the advent of Joseph Chamberlain and his Liberal Association party lines had hardened to such an extent that an independent like Hughes was becoming very nearly an anomaly. The candidate, Hughes complained in 1878, was at the 'mercy of a party organisation with a cut-and-dried bundle of pledges to be swallowed on pain of party ostracism'. By 1887 his bitterness on the subject had grown so great that, as he told Lowell, he was 'coming more and more round to Goldwin Smith's faith that our English-speaking race will have to consider whether government by party is really the last and highest word in human affairs'. Co-operation seemed to him the 'solution in politics as elsewhere', for only through co-operation could one get statesmen who ruled by 'hope' and 'self-sacrifice', not by 'fear and greed', and who would be concerned with the manner in which they secured the 'consent, acquiescence, enthusiasm' of their constituents.[38]

The question of Hughes' return had, however, become largely academic. 'I doubt if I shall ever return to the House', he wrote Lowell in 1880 'as my views on the Church question make me an almost hopeless candidate in the North of England,[39] and my support of co-operation a perfectly hopeless one at present in the South'. Two years later he told Lord Ripon that 'unless a vacancy had occurred at Rochdale or possibly one or two other northern towns where co-operators rule the roost I should not have a chance of getting back into the House even if I had seen my way financially'.[40]

It remained only for a Kansas editor to provide a final ironic commentary on Hughes' long fight for liberal causes.

'Thomas Hughes', wrote the editor, introducing an article by Hughes' son George, many years later, 'was a hide-bound conservative, a member of the landlord class of England, and a staunch supporter of the British aristocracy. His son, coming to America, has breathed the air of independence of thought and action, and has aligned himself with the progressive elements of the country'. [41]

6

Perhaps the most decided rebuff came at the 1881 Co-operative Congress, when Holyoake attacked the *Manual of Co-operators*, which Hughes and Neale had prepared at request of the Congress two years earlier. Holyoake's attack began in the initial meeting of the Central Board:

'It can only be regarded as *their* manual and can only be published as representing *their* opinions. Published officially, it would convert our entire union into a theological body, and terminate that neutrality which has hitherto been our distinction and our strength. . . . This book is an intentional manifesto of religious opinion and must be rejected. . . .'

Lloyd Jones sprang to Hughes' defence, declaring that 'the best work that has ever been done for Co-operation lies between its covers'. But Holyoake was not to be mollified, and on 7 June, the second day of the Congress, when Hughes himself was in the chair, brought up the *Manual* once more:

'We are asked to make a new departure in Co-operation', he warned the delegates, 'and the nature of it ought to be stated. This practically hands over the whole of the Co-operative body to the Church of England.'

Cries of 'Time' and 'Shame' were followed by Lloyd Jones rising to his feet to defend his old Christian Socialist leader: 'The words I have just listened to', he said with sorrow, 'have given me more pain than anything I have ever heard in connection with the movement.'[42]

Holyoake's feelings were echoed by many others who disapproved of the views which Hughes and Neale had so long expressed both in Congress and in print that co-operative banking and production were as essential parts of the movement as co-operative consumption. That these views, rejected by the C.W.S., should now be embodied in a manual for co-operators seemed a monstrous perversion of realities. But the moral force of Hughes carried the day and the *Manual* was published.

Hughes himself felt bitter about the whole affair. Holyoake said he 'was so indignant that, being in the chair, he refused to call upon me to move a resolution officially assigned to me upon another subject'.[43] Holyoake apologised to Hughes, but Hughes regarded it as 'an attempt to butter me, like the sneak he always was'.[44] Not until twenty years after Hughes' death, when the

Manual was re-edited, were words written which might have tempered his anger at this direct repudiation of his long efforts on behalf of Co-operation. The *Manual*, said the twentieth-century editor, was

'the rock on which the structure of the movement should be reared; and a response to its teaching will supply the most effective antidote to the gross materialism which in later years has eaten like a canker into the movement, obscuring its vision and retarding its progress'. [45]

Indeed, it looked as if Hughes had feeble hopes for the future of England in 1881, and it is little wonder that, sitting by the bedside of the dying Dean Stanley, he should 'betray, without intending it, some of that despondency which the present state of affairs both in Church and State has produced on so many English minds'. [46]

NOTES

[1] *New York Tribune*, 21 June 1871.

[2] New York Public Library, Berg Collection, letter of Hughes, 12 Jan. 1877.

[3] W. J. Davis, *The Trade Union Congress* (London, 1910), 41.

[4] Sheffield University Library, Mundella to R. Leader, 21 March 1874.

[5] *ibid.* See also *Hansard* clxxxii (1700 ff.). Hughes was asked only an hour or two before the names were submitted to the Queen.

[6] Bishopsgate Institute, Howell Correspondence, Hughes to Howell, 25 March 1874.

[7] *ibid.*, Hughes to Howell, 13 Jan. 1875.

[8] *Parliament Sessional Papers*, *Reports of Commissioners*, 1875, xxx.

[9] Letters, Hughes to Fanny Hughes, 9 Dec. 1874 and several undated.

[10] S. and B. Webb, *History of Trade Unionism*, 253.

[11] Bishopsgate Institute, Howell Papers, 13 July 1876.

[12] *Report of the Sixth Co-operative Congress* held at Halifax, 6, 7, 8 April 1874.

[13] For whom see P. Redfern, *J. T. W. Mitchell* (Manchester, 1923). Mrs. Webb called him 'the most remarkable personality that the British Co-operative Movement has thrown up', *My Apprenticeship* (1926), 359 ; C. R. Fay describes his work as 'forming a pattern which was rough and rather quarrelsome at the edges but very strong at the centre', *Co-operation at Home and Abroad* (2nd edition, 1948) ii, 19.

[14] The three factories acquired by the C.W.S.— a biscuit works at Crumpsall, a boot and shoe factory at Leicester, and a soap works at Durham—were all worked on the principle of a bonus to labour employed there. The principle, adopted on 16 Nov. 1872 before they were in operation, was abandoned on 19 June 1875, William Nuttall, one of its principal advocates, voting against it. P. Redfern, *The Story of the C.W.S.*, 79–80.

[15] In 1872 Hughes had helped to found, and become chairman of the Coal Co-operative Society, a co-partnership which was to pay a 5 per cent dividend

and reduce the cost of coal to consumers. *The Times*, 16 Oct. 1872, 6. Lowell Papers at Harvard, Hughes to Lowell, 25 June 1876; Potter, *The Co-operative Movement in Great Britain*, 134; notes for speeches in Hughes' papers.

[16] N. P. Gilman, *Profit-sharing between Employer and Employee*, 265. *Report of the Seventh Co-operative Congress* held in London, 1875, 21.

[17] B. Jones, *Co-operative Production*, ii, 549.

[18] *Report of the Ninth Co-operative Congress* held at Leicester, 2, 3, 4 April 1877.

[19] Letter, Hughes to R. Newton, 1 Aug. 1879; Potter, *The Co-operative Movement in Great Britain*, 134. As B. Jones points out in *Co-operative Production*, ii, 680, the association did not take sufficient heed of rapidly impending change: polished and painted woods superseded carving and gilded mirrors. Hughes had to resign from the directorate with Newton, to be replaced by Applegarth, Jennings, and Standley.

[20] *New York Tribune*, 28 March 1876; letter, Hughes to Fanny Hughes, 6 Dec. 1874.

[21] D. Hughes, *Memoir of Jane Elizabeth Senior*, 172; letters, Hughes to Fanny Hughes, 23 Sept. 1867, Hughes to Jeannie Senior and Jeannie Senior to Hughes, 8, 12, 23 Jan. and 9 Feb. 1876; Lowell Papers at Harvard, letter, Hughes to Lowell, 25 June 1876.

[22] F. D. Maurice, *The Friendship of Books*, edited with a preface by Thomas Hughes (London, 1874).

[23] Charles Kingsley, *Alton Locke*, with a preface by Thomas Hughes (London, 1876); *Macmillan's Magazine*, March 1877, 337 ff.; letter, Jeannie Senior to Hughes (undated).

[24] Letters, Hughes to Jeannie Senior, and Jeannie Senior to Hughes, 16, 23 Sept. 1872.

[25] *Athenæum*, 15 Feb. 1873; Norton (ed.), *Letters of J. R. Lowell*, ii, 92.

[26] *Dublin Review*, Oct. 1873, 525.

[27] Lowell Papers at Harvard, letter, Hughes to Lowell, 21 June 1877.

[28] Printed in the *Report of the Ninth Co-operative Congress* held at Leicester, 2, 3, 4 April 1877.

[29] *The Times*, 10 and 13 Aug. 1877. *Official Report of the Church Congress at Croydon* 1877, 492.

[30] *Westminster Review*, April 1880, 54; *Spectator*, 3 April 1880, 437.

[31] *Report of the Tenth Co-operative Congress* held at Manchester, 22, 23, 24 April 1878.

[32] P. Redfern, *The Story of the C.W.S.*, 418–419.

[33] *The Labor Question and other Vital Questions*, 7; T. Hughes and E. V. Neale, *A Manual for Co-operators*, prepared at the request of the Co-operative Congress held at Gloucester in April 1879, xiii.

[34] Lowell Papers at Harvard, letter, Hughes to Lowell, 24 Oct. 1878. Lowell, more conservative than Hughes, came to disagree with him about Disraeli. In 1875 he told Hughes that 'barring Dizzy' he would be a Tory, as 'I would not give up a thing that had roots to it, though it might suck up its food from the graveyards'. In 1878 he came round to the point of view from which he could write that the prejudice against Disraeli was 'medieval': Disraeli's policy had restored the prestige of England: 'as I back the English race against the field, I am not sorry for it'. Norton, *Letters of J. R. Lowell*, letters 15 Feb. 1875, 17 Nov. 1878.

[25] Lowell Papers at Harvard, letters, Hughes to Lowell, 25 June, 25 Oct. 1876, 24 Oct. 1878; letter, Hughes to Fanny Hughes, 12 Oct. 1874; A. G. Gardiner, *Life of Harcourt* (London, 1923), i, 254 ff. Hughes had once at least in the past been friendly to Harcourt. 'As a barrister and an Englishman' he congratulated him for defending Colonel Crawley in 1863 without taking a fee. Moreover, despite Tom's bitterness, Fanny was on terms of friendly correspondence with Harcourt, and when the latter married Lily Motley the Hugheses became occasional visitors at their home. But Hughes and the witty, audacious Harcourt were temperamentally too far apart to get along, even when, as often happened, they agreed politically. Hughes' references to him in later years are less bitter than those of the 'seventies, but are seldom without an acid touch. Harcourt was behaving with patience, and courtesy at the Home Office, he told Lord Ripon in 1881, 'which is the more telling from being unlooked for'. In 1890 Hughes told Lowell that Lady Winchelsea was the daughter of E. Harcourt, 'elder brother of Sir William but worth 50 of him'. Gardiner, *Life of Harcourt*, i, 157, 265; Ripon Papers in the British Museum, Add. MSS. 43,531, letters, Hughes to Ripon, 19 May, 22 June 1881; letter, Hughes to Fanny Hughes, 1 Dec. 1874; Lowell Papers at Harvard, letters, Hughes to Lowell, 23 Jan. 1877 ; 20 June 1890 (Mrs. Rantoul Collection).

[36] Notes for speeches in Hughes Papers; Lowell Papers at Harvard, letter, Hughes to Lowell, 23 Jan. 1877; *The Times*, 9 Dec. 1876; 8 May 1877.

[37] *New York Tribune*, 11 June, 5, 16 Dec., 1, 1878; letter, Fanny Hughes to Alexander Macmillan, 26 Nov. 1879, in the possession of Macmillan and Co.; *True Manliness*, xx–xxi; Norton (ed.), *Letters of J. R. Lowell*, ii, 123; *Co-operative Congress for 1880 Report*, 42. A speech which Hughes delivered on 19 July 1879 on the occasion of the laying of the foundation stone of the London branch of the C.W.S. building on the corner of Hooper and Rupert Streets did him great harm, for he dwelt upon the 'solemn responsibility' of the movement for being 'trustees for the savings of the poor', and castigated the 'fierce and reckless competition against which this building will be a protest'.

[38] Lowell Papers at Harvard, letter, Hughes to Lowell, 25 Oct. 1876; Brown, *True Manliness*, xx.

[39] His speeches at Sion College 18 March 1877, and his address at Hull in the December of the previous year, were both reprinted in this book, *The Old Church. What Shall We Do With It?* (London, 1878). This collection of his views on the necessity of preserving the established church was a direct assault on the Liberation Society.

[40] Brown, *True Manliness*, xxi; Ripon Papers B.M., Add. MSS. 43,531, letter, Hughes to Ripon, 25 Aug. 1882.

[41] Note in Hughes' Papers.

[42] *Report of Proceedings at Co-operative Congress*, 1881, i, 2, 3, 49.

[43] J. McCabe, *Life and Letters of G. J. Holyoake* (London, 1903), ii, 37; Holyoake, *Bygones worth Remembering*, ii, 113.

[44] Ripon Papers, B.M. Add. MSS. 43,531, Hughes to Ripon, 21 June 1881.

[45] T. Hughes and E. V. Neale, *Foundations: A Study in the Ethics and Economics of the Co-operative Movement*. (Revised by A. Stodart and W. Clayton) (Manchester, 1916), preface.

[46] *Harper's New Monthly Magazine*, Nov. 1881, 919.

CHAPTER FOURTEEN

Tom Brown in Tennessee, 1878–1892

MEANWHILE Tom Browns had been streaming from the
public schools with little to offer an industrial society
beyond a capacity to play cricket or write indifferently
on classical models.[1] Many of them no longer wished to embrace
a clergyman's calling, and in a scientific world their accomplishments were poor. The slump of the 'seventies, the rise of Germany
and America to commanding positions in the world markets, the
recruitment of an executive class from other, more vocational
schools, the increasing dominance of a secular-minded working
class: all made the superfluous middle-class Tom Browns feel like
displaced persons in England.

'First rate human material was going hopelessly to waste, and
in too many cases beginning to turn sour, and faint, instead of
strengthening the national life.' So Hughes diagnosed the malaise,
estimating that 'something like half' the boys leaving public
schools were so affected. The 'spirit of our highest culture and
the spirit of our trade do not agree together. The ideas and habits
which those who have most profited by them bring away from
our public schools do not fit them to become successful traders',
he lamented.[2] Nor could these Tom Browns, by their very caste
training, find a place in the handicrafts. The Saturday Review's
verdict was that if schools did not fit their pupils for a society in
which they had to find a place, then either the schools or the
society must be at fault.[3] Hughes would not admit that there was
anything wrong with the schools, but blamed the society, which
refused to allow the Will Wimbles and Tom Browns to be
absorbed into the nation. The public-school boy needed an environment 'where what we have been calling the English public
school spirit . . . shall be recognised and prevail'.

His remedy was to create such a society for them. This society
should be based on an outdoor manly life, where, by working
with their hands, Tom Browns would find their rightful *métier*.
Such a colony, by spreading Englishmen abroad, would create

'a new feeling of loyalty to the old country ... all around the world'.[4] This scheme, a fusion of all he had ever learnt from Kingsley, from Carlyle, and indeed from Emerson, was, as he told his wife, 'the last castle in Spain I am ever likely to build'. To Lowell he wrote, 'How much my heart is in it, I can't tell you.'[5] His colony was to be a community, tightly organised to prevent the evils of modern competitive society.[6] It was to have its own store, its own common church, both set 'in the quiet comfort and repose' of an 'old-fashioned village in England'. It was not to be a money-making project, for Hughes looked 'with distrust rather than with hope on very rapid pecuniary returns'. Riches would spoil a community designed to house gentlemen and ladies, where all would 'to some extent' work with their hands, and where even the humblest would be cultured enough to meet princes. 'The English distemper', Hughes concluded, 'is a determination of blood to the head and heart, and the remedy is to carry it to the extremities.'

I

The extremities, for Hughes, were the United States of America. His earlier preference for Canada had by 1874 weakened to indifference as to whether his son stayed 'under the old flag or goes over the border'. Five years later he asserted that 'the most patriotic thing an Englishman can do just now' was to become an American. The crucial importance of Anglo-American ties was, for Hughes, emphasised by the building of the Canadian Pacific Railway, which was drawing Canada away in another direction.[7]

At this very time an ideal site presented itself on the Cumberland Plateau of Eastern Tennessee. It had been originally surveyed by a group of Boston financiers for a similar venture to alleviate an industrial depression on the Eastern seaboard. Chosen in May 1878 after four excursions covering some 20,000 miles, the site was abandoned when the American industrial depression ended and the Boston financiers lost interest in their distressed mechanics. The projector, Franklin W. Smith, thereupon brought the site to the notice of Hughes and his English coadjutors.[8] Hughes sent over John Boyle [9] (first cousin to the Earl of Glasgow, and one-time guardian to the Earl of Bute), who surveyed the country, was delighted with its timber and minerals, and told

Hughes of its potentialities as a farming centre. Peanuts, tobacco, vegetables, fruit, and grazing herds of cattle were to be conjured by Tom Browns out of a land which had hitherto supported nothing but poor whites and Negroes, who lounged among rhododendrons, azalias, and twenty-feet-high magnolias.

Boyle was an impressive figure. Gladstonian in appearance, he was generally supposed to be the original of Mr. Giles in Disraeli's *Lothair*. He and Hughes, together with Henry Kimber,[10] an English railway magnate who had much experience of similar successful settlements in Natal and New Zealand, confidently envisaged a settlement which would help join North and South.[11] All three listened most receptively to the agent of the American company, one Cyrus Clarke, of Newcastle, Pennsylvania.

So the American and English groups merged into the Board of Aid to Land Ownership, with Hughes as president. The Board's seal bore the crossed flags of both countries. But though Franklin W. Smith and the Boston office continued to figure on the Board's prospectus, the control passed more and more to the English group, who supplied £150,000 worth of capital to buy a 7,000-acre tract at the beginning of 1879. In the centre of this tract a new town called Rugby was to arise, and on an additional series of scattered lots, numbering some 33,000 additional acres (which cost the Board from 20 cents to 2 dollars an acre), farms were to be laid out. On 22 January 1879 the Board was formally incorporated under the laws of Tennessee, and Cyrus Clarke was empowered to make contracts for the erection of the town which was to rise in the wilderness. As purchasing agent for the Board, Cyrus Clarke began to busy himself bonding a further 360,000 acres for future purchases by the Board. Settlers were to be lent money at 6 per cent interest in order to buy land; boarded and taught to farm at a cost of from £60 to £70 a year; and allowed to do piece-work while they learned.[12]

2

At this point Hastings Hughes heard of his brother Tom's purchase. With a scepticism born of his own losses and a knowledge of Tom's trusting nature, he wrote to John Forbes, the great American railway magnate, who had entertained Tom so royally nine years before and taught him songs like 'Marching through

Georgia' and 'John Brown'. Forbes' reply was enough to confirm his worst suspicions: Tom had been duped. He replied to Forbes in February 1879 that he felt sure that Tom and Boyle 'do not know all the antecedents of the principal men they are dealing with': 'I fancy that psalm singing old humbug quite impressed him with his honesty'.

Hastings was not one to allow his brother to harbour an illusion too long, and promptly warned him against Clarke, and told him that he had paid too much for his land. 'Poor dear old boy,' wrote Hastings to Forbes describing the scene; 'he was evidently much cut up at being obliged to suspect anyone with whom he was having dealings of not being as trustworthy as himself.' Hastings, who always referred to Clarke as 'the Deacon', was told by both Tom and Boyle that he was 'unnecessarily suspicious' and that as checks to any jobbery the two young Boyles were to travel to the settlement to watch operations. All this made Hastings 'awfully sick', and as he was speaking to Tom he

'had a horrible vision of the Deacon summoning those two boys [i.e. the Boyles] and the rest of the infant settlement to family prayers, and after breakfast riding out to meet the man who would have the contract for that hotel, etc., and wanting to know exactly what he was to have out of the job.'

Even if the land could be made to pay for its development, there was no chance of its doing so with Clarke around. Yet if Tom and Boyle were quit of him they probably could not go on at all, 'and so I feel very low, and helpless'.

Hastings felt even lower the next day. Boyle in America had, he heard, discovered that Clarke had been cleared of alleged misdoings and that he was an intimate of Baring's agent, and therefore presumably solvent. 'The long and short of it is that both Mr. Boyle and Tom think that I am a busybody who has thrown stones at a saint.' Tom presumably still believed that Clarke was getting only a small commission on the sale of lands acquired by him and his friends 'at 2 dollars per acre (a bargain) with the view of settling distressed Boston mechanics on it', lands which they were now shy of holding as a speculation, since they had bought them only for philanthropic reasons.

'And now, God forgive me,' Hastings concluded to Forbes, 'I feel pretty sure that the man is getting about 25% commission out of the job (and contemplating further jobs) and if it is brought home to him he can turn round and say "you knew I was to have a commission".' [13]

The most that Hastings' warnings effected was to get Tom to have Tom Brassey ask his Boston agent to investigate the matter.[14] By the time, over a year later, that Hastings, now in America, had been able to confirm his worst suspicions on the spot and even the *Tribune* had publicly warned Hughes that middlemen 'are apt to gobble up the biggest share of the profits from both sides',[15] it was too late. Clarke had become the first American manager for the Board of Aid, and had convinced Hughes that he had made 'very favourable terms' for the future purchase of the colony's additional 400,000 acres. Though Clarke was soon superseded by John Boyle as manager, and though Hughes eventually ceased purchasing land from Clarke, it was not until the autumn of 1881 that Tom came to realise that the 'old psalm-singing Pennyslvanian', as he himself called him in 1884, had cheated him.

3

For a while Hughes supervised his new colony from a distance. Within a year and a half of the original purchase there were 120 settlers building in the wilderness, whom Tom showered with advice from across the Atlantic. Boyle, his representative, was to watch finances, to be sure there were accommodations when the settlers arrived, and to check up on Smith's handling of purchases and titles, building the hotel and the road to the station, and starting the store, which was, against Cyrus Clarke's advice, not to be a monopoly of the Board. Above all, money needed for buildings shouldn't be wasted on 'canyon paths', etc.[16] Then, unable any longer to resist seeing for himself what was going on, Hughes set sail for America.

Arriving in New York on the *Germanic* on 21 August 1880, accompanied by the Earl of Airlie, Lord Ogilvie, and others interested in the colony, he was met by Franklin W. Smith on behalf of the American members of the Board, and a whole host of reporters, to whom he talked freely and enthusiastically about his colony at his Fifth Avenue hotel headquarters. He came, he said, to work, not to 'blarney' around, and, after a few days in Newport, would go on to Rugby, where 300,000—400,000 acres of land were waiting for purchasers.[17] He was immediately besieged by offers of hospitality, help, and advice, from interested parties all over the country. Such diverse individuals as an Australian, an Englishman living in Kentucky, a minister from

Pittsburgh, and a man from Constantinople wrote to inquire about making their homes at Rugby. Memphis wanted Hughes to take an excursion to West Tennessee to celebrate 'the blessings of health, abundant crops and remunerative labour' there, and a semi-illiterate octogenarian from the same state offered him hospitality, though he had no 'grannite and marble Palaces' to show. Alabama and Georgia called attention to their mineral, timber, and coal resources. The retired senior clerk of the Public Record Office offered to help the colonists in New York, and someone sent two 'unusual' letters of introduction to railroad presidents. The bishop of Tennessee proffered Hughes hospitality at Sewanee; the Director of the Kentucky Geological Survey invited him to visit the Kentucky farm country, and the vice-president of the Southern Railway sent him a special car to come to Cincinnati on 7 September. Among his mail there was even an offer by an American publisher, Harper's, to pay him royalties in America, which perhaps somewhat mollified his feelings about 'the unblushing way in which we poor devils are used by those sons of Mammon'. Among all these enthusiastic attentions two warnings—one from a Vermonter who said 'English well-to-do farmers find it not very easy to conform to American circumstances', and the other from a Tennesseean, who claimed Hughes couldn't get half what he had paid for his land, which was too thin to support any but a few poor, isolated, ill-educated mountaineers—passed, one imagines, unnoticed.[18]

Ignoring for the moment dozens of request from near and far to visit and speak, Hughes made directly for Tennessee at the end of August, in a state of benign satisfaction. The Cincinnati Southern Railway, on which he travelled south from Cincinnati, seemed to him a triumph of *l'audace* since its construction involved, because of the nature of the country, tremendous engineering feats. Such boldness, characteristic of the time and country, would, however, be justified: coal-mines were opening all the way to Chattanooga, tobacco was looking for a market, and fruit was waiting to be grown. The Negroes met on the trip all seemed to Hughes fun-loving and kindly, and, despite what he had heard about the Ku Klux Klan, were apparently on good terms with the whites. Hughes' reception committee at the station for Rugby was just the sort of thing he had been looking forward to: five Englishmen, all public-school men from Rugby, Eton,

Harrow, and Wellington, decked in boots, broad straw or battered felt hats, and flannel shirts of all colours.

4

Hughes found Rugby laid out and the hotel—called the Tabard as it supposedly had banisters from Chaucer's original Tabard Inn —built, but not furnished. Everyone was crowded into one cottage, including two ladies, but Hughes enjoyed 'roughing it'; and there was afternoon tea to make him feel immediately at home. Sitting on the verandah, he gushed in frank romantic vein:

'Above, the vault is blue beyond all description, and studded with stars as bright as though they were all Venuses. The katydids are making delightful music in the trees, and the summer lightning is playing over the Western heaven; while a gentle breeze, cool and refreshing as if it came straight off a Western sea, is just lifting, every now and then, the corner of my paper. Were I young again,—but as I am not likely to be that, I refrain from bootless castle-building and turn in in this "enchanted solitude".' [19]

During the following days—he was in Rugby off and on somewhat over a month—Hughes had much chance for observation, and his reactions were almost universally favourable. True, there was much moon-shining, and the natives, who tended to be dirty and addicted to violence, seemed to prefer hunting and loafing to dollars. But they were actually very likeable, and could be educated, particularly the Negroes, who, never mean or depraved, wanted to educate themselves, and were more patient, obedient, and less interested in hunting than the whites. There was also, perhaps, too relaxed an atmosphere in the colony, too much blacking of boots and emphasis on good food. But men needed a place and time for being slack, and Hughes was charmed by the merry young people going by in free-and-easy clothes on this 'last frontier for loafing', while their parents sat in rockers on the verandahs and looked at the view. Since houses couldn't be built until titles were perfected, there was nothing wrong in making a tennis-court first. Hughes enjoyed the tennis—the story is that he named Rugby while watching a match—and encouraged shooting and swimming as well. There were, he felt, plenty of ambitious colonists to make a success of the place when given a chance, including a prominent horseman who planned to breed fine steeds, an Englishman home on pension from India who

planned to raise tea and coffee as in the Himalayas, and Hughes'
favourite settler, Amos Hill, the 'Forester', who had started an
English garden to prove that with hard work one could grow
water-melons, cantaloupes, tomatoes, lima beans, cabbages,
sweet potatoes, beets, and squash. Arrested for poaching in
England, Hill had come to the United States thirty years previously, and had distinguished himself in Hughes' eyes by preaching to the rebels against swearing when he had been a war
prisoner, and by refusing to fire a shot even when exposed to great
danger. Loving the United States, he planned to buy a place in
Rugby, to be called Newnham Paddocks, after the estate where
he had been a stable-boy. Such men, Hughes felt, deserved to
have such as himself black their boots rather than the reverse.[20]

5

If Hughes had any moments of doubt or fears that his swans—
'visions, already so bright, of splendid crops, and simple life, to
be raised and lived in this fairyland' [21]—might prove geese, they
were dissipated by the great ceremonial opening of Rugby on 5
October.

They foregathered on the day before. Over eighty guests from
North and South braved a downpour of rain to attend. The
Mayor of Chattanooga, citizens of Knoxville, and Bishop Quin-
tard of Tennessee came by morning train. Hughes wrote:

'If they had all been Englishmen on a pleasure-trip, they could not have taken
the downpour more cheerily. . . . They dined and chatted and smoked in
the verandah, and then trotted off in *gum* coats to look around at the walks,
gardens, streets, and cots, escorted by "the boys".'

Another party, delayed by the breakdown of a freight train,
arrived an hour before midnight, singing 'John Brown's Body'—
'a set of as stalwart good fellows as ever sang a chorus or ate a
beef-steak at midnight'.

On the opening day the Bishop held a service at eleven in the
morning. The congregation sang 'Jerusalem the Golden', with
two psalms: 'Lord who shall dwell in thy tabernacle' and 'Except
the Lord build the house'. After the service they dispersed to
various parts of the settlement, some to fish, others to the tennis-
ground 'to see some set played which would have done no dis-
credit to Wimbledon'.

Hughes himself made a characteristic speech, pointing out that this was 'a swarming time of the race, a time of great movements of population, which no human power can check, which may either be left to work themselves out by rule of thumb, or ordered and directed from the first on distinct principles'.[22]

Eleven days later, J. W. Harper described it as the initiation of Britain's second period of colonisation in America.

A day or so after the opening Hughes left Rugby for Cincinnati, Toronto, Chicago, Boston, Philadelphia, and New York. He had already during his stay at Rugby visited Chattanooga and Knoxville, attended by a committee that called for him on a special train, and had twice spoken in Cincinnati: once at the opening of the Cincinnati Exposition on 9 September, and once on Sunday 3 October, at Pike's Hall, before 1,110 members of the Young Men's Mercantile Library. Though Hughes did not approve of Sunday lecturing, he had not been able to resist the invitation of the Rev. Charles W. Wendte to speak to such a large audience in the 'wickedest city on the American continent', a city whose Sunday—'the most depraved that our country can show'—found 5,000 brothels and saloons and no churches open.[23] After leaving Rugby he journeyed to Chicago, where he was given an 'elegant' dinner by the Literary Club on 8 October at the Grand Pacific Hotel and stayed under the 'semi-English' roof of the Rev. Brook Hereford. On 22 October he received an LL.D. from Haverford College and spoke informally—the *Tribune* reported that he 'leisurely lolled upon the reading-desk'—on Dr. Arnold. In New York, where he spent his last ten days, Hughes spoke twice at Cooper Union—on 1 November before the Farmer's Club on Rugby, and 5 November before working men on co-operation—and was entertained at a reception at the University Club on 8 October and at a big dinner at the Lotus Club on 30 October. Whitelaw Reid had invited 120 people, including, as he told Hughes, 'some people worth seeing', to the Lotus Club dinner, thus giving Hughes an opportunity to talk about his colony where it would do the most good. Hughes availed himself of the opportunity at great length, and received a rousing welcome from, among others, Reid, Hewitt, and Chauncy Depew, who said that he represented more of the 'superiority of manhood over birth than any Englishman we have ever had among us'.[24] On 7 November Hughes was on the *Germanic* en route for England, leaving his colony to be run by John Boyle with help from Cyrus Clarke, Franklin Smith, Amos Hill, and Hastings Hughes, who had Tom's power of attorney.

While Tom was still in America he showered Hastings with letters of advice and encouragement. Finances were admittedly shaky, and Hastings must keep spending down and make no rash promises to anyone. Indeed, company funds were temporarily exhausted, so that unless money was made by sales or new subscriptions to the stock, Hughes would personally have to meet the notes on the last advances with cash secured in New York. Yet the future held indefinite promise if the next decisive year could be successfully negotiated. Both the land and the shares of the Company would, with a little care, be a good investment, and Hughes showed his confidence by buying five lots himself. All was coming out 'far better than I had ever hoped', he wrote jubilantly to Lord Ripon from the boat that was carrying him back to England: he could 'scarcely have picked better men' for colonists 'had I had the choice', and the store was already making 2000 dollars a month.[25]

6

All through the winter and spring Hughes was busy sending colonists to Hastings and propagandising for his settlement through speeches at the Working Men's College and elsewhere. In April 1881 Macmillan brought out his *Rugby, Tennessee* (giving Hughes all the profits but a 'modest percentage to pay costs out of pocket', in order that he might use the money for 'needed public buildings and improvements at Rugby'), which told the public in detail what they would find at Rugby. If a boy brought to the colony, Hughes informed his readers, a few clothes, a gun, a fishing-rod, fifteen pounds, a little intelligence, and a willingness to work hard with his hands, he could easily get along and earn a livelihood by his own efforts. The colony, with its cultivated society, its library, and other places of recreation and study, would take care of his leisure moments.[26]

In the meantime the Board of Aid had issued a pamphlet in America describing the colony.[27] Much publicity had been coming from other sources: from *Harper's Weekly*, which ran three articles on Rugby; from the *Spectator*, the *Saturday Review*, *The*

Times, the *New York Tribune*, and other magazines and news-papers. Not all of this publicity was favourable. *Harper's* found that 'life-long residents' of northern Tennessee were surprised 'at this attempt to redeem these low-priced mountain lands, from every foot of which the timber must be cleared, and which set at defiance all preconceived notions in favour of bottom-lands', and thought that there were 'still . . . many arguments' in favour of Iowa—where there was already an English colony—and Colorado, 'which offer ready-cleared lands'. The *Saturday Review* had the same doubts, adding that there seemed little reason to think that boys who couldn't make good in England would do so in Tennessee, especially if Hughes kept deprecating the idea of making profits. But even the *Saturday Review* recommended the colony. Other organs of opinion were all similarly enthusiastic about the beauty of the location, the climate, and the possibilities for development that Hughes' infectious idealism might turn into realities. Neither *The Times* nor the *Spectator*, incidentally, thought the colony could remain distinctively English if it were to succeed; nor did it need to, since the 'world is to belong to the "Anglo-Saxons" '.[28] As a consequence of all this publicity, a steamship company advertised through rates via Liverpool and Philadelphia to Rugby, and eventually—though the colony never had more than 300 residents at a time—over 1,000 settlers found their way to Tennessee.

7

For nearly a year after Hughes' visit the prospects of the colony seemed to justify all the public enthusiasm. By the spring of 1881 the hotel was running as a first-class establishment and drawing such visitors as Charles A. Dana, who wrote to Hughes for accom-modations for his daughter and children. The commissary, started in October, netted 900 dollars in its first three months, though the original rude log store, costing 3,000 dollars, had to be replaced in 1881. Christ Church, with its stained glass, its altar hangings embroidered in a convent in England, and its imported organ, was finished or nearly finished. There was a 2,000-dollar library of 7,000 books contributed by thirty-eight publishers and public societies (Chicago, for whom Hughes had done so much, did not contribute) and shipped free by the Pennsylvania Railroad. The road from Rugby to the railroad station at Sedgemoor, later called Rugby Road, was being built at a cost of 30,000 dollars; a saw-mill and brick-kiln had been erected; and there were tennis and other sports, a dramatic club, and, beginning in January 1881, a monthly magazine called *The Rugbeian*.[29]

In November 1880 a writer for *Harper's* had given a very cheery picture of the colony. He found there a forty-five-year-old school teacher, his rosy-cheeked wife, and seven boys, 'veritable Tom Browns everyone', who were happy to have escaped from unemployment and high rent; a young aristocrat 'making bread in the washbowl from an entirely original recipe, in which flour, baking-powder, and saleratus entered as equal components'; and a 'strange medley' of the 'luxurious' and 'indispensable' among an earnest crew of young men about to depart, axe in hand, 'to seek the vitals of the monarchs of the forest'.[30] *The Rugbeian*, which started as a rather pretentious literary magazine, somewhat given to long essays and sermons, was equally satisfied with the spirit of the place at Christmas: the settlers had already shown that Rugby was nearer to their hearts than their own success, thus proving 'themselves to belong to good old stock which has taken in hand the best part of this little planet'. The contented note continued to sound through the spring, especially when, in May, Hughes' eighty-four-year-old mother—the 'graceful realisation of the ideal of an old English lady', as the *Tribune* called her [31]—arrived to spend the last years of her life in a home, Uffington House, that she was to have built for her at Rugby. The coming of summer brought a final burst of confidence: Rugby was now a town, and *The Rugbeian*, transformed into a weekly, reported that the inhabitants celebrated the 4 July standing proudly 'shoulder to shoulder'.

8

There had, however, already been ominous warnings that all was not well. Complaints that no one worked and that landsharks had cheated the colonists were frequent. Magazines and newspapers began to print disparaging stories, one of which asserted that the colony was a failure and was moving to Minnesota. By midsummer the complaints had grown to a swelling chorus of accusations against the Board for allegedly unloading inferior land on the colonists at great profit. The *Cincinnati Commercial* circulated a rumour that the colony was in decay as a result of restrictions imposed by the management, and that Hughes had deserted. The 'cattle king of Allegheny county' gave it as his opinion that 'someone ought to lock up Tom Hughes before he does any more mischief'. No wonder Tom wrote in consternation to Lord Ripon on 14 July that affairs in his American settlement were 'all going wrong'.[32]

Worse was to follow. On 20 August typhoid broke out as a result of 100 days of drought, killed seventeen people, stopped land sales, and ended any hope of turning Rugby into a popular summer resort. Only more money and a change of management —the end of 'Lord God Almighty' Boyle's unpopular reign— could save the colony, *The Rugbeian* asserted desperately by the autumn:

> 'Everything that mismanagement and incapacity could do to kill the place has been tried with a laudable persistency worthy of a better cause, and the Board of Aid Office has long been a byword for snobbish incivility.'

But it was already too late. In January 1882 the Board admitted that they were at the end of their rope: they had not counted the cost, and now there was no money to carry on. On 21 January *The Rugbeian* wrote a bitter epitaph on the colony's first year and a half of existence:

> 'Rugby's start, course, and failure, so far as its good will and "shoulder to shoulder" principles, once so belauded, are concerned, will now be an interesting study for the psychologist, and further, serve to point a moral, if it should fail to adorn a tale. Truly a very ridiculous mouse have these Cumberland mountains brought forth.'[33]

In assessing the causes of the disaster in February, *The Rugbeian* repeated its accusations against the Board of Aid and its Rugby manager, Boyle, whose policy 'has brought Rugby so low', and urged Hughes, who was too much in England and too English to know American conditions, to get an American as manager: the colony, it said, 'had been simply strangled by . . . want of tact, of business insight, and *appreciation of the spirit of the country we are living in*'.[34] There seems little reason to dispute these charges. The Board, which meant either the snobbish, punctilious, and dictatorial Boyle or men 3,000 miles away and unfamiliar with American conditions, ran things as it pleased, and did it badly. On the one hand, it permitted the colony too little self-government; on the other, it supervised the idle insufficiently. Hughes' cherished combination of organisation and freedom became in practice autocracy and licence. The Board had certainly paid too much for the land it had bought—almost three times the value of the surrounding land—and, what was worse, did not often have clear titles. Overlapping claims brought frequent injunctions—there were fifty-two out against the settlers at one time—and the inhabitants, without deeds, were in a panic. Even Hughes admitted laconically later on that the Board had had 'defective information supplied them at the outset'.[35] Clarke was not the only scoundrel: one such told Hastings Hughes he was a brother-in-law of Lord Cholmondeley, but gave himself away by pronouncing it as written, instead of 'Chumly'. Further, the Board had grossly over-estimated the productivity of the land and the usefulness of mineral deposits and timber. Behind all these difficulties, however, lay a more basic one: the calibre of the settlers attracted to Rugby.

As Colonel Killebrew, Tennessee Minister of Agriculture, whose report Hughes appended to his book, made abundantly clear, these Tennessee mountains could only be turned into a productive farming, grazing, and manufacturing centre by the hardest kind of work. And Tom Hughes, with his quixotic belief that materialism, selfish individualism, and the psychology of the market-place could best be overcome in post-Civil-War America by upper-class English boys fed on the husks of Arnoldian idealism, did not attract to his colony those willing to contribute such efforts. 'It was a very common idea in the early days', said the *Plateau Gazette*—one of the successors to *The Rugbeian*—in 1884, 'that the Rugby colony was a "society" or a "Brotherhood"', entry to which could be obtained only by pronouncing some 'shibboleth'.[36] That 'shibboleth' seemed best known to upper-class ne'er-do-wells, younger sons who had taken to drink and whose family thought the 'teetotal' colony would reform them. Young Willie Hughes gave a graphic picture of one of these Englishmen in San Antonio in 1884: he

'belongs to a titled family, and I think his name is in the blue-book. He hasn't a cent, and won't work, but just gets what he can out of everyone. . . . He has a most gentlemanly face, but his light London suit is beginning to look shabby, and matches the dirty white shirt with no tie or collar very well. He got into a scrape in England, I suppose, and got kicked out'. [37]

CHRIST CHURCH, RUGBY, TENNESSEE

THOMAS HUGHES PUBLIC LIBRARY, RUGBY, TENNESSEE

Whether such boys were remittance men (with allowances from home) or had no money at all, they neither could, nor wanted to be farmers. They enjoyed the Rugby life with its dramatic performances, tennis, archery, football, baseball, Isthmian games, horseback-riding, and jolly walks in beautiful parks among pet deer. They even liked to grumble and write to the papers. But not work. The Rugby library was full of little-read farm manuals. And most of them didn't care whether the colony throve or not: as one Rugbeian wrote, the colony did not fail: it never had any vitality. Tom Hughes' son George, when he visited the place later on, found a 'community full of an ideal and empty of real wanting to be there and do something'; the settlers talked much of being Tom Browns, but had as little knowledge of what it meant as did 'the business men who unloaded the scenery at a profit'. The only *esprit de corps* that these 'dukes incognito', these 'lords in mufti', possessed, was class consciousness. They despised the natives, with whose methods they would have to cope if they were to succeed, for being different and for prizing freedom above the wages of tenantry, and they liked their Yankee associates little better. Always English, the 'House' meant to them the English Parliament, and prices remained in shillings and pence.[38]

The *Plateau Gazette's* ironic picture of the community, written two years after the disaster, sums up the situation with graphic finality:

'For a long time the poor colonists endured the torments of hades. They are Englishmen of culture and refinement, and at one period their supply of Worcester sauce became exhausted and their agonies were terrible to witness. But even this disaster was followed by a greater. This was the failure of London *Punch* to arrive on time, and it was, indeed, a gloomy outlook for the struggling colonists, particularly as one of the ladies of the party, nearly related to the nobility, was bitten on the back of the neck by a mosquito. Then, again, the country was not favourable for the playing of lawn tennis. This, of course, had a most depressing effect on the pioneers in culture, high art and mutton chop whiskers.

'It was also discovered that the quail were not tame enough to be shot on the ground. All this was, of course, discouraging to sportsmen not accustomed to shooting them on the wing, and strong men in English shooting jackets wept at the heartless refusal of the vivacious quails to remain on the ground long enough to be shot in good old English fashion. The plum pudding and oil gave out early in the summer. The settlement was six miles distant from the nearest saloon, and when they reached it they were obliged to listen to the shrill voice of Tennessee farmers, who absolutely refused to drop a single "haitch".' [39]

9

Tom Hughes was heartbroken at the turn of events. As early as September 1881 he foresaw the worst, and felt both alarm and guilt.

'It was a rash undertaking at my age,' he told Lord Ripon, 'but as you know I am hot-headed more or less and the thing seized on me mightily. . . . I have risked in it more than I should have done (but that again is my temper) and have sorely repented it, though my dear brave wife like herself, though the whole thing was against her wish, has entirely pardoned it.' [40]

When the crash came in January 1882 he reached the nadir of his existence. His financial losses were so heavy that he had to rent his London home and ship his youngest son George to America without the help his other children had received. Sir Henry Kimber reports that he passed 'through a period of intense suffering', and his son speaks of him as a 'man busier and more alive than most' living in 'the hell of depression'.[41]

10

But he rallied manfully. When his 'heart was in anything' he did not, as he told Lord Ripon, count the cost, and he was still ready to throw future earnings into his colony.[42] Fortunately—or unfortunately—he found friends like Goldwin Smith, Lord Ripon, and Sir Henry Kimber willing to help save his reputation and his dream. Kimber, deciding when he visited Rugby that people had simply 'lost their nerve and consequently their judgement', and that things weren't so bad, went out and raised 275,000 dollars. Lord Ripon personally contributed £1,000, and in the spring of 1882 the colony was put back on its shaky feet. On 4 May, Robert Walton, an American, was installed as manager. Boyle and Clarke disappeared from the scene, though the latter apparently stayed on in Rugby for some years, and was eventually killed 'when his team of little cream coloured mules ran away down a steep mountain road and he was thrown from the buggy'.[43]

For a time it appeared that the situation could be saved. The summer of 1882 was a good one, and the colonists took heart, feeling that they were on probation. Though there was a great need for new recruits, the settlers were determined to have no more Will Wimbles, but workers who would clear the land and who would become American citizens. Any impression that Rugby was still a brotherhood, requiring of those who wished to come there 'some application, differing from that of other communities in America', was, declared the *Plateau Gazette*, false. 'We emphasise as strongly as possible that Rugby, with Chicago, Cincinnati, New York or elsewhere, is open to all, the "Almighty Dollar", and the "trade dollar" with a small discount being the only Shibboleth we have.'[44] In 1883 and 1884 the colonists, confident that the Board saw 'difficulties and objects very differently' and that the town was convalescent, began to show signs of renewed vigour. *The Rugbeian*, which had stopped publication in October 1882, was revived as the *Plateau Gazette* in July 1883 (and again, after lapsing from June to August, as the *Rugby Gazette and East Tennessee News* in the autumn of 1884). Several manufactures were started, a canning plant and the Rugby Brick Tile and Terra Cotta Works; and in January 1885 the Arnold School was opened with six pupils, featuring science, languages, mathematics, and philosophy, and cultivating manliness 'and an interest in the purity of the moral atmosphere of the school, as even better than knowledge'.[45]

Tom Hughes' spirits revived almost immediately. He was perhaps more cautious in 1884 than he had been in 1881 in advising young men how to try their fortunes in America. His nephew, he wrote in the introduction to *Gone to Texas*,[46] had learned through 'contact with the hard facts of brush and prairie farming' that life in Texas was more difficult than he had imagined: he couldn't, as he had hoped, simply import English sheep and immediately 'teach the natives how to do their business better'. A boy coming to America must not allow the 'cheery tone of glowing circulars' to blind him to the facts. If he came looking for fleshpots, he would only add 'one more to the long roll of young Englishmen who drift away to the gambling and drinking saloons, which unhappily are to be found in abundance on the outskirts of civilisation in every new country under the sun'.[47] But Hughes' old confidence in his colony had returned.

'You will I know rejoice to hear', he told Lowell in 1884, 'that we are getting to the end of the cloud of rascally law suits which the old psalm singing Pennsylvanian who managed the land buying and laying out at Rugby left us as a legacy when we turned him off nearly three years ago. . . . I expect we shall beat the lands sharks all along the line, though by the time we are through the land will have cost about treble its nominal price.' [48]

During the next three years Hughes continued to warn prospective emigrants of ticket scalpers, of 'hiring out' as against buying, of the temptations to drink and the need to work, and of the difficulties to be expected in a country where the ranches were all owned by the rich and where it took six years to develop orange-groves and three or four to make vineyards pay.[49] All through the 'eighties Hughes held on to his lands; and he invested in the canning company stock in 1882 and in that of the pottery company—fifty shares—in 1885. Every year from 1883 to 1887, when his mother died, he visited America solely to see her and his colony. In 1884 he managed also to get to Mexico to see his son Jim, and his letters to his doubting wife at home convey much the same sanguine enthusiasm as do those written before the disaster.

II

On most of his trips we catch mere glimpses of Hughes: in 1883 at the New York Stock Exchange telling the brokers how he thought 'prosperous bulls' meant Englishmen, and in 1885 at Association Hall, New York, where he came with Hewitt, with whom he was staying, to lecture on Lowell.[50] But the 1886 jaunt we have in detail. He sailed on the *Aurania* on 12 August, the same boat that 'our dear Matt' had travelled on. Oliver Wendell Holmes was aboard, and Hughes spoke of him as tottering to his chair, from which he made a speech and read a poem. In good spirits, Hughes tried his hand after many years at a piece of fiction suggested by a gambling altercation on the *Servia* the previous year. His chief difficulty with his 'Steamboat farce' was to get some love interest into a tale of gamblers who accused a reformed gambler of smuggling, and to 'make virtue triumphant'. In New York he was shocked by an indecent song, which in his day would have caused the women, he said, if not the men, to walk out. He would have liked to visit Forbes and to go to the Saturday Club in Boston, now that Lowell and Holmes were back, as it was 'the best thing in America so far as I have seen'. But since he wanted to sail on 25 September, he had time only for Rugby.[51]

Arriving there on 1 September fresh from reading *Vanity Fair*, which he had not read since he and his wife pored over it together on their honeymoon, and which he now found a 'terrible book', he was greeted with the troubles of his mother (who found Tom's yearly visits anything but adequate) over her hens and fruit-trees. But soon he was happily reading George Herbert, 'dear quaint deep old dear', listening to a church service without ritualism, deploring Moody & Sankey hymns, and contemplating the Englishmen who peopled Rugby: the Dyers and Marshalls; scapegraces like young Mytton, who hoped to make good; Milman, the nobleman's valet who was now a farmer; and Dr. Kemp, whom he liked as he did all enthusiasts, though this particular enthusiast also had patience and thoroughness, and was a genius at growing grapes. He found Rugby peaceful and prosperous: the new hotel was being built, the vineyard experiments were prospering, and a new man was starting a poultry-farm.

He was even rewarded by a visit from his son George (Plump), to whom he had not said a word about coming, badly as he had wanted to see him. Tom promised not to 'influence Plump to his disadvantage to come and fix himself here', both because George had earned the right to decide for himself and because, Tom knew, Fanny was against the idea.

'But this I think I have a right, indeed a duty to do—I shall take him round and show him my several plots here, all of which are in capital order now, including the vineyard which has done splendidly, and the Commissary (or big shop) which pays me regularly 6% on the outlay.'

He would offer George the management or ownership up to £1,000. George could not do better, Tom felt, than settle at Rugby. 'Up to this year I should have had great doubts but now I have none at all.' [52]

George seems to have had a good deal of his mother in him. The next day he 'arrived by the hack, unshaven, red eyed and gaunt, but as hard as nails and in excellent condition and spirits'. He sat on the verandah and read the *Spectator*, talked volubly and occasionally eloquently, looked over the situation shrewdly, and then decided firmly, as had Hastings' son Willie a few years before, that he would have none of it. [53] Tom Hughes took this rebuff in characteristic fashion. If his son preferred being a cattle-man in Texas, that was all right with Tom, and though he warned him—with rather poor grace—not to try to handle too much land, he sent him in the next few years yearly 3,000 dollars to pay off mortgages on a farm and grazing land George had bought with Tyrone Power and two other men.

'I am very glad', Tom told Lowell, 'he went in bravely for the healthy new life on the soil instead of pining and half starving in a profession—into trade as at present conducted on both sides of the water I wouldn't let a son or any boy go if I could help it.' [54]

12

George's decision was certainly the right one. For, despite appearances, Rugby never really revived. The basic difficulties of the poverty of the land, which could never supply the eighty-acre holdings with enough feed to raise cattle successfully, and the inadaptability of the settlers remained. Moreover, transportation rates were too high, markets too far, and access to the railroad limited by absence of a rail spur or even an all-weather road. The effort to get new settlers on the land failed. 'Nobody will now believe, no matter who certifies to the contrary,' said the *Rugbeian* prophetically in August 1882, 'that Rugby is anything but a disastrous failure.' The bad publicity that the American papers, and even more the English ones, continued to give the colony made it impossible to reverse public opinion. The Board even tried, without success, to import French Canadian and German peasants. Of 106 land sales made during the first six years, seventy-four were in the first two: the majority being sales of town sites, not of farms. With each transaction the price dropped: in 1883 forty dollars was asked for land that had once brought seventy-five dollars. The manufacturing plants, carried on by inexperienced men, fared even worse than did the farms. Since there were never enough tomatoes to can, all that was ever produced by the canning factory were the labels. Finally, the renewed effort to make Rugby a summer resort ended when the New Tabard Inn, built in 1887 to replace the original Tabard that had burned down in 1886, also burned to the ground without insurance.[55]

13

Though the farmers struggled along for a time in a half-hearted way, in 1891 the inevitable happened. The settlement collapsed, and the Board of Aid sold its holdings to the Rugby Tenn. Co.

Ltd. of England. An American company—the Rugby Land Co. —took over in 1899, and in 1920 the land was sold to a Cincinnati capitalist. Today there are still a few houses of the old settlement in Rugby (especially Mrs. Hughes' Uffington House, the church, and the Lindens, where the last manager's descendants live), nestling in forsaken beauty among almost deserted English parklands, which are threatened by the encroachments of a lumber company that bought much of the land from the Cincinnatian's heirs.

Tom Hughes was spared at least this last threatened commercialism of his dream. But he lived long enough to see the Board of Aid transfer the Rugby property to the 'New Company', which meant the end of the Rugby experiment. In 1892 he sold his own 'several plots', dividing the money realised on the transaction with Dr. Blacklock of the Arnold School and Robert Walton, who had, as he said, done all the work on them. To the very last, however, he remained sanguine, regretting only that he would never again get to Rugby, the visits to which had been the 'greenest spots' of his life. The hard life, he wrote the remaining Rugbeians, would ultimately be a blessing. 'Good seed was sown when Rugby was founded and . . . some day the reapers, whoever they may be . . . will come along with joy bearing heavy sheaves with them.' Though he himself was nearing 'the psalmist's limit of three score and ten', and would never live to see it, some day a 'righteous and prosperous colony' would rise 'in those fascinating mountains'.[56]

NOTES

[1] As G. M. Young says, 'The great Victorian omission had to be made good, and the executive class educated up to the level of the demands now making on it in a trained and scientific world', *Victorian England* (Oxford, 1937), 164–165.

[2] T. Hughes, *Rugby, Tennessee*, 3, 6, 7, 12.

[3] *Saturday Review*, 10 Sept. 1881, 352.

[4] T. Hughes (ed.), *G.T.T. Gone to Texas* (London, 1884), xi.

[5] Brown, *True Manliness*, xxi; Hughes, *Vacation Rambles*, 193.

[6] He was anxious not to give his listeners the idea that he sympathised with the State Socialism of Karl Marx, with which he had 'no sympathy whatever'. 'We have no vision whatever to realise of a paternal state, the owner of all property, finding easy employment and liberal maintenance for all citizens,

reserving all profits for the community, and paying no dividends to individuals . . . . We are content with the laws relating to private property and family life as we find them.' He told his brother Hastings: 'Above all things my dear fellow don't shock people, keep to beaten ruts and commonplaces—we can build up a community such as we want to see far more surely by showing everyone that we are ajog trot every day folks, who want to go on just as like their neighbours as possible consistently with their co-operative ideas, which they don't want to force on unwilling folks but just to let grow quietly'; letter, Hughes to Hastings Hughes, 15 Nov. 1880, in Rugby Papers.

[7] Lowell Papers at Harvard, letter, Hughes to Lowell, 17 May 1874; Hughes (ed.), *G.T.T. Gone to Texas*, Preface; T. Hughes, *Rugby, Tennessee*, 117–119.

[8] *New York Tribune*, 5 Nov. 1880.

[9] See L. H. Dorehill, *Rugby Advertiser*, 26 Oct. 1923.

[10] Henry Kimber (1834–1923) was a member of parliament, vice-chairman of the Capital and Counties Bank, chairman of the Colonist Land and Loan Corporation, chairman of the International Financial Society, and chairman of the South Indian Railway. He owned a settlement in Natal, where two of his sons lived, and dispatched many emigrants from his own constituency of Wandsworth (which he represented from 1885 to 1913) to the Manchester Block Settlement in New Zealand, which covered 106,000 acres, and returned all the promoters' capital with interest.

[11] Hughes wanted to 'show respect and good will for a people of English blood who fought through one of the gallantest fights of all history, against overwhelming odds, though for a bad cause', Hughes, *Rugby, Tennessee*, 119.

[12] For detail on the Rugby settlement see M. B. Hamer, 'Thomas Hughes and his American Rugby', *North Carolina Historical Review*, v (1928), 391–413; 'The Correspondence of Thomas Hughes concerning his Tennessee Rugby', *North Carolina Historical Review*, xxi (1944), 203–214; W. H. G. Armytage, 'New Light on the English Background of Tom Hughes' Rugby Colony in Tennessee', *East Tennessee Historical Society's Publications*, xxi (1949), 69–84; 'Public School Paradise', *Queen's Quarterly*, (Kingston, 1951), lvii, 530–536.

[13] Letters, Hastings Hughes to Forbes, 12, 13, 14 Feb. 1879, in Rugby Papers.

[14] Letter, Hughes to Thomas Brassey, 5 March 1879, in Berg Collection of New York Public Library.

[15] *New York Tribune*, 2 Aug. 1880.

[16] Letters, Hughes to Boyle, 19 April, 26 May 1880; Hughes to Smith, 18, 21, 22 June 1880, in Rugby Papers.

[17] *New York Tribune*, 22, 23 Aug. 1880.

[18] Letters in Rugby Papers; Lowell Papers at Harvard, letter, Hughes to Lowell, 3 Jan. 1870.

[19] Hughes, *Vacation Rambles*, 186; letters in Rugby Papers.

[20] *The Times*, 6 Dec. 1889; Hughes, *Rugby, Tennessee*, 130; Hughes, *Vacation Rambles*, 187 ff.

[21] Hughes, *Rugby, Tennessee*, 193.

[22] Hughes, *Vacation Rambles*, 222–228; Hughes, *Rugby, Tennessee*, 92–94.

[23] *New York Tribune*, 12 Sept. 10 Oct. 1880; *Harper's Weekly*, 6 Nov. 1880, 709; letters in Rugby Papers.

[24] *New York Tribune*, 9, 23, 29 and 31 Oct. 1880; letters in Rugby Papers.

[25] Letters in Rugby Papers, 7, 12, 15 Oct. 1880; Ripon Papers in British Museum, Add. MSS. 43,531, letter, Hughes to Ripon, 14 Nov. 1880.

[26] Hughes, *Rugby, Tennessee*, 10 ff.; *The Times*, 6 Dec. 1880, 8; letter, Hughes to George Macmillan or George Grove, 12 April 1881, in possession of Macmillan and Co.; letters in Rugby Papers, 12, 18, 23 Dec. 1880; 4, 29 Jan. 1881, 21 March 1881, 5, 17 April 1881, 19 May 1881.

[27] *Rugby, Morgan County Tennessee, Settlement* (Cincinnati, 1880).

[28] *Harper's Weekly*, 16 Oct. 1880, 709; *Saturday Review*, 11 Dec. 1880, 729; *New York Tribune*, 2 Aug., 5 Nov. 1880; *The Times*, 14 Sept. 1880; *Spectator*, 30 Oct. 1880, 1374.

[29] Letter, Dana to Hughes, in Rugby Papers; *The Landmark*, Nov. 1932, 'Thomas Hughes in America', by Mary Blake Ringold.

[30] *Harper's Weekly*, 16 Nov. 1880, 709.

[31] *New York Tribune*, 25 May 1881.

[32] Ripon Papers in the British Museum, Add. MSS. 43,531, letter, Hughes to Ripon, 14 July 1881.

[33] *The Rugbeian*, 21, 28 Jan. 1882.

[34] *The Rugbeian*, 25 Feb. 1882.

[35] *Rugby Gazette*, 20 Sept. 1884.

[36] *Plateau Gazette*, 10 Jan. 1884.

[37] Hughes, (Ed.), *G.T.T. Gone to Texas*, 88.

[38] *North Carolina Historical Review*, v, 407–409; letter, George Hughes to Robert Walton, 8 March 1926, in Rugby Papers.

[39] *Plateau Gazette*, 13 Oct. 1883.

[40] Ripon Papers in the British Museum, Add. MSS. 43,531, letter, Hughes to Ripon, 14 Sept. 1881.

[41] *Rugby Gazette*, 27 Sept. 1884; letter, George Hughes to Walton, 8 March 1926, in Rugby Papers.

[42] Letter, 12 Dec. 1881, Ripon to Hughes in Hughes Papers.

[43] Letter, Mrs. Robert Walton to Edward C. Mack, 8 Nov. 1946; *Rugby Gazette*, 27 Sept. 1884.

[44] *The Rugbeian*, 15, 24 July, 29 July, 5 Aug. 1882; *Plateau Gazette*, 10 Jan. 1884.

[45] *Rugby Gazette*, 20 Dec. 1884.

[46] To be more accurate, he 'recast' the manuscript of Hastings' introduction in his 'own name and way'. For Hastings had the original idea to publish his own son's letters in England to encourage English boys just about to leave school. No names were to be mentioned. Then Tom took them 'under his wing', added names and statistics, and made a book which he hoped might sell both in England and America. Letters, Hastings Hughes to George Macmillan, 29 March, 1884; Tom Hughes to George Macmillan, 29 Jan., 3 March 1884.

[47] *G.T.T. Gone to Texas*, ix, xiii.

[48] Lowell Papers at Harvard, letter Hughes to Lowell, 29 June 1884.

[49] Hughes, *Vacation Rambles*, 233, 248–249.

[50] *New York Tribune*, 7 Sept. 1883, 8, 30 Sept. 1885, 5.

[51] Letters, Hughes to Fanny Hughes, 12, 14, 20 Aug., 7, 11 Sept. 1886.

[52] Letters, Hughes to Fanny Hughes, 1, 3, 4, 6, 11, 14, 16 Sept. 1886; letter, Margaret Hughes to Walton, June 1883, in Rugby Papers.

[53] Hughes, *G.T.T. Gone to Texas*, 131; letter, Hughes to Fanny Hughes, 19 Sept. 1886.

[54] Letter, Hughes to George Hughes, 23 April 1888; Lowell Papers at Harvard, letter, Hughes to Lowell, 26 Dec. 1889.

[55] *North Carolina Historical Review*, v, 404; Miller, Ernest I., *The English Settlement at Rugby, Tennessee* (Knoxville, Tennessee), 26 May 1941; *The Rugbeian*, 5 Aug. 1882.

[56] Letters, Hughes to the Rugby Colony, 7 Dec. [1891] (?). 8 Oct. 1892 in Rugby Papers.

CHAPTER FIFTEEN

Wig Over One Ear, 1882–1896

'Y ES,' Hughes told Lord Ripon, 'I was more or less seedy after getting back from the U.S.—giddy and inclined to go like a drunken cove in the streets—but never enough to make any real difference in one's ways.' He continued:

'I take it as simply a phase of the disease A.D. and as I am a good deal nearer 60 than 50 it is time I got some kind of warning. I am now much better—in fact well I think—I wish my wife were, but the long winter, only just over, told on her sadly.

'I meant to have written a long gossipy letter but must close now, as I am sorry to say I have a very troublesome and onerous business on my shoulders in connection with my American settlement which is all going wrong—wish me well through it: Twenty years ago it would have been light but now it is a very heavy and sorrowful burthen.' [1]

About this 'troublesome and onerous business' Hughes soon had more to say:

'Thanks for your kind words about my settlement . . . whether it will pull through seems doubtful with this unlucky fever coming on the back of the drought which has destroyed almost all such crops as there were in the first year. My anxiety as to the fever is nearly over as the reports are all good now— but in other ways the place is going through great trials. . . .

'If it fails, we shall be really poor for some years at any rate, so she, to meet the worst at once, has let the house for six months from Nov. 1st, and we shall spend the winter economising by the sea, most likely at Eastbourne.'

Although the troubles of the Rugby experiment must have been a blow, forcing him to leave his charming house in London's West End, he had not lost faith in the needs which had called it forth, and concluded, 'I am going to give our youngest boy a thorough training as a farmer in view of the future. I hoped he would take orders, but am giving that up.' [2]

Some idea of the financial loss in which Hughes was involved and the change which it made in his own life is revealed in a letter written on 13 November 1881:

'The cloud into which we were passing has by no means lifted yet, but it is not as dark as it seemed then. The fever has abated in the settlement, and I have lost no one but that is all that can be said.

'The place has received a blow from which it will take years to recover if it ever does, and in any case the founders must be very heavy losers. My own loss I can't put less than £7000, which makes me a really poor man again at a time when it is hard to recover. I had no right to risk so much—too true—but I never could count the money cost, when my heart was in anything, as you may think, the bitterest drop in the cup has been to feel what the loss entails on my wife and children—none the less bitter because of the noble way in which they have all borne it—not a word of complaint or repining has come from son or daughter, and even after a long life's experience of her I am astonished (and deeply humiliated) at my dear wife's courage and bright and loving sympathy.

'She has left her house, and with it the only life she is used to as though it were a light thing, quite natural, almost a pleasure! to begin life again and start new roots! No one knows what a true wife can be till they get into such deep waters by their own fault.

'Why do I tell you all this? My dear friend, I hardly know, except it be from a sort of instinct which turns at such times to those with whose lives one's own had been much bound up, in a vague kind of craving to unburthen ones self to someone. I have not said anything of this to any man, and should not to you, but I felt that I must write sooner or later, and nothing else would come to my pen's end—and I feel that the effort has been a relief which I know you will be glad should have come to me.

'I know well there is some lesson which God means I should learn from this trouble, and which in part I think I have learned. For the rest I wait reverently and I hope patiently for further light. It was you and your wife who came to us in our greatest trouble twenty years ago, and you will bear with me now if I seem morbid.'

He went on to sketch the efforts he would have to make:

'As to the future—I have given up of course all idea of getting back into Parliament and have done the last thing I ever thought to do, applied for a place. So you may see me a police magistrate or something equivalent when you come back. Meantime I shall be writing again, chiefly the long abandoned pot-boiler! Fiction, which would be the most profitable, I have long felt an aversion for which I doubt if anything can overcome—besides I am too old for it now. All unpaid work (of which my hands have always been too full perhaps) I give up except Co-operation, which I can't quite leave just now, the time being too critical. Our Union (to which you gave such timely advice) is at the parting of the ways, and no one who wants it to take the right turn can take off his hand—I must remain too at the Working Men's College until they can find a suitable successor. There—I hope I never wrote you a letter so full of myself before, and I certainly never will again.' [3]

So to lodgings at Eastbourne the Hughes family went for the winter of 1881. Hughes, ever unwilling to intrude his troubles on even his closest friends, continued to write to Ripon with scarcely a hint of his own fortunes. On 12 May 1882 he confessed, '. . . our affairs look rather better, but one has no mind to think of them still less to trouble other people about them, when the country is in such troubled waters'.[4] His old friend Goldwin Smith, now at Toronto, came over to the Co-operative Congress held at Oxford in June. The two nephews in Mexico were doing well. The London house was let to Sir A. Eden. Most important of all, Hughes got 'a place', and on 27 July could write and inform Ripon that he had been made a county court judge, declaring, 'As I am definitely out of politics, there is no work I would sooner do in which I could be more useful.'[5]

So before the next winter came round Hughes migrated to Chester, to be near his circuit. He resigned from the Co-operative Union and wrote again:

'Politics and all public action connected with them are of course over with me now I have accepted the county court—I never thought that I should have borne the change so tranquilly, but I am really inclined to rejoice in it. Unless a vacancy had occurred at Rochdale or possibly one or two other northern towns where co-operators rule the roost, I should not have had a chance of getting back into the House even if I had seen my way financially and even in the House now, what possible good could I have done, the first duty of a loyal Liberal being to hold his tongue.'[6]

I

The old town and cathedral of Chester, with its Roman Wall and historic associations, proved the opiate he needed. He confessed, 'They have a strange charm which is I think added to by the feeling that one has done with active politics.'[7] There were moments of loneliness. His six surviving children—his son Jack died after a mysterious paralysis in 1888—were seldom with him except at Christmas, and only George provided him with grandchildren.[8] But on the whole he was happy, and wrote encouraging letters to Ripon, then Viceroy of India, transmitting glowing accounts of his sons and nephews in Mexico. He told Ripon:

'Our eldest boy has come back since my last [letter] to you. It is a wonderful pleasure to have him and see what a splendid specimen of the Western Man he has grown into, but I fear I shall have great difficulty in installing anything like sound principles as to co-operation into him.'[9]

To Chester he could return after the round of Common Law actions, summonses under the Debtors Act, and employers' liability cases which absorbed his time as he travelled on circuit through the mining centres of Stockport, Ashton-under-Lyne, and Macclesfield. At Chester he was able to fortify himself to

deal with barristers whose formal eloquence proved too much
for his patience, and to bear increasing afflictions of gout and
rheumatism.[10]

The existence of renting other people's houses—first at 11
Stanley Place, then at 2 Sandowne Terrace—ended in October
1885, when he and Fanny moved into a house they had built in
Dee Hills Park. This house (to which Fanny added 'a turret and
bow windows' in 1890) lay behind wrought-iron entrance gates
with the letters T.H. and F.H. embodied in the design, looking
down over a terraced garden to the River Dee.[11] He told
Lowell:

'Out of the windows of my den I look right over the Cheshire vale to the
Packforten hills on the East & the lordly castle of the Tollemaches perched on
the spur; & over the gleaming Dee and green water meadows to the woods
& spire of Eaton on the South; while to the west (which I must go out on to
the stair-case to contemplate) lie Chester Castle & Cathedral with the Welsh
Moels on the horizon—there is nothing more delightful in the way of an all
round view anywhere that I know, & it don't seem to me that the democratic
republic will have an easy task in remaking it all.' [12]

The house that she had 'made', Hughes told his wife, was 'the
sweetest home in all England', though he couldn't quite believe,
with his luck, that they would be allowed to have 'perfectly
happy arrangements' there.[13] His sense of the past was very
much with him as he built this last home. The mottoes of both
his and the Senior family and their joint escutcheon were woven
into the design of a three-panelled oak mantelpiece in the lounge,
and were repeated in heraldic colours in the stained glass of two
windows on the staircase, the four long lower panels of which
depicted four of Tennyson's heroines: Enid, Vivien, Elaine, and
Guinevere. Hughes called his home Uffington House (the name
Tom's mother had also given her Rugby, Tennessee, home), thus
bringing his life full circle to its Berkshire beginnings.

2

The way his wife throve in a new home in the 'evening of her
life' delighted him. Humdrum as it sometimes was, he liked his
work as a judge, which was 'not at all an unsatisfactory one upon
which to spend one's remaining years of active life', and which,
he hoped, would be the means of 'spreading the respect for &
confidence in law' and 'inspiring some hope in poor folk'.[14] He

had no desire to be young again. Even his dreams were now pleasant. Before he was sixty

'if I had to make a speech I couldn't say what I wanted to say, and often could say nothing at all: if I had to fight I could never hit out: if riding, I could never get my horse to go at a fence: and when I committed crimes, was powerless either to escape or confess. . . . But all this is reversed in the last few years. . . . I now make speeches, especially replies, in some of the many controversies of my life, which come up again and again in my dreams, of the most convincing kind. . . . Moreover, my morals have so improved that I am now almost always on the right side, and have not committed a felony for I don't know how long.' 15

Tom was mellowing. As his dreams suggest (Tom knew enough about the subject to realise that since 'moral responsibility' ceases in dreams they could be very revealing), the competitive pressure was removed. Hughes no longer felt, except at moments, that he needed personally to set the world to rights. His son noted the difference in 1885 or 1886.

'It was not that he would not box [debate] it was rather that one did not think of it as one looked at him. I noted with a shock, I remember, that I did not look up to my partner as I used to do when he rowed on the Dee, and first discussed the People's party programme in his cunning breezy way. But the shock left me when I looked into his eyes; something in love, in understanding had permeated his expression which words fail me to describe. No I did not want to box, to throw down the gauntlet of my own opinions and beliefs; I rather wanted to find out what that outward visible sign in his face meant.' 16

Tom could now take the long view, as indicated in a very revealing letter to Alexander Macmillan in 1892. Macmillan ought no longer exert himself, Hughes said,

'but sit back easily in your big arm chair and think over no end of good times, and as well spent a life as all but prophets like Maurice can reckon over in this tough old world—and then too the dear prophet was quite unable to think of any good times he had ever had or good he had done, but only of the wickedness the poor old world had blundered into, which he had been sent especially to pull her out of and hadn't done it. So after all we are better off in our seventies than the prophets on this side the veil, however it may be on t'other.' 17

As for 't'other', Tom had the solid core of his religion: expectance of immortality, which the novelty that 'perpetually attends life' hints of, and faith in which 'must rest on the man's own assurance that he can fill a larger theatre than he is allowed here': 'we have our identity in the success of that to which we belong

. . . . He who is good for anything ought not to calculate chances of living or dying.' [18] What the loss of his faith would have meant is evident from his comment in 1889 on the doubts that assailed Leslie Stephen:

'Alas when a man has drifted from his old moorings, and lost his compass in the invisible, without giving up his longings for victory and truth and love in the visible creation, the rest of his pilgrimage cannot but get sadder and sadder.' [19]

3

Neither Tom's increasing mellowness nor his judicial wig, however, really subdued him. Just as he would impatiently silence lawyers in disgust over the pettiness of the cases which they argued before him, so he would flare up on any question that touched his vital beliefs. 'Blow Mrs. Grundy,' he told Alexander Macmillan; 'we didn't heed her much in the 'forties, and I have been strengthening in that belief ever since.' [20]

His retirement, so called, from the Co-operative Union was typical of the man. He declared that he would accept a testimonial only if no one paid more than a penny. When £1,200 was collected—a sum which later grew to £1,500—he knew that the conditions had not been kept. 'It is rather a trial for me', he told Ripon, 'as I have always protested vehemently against testimonials and preached that work should be its own reward.' [21]

In a blaze of eloquent denunciation, he warned his listeners:

'The critical time has come. One universal cry of distress is going up from every great trade and industry in the land. What is that cry? Surely my friends, the strangest that ever went up from any great trading community. "Too much corn, too much cotton, too much labour, too much wealth" while two-thirds of our people are underfed, badly clothed, miserably housed. Power is rapidly passing into their hands. How long, with all their patience, can this state of things last?'

He continued:

'With the trumpet-tone of the advance of 1849–50 still sounding in my ears, I seem to listen in vain for the true ring in these later days. I have seen old comrades disappearing, and often their places filled by those in whom the electric spark has never been kindled, who neither believed, nor loved, nor hated as they must believe, and love and hate who would win this battle.' [22]

Far from withdrawing from the movement, Hughes seemed to plunge even deeper in order to overthrow the dominance of the

C.W.S. and bring about co-operative production. To this end he submerged his feelings to work in close alliance with Holyoake: so much so that Holyoake's biographer acknowledged that 'Hughes was the dynamo of the co-partnership group'.[23]

When the Leicester employees of the C.W.S. left to set up a small factory of their own, Hughes proposed a strong resolution directing the C.W.S. to 'put their house in order'. Holyoake's support, as president of the 1887 Congress, enabled them to obtain 107 votes, but the C.W.S. polled seventy-nine more to defer the whole question to the next congress.[24] Hughes argued that the C.W.S. should be the agent for every independent producer society, and that unless production in the C.W.S. factories was organised along profit-sharing lines 'we may see our distributive societies drifting back into the old competitive groove, ignoring their principles, and becoming nothing better than cheap shops'.

For Hughes was tired of the perpetual endorsement of the principle of profit-sharing without corresponding action, and hit out fiercely:

'Two roads lie before,' he warned his hearers, 'along both of which we cannot travel, and of which it is extremely important that we should choose the right one.'

Urging that the existing productive societies belonging to the C.W.S. should be reorganised as self-governing workshops, he continued:

'You cannot give men a share in the profits, and not do it. Is one right and the other wrong? If one is right and the other wrong, say which is right and which is wrong, and stick to the right and give up the wrong'.

And the temperature of his feeling may be gauged from the ringing conclusion of his speech:

'If you deny the cardinal doctrine of self-governing and profit-sharing workshops, I . . . will retire from the Co-operative Union.'

What made the situation even more incongruous was that Neale, hitherto a close ally of Hughes, actually seconded the amendment to defer Hughes' proposal to the next congress.[25] Hughes was perplexed, and wrote to Holyoake:

'What could have possessed Neale? I never was more dumfoundered than when he got up to second the *amendment*! Now I shall just leave them to stew in their juice, hoping that you will take care to make it pretty pungent for them.'[26]

One of the producer societies in which he had taken a financial and personal interest for the previous seventeen years showed its appreciation of his efforts by naming its new engine the 'Thomas Hughes'.[27] This—the Hebden Bridge Fustian Manufacturing Society—also elected Hughes as its delegate to the subsequent congresses.

As its delegate, Hughes protested at Dewsbury in 1888 against the competition put up by the C.W.S. factories. Neale was the president of that congress, so a fresh pronouncement on profit-sharing was inevitable, and a resolution in favour of it was passed by 213 votes to 160.

4

His Indian Summer was also darkened by the clouds that gathered around the English political scene. A number of new elements in the political situation conspired to vex him. There was

'the heathen idea of external aiding and disciplining of the citizen and raising him by law.

'The Trade Unions have gone all wrong. Their union is centred in their Parliamentary Committee, which has no other function (nor has their Congress) but to propound and support Acts of Parliament dealing mostly with subjects quite outside their sphere; for the good reason that within it they have long ago got all that they are fairly entitled to. I left them altogether nearly ten years since now, seeing how wrong they were going.' [28]

There was the growing movement towards State Socialism, which he could not tolerate. But chiefly there was the decision of the Liberal party to adopt Home Rule, a decision which lost Gladstone the friendship of Hughes.

In the election of November 1885 he campaigned for W. E. Forster in Bradford, venting his anger on 'the young swashbuckler' Randolph Churchill; then leading 'the great phalanx of the Tories . . . by the nose into a thoroughly scandalous and disgraceful alliance with the Irish'.

As the Irish problem became more acute, Hughes was more and more inclined to treat the Irish in the way the North had treated the South in the American Civil War. He wrote to Ripon in the spring of 1886:

'It seems to me as if the Devil had succeeded in tempting Gladstone on his weakest side, and that he has been able to cast a glamour over the mass of

Liberals which may, or rather which must, bring us into fearful difficulties ..
apart from all other considerations, the shame of deserting the scattered loyalists
all over Ireland and leaving them to the tender mercies, not even of Parnell &
Co., who will soon be shoved aside, but of the Invincibles, makes me fairly
turn side.'

And turn side he did. Along with Joseph Chamberlain, whom
he had once feared, and Hartington, whom he particularly admired, he became a Liberal Unionist. In the summer of 1886 he
helped defeat a Gladstonian Separatist standing for Parliament in
Chester. The question of Home Rule for Ireland, he declared,
was 'the most momentous which has ever been; or can be'.[29]

That this meant breaking old political and personal ties Hughes
realised. He 'spent some sad hours', he told Lord Ripon, 'rum-
maging among the letters of old friends and lamenting' his growing 'estrangements from the few that remained'. With Lord
Ripon himself there was almost a breach, when, in May 1888,
Hughes vigorously and intemperately protested against Ripon's
talking on the Irish question in the Co-operative Hall at Dewsbury
while the Co-operative Congress was in session. Fortunately
Lord Ripon, though 'grievously' tempted by Hughes' 'needlessly
aggravating tone' to defy him, postponed his meeting, and
Hughes was—characteristically—contrite and apologised on the
instant.[30]

With Gladstone the break was irreparable.

'That terrible old man', he wrote his wife in the autumn of 1886, 'gets worse
and worse and I heartily wish he would join the Church of Rome on this trip
and be made a Cardinal, or at any rate end his days in Bavaria, or anywhere
else equally far "from the land he so misunderstands" as Henry Granfill puts it—
I never could have believed that a man of his superb intellect and genuinely
religious mind (as his must be I think though utterly unlike my own idea of
what religion means) could have so absolutely destroyed every vestige of respect
and admiration in the minds of those who look at politics (I hope) from ground
quite outside the lines of party.' [31]

Hughes had additional reasons, of which he was quite unaware,
for being angry with Gladstone. The fragmentation of the Liberal
party destroyed it as a mediator between labour and the country,
and soon labour was to have not only its own party but also its
own representatives in Parliament. So the need for men like Tom
Hughes disappeared.[32]

He was also 'astonished and not a little troubled' that so many of
his American friends—'men who had passed through and borne

the burden of the War of Secession'—were saying about the Irish, 'Oh, you had better let them have their own way'. Hughes, disgusted with America's infatuation with money, hoped that God would 'put his hook in Demos' nose and his bridle in his lips' by raising up another Lincoln. This disgust, no doubt, led him to

'say something about this "Westward Ho" gadfly which seems to have bitten young England with a vengeance. . . . I am startled, not to say alarmed, at the number of letters I get from parents and guardians . . . of youngsters eagerly bent on cattle ranches, horse ranches, orange groves in Florida, vineyards, peach and strawberry raising, and I know not what other golden dreams of wealth quickly acquired in the open air, generally with plenty of wild sport thrown in.'

He warned such parents and guardians that life in the West was 'really hard manual labour and rough board and lodging', and that 'they had better look the thing round twice or thrice before starting'. The experience of Tennessee had obviously bitten deep.

Over India, on the other hand, he had been optimistic ever since Lord Ripon went there, feeling that, redeemed by England, 'a self governing country and an integral and satisfied branch of the Empire of the future' would yet be established there. So, too, his ultimate belief that England itself could 'come out right side up' expressed itself in letters to Lowell.

'The national conscience is wonderfully better in all ways than I can ever remember it,' he remarked in 1887. 'On the whole there is not, nor ever was, a nation that kept a more active conscience, or tried more honestly to do the right things all round according to its lights.'[33]

Slowly he drifted towards a conservatism of the sentimental. By 1892 he could write in the *Spectator* that the Conservatives had done more for social legislation than the Liberals. For the Liberals generally wasted their time 'in tinkering at the machinery by which social good was achieved—shorter parliaments, paid members, one man one vote; while the Conservatives, though they might oppose alterations in the machinery, used it with success in improving the conditions of life for the poorer classes of our people.'[34] Ruefully he confessed that the new radicals thought of themselves as 'the real rulers of the nation' and wanted everything done for them by legislation: Gladstone and Chamberlain making matters worse by listening to 'Hyndman and Co.', who wished to equalise property by fiat.[35]

5

Nor did the new radicals look with a kindly eye on Hughes' own intrusions into their activities. 'Tom Hughes by his dogmatism and violence has thrown the whole question of profit-sharing back for at least ten years,' lamented J. J. Dent to Benjamin Jones just before the 1889 Congress at Ipswich. 'But', he continued, 'Tom Hughes has lost money in the movement, and you had better not have a hit at him in your address. The Southern Section look on him as their leader. I confess I am glad he is not here.' [36]

This impression of Hughes was fairly general among the younger middle class allies of the Co-operative movement, who were superseding Hughes and Neale as leaders. Beatrice Potter (who made the Glasgow Congress of 1890 an occasion for meeting Sidney Webb, and the Lincoln Congress of the following year an opportunity for getting engaged to him) was engaged on a history of the movement. In her book, published in 1891, she distorted the outlook of both Hughes and Holyoake, calling them 'individualists' who did not agree with the distribution of profits to consumers. Her Fabian worship of collectivism led her to dismiss the self-governing workshop as lacking not only the managerial ability, but also the workshop discipline, knowledge of the market, and industrial adaptability to survive in a world of constantly changing processes.[37] So it was not surprising that the president of the 1891 Congress, A. H. D. Acland,—a Rugbeian and an Oxford don—should deprecate the 'wordy warfare' which had hindered the progress of the C.W.S.[38]

But Hughes was unmoved by all this. 'I am not sure', he wrote to Holyoake 'that the time has not come to take off the gloves with Mitchell and his tail.' [39] Neale's death in 1892 meant that the Co-operative Union had to appoint a new secretary. They chose J. C. Gray,[40] son of a Baptist minister at Hebden Bridge, and one-time secretary of the Hebden Bridge Fustian Society. To influence him, Hughes proposed to Holyoake that they should both stay at the same hotel before the Congress of 1893, going on to propose that the C.W.S. should either be expelled from the Union or else that the Union should withdraw its holdings in the C.W.S., 'that stronghold of the devil'. Though such radical proposals did not actually find their way to the agenda of that Congress, Hughes and Holyoake both gave warm approval to the Scottish Wholesale Society's adoption of co-partnership, and urged the C.W.S. to follow its example. It was symptomatic that Beatrice Potter (now Mrs. Webb) should lead the opposition to this in a speech which asserted that co-partnership was 'a meaningless term', dismissing Hughes' demands as archaic.[41]

Hughes' anger against Mitchell knew no bounds. In 1894, when the Co-operators deputed Mitchell to unveil the bust to Neale which they had erected in St. Paul's, he flared out, threatening to write to *The Times* against the monstrosity of Neale's chief opponent being so honoured. Holyoake agreed, and wrote to Gray that the eulogy should more fittingly have issued from the lips of Hughes, Lord Ripon, or J. M. Ludlow. But Mitchell himself had not much longer to live, and died in the following year. Hughes was determined to seize this chance to gain for his ideas more emphatic endorsement by the Congress. 'It will probably be our last chance of getting the Union back on to the original and only safe lines,' he told Holyoake. The younger generation who advocated profit-sharing were, however, weary of the persistent endorsement of the principle of profit-sharing by Congress, and preferred to perfect and strengthen existing co-partnership societies, so that by practice, precept would be more effective.[42]

Swayed by this, the old warrior acquiesced in the establishment of a round-table conference to discuss the differences between the two wings of the movement. But in the year that the report appeared, the old fighter had left the ring.

6

As a compensation for the darkening shadows that were falling over Co-operation, light seemed to be breaking in at last upon the Established Church. Lay participation in counsel and work, for which Hughes had laboured so hard in the Church Reform Union, became in 1885 an accomplished fact, when, on 8 July, the constitution of a House of Laymen for each province was formally approved by Convocation. The first Canterbury House met on 16 February 1886, and the corresponding York House met for the first time on 20 April 1892. Though neither of these houses possessed any constitutional status, their deliberations undoubtedly contributed to the settlement of problems of ritual and patronage in the last decade of the century.[43]

A further source of comfort to Hughes was the increasing tendency of the Church to recognise the labour world. By 1887 he could 'score' a fifth bishop willing to speak at a Co-operative Congress, while many more were friendly. Moreover, in 1889 there arose within the Church a movement which stemmed directly from Maurice, the Christian Social Union: founded by Henry Scott Holland and Charles Gore.[44]

Hughes was delighted with the Union, which seemed to him to offer proof that the Church was not 'drifting back into mediaevalism but is ready to go into the ring and face the 19th Century devil with the gloves off', and he both accepted a position on its Executive Committee in 1891 and agreed to write for the first volume of its new *Economic Review*. The *Review*, he told George Macmillan, might

'just as well be called Christian Socialist and form a continuation of our old tracts—indeed I have told them that they are wrong not to add the 'ist' at once to their name and face the music.'

But 'your (or rather our) Chairman', he wrote the Union with much of his old gusto,

'don't seem to care about the 'ist', though he ought to have wacked you with his crozier (if he has one—our Bishop has, and a cape! and a mitre!! but he is a good Christian Socialist nevertheless), and made you all toe that line however much you winced. . . . And the Economic! What a name for our organ! We don't want Economy or Economists, but spendthrift fellows (and women) who will spend first themselves and then their own goods and then all the goods of other folk which they can lay hands on without thieving on the cause.' [45]

Hughes was perhaps somewhat over-optimistic about the Union, whose sedate members were not used to Hughes, and made him feel his letter had been 'abominably swaggering and insolent'. But Christian Socialism had come to stay, if only on the fringes of the Church. When the Union lost its drive, its place was taken early in the new century by the Church Socialist League. And in 1920 the Industrial Christian Fellowship was formed, which has worked more closely with labour than has any group since early Christian Socialist days.

7

Active as he was in these years both on and off the judicial bench, he was more and more seeking spiritual refreshment in the world of his youth. His *Early Memories for the Children*, written in 1890 (though never completed because of the death of his son Jack, for whom they were written), was frankly auto-biographical. His 1891 introduction to Lowell's works, his 1892 preface to Marriott's lecture on Kingsley, his 1893 article on Neale, his 1891 and 1894 talks at Rugby, and his many speeches before Co-operative and Church congresses are unabashedly personal, stressing the events in which he had played a part. There was nothing that Hughes liked more than to feel that he was drawing together the threads of his life. He was particularly pleased to have his old college—Oriel—brought close to the Co-operative movement through the scholarship given him as a testimonial in 1884. And in 1894 he dedicated what 'in all human likelihood' would be his last book—a reprinting of the *Manliness of Christ* with three Rugby addresses added—jointly to Rugby and the Working Men's College in the hope that a connection would grow between the two.

Hughes' willingness to turn to biographical writing stemmed largely from this growing desire to relive in memory the half-century of his youth and maturity. Hughes refused, indeed, to write on men whose lives were not a gateway leading back to his own experience and sympathies: on Dean Stanley [46] because he was 'perfectly unacquainted' with the 'courtly' and only 'outside-wardly' familiar with the theological side of his life; on Howard, about whom he had 'only the slightest knowledge'; and on Froude, who 'was always a profound puzzle to me', though 'I liked him very much and his works almost more'.[47]

The four subjects he chose were nineteenth-century English and American figures, all but one of whom—David Livingstone —he had known, and with two of whom—Bishop James Fraser and Daniel Macmillan—he had been on terms of some intimacy. And they were all men with whom he had much in common. Macmillan, a friend from Christian Socialist days, had had spiritual and vocational struggles not unlike Hughes' and coincid-ing with them in time. Fraser, an idealistic and practical-minded Broad-Churchman, the first bishop to speak before a Co-operative Congress, had been Hughes' Oxford tutor and a lifelong friend. Peter Cooper, industrial pioneer, philanthropist, and founder of an American working-men's college—Cooper Union—was, though a less familiar type to Hughes, very much a man after his own heart. And Livingstone, who opened up darkest Africa and planted English trading companies and missionaries where they could win the natives to true religion and Africa from the Boers, was the perfect example of those whom Hughes believed sent by God to help the English civilise the world.

Hughes wrote the books on Macmillan and Fraser, to whom he was closer, with a good deal less reluctance than the other two, consequently experiencing much less difficulty and much more pleasure in writing them. Fascinated by Macmillan's diaries when they were shown to him by Alexander in 1880, he immediately agreed, as requested, to 'select and weave them into a story', which would exclude business and family matters and concentrate on Macmillan's way of looking at life. Though Hughes had some trouble gathering and putting together his material, the book, written during the year of his Rugby troubles, was finished by the spring of 1882, and would have been 100 pages longer 'were I to follow my own wish'.[48] The suggestion to write a memoir of Fraser, the third of Hughes' biographies, came from Mrs. Fraser and Tom's son-in-law Cornish early in 1886, when Hughes had hoped he would be able to use his leisure hours for his 'family house-book' (the *Early Memories*), the 'only literary work for which I have any hankerings now'; and he consequently considered himself an 'ill-fated cove'. But he rushed immediately to see Mrs. Fraser. In a week he had agreed to do the job, feeling, with his usual exuberant optimism, that within two months he would have

'got through and mastered the 15 vols. (about 6 inches thick each) of his addresses, speeches, rows with mad parsons etc. which his wife collected and which with other materials such as letters and reports on Education in the U.S. etc. fill a big trunk'.

Within four months he had not only been through the material but had written seven chapters and, 'much taken with' them, was sure the book would 'come out very well'. From America, where he continued to work on it, Hughes wrote exuberantly to his wife that 'unless I am quite mistaken this life of Fraser will be a very bright taking book and will turn in a lot of money'. *James Fraser* was finished in October, eight months after Hughes had agreed to write it. Perhaps a little less haste might have spared Hughes an indignant letter from Gladstone, objecting to Hughes' confusing him with a William Gladstone who had subscribed to a Confederate loan.[49]

David Livingstone, the last of Hughes' biographies, was much less a labour of love, Hughes having agreed to do it in the summer of 1887 only because Macmillan wanted him to initiate their series of English Men of Action. Having agreed, he nearly backed out when he found 'what a lot of lives of the fine old explorer had already appeared'. And, knowing little about Central Africa or the intimate facts of Livingstone's life, he had great trouble getting to work and was constantly asking Craik for help about details, especially of a personal kind. Nevertheless, he ground out the book within less than a year—in September he talked of having it 'practically finished' on his return from America—and was, characteristically, 'pleased and think the book will come out very well'. The book was, he felt, a timely one.

'Surely never was there such a moment for getting out the life as this', he wrote in July 1888, 'when the suspense about Stanley is at its height, and the late doings of the Arab slave hunters on Lake Nyassa, and the Portugese on the Zambesi, are jeopardizing not only Livingstone's work but all that the English and Scotch missionaries and trading companies have accomplished since his death. I am preparing a few pages on this text for the finish, or for a preface if you think of having prefaces to the series.'

The book did not appear until 1889.[50]

The biography of Cooper had the most unfortunate and the most complicated history of the four. When Abram S. Hewitt (the 'old original's literary son', as Hughes called him) asked Hughes to undertake the task in the autumn of 1884, he agreed to do so mostly as a favour, having not 'much interest' in or knowledge of the subject. The work proved trying. Hewitt, who had agreed to collect the material, showered him with comments on the erratic character of the Coopers, with documents and autobiographies, and with background material, including McMaster's and Higginson's histories of the United States. 'Cooper's Reminiscences' Hughes found an 'infinite wilderness of undigested notes', and the rest of the 'ms., and other materials which were shunted on me, a frightful muddle'. Moreover, though Hewitt liked the first chapter, which Hughes sent him in November 1884, approved of his scheme for the remainder, and insisted that the 'book must be yours, and not edited by me or by anyone else', it was soon evident that cross purposes were at work.

'There is some difference of opinion in my family', Hewitt wrote in December, 'which I think cannot be well settled until you get further on with the work. I think you are on the right track, and I like the style and spirit of it very much. Mr. Edward Cooper Peter's son agrees with me, but he would like to see more of it before he comes to a final decision. It does not seem to strike Mrs. Hewitt as altogether in accordance with her idea of what should be said with regard to her father; but I think she is misled by that sentiment of reverence and love which does not tolerate the idea of any imperfection, either in character or action.' [51]

Nevertheless, Hughes plodded ahead. What he thought were the 'critical chapters'—on 'religious views etc.'—he had thrashed out with Edward Cooper when he came to America in 1885, leaving 'under the impression' that though Cooper's daughter, Amelia Hewitt, might not approve, 'she had no intention of putting on a veto'. The difficulties with sources were finally ironed out at the cost of a 'year's work in leisure hours', and Hewitt and Rossiter W. Raymond of Cooper Union, who were to do several chapters, finally produced their contributions. By the end of 1885 the book was finished. Hughes was even pleased with it, having found that the work 'grew on me very much, and at last I found the quaint old gentleman a most attractive as well as eccentric piece of human nature'. Advertisements were out, and publication waited only for Hewitt to give the final word from across the water.[52]

That word, however, never came. 'I can't think what has happened to Hewitt,' Hughes wrote Macmillan on 27 February 1886; 'suppose Mrs. H. has objected to some of my disclosures of the many eccentricities of her excellent father.' [53] Mrs. Hewitt had found a whole host of things wrong with the book: it was full of inaccuracies, badly arranged, done 'in a flippant manner',[54] and in general unsatisfactory as a tribute to her beloved father. Hewitt ordered Hughes to halt publication. Fifty copies were struck off, all but a few of which, in Hughes' possession, were sent to New York and stored in boxes in the basement of the Cooper house at 9 Lexington Avenue. Until recently, when Cooper Union began distributing them, no library in the world had a copy. The book is not contained in the Macmillan list of publications.

Hughes took this rebuff with amazing calm and good nature, though even his patience might have been taxed had he known that, nearly a year before, while he was still feverishly at work, Hewitt had already expressed doubt, in a letter to the publisher, George Putnam, whether the book would ever be published.[55]

Hughes' one desire seeemd to be, as he told his publishers, not to have a 'quarrel with Hewitt . . . added to the debit side of the account'. He had 'no wish', he wrote Hewitt, 'but to wipe up the whole mess in the manner most acceptable to Ed and your wife, with whose reverence for their father's memory as I have always told you I most heartily sympathize'. He accordingly worried even about the fifty copies, since some 'penny-a-liner' might get hold of one and print 'long extracts from the objectionable (to your wife and Ed) parts just strung together by a sentence or two'. 'Three New York ladies' had read Mrs. Hughes' copy and would no doubt talk about the book to Mr. Appleton, the publisher, on the trip back to New York, increasing the danger of public comment. As to pay, Hughes was at first, as he told Macmillan, 'too proud (or foolish) to make any charge', since 'the arrangement was that I was to have all profits', and there were none. He had, he wrote Hewitt, undertaken the task 'as your friend without any wish to make money out of it', and would at most—if it would make Hewitt 'feel more comfortable' —accept pay for his labours plus '£25 or £50 . . . to show that *you* are satisfied'. The figure finally agreed on was £250, and Hughes was off for America in August in the best of spirits, deep in the Fraser book.[56]

Hughes' three published biographies received good notices, especially the *Daniel Macmillan*, which the *Athenæum* found one of the most satisfactory biographies in its recollection, and the *James Fraser*, which the *Scottish Review* thought could not be praised 'too highly'.[57] Yet the first edition of even the *Fraser* lingered on Macmillan's shelves six months after publication, and only the *Livingstone* was in print in 1928. They are, in truth, none of them distinguished books, despite occasional vivid portraits and evidences of Hughes' old narrative skill.

Hughes' conception of a biographer, shared by many of his contemporaries, was that of a recorder and editor, who laced quotations to narrative, interspersed by moral comment. There is little analysis or interpretation in Hughes' books, little effort to penetrate into the mind and heart of either Cooper or Fraser, and no attempt is made to place them in relation to their environment. Even within such self-imposed limits Hughes was in too big a hurry to do a first-rate job. All his books were written in parts, which were sent on to the publisher as Hughes finished them, and which were then revised in accordance with the space Macmillan permitted him or the necessity for adding new material. Moreover, Hughes felt cramped by facts, which he was too impatient to collect and organise carefully. How much exact accuracy bored him is illustrated by an amusing letter to his publisher in 1888, when a Professor T. Schmidt of Lichtenfelde, who was editing *Tom Brown's Schooldays* with German notes, found that Hughes had attributed to Rowe a line that belonged to Shenstone. Hughes was annoyed, particularly as he found two other 'fat' mistakes just in glancing at a few pages of his book:

'Fancy an old spectacled Teufelsdrockh enjoying himself over such slips as these—surely this Herr Professor might have found some more desirable subject for his infernal notes! Can't you make him pay or frighten him somehow. There may be 50 other blunders for aught I know.' [58]

His books are as a result formless and often inaccurate. Mrs. Grundy supplied the finishing touch. Hughes' reluctance to reveal the intimate, the unpleasant, and the discreditable, had grown stronger with the years, and was certainly not diminished by what happened to the Cooper book. Even in *Daniel Macmillan* and *Peter Cooper* he had assumed that the 'veil' should be drawn back from 'those relations which most shrewdly test' manhood only if what was behind the veil was 'pure and of good heart' and would 'send the reader back to his own fireside a gentler, braver, brighter man'. There were 'too many stains visible in the stream of life as it flows solemnly on carrying each generation away towards the ocean which shall cleanse it at last, for any of us heedlessly to turn in another tainted rill, be it never so slender'.[59] When one adds to such feelings Hughes' natural blindness to the weaknesses of men, particularly when they were his friends, it is little wonder that his portraits are flat and bloodless.

Read together, these biographies are not so much portraits of four very different men as a composite drawing of the ideal man of Hughes' imagination. We have already observed how Hughes transformed King Alfred and Jesus into muscular Christian heroes. Now, working with four sympathetic figures out of his own past, at a time when he was pulling together the threads of his life, Hughes succumbed to the temptation to sketch them as four aspects of his long-cherished dream of manhood. None of the four was exactly the hero the future demanded—with Cooper,

Hughes was quite specific about this—but each embodied, as did the figures in Carlyle's *Heroes and Hero-worship*, most of the attributes that the hero ought to possess. Whether or not they were self-made as were Cooper and Macmillan, they were all ardent, downright, thrifty, and ambitious men, who loved work. No great students, they loved games and rough sports—Cooper and Macmillan got little chance to play games—and could be boyish and playful as well as serious. But there was a deep and serious faith behind the playfulness that coloured their lives and made them cheerful, reticent, and courageous. This faith was never dogmatic or narrow—there was even doubt as to whether Cooper was a Christian—but it envisaged God as the lover of all mankind. In His service they disciplined themselves to strive primarily for the good of humanity, which He loved, and, being practical men and fighters, not theorists, they had good deeds to show for their efforts. These efforts were always directed in early life towards helping their mothers and later towards aiding the industrious poor, who needed to be educated and protected in a fatherly way both from the rich and from their own baser natures, easily perverted by those who preached destructive revolution, or rights without duties. Whether through publishing, or building a working men's college, or working as a clergyman with co-operators, or as an explorer with heathen savages, these four heroes dedicated their lives to furthering God's will on earth. Like Dr. Arnold and Maurice and Lowell—and Tom Hughes—they were the humble agents of God's mission to the century.

8

Even before he undertook the last of his biographies it is evident that Hughes' urge to write for publication was diminishing. 'Mere article writing is demoralizing and unsatisfactory in many ways,' he wrote his publishers in 1887. And the writing of books was little better. After he had finished the *Livingstone* he would

'settle down to my great (posthumous) Anglo-American Novel, and cease to trouble publishers or printer's devils on this planet—or I should guess on any other, not seeing (as at present advised) how there will be any use for us in the new earth "wherein dwelleth righteousness". . . . Loafing in this sun [Rugby, Tenn.] is the best business here below, you bet! Blow writing and publishing!' [60]

Hughes did not, of course, stop doing either. Between 1890 and

1894 he wrote a number of articles—on Lowell, on Kingsley, on Neale, and on Rugby (for both the Rugby paper, the *Sybil* and the *English Illustrated Magazine*), and reprinted two of his earlier books, *The Scouring of the White Horse* and the *Manliness of Christ* (with new material added), though he couldn't imagine why 'up to date readers who batten on "Marcelle", "The Fabian Essays" and "Dodo"' would want 'my old world thoughts on such subjects'.[61] But the *Livingstone* was, except for the fragmentary *Early Memories*, his last book, and the shorter pieces grew fewer and fewer. As for the *magnum opus*, the Anglo-American novel, it never, posthumously or otherwise, troubled publishers or printer's devils. If Hughes wrote any of it—he mentions working on it in one of his letters—no remnant appears to exist. By 1894 he had plainly written himself out. 'I have written again & again in English periodicals', he wrote in response to a request for a piece on Arnold, the Socialist Movement of 1848 or the American Civil War, 'and don't care—or indeed think it honest—to dish up old material for your readers.' It was perhaps better, anyway, to hold one's tongue if one wanted to keep any self-respect in this 'well meaning but blatant generation'.[62]

Except for this reluctance to put pen to paper, there is little evidence that Hughes' powers were declining as he entered his seventies. His letters indicate no muffling of his youthful vibrancy, and he continued to work like a dynamo. In December 1894 he insisted, characteristically, that he could write an introduction to the Bishop of Chester's book on the catechism in two days.[63] His health, buttressed by a strong athletic body, remained almost perfect to the end. Lowes Dickinson painted his portrait at forty and then again at seventy. The latter portrait, which was paid for by subscription—or almost, since the subscriptions evidently ran short [64]—and presented to Fanny Hughes as a surprise, showed Tom Hughes to be remarkably unchanged in thirty years. Though he had fewer hairs, and those white, he was the picture of robust, fresh-faced health. In October 1895 he subscribed to the *Economic Review* for four years, his only worry being that *they* would not last that long.[65]

9

In his last years he was an inspiring figure. David Nelson Beach, who met him in 1894, said it was 'like going up into the

Delectable Mountains, or into the Mount of Transfiguration. He talked like a man inspired.' Even Tom's son George, who disagreed with his father about Co-operation, was much impressed when the old man spoke of the futility of political victories unless they hastened 'the binding of all humanity to God the Father, in perfect love, in perfect understanding'. This union, Tom continued, could only be achieved through the 'laws for human conduct which the Master lived and died, for the most part in agony, to proclaim'. 'When he uttered such words,' George confessed, 'the expression of that enthusiastic wholesome boxer seemed to become sublime.' [66]

On 26 November 1895 Tom wrote to the Rev. C. E. Escreet, who had invited him to be his guest at the forthcoming Co-operative Congress to be held during Whit week the following year at Woolwich:

'I am well past seventy, the psalmist's age of man: I have rather lost touch with the Union. So it is quite on the cards that I may not be named as a delegate by any of the associations in Union. But "save as aforesaid" (as we used to say in equity pleading) i.e. *if* I am still alive, *and* elected to go to Congress, I shall have great pleasure in being your guest. Nothing makes my last years so hopeful and cheery as seeing how many parsons are coming out fair and square for Christian Socialism. I have been sure for these last fifty years or thereabouts that in no other way can our country (or indeed any other) be saved, and by this way she may and will be.' [67]

But a month later, in December 1895, he had a series of colds, and the doctor sent him to rest at Torquay. Though the rest seemed to revive him, on 19 February 1896 he and Fanny went to Manchester to save him 'some travelling for part of his circuit. He has to be taken care of', Fanny wrote.

Tom wanted to write a memoir of Alexander Macmillan—who had died in January—but Fanny lamented, 'Alas, he must write no more; it tries him more than holding courts.'

In March he had another cold, and on the 19th set out to recuperate in Italy. But he only got as far as Brighton, when congestion of the lungs overtook him. On Sunday morning, three days later, he seemed better, and said he had passed an excellent night and would pull through. But once again his sanguine temperament overreached itself, for within a few minutes he was dead. The heart that had beaten so warmly for so many good causes had failed him at last.[68]

10

At his own request only his family and a few friends followed his body to its grave. His meagre estate of £8,412 was mute testimony to his generosity and concern for others. As the *Spectator* wrote, Tom Hughes' death 'will probably have caused a more diffused and general feeling of personal grief than would have been caused by any other death that could have taken place'.[69] All over the world people rushed to offer homage. One Boston journal paid him what they considered the supreme compliment by declaring he had an 'American soul in an English body'.[70] Old Rugbeians, whose Alma Mater was soon to possess a statue of Hughes by Brock, collected a memorial fund for him. And twenty-five American educators, including Nicholas Murray Butler, Charles Eliot, William Harper, Lyman Abbott, Seth Low, and Timothy Dwight, urged their fellow-countrymen to contribute to this memorial.[71] Among the host of articles about him at his death there was but one dissenting voice, that of his old enemy, the *Saturday Review*. Under the guise of 'an old Friend' the writer reduced Hughes' genial love of meeting boys to an insincere formality; called *Tom Brown* shallow and the *Vacuus Viator* letters garrulous and exasperating; accused Hughes of intolerance, of holding the floor whether anyone wished to listen or not, and even of cheating to prove a point; stated that he had been a failure 'in every walk of life' after his first success, including his role of judge, in which his rough-and-ready justice became a byword for reversal; and ended by saying that Hughes had 'absolutely no imagination and his sense of humour was perverted'.[72]

11

A fitting written memorial was not, however, forthcoming. Hughes had survived all his brothers and sisters except one, three of his nine children, and almost all his friends except Ludlow and Llewelyn Davies. On one of the two latter, it seemed evident, rested the task of writing his biography. Davies thought Ludlow ought to do it, but Tom's oldest son, Jim, preferred some third person, who would be less inhibited in describing what Tom 'aimed at'.

Mrs. Hughes decided that there should be no memoir at all; [73]

'Several times in late years,' she wrote George Macmillan, 'my dear husband told me he never wished any memoir or letters of his published so that I feel I can never wish anything of the kind done in my lifetime. Our old friends Lord and Lady Ripon are now here for a couple of days and yesterday talking of him with Lady Ripon she said he had told her how he should object to any memoir and that he thought too many were written.'

So Ludlow had to be satisfied with an article in the *Economic Review*, and Davies with another in the *Dictionary of National Biography*. There the matter rested for half a century.

Tom's sons did not carry on his work. One of them—George —became, even before Hughes' death, a believer in Henry George's single-tax scheme, so ruinous to the gentry whom Hughes admired. Another—Arthur—went in just the opposite direction, becoming a cynical, disillusioned disciple of Herbert Spencer, a hedonist and a lover of Italy and Germany. Though Hughes tried to conceal his disappointment, he could not help disparaging Arthur's oscillations between Shelley and Spencer, and apologising for George's 'state socialism' as 'a reaction perhaps from the intense individualism and dollar-worship' around him. His grandson, who came to England as an American soldier in the Second World War, has seen Labour come to power, but primarily through the efforts of the trade unions, which Hughes hoped would disappear, and under slogans of government intervention and ownership, of which Hughes disapproved. The Co-operative movement, though highly successful, has not developed production as a laboratory of Christianity. Neither the Church, nor the public schools, nor the empire have become mirrors of Hughes' dreams. Over and above all these things, the world has moved not closer, but farther from freedom and order based on individual initiative and Christian discipline and love.

Yet consignment to oblivion can be premature, as this book has tried to show. And defeat can be temporary. Actually, Tom Hughes' work has not been without effect on English life even during the last half-century. And the world is not in such a happy state today that it can afford to ignore those who, like Tom Hughes, would lead it in different directions. Hughes' basic ideas and feelings were not the sort to be withered by time. They were sound in his day, and they might well be found sound in ours, as we return, after a long and painful journey, to some of his major premises. They might even win a hearing once denied to them.

Do they deserve such a hearing?

NOTES

[1] Ripon Papers, B.M. Add. MSS. 43,531, Hughes to Ripon, 14 July 1881.

[2] *ibid.*, 14 Sept. 1881.

[3] *ibid.*, 13 Nov. 1881. This is the only long record extant of the impact of the Rugby Disaster upon Hughes.

[4] *ibid.*, 12 May 1882.

[5] *ibid.*, 27 July 1882.

[6] *ibid.*, 25 Aug. 1882.

[7] *ibid.*, 21 Sept. 1882.

[8] He gave £1,000 to Jim in 1886.

[9] Ripon Papers, B.M. Add. MSS. 43, 531, Hughes to Ripon, 9 May 1883.

[10] Letter, to Edward Mack from George Hughes; *Green Bag*, Sept. 1896, 375; *The Times*, 27 Dec. 1892, 9; 16 Feb. 1894, 10. His circuit included five towns in Cheshire, two in Lancashire and one in Shropshire.

[11] Letter to Edward C. Mack from the present owner, Ambrose Roberts, May 12, 1946. The gates were commandeered by the Government during the Second World War.

[12] Lowell Papers at Harvard, Hughes to Lowell, 25 Nov. 1885.

[13] Hughes to Fanny Hughes, 20 Aug. 1886.

[14] Ripon Papers in the British Museum, Add. MSS. 43,531, letters, Hughes to Ripon 25 Aug. 21 Sept. 1882, 10 Jan., 9 March 1883; Lowell Papers at Harvard, letter, Hughes to Lowell, 7 Sept. 1882, 19 July 1888.

[15] Hughes, *Early Memories for the Children*, 66 ff.; Hughes, *Vacation Rambles*, 309.

[16] Letter to Edward Mack from George Hughes.

[17] Graves, *Life and Letters of Alexander Macmillan*, 384.

[18] Notes for Speeches in Hughes Papers.

[19] Lowell Papers at Harvard, letter, Hughes to Lowell, 1 Sept. 1889.

[20] Graves, *Life and Letters of Alexander Macmillan*, 384.

[21] Ripon Papers, B.M. Add. MSS. 43, 531, Hughes to Ripon, 9 March, 1883.

[22] Hughes, *Address on the Occasion of the Presentation* . . . (Manchester, 1885). The presentation, with Bishop Fraser in the chair, was held in the Balloon Street meeting-room. An Oriel Scholarship in his name, a watch, and a casket of jewels were presented to Hughes, whose speech was well reported ; see P. Redfern, *The Story of the C.W.S.*, 124–125.

[23] J. McCabe, *Life and Letters of G. J. Holyoake*, ii, 240.

[24] Report of the Co-operative Congress of 1887; J. McCabe, *op. cit.*, ii, 234.

[25] A possible explanation is that since he was to be president of the next congress, he could therefore guide its discussions.

[26] McCabe, *op. cit.*, ii, 234.

[27] Joseph Greenwood, *The Hebden Bridge Fustian Manufacturing Co-operative Society* (1891), 13, 19.

[28] Ripon Papers, B.M. Add. MSS. 43, 533, Hughes to Ripon, 19 May, 1885.

[29] Letters, Hughes to Fanny Hughes, 12–14 Aug. 1886; Forster to Hughes, 11 Nov. 1885; Hughes to Craik, 6 July 1886 (in possession of Macmillan & Co.); Lowell Papers at Harvard, Hughes to Lowell, 25 Nov. 1885; Wolf, *Life of Ripon*, ii, 181; *The Times*, 11 Nov. 1885, 4; Hughes, *Vacation Rambles*, 247; *Forum*, Sept. 1889, 1.

[30] Wolf, *Life of Ripon*, ii, 181 ff.

[31] Letter, Hughes to Fanny Hughes, 10 Sept. 1886.

[32] *English Historical Review*, lxv (1950), 51.

[33] Wolf, *Life of Ripon*, ii,1 56; Parrish Collection at Princeton, letter of Hughes, 15 July 1890; Lowell Collection at Harvard, Hughes to Lowell, 20 June 1890 (Mrs. Rantoul Collection), 25 April 1891 (Mrs. Rantoul Collection), 30 Jan. 1887; *Vacation Rambles*, 332.

[34] *Spectator*, 6 Aug. 1892.

[35] *The Times*, 17 Feb. 1886, 7, 16 Feb. 1894, 10; *Economic Review*, Oct. 1914, 381.

[36] Beatrice Webb, *My Apprenticeship* (London, 1926), 372. J. J. Dent was a bricklayer who in 1883 had been elected secretary of the Working Men's Club and Institute Union, and in 1893 was appointed Co-operative Correspondent to the Board of Trade. B. Jones was for many years general manager of the London Branch of the C.W.S., helped Beatrice Potter in her researches into Co-operation, as well as being co-author (with A. H. D. Acland) of *Working Men Co-operators* in 1884. His *Co-operative Production* (1894) is the fullest and most comprehensive account of the various societies in English.

[37] B. Potter, *The Co-operative Movement* (1891).

[38] A. H. D. Acland, a curate who had relinquished his orders to become secretary of the Oxford University Extension Movement. He and his wife played a great part in Co-operative work, especially after he was elected M.P. for Rotherham in 1886.

[39] J. McCabe, *Life and Letters of Holyoake*, ii, 239.

[40] J. C. Gray (1854–1912) was trained as a clerk in the audit office of the Lancashire and Yorkshire Railway Company. After a period as General Secretary of the Hebden Bridge Fustian Society from 1874 until 1883, he became assistant to Neale at the Co-operative Union. He was, like Neale, an enthusiast for Co-operative Production, and at the Plymouth Congress in 1886 he read a paper on the subject which was unanimously adopted by Congress, the C.W.S. abstaining. His proposals for the amalgamation of co-operatives into a single national society are given in S. and B. Webb, *The Consumers' Co-operative Movement* (London, 1921), 307–309.

[41] J. McCabe, *Life and Letters of Holyoake*, ii, 238.

[42] *ibid.*, 241–243.

[43] F. W. Cornish, *A History of the English Church in the Nineteenth Century* (London, 1910), ii, 326–327.

[44] H. Scott Holland (1847–1915). A companionable Oxford Don who was the centre of the active group that produced *Lux Mundi* in 1889. He took a great part in founding the Christian Social Union and edited its journal—*The Commonwealth* from 1895 until 1912; E. Lyttleton, *The Mind and Character of Henry Scott Holland* (1926). Charles Gore (1853 to 1932). Gaunt and wiry, his belief in community life led him in 1892 to found the Community of the

Resurrection. He wrote the essay on 'The Holy Spirit and Inspiration' in *Lux Mundi* in 1889, and was later Bishop of Worcester and Birmingham and Oxford; G. I. Prestige, *Charles Gore*, 1935.

[45] Letters in possession of Macmillan & Co., Hughes to George or Fred Macmillan, 12 Dec. 1892, *Economic Review*, Oct. 1914, 381.

[46] *Harper's New Monthly*, Nov. 1881, 911, contained an article of Hughes on Stanley, it is true, but it was reminiscences. The International Index attributes a *Quarterly Review* of Prothero's *Life of Stanley* in 1894 to Hughes, but the learned nature of the review, its absence of personal references, and its distrust of a plethora of combative latitudinarians in the Church make such authorship unlikely.

[47] Letters, Hughes to Craik, 15 June 1887, Hughes to Fred Macmillan, 1889, Hughes to George Macmillan, 19 Oct. 1894, in possession of Macmillan & Co.

[48] Graves, *Life and Letters of Alexander Macmillan*, 351–352, 362–363; letter, Hughes to Fred Macmillan, 5 June 1882, in possession of Macmillan & Co.

[49] Letters, Hughes to Fred Macmillan and Craik, 5, 18, 29 March, 16 April 1887; to Craik, 6 March 1886; to George Grove, 26 June 1886; to Alexander Macmillan, 27 Feb. 1886, in possession of Macmillan & Co.; Hughes to Fanny Hughes, 6 Sept. 1886; *The Times*, 11 March, 1887, 10.

[50] Letters, Hughes to Craik, 1 Aug. 1887; to Alexander Macmillan, 14 Sept. 1887; to Fred Macmillan, July 1888, in possession of Macmillan & Co.

[51] Cooper Papers at Cooper Union, letters, Abram S. Hewitt to Hughes, 28 Oct. 1884, 11 Nov. 1884, 6 Dec. 1884; Hughes to Hewitt, 3 March 1886; Lowell Papers at Harvard, letter, Hughes to Lowell, 25 Nov. 1885; letters, Hughes to Alexander Macmillan, 1, 4 June 1885, 4 June 1886, in possession of Macmillan & Co.

[52] Letter, Hughes to George Grove, 14 Nov. 1885, in possession of Macmillan & Co.; Cooper Papers at Cooper Union, letter, Hughes to Hewitt, 3 March 1886.

[53] Letter, Hughes to Alexander Macmillan, 27 Feb. 1886, in possession of Macmillan & Co.

[54] Hewitt Papers at Cooper Union, letter of Hewitt's, 16 Dec. 1890.

[55] Cooper Papers, letter, Hewitt to George Putnam, 11 June 1885.

[56] Cooper Papers, letters, Hewitt to Hughes, 24 May 1886. Hughes to Hewitt, 3 March 1886; letters, Hughes to Alexander Macmillan, 4 June, 8 July, 1886, in possession of Macmillan & Co.; letter, Hughes to Fanny Hughes, 15 Sept. 1886.

[57] *Athenæum*, 19 Aug. 1882, 233, 28 March 1896, 414, 12 March 1887, 343; *Westminster Review*, Aug. 1887, 647; *Scottish Review*, Nov. 1882, 175, April 1887, 419, July 1889, 293; *Saturday Review*, 2 Sept. 1882, 320, 26 March 1887, 458.

[58] Letter, Hughes to George Macmillan, 22 Feb. 1888 in possession of Macmillan & Co.

[59] Hughes, *Memoir of Daniel Macmillan*, 178; Hughes, *Life and Times of Peter Cooper*, 221.

[60] Letters, Hughes to George Macmillan, 21 June, 14 Sept. 1887, in possession of Macmillan & Co.

[61] Letter, Hughes to Fred Macmillan, 22 May 1894, in possession of Macmillan & Co.

[62] Letter, Hughes to Horace Scudder, 8 Jan. 1894, at Harvard.

[63] Letter, Hughes to George Macmillan, 21 Dec. 1894, in possession of Macmillan & Co.

[64] Letter, Hughes to Fred Macmillan, 27 June 1894, in possession of Macmillan & Co.

[65] *Economic Review*, Oct. 1914, 381 ff.

[66] Letter to Edward C. Mack from George Hughes.

[67] *Co-operative News*, 28 Dec. 1895.

[68] *The Times*, 24 March 1896; letters, Fanny Hughes to George Macmillan, 18 Dec. 1895, 19 Feb. 1896, in possession of Macmillan & Co.

[69] *Spectator*, 28 March, 1896, 435.

[70] *Literary World*, April 1896, 104.

[71] *School Review*, June 1897, 409.

[72] *Saturday Review*, 28 March 1896, 320.

[73] Letters in possession of Macmillan & Co., 12 and 14 May 1896.

CHAPTER SIXTEEN

Proper Pedestal

IN public life most men need a platform. Tom Hughes had too
many. His old law tutor said he had 'seven times more irons
in the fire and that he heated them all seven times more than
anyone else'. Cricketer, author, boxer, lawyer, politician, co-
operator, church reformer: he was a great all-rounder, whom
later generations of Tom Browns have tried to emulate. Yet *Tom
Brown's Schooldays* probably had more influence on his contemporaries than all his manhood accomplishments put together.
And this was first published anonymously.

I

The mercantile middle class, riding in Thackeray's phrase to
'manly opulence', took Tom Brown to its heart. Seventy
editions were run through in his lifetime, projecting a picture
which stirred two generations.

Seven years after it was published, Fitzjames Stephen wrote:

'Tom Brown and his imitators, and those from whom Tom Brown drew his
inspiration, had so glorified football and cricket, and had mixed up Dr. Kingsley's theories and Dr. Arnold's practice into a composition so attractive to a
considerable portion of the public, that the public schools had come to be invested in the eyes of the world at large with even more than usual of that halo
which individuals are always prone to throw over places in which they have
passed a pleasant and important part of their lives.' [1]

Leslie Stephen followed nine years later with the comment:

'Neither the British jury, nor the House of Lords, nor the Church of England,
nay, scarcely the monarchy itself, seems to be so deeply enshrined in the bosoms
of our countrymen as our public schools.' [2]

But the Rugby Hughes extolled was misinterpreted by most of
his middle-class readers. Tom Hughes hoped that public schools
would nourish crusaders for the Christian life, Arnoldians who
would fight for Saxon simplicity against Norman guile, true followers of Christ and King Alfred; but his middle-class readers

279

saw only Tom Brown the potential pro-consul. It was so easy a message to misinterpret. Where Tom saw such schools as nurseries of social servants, his middle-class readers saw them as training-grounds for sahibs. Unwittingly, he touched a vein of class sentiment, which erupted, not only into such literary phenomena as *Beeton's Boy's Annual*, but into yet more public schools which were far from fulfilling the wishes of either Arnold or his disciples.

Tom himself was worried by such consequences. He publicly deplored the over-emphasis on games which caused the 'training and competitions [for] them to outrun all rational bounds' and led to professionalism. He acknowledged that an athlete could be both a brute and a coward, since games tested only skill and strength. To idolise such athletic success, he conceded, led to obsequiousness and cauterised the growth of independence and idealism: necessary virtues in a materialist age. Moreover, the over-production of Tom Browns in such schools posed a serious social problem, for their rock-like resistance to change in all forms made them social misfits in a society which was calling for an *élite* with technical knowledge.

So Tom sank his fortune in the Tennessee hills to provide an opportunity for unwanted Tom Browns to show the world that they were not amusing anachronisms. As proof of this, he not only called his settlement Rugby, but dedicated his last book half to Rugby, and half to the Working Men's College. The frequent recurrence of public-school boys in his accounts of the settlement reveals his delight that such manly products had now found their proper vocation.

2

Just as he had written *Tom Brown's Schooldays* for his eldest son, so he looked to the manly life of the West to make men of his other sons. Even his own mother followed his star, and went out to spend her last days in a house which Hughes had built and christened Uffington. He told Ripon in 1883 how wonderful 'a specimen of western man' one son had grown into, but added, 'I fear I shall have great difficulty in installing anything like sound principles as to co-operation into him'. Jim on the Rio Grande amongst his 'crocodiles, white cranes, beavers, wolves and all manner of strange birds and beasts' was a constant source of delight to Tom. 'The life brings out all there is in a fellow, and I am glad and proud to recognise what fine stuff there was in him to bring out'.

Though the Rugby settlement languished, nothing could shake Hughes' belief that ranch life was the real outlet for boys of the Tom Brown type. Writing of a young Haileyburian (who might have been his own son), scarcely emancipated from his high collar and white clothes, then cropped and tanned by two years in the saddle on a Rio Grande ranch, he observed:

'At home he might by this time be just through responsions by the help of cribs and manuals, having contracted in the process a rooted distaste for classical literature. Possibly he might have pulled in his college boat, and won a plated cup at lawn tennis, and all this at the cost of say £250 a year. As it is, besides costing nothing, he can cook a spare rib of pork to turn on a forked stick, hold a bull-calf by the tail, and is voluntarily wrestling (not without certain glimmerings of light) with *Sartor Resartus*. Which career for choice? How say you, Mr. Editor?' [3]

Of the hundred or more experiments in community founding, this Tennessee venture, though one of the most significant, has also been one of the most ignored. For like its fore-runners, it was the reflection of a fundamental social movement in England: a legitimate successor of the communities of Frances Wright and Robert Owen.[4] Like these and countless other essays in community founding, it drew to the expanding West men and women with the very qualities needed; qualities like individualism and a sense of freedom. Though it collapsed through the weaknesses of its members, Rugby Tennessee had fired others. E. W. Marland, the great oil imperialist, was one,[5] and Arthur Dyer, the Rugby colonist who later discovered micanite insulation was another.[6]

His project also co-incided with the entry of the largest number of immigrants hitherto recorded in the history of the United States—nearly 800,000 as the venture was taking shape: a number in which the British element constituted nearly a quarter. And as we have seen, Tom Hughes realised and encouraged this great demographic distribution of what he called 'the Anglo-Saxon brotherhood'. His persuasive and much-publicised exhortations were undoubtedly a factor to be considered in its assessment.

Nor should the minute scale of his venture, like the minute scale of his essays in producer co-operation, induce an under-estimation of its importance. For, as a distinguished French

observer remarked in 1928 of some of the other essays in community founding:

'I do not even consider it unlikely that either this century or the
next these communitarian associations—or integral co-operative
societies if you like—may occupy as large a place in the world as
the religious communities did in the middle ages.' [7]

3

The Tennessee adventure was also, for Hughes himself, an
attempt to salvage the social beliefs of his youth, when he and
Kingsley had set out to capture the Socialist movement from the
secularists. It was singularly apt that the first headquarters of their
essays in co-operative production should be in Charlotte Street,
first made famous by Robert Owen. For, by capturing the
secularist legacy of Owen, they did, in large measure, instil a
Christian leaven into the Co-operative movement. That this
leaven did not permeate the whole was, as we have seen, due
partly to the stolid resistance of the C.W.S., and partly to the
wilful rejection of producer co-operation by a later generation of
middle-class allies. These later allies, of whom the Fabians were
most influential, regarded Hughes' 'fair vision of a brotherhood
of workers' as 'an indescribable industrial phantom'.[8]

Yet for all the Fabian worship of the statistics and facts of consumer co-operation, ample as they were when Beatrice Potter
was writing her study of the movement, neither the Fabians nor
their successors, the quantitative-minded economic historians,
under-estimated 'the deep interest which they [the producer
societies] stirred in men of good will unwarped by dogmatic individualism'.[9] For though the pilot ventures in co-partnership
established by Hughes and his colleagues would hardly be visible
on a map of late nineteenth-century industrial Britain drawn on
the largest possible scale, nevertheless they served to nourish a
concept which may yet supplant the State Socialism of the early
twentieth century: a concept far more capable of exciting those
industrial incentives which the bureaucratic State of the Fabian
imagination has so far failed to provide. That concept, a func-
tional democracy of co-operative producers, excited the attention
of such men as A. J. Penty, A. R. Orage, and the early G. D. H.
Cole, as well as others, like R. H. Tawney and M. B. Reckitt,
whose inspiration stemmed more directly from Gore and Maurice.

Glimmerings of the concept lay behind the summons of the first Co-operative Congress by Hughes and his fellow-enthusiasts for co-operative production in 1869, and their attempt to transform it into a Parliament of Democratic Industry. That Beatrice Webb should so emphatically reject the claims made for the Co-operative Congress over the C.W.S. is itself proof of the contagious enthusiasm felt by Hughes and his colleagues who, had they had their way, would have created a labour bank to finance productive co-operation to supply the C.W.S. Hughes was as emphatic an opponent of the servile state and the dominance of an intellectual bureaucracy as any of the Guild Socialists, and as great a realist as Peter Drücker when he pleaded for the end of economic man, of man as a creature of circumstance and an instrument of exploitation. And had his group obtained control of the *Co-operative News*, founded two years after the first congress had met, they might have secured an effective organ of propaganda for their ideas.

The ideal of co-operative production and profit-sharing excited three white papers: the first within two years of Hughes' death and the other two early in the twentieth century. But Fabian State Socialism, with its irresistible centralised bureaucracy, was in the ascendant: managers, intellectuals, and trade unionists were all convinced of its mechanical efficiency, and ideals were stigmatised as utopian. Now, however, the Co-operative Party have seen that nationalised industries are too big to be run from one centre, and in 1951 A. Stewart and W. P. Watkins revived the idea of producer co-operatives. National Boards, they argue, instead of controlling the industry, should lease its mines to co-operatives, drawing rent from the profitable ones, and granting a subsidy to those mines where production at a loss is regarded as a national necessity. By this means the individual might feel that he has an integral function to fulfil in industry.[10]

4

Industry was, in Hughes' eyes, God's laboratory. Like Emil Brunner of our own day and generation, he insisted that God wanted man to use his intelligence in order to rise above nature and subdue the earth, for God created man in His own image. The whole extension of man's natural faculties—the fortified fist expressed in the hammer, the prolonged arm in the crane, and the extended foot in the steam engine—were the mere technics of progress. The harder mastery of the brute nature, the wolfish competitive spirit of Victorian society, Hughes hoped to see accomplished by co-operative production on Christian lines.[11]

His re-statement of the revolutionary nature of the Christian faith appeared in the book which he and Neale wrote in 1879. He saw that secularism increased coercive law, and broke with the trade unions on that issue. He crusaded against both the oligarchic misuse of power by plutocrats and bureaucrats, and the ochlocratic fanaticism which denied subordination.

By his layman's faith he helped to keep alive the burning zeal for social reform which had almost been extinguished in the hierarchised establishment like Barchester. Christian Socialism was derided by the Church. Canon North Pindar says it was 'taken up by the few, who for a testimony were content to wear strange patterned and ill-fitting trousers made in the workshops of the C.S. tailor'.[12] Such a remark is evidence enough of the divorce of the Church from working men in the middle of the last century.

The work of the Christian Socialists did much to bridge this rift, though they could not prevent it getting wider as the century progressed. To this bridging process the life of Tom Hughes was dedicated. He helped to keep alive among the laity the sense of moral values which stemmed directly from Christianity by creating a hagiography for his age. Tom Brown and King Alfred were, like their creator, very angular Saxons, rooted in the soil and religion of centuries. And in his social teaching Hughes went farther than either Kingsley or Maurice. For, as the empiric man of action of the group, Hughes carried into his political life the teachings of Maurice, often, as we have seen, against the wishes of Maurice himself.

Hughes also bridged the gap between the work of Maurice and that of S. D. Headlam, which stemmed directly from it. Headlam's Guild of St. Matthew, formed in 1877 to study political and social questions in a Christian light, attracted C. W. Stubbs, W. E. Moll, A. L. Lilley, C. E. Osborne, Conrad Noel, Percy Dearmer, and J. G. Adderley. Hughes took an active part with Scott Holland in the establishment of the Christian Social Union, a body to which William Temple was to adhere early in the twentieth century. Both Stuart Headlam and Scott Holland were, in a real sense, Tom Browns of the first generation, for both were taught at Eton by William Johnson Cory, also a Christian Socialist. The debt both owed to Maurice was further emphasised by the christening of Maurice Hostel at Hoxton, founded as an embodiment of the principles and aims of the C.S.U.[13]

5

Tom Hughes was not afraid to utter truths because they were commonplaces, nor to express feelings because they were obvious. To him, the end of life is the happiness and deepest fulfilment of all human beings. This, and not denial of impulse and retreat from the world, is what Hughes meant by spiritual as against material ends. And happiness could be brought about ultimately only through the agency of free individuals working together for their own betterment and that of society. Hughes did not need our bitter experience to know the folly of relying on discipline imposed from above or on the automatic workings of economic forces to accomplish the ends he sought; nor was he tempted to over-estimate the help of technical knowledge or institutional planning. He knew no less than did St. Paul that 'there was something to be said for hope and love', and an almost equal amount for self-discipline. A society that counted on individuals to accomplish what no little Cæsar could achieve, required, he was fully aware, individuals capable of willing the good of society as well as their own good, and mature enough to act on their beliefs.

But to what extent are most men capable of such willing and acting? Tom Hughes' naïve faith in the goodness of man and the universe, which led him into so many frustrating experiences, seems to us almost wilful blindness. If recent history and the discoveries of science have taught us anything, it is to temper our enthusiasm about ourselves and to refrain from easy assumptions about the benevolence of things in general. Yet has not our pessimism gone too far? The psychologists now assure us that, though man may be full of hate and selfishness, he is not inevitably so; the healthy or normal human animal is capable of both love and self-control. Moreover, whatever the disparity between our ideals and the purposes of the universe, human fulfilment must remain our highest aim. And such fulfilment can be achieved only through institutions that will fan the small spark of man's virtue and demand its exercise. Across the span of half a century Tom Hughes speaks to us living words.

Moreover, the man behind the words, the personality of which they were the natural expression, emerges with equal freshness from the mist of years. And as the protagonist of an ever-recurring drama, as the human instrument of social change, he offers us valuable lessons in human behaviour.

There has been no attempt in this book to suggest that Tom Hughes was a heroic protagonist. Ludlow touched on a group of his weaknesses when he called Hughes hasty, over-sanguine, and so trustful that he was easily taken in by rogues: always to some extent a boy, he was both too outspoken and too soft-hearted to be eminently effective. Probably more disturbing to us are certain narrownesses and intolerances. Hughes paid the penalty for knowing the truth, a penalty that was the greater since a good deal of the truth that he knew was the limited truth of a Victorian gentleman. His son George said that Hughes was a benevolent egotist who could 'understand at' but never really comprehend hostile points of view. He was angered by 'flippant scepticism' and by deviations from the Victorian moral code, bored by art and by most classical music, and impatient of foreigners, foreign ideologies, metaphysics, and the higher reaches of thought in general. Above all, Hughes often seems unwilling to face unpleasant truths or to look squarely at reality. His letters and speeches are full of his hopes in detail, but when reality has blown these hopes sky high, the whole subject usually gets only a passing mention. It was thus with Briggs & Co.'s failure no less than with the shattering of his Rugby hopes. Tom Hughes was a Victorian in no way more typically than in his ability—which the Victorians called faith—to see only what he wanted to see.

Tom Hughes' deficiencies do not, however, loom very large in the total picture, and were more than balanced by attractive qualities, of which they were, indeed, often but the obverse side. Above all, Tom Hughes was a man whom the world could take to its heart. As Ludlow said, 'No one who had any genuineness in him could know him without loving him', and the *Spectator* asserted that his very presence made one feel 'that the air was lighter and the clouds upon the move'.[14] His warmth, his honesty, his charm, and his easy grace of manner lend their tone to the smallest no less than the greatest of his acts. Naturally tolerant except where basic beliefs or prejudices were involved, he favoured compromise and accommodation over fanaticism. Modest to a fault, he preferred to praise the wares and boost the egos of others rather than to further his own aggrandisement. 'To ask anything of Tom Hughes', as the *Spectator* wrote, 'was to make him think better of you at once.' [15] No wonder that he could rally a heterogeneous collection of oddities around the Christian Socialist banner, infuse the spirit of Tom Brown into a whole generation, win the confidence of hard-boiled labour leaders, and draw hundreds of men after him into the Tennessee wilderness. Tom Hughes may have trusted too easily and thus limited his own effectiveness; but in compensation he drew other men's trust and support for new social goals.

In pursuing these goals, Tom Hughes exhibited a staunchness that often approached the heroic. Behind his gaiety and easy friendliness was a tenacity that never for a second slackened its grip on the purposes he set for himself. Here his very deficiencies came to his aid. Out of blind faith he drew strength, and out of a refusal to look too steadily into the abyss he plucked courage. Life could not touch him: one failure was but the springboard for another hope. All through his life he strove passionately and ardently for those things in which he believed, deterred neither by the prejudices of the class to which he belonged nor by the strength of the forces arrayed against him. And in the end persistence sometimes won what love and good-fellowship alone could not have accomplished.

Were Tom Hughes alive today he would, as his son wrote, 'be boxing overtime'. The current spectacle, with its outer chaos and inner confusion, would surely sober him. But the overconsciousness of motive and the uncertainty of purpose that have led to our modern failure of nerve would leave him untouched. Tom Hughes would still know which way to head, and would be trudging straight down the road that leads there, perhaps drawing with him some of the faint of heart. It would be good to have him with us.

NOTES

[1] *National Review*, Nov. 1864, 280.

[2] *Cornhill Magazine*, March 1873, 283.

[3] *Vacation Rambles*, 238.

[4] For which see Mark Holloway, *Heavens on Earth* (London, 1951).

[5] J. J. Mathews, *Life and Death of an Oilman* (Norman, Oklahoma), 10–13.

[6] L. H. Dorehill, *Rugby Advertiser*, 26 Oct. 1923.

[7] Charles Gide, *Communist and Co-operative Colonies* (trans. E. F. Row) (London, 1930), 216.

[8] B. Potter, *The Co-operative Movement* (1891).

[9] J. H. Clapham, *An Economic History of Modern Britain* (Cambridge), ii, 144–145.

[10] For a bibliography, see *Report on Profit-sharing and Co-partnership in the United Kingdom*, H.M.S.O. Cmd. 544 (1920), with the two previous White Papers, Cmd. 6496 of 1902 and Cmd. 7458 of 1894. Of the 133 schemes shown in the first-named report, eighty-one were started since 1900 and sixty-seven since 1915. G. D. H. Cole's study of the Co-operative Movement, published in 1951, carries the argument further.

[11] Karl Brunner, *Christianity and Civilisation* (London, 1949).

[12] Abbott and Campbell, *Life of Jowett* (London, 1897), i, 135–136.

[13] M. B. Reckitt, *From Maurice to Temple* (London, 1947).

[14] *Spectator*, 28 March 1896, 443; *Economic Review*, vi, 1896, 312.

[15] *Spectator*, 28 March 1896, 443.

APPENDIX

The Story of the Autobiography of Tom Hughes

IN 1880 Lothrop and Company of Boston collected a number of the choice remarks of Tom Hughes under such headings as 'Ambition' and 'Courage' between the covers of a book called *True Manliness*. Prefaced by some remarks of Lowell's, this volume contains the first extended account of Hughes' life yet to appear anywhere in print: an account moreover that has an added interest in being written by Hughes himself.

The story of the publication of this autobiographic piece, and especially of the repercussions that eventually followed, is both amusing and somewhat mysterious. Requested to write a short notice of Hughes' life, Lowell had asked Hughes for the facts and dates.

'His answer was an autobiographical letter which I found so interesting that I resolved to print it, omitting only a few intimate allusions natural in such a communication, but with which the public has nothing to do. My temptation was the greater that the letter was not intended for publication, and had, therefore, that charm of unpremeditated confidence which is so apt to be wanting in more deliberate autobiographies.'

Lowell had, he said, purposely waited until Hughes was where he could not be reached and would be unable to object.

'I fear that friendship may have tempted me to an unwarrantable liberty, but I could not bring myself, even at the risk of seeming indiscreet, to deny to others what had given me so much pleasure.' [1]

Lowell surely had reason to be worried. Hughes had been perfectly willing to write Lowell 'a sort of memoir of myself being moved by the notion of telling you more of my life'; indeed, since 'it is one of the greatest pleasures of life to be known to one's friends', Hughes was glad rather than sorry to have been 'moved by the horrid little stout slow speaking Yankee to deliver myself of this long screed which, monstrous in size as it is will not I feel confident bore you'. But he plainly did not intend that the letter, which divulged 'more than I have ever told before of my secret thoughts my works and ways', should be seen by any but Lowell's eyes. Since an account of his life was demanded by the public—though Hughes still hoped the plan could be squelched altogether—Lowell was to use the letter as the basis for a piece of his own, which would 'give only the driest and meagrest facts and dates'. 'I am *quite* sure', Hughes wrote Lowell, 'that nothing you can write will add to my love for, and debt to, you—or, I am nearly sure, can lessen them.' Hughes had reason to be confident about this, since he had told Lowell explicitly that at 'our time of life . . . the liking for seeing or hearing anything about oneself (if it ever was strong in me, as to which I am very doubtful) has got very weak indeed—One knows too well what a poor kind of cuss one is at the best, and gets more and more to wish to do one's quiet day's work in one's quiet corner, as the days draw in.'

Lowell had himself stated in print that Hughes hated 'the idea of being presented in any guise to the public'.[2] In 1889, when requested to write a memoir of himself for an American edition of *Tom Brown's Schooldays*, Hughes refused, 'as it happens that nothing in modern literature, or rather journalism, offends me more than the pandering to the unhealthy curiosity of the public as to the private lives of our contemporaries'.[3]

There were, nevertheless, no protests from Hughes when the book appeared nor was there at any time any censure of Lowell. The public learned about Tom Hughes, and Tom Hughes evidently accepted the fact gracefully. What really happened, astonishingly enough, was that Hughes apparently never saw the book. He seems not to have questioned Lowell about it, and Lowell, possibly fearing Hughes' reaction, seems never to have mentioned it, or to have had the publishers send Hughes a copy. Not till fourteen years later, when Lowell was dead, did a copy find its way into his hands.

Hughes was then—somewhat belatedly—furious:

'I found a copy of a Yankee book here on Manliness', he told George Craik (husband of the author of *John Halifax, Gentleman*) of Macmillans on 2 October 1894, 'made up of extracts from my writings, with a short introductory letter of Lowell's covering a long letter of mine to him of which I can't remember having ever sanctioned the publication. It is one of Lothrop of Boston's "Spare Minute Series", title "True Manliness", no dates given.' Two days later he added, 'Lowell never told me he had given a copy of the letter in the preface to anyone and I should certainly have objected to publication had I known of the intention. And why do they wait till after Lowell is dead so that I can't know what he did ?'

As he thought about the matter, Hughes grew angrier and angrier, and surer and surer that Lowell was not to blame. If three-quarters of this intimate letter to a 'dear friend is now published, entirely without my leave', it must also have been 'I *believe*', without his.

'If not, i.e. if they really had his leave, they would have published 12 years ago, or at any rate in his lifetime. . . . No doubt he said, "mind you must get Hughes' consent before you print this, or I don't agree till you have got it to your printing my introductory note" . . . I should be glad to punish these Yanks if I can and would even pay to the cost of proceeding over there for an injunction and an account of sales etc. It is rather too strong even in these days that a fellow's confidential chat about himself to an intimate friend should be any scamp's property with "by your leave", or even "d— your soul", if he can only get a copy.'

That Hughes could have assumed that the book was new in 1894 is understandable enough. But how he could have been so sure, after reading Lowell's explicit statement in the preface, that Lowell had not authorised publication is hard to comprehend. Possibly he thought the words about indiscretion and unwarrantable liberty were a mere literary device, since he could imagine almost anything that absolved a friend from the implication of betrayal. If he ever learnt the truth, his thoughts have not been recorded. Macmillan told him to write to the publisher, and though Hughes was not sure he could address 'your brother of books at Boston' as '*dear* Sir', he apparently did so. He also petitioned his lawyer friend Cadwallader in New York 'to see if he could do anything in the way of injunction or damages'. But their answers—if they answered—are not extant.[4]

If Hughes was safely out of reach during those summer days of 1880 when Lowell was planning his biographic scoop, it was because he was on the ocean on his way to pay his second visit to America.

NOTES

[1] Brown, *True Manliness* preliminary note.

[2] *ibid.*; Lowell Papers at Harvard, letters, Hughes to Lowell, June 1880, two undated, probably June and July 1880.

[3] *The Critic*, 20 July 1889, 34.

[4] Lowell Papers at Harvard, letters, Hughes to Lowell, 22 March 1873, 17 May 1874, 23, 25 June 1876, 7 Aug. 1880; New York Public Library, letter of Hughes to Cadwallader, 12 Nov. 1894; letters of Hughes to George Craik, 2, 4, 11 Oct. 1894, in possession of Macmillan & Co.

BIBLIOGRAPHICAL NOTES

THE chief manuscript sources for this life of Thomas Hughes are the following:

1. Hughes Papers belonging to his son George Hughes in Topeka, Kansas. These consist of Hughes' letters to his wife, a journal written during his college days at Oxford, a host of miscellaneous letters chiefly to or from Hughes, notes for speeches, etc.
2. Rugby, Tennessee, material. This consists of letters, many by or to Hughes, chiefly on the subject of the Rugby colony, as well as much useful manuscript and printed material about Rugby.
3. Papers of the first Marquess of Ripon in the British Museum.
4. The James Russell Lowell Papers in the Harvard University Library.
5. The letters of Hughes to various members of the firm of Macmillan & Co., in London, owned by the latter.
6. Letters from Hughes to George Howell in the Bishopsgate Institute, London.

There are also a few letters of Hughes in the Morris L. Parrish collection at Princeton, in the Cooper Union Library, in the Pierpont Morgan Library, in the Henry W. and Albert A. Berg and other collections of the New York Library, in the Library of Congress, in the Gladstone Papers at the British Museum, the Mundella Correspondence at Sheffield University, the Huxley Papers at the Imperial College of Science and Technology, London, and at Rugby School.

Among published works, Hughes' own books and articles have been, of course, the primary source. Much of this material—articles, speeches in Parliament, and reports as correspondent of the *New York Tribune*—is, though invaluable to a biographer, necessarily ephemeral. The list below contains only books, articles that have been reprinted, and speeches published in pamphlet form. References to other items will be found in the footnotes.

Address on the Occasion of the Presentation of a Testimonial in Recognition of his Services to the Cause of Co-operation, 6 December 1884. (Manchester, 1885.)
'Account of the Lock-out of Engineers in 1851–2' in *Trades' Societies and Strikes*, 1860.
Alfred the Great, London. Part I printed Oct. 1869. Part II printed Nov. 1869. Part III printed Dec. 1869. Volume made up from parts 1869 to 1871. First reprinted as a volume June 1871. Reprinted 1873, 1874, 1877, 1881, 1887, 1901.
In America, four editions by four publishers were in print by 1899.
'The Ashen Faggot, A Tale for Christmas', in the third edition of *The Scouring of the White Horse*, London, 1889 (originally published in *Macmillan's Magazine*, Jan. 1862).
The Cause of Freedom : Which is its Champion in America, the North or the South ? published by the Emancipation Society, 65 Fleet Street, London, 1863.

Church Reform and Defence. An address delivered in Wadham College Hall, Oxford, on Advent Sunday 1886, on the invitation of the Oxford Layman's League for Church Defence.

Co-operative Production. An address delivered at the Co-operative Congress held at Carlisle, May 1887. (Manchester, 1887.)

David Livingstone in Macmillan's 'English Men of Action', March 1889, reprinted July 1889, 1898. In print in America in two editions by 1899.

Early Memories for the Children, London, 1899.

This, written in 1890, was privately printed as 'by the author of *Tom Brown's Schooldays*'. In 1925 it was re-edited by Henry C. Shelley, and printed in the *Cornhill Magazine* as 'Fragments of Autobiography, Early Memories'.

History of the Working Tailors Association, 34 Great Castle Street [signed] H. (London, 1850). Tracts on Christian Socialism, ii,

James Fraser, Second Bishop of Manchester, A Memoir, 1818–1885, Feb. 1887, reprinted March 1887. 2nd ed. (electrotyped), 1888, reprinted 1889.

King's College and Mr. Maurice No. 1. The Facts, 'by a Barrister of Lincoln's Inn'. (London, 1854).

A Layman's address to Rugby School, Quinquagesima Sunday, 8 Feb. 1891 (London, 1891).

A Layman's Faith. (London, 1868.) This is a reprint of 'Religio Laici'.

Lecture on the History and Objects of Co-operation. Delivered in Manchester, 22 April 1878. (Manchester, 1878.)

Lecture on the Slop System, especially as it bears upon the females engaged in it. (Exeter, 1852).

Life and Times of Peter Cooper. (London, 1886.)

The Manliness of Christ. London, 1879, reprinted 1880. Edition of 1894 has three additional addresses by Hughes, 1907.

A Manual for Co-operators, prepared jointly with E. V. Neale, at the request of the Co-operative Congress held at Gloucester in April 1879. 1st ed., 1881, revised 1888, further revised by A. Stodart and W. Clayton in 1916.

Memoir of a Brother, 1st ed., Jan. 1873. Reprinted March (twice), April, June, July, and Nov. 1873, 1882. Published in America by Houghton, Osgood and Co. in 1873.

Memoir of Daniel Macmillan, 1st ed. printed July 1882, reprinted with corrections Oct. 1882. 2nd ed., Dec. 1882. A shilling edition from plates published in 1883.

The Old Church. What Shall We Do With It? (London, 1878.)

'Religio Laici', 1st ed. printed May 1861, reprinted May, Aug., Oct. 1861. Afterwards published in a volume *Tracts for Priests and People* by various writers.

Rugby, Tennessee, being some account of the settlement founded on the Cumberland Plateau by the Board of Aid to Land Ownership . . . with a Report on the soils of the Plateau by . . . F. W. Killebrew. (London, 1881.)

The Scouring of the White Horse, or the Long Vacation Ramble of a London Clerk, by the author of *Tom Brown's Schooldays.* 1859 (two editions), 1889. Republished Blackie (1925), two editions.

'The Struggle for Kansas', in *A Sketch of the History of the United States* by J. M. Ludlow. (London, 1862.)

Tom Brown at Oxford. By the author of 'Tom Brown's Schooldays'. In three vols. 1st ed., Nov. 1861 (Cr. 8vo), reprinted Nov. 1861; 2nd ed. (stereotyped plates), 1864 (1 vol., Cr. 8vo), reprinted 1865, 1869, eight illustrations added to part of this edition 1871, 1872, 1874, 1875, June and Dec. 1877, 1879, 1880, 1883, 1886; 3rd ed. (electrotyped plates), 1889, 1903.

In America, the first part was printed as *Tom Brown at Oxford*; *A Sequel to School Days at Rugby* by Ticknor and Fields in 1858–60, and sold at one dollar. Harper and Bros. sold the same 'premature version' for 38 cents. The full American edition was not published until 1871 by Ticknor and Fields. New editions were published by Macmillan and Harper in 1870. By 1899 there were twelve editions in print by twelve publishers.

Other English publishers include Routledge (1905) and Nelson (1914, 1932, 1935), and a French translation was published in 1881.

Tom Brown's Schooldays 'by an Old Boy'. Cr. 8vo. 1st ed., 24 April 1857; 2nd ed. July; 3rd ed. Sept.; 4th ed. Oct.; 5th ed. Nov. 1857; 6th ed. (with a preface on bullying added, which was printed in all subsequent editions), Feb. 1868.

All the above were Cr. 8vo, printed by R. Clay of Bread Street Hill, and published at 10s. 6d. A Fcp. 8vo edition at 5s. was printed 1859 and reprinted 1861, Feb. 1865.

In 1869 the first illustrated edition was published (the Pott Quarto) with engravings by Arthur Hughes and S. P. Hall in the text, and a frontispiece engraved by C. H. Jeens from the C. F. Watts portrait of Thomas Hughes.

Other editions published by Macmillans up to 1889 were: Cr. 8vo. ed. at 6s. (reprinted from Fcp. plates), 1871, 1872, illustrations added 1874; new ed. reset and stereotyped, also at 6s., 1874, reprinted 1877, 1878, 1879, 1880, 1882, 1885, 1888; new ed. 1889; med. 4to. printed 1882, reprinted 1884, 1886 at 6d. Also bound up with three other works in a volume known as 'People's Editions'; Golden Treasury at 4s. 6d. first printed 1868, reprinted 1870, 1873, 1876, 1880, with new headlines 1885. Pott 8vo. at 2s. printed July (twice) and Nov. 1865, June and Oct. 1869, 1870, 1872, 1873, 1874, 1875, 1877, 1878, 1879, 1880, 1882, 1883, 1885, 1886, 1887.

American editions began under two titles, *Schooldays at Rugby*, by an Old Boy, and *Tom Brown's Schooldays at Rugby*, both published in 1857 by Ticknor and Fields. The first title was republished 1858–1860, and again in 1861 (author's ed.). The second title was republished in 1869 by Fields, Osgood and Co. The first edition called *Tom Brown's Schooldays* was that published by Harper at 50 cents in 1870. After this date, and until 1899, there were 23 separate editions by as many publishers. This does not include such bowdlerisations as *Brown and Arthur: An episode from Tom Brown's Schooldays . . .* arranged for the press by a mother, published by West and Johnston from Richmond (Va.) in 1861.

Macmillan editions after 1889 include those of 1890, 1892, 1896 (illus. by Edmund J. Sullivan), 1901, 1903, and 1905 (6d. edition). Then a gap till 1916 (illus. by J. Macfarlane), 1923 (illus. by Edmund J. Sullivan), 1923 (*American Pocket Classics Series* with introduction by Charles S. Thomas), 1926, 1929 (July and Oct.).

Other English publishers besides Macmillan began to issue it after 1892.

Pitman's (1892, in easy reporting phonography), Dent (1903, illus. by T. H. Robinson), Collins (1903, 4-coloured illustrations) (1904, *Handy Pocket Library*), Routledge (*New Universal Library*), Amalgamated Press (1905, *Harmsworth Library*), Long (1905, *Library of Modern Classics*), Dent (1906, *Everyman's Library*), Collins (1906, *Home Library*), Milner (1906, *Camp Library*), Nimmo (1907), Cassell (1907), Frowde (1907, Oxford ed.), Chambers (1908, *Standard Authors*), Nelson (1908), Ward Lock (1910), Dent (1911, illus. by Louis Rhead), Routledge (1912), C. H. Kelly (1913, illus. by Paul Hardy), Sidgwick & Jackson (1913, preface by Lord Kilbracken, with introduction, notes and illus., ed. by F. Sidgwick), Black (1914), Chambers (1917), Frowde and Hodder and Stoughton (1917), Ward Lock (1920, 1921), Harper (illus. by Louis Rhead and introduction by W. D. Howells), Hayes (1923, *Rosebery Series*), W. Scott (*Carnarvon Series*), Nelson (1923, *Standard Books*), Harrap (1923), Sidgwick & Jackson (1923, 2nd ed. of ten years before), Collins (1924, *Masterpiece Library*), Black (1924, 4 colour illus. by Nicol Laidlaw), Epworth Press (1926, illus. by Paul Hardy), Collins (1927, *Boys' and Girls' Library*, 1928, *Silver Lion Library* and *Story Hour Library*), Low (1929), Collins (1929 *Red, Lion Library*), R.T.S. (1930), Pilgrim Press (1930, *Prize Library*), Nelson (1932, *Famous Books*), Ward Lock (1932, re-issue of 1910), Collins (1933, *Canterbury Classics*, illus. by H. Copping), Marshall, Morgan & Sons (1933), Collins (1935, *Albany Classics*, illus. by H. Copping), Hutchinson (1935), Foulsham (1935, *Boy and Girl Library*), Nelson (1935, *Winchester Classics*, re-issue), Juvenile Publications (1936, *Martyn Library of Juvenile Books*), Collins (1937, *Pocket Classics*), Seeley, Service (1938, illus. by L. Speed), Collins (1939), Dent (1944), Gawthorne (1947), Studley Press (1947), Ward Lock (1949, *New Prize Library*).

True Manliness. Selections from Hughes' writings made by E. E. Brown, with an introduction by James Russell Lowell, Boston, 1880.

'Truth'. A poem in *Lays of the Sanctuary and other Poems*, edited by C. G. de M. Rutherford. (London, 1861.)

Vacation Rambles. (London, 1895.)

'Working Classes in Europe', in *The Labor Question and Other Vital Questions*, N.Y., n.d., essays by Hughes, Thomas Brassey, E. A. Freeman, Judge Cooley and others.

Young Heroes of the Civil War, Old South Leaflets, viii, 181, Boston, n.d. Published originally in *Macmillan's Magazine* in January, 1866, under the title 'Peace on Earth'.

Hughes also edited a collection of letters from his nephews in Texas called *G.T.T. Gone to Texas*, London (May and Dec.) 1884; *The Trades' Unions of England*, by M. le Comte de Paris, London, 1869; and *Friendship of Books*, by F. D. Maurice, London, 1874 (two editions), 3rd ed. 1880, 4th ed. 1889, to which he contributed a preface. He wrote introductions, prefaces or prefatory memoirs to the following:

Alton Locke, by Charles Kingsley. (London, 1876, 1881.)
The Biglow Papers, by James Russell Lowell. (London, 1859, 1880.)
Charles Kingsley, Novelist, by J. A. R. Marriott. (Oxford, 1892.)
Gilbert Marlowe and other Poems, by William Whitmore. (Cambridge, 1859.)

Guide Book to the Canadian Dominion, by Harvey J. Philpot. (London, 1871.)

The Poetical Works of James Russell Lowell. (London, 1891.)

For biographical purposes the *Vacation Rambles*, the *Memoir of a Brother*, *True Manliness*, and *Early Memories for the Children* are the most useful of Hughes' works, containing as they do autobiographical material and letters. A few of Hughes' letters have been printed in the *Economic Review* ('Some Letters of Thomas Hughes', Oct. 1914) and others in the *North Carolina Historical Review*. Others are printed in the *East Tennessee Historical Society Publications* ('The Correspondence of Thomas Hughes concerning his Tennessee Rugby', by Marguerite B. Hamer, July 1944) and W. H. G. Armytage ('New Light on the English Background of Tom Hughes' Rugby Colony in Tennessee,' 1949). A great many letters appear in the biographies of other men, notably in *The Life and Letters of Alexander Macmillan*, by Charles L. Graves (London, 1910); in *The Life of Frederick Denison Maurice*, edited by his son Frederick Maurice, 2 vols. (New York, 1884); in *The Life of the First Marquess of Ripon*, by Lucien Wolf, 2 vols. (London, 1921); in *The Life and Letters of George Jacob Holyoake*, by Joseph McCabe, (London, 1908); and in *Sixty Years of an Agitator's Life*, Holyoake's autobiography (London, 1892).

There has been no biography of Thomas Hughes. Llewelyn Davies' article in the *Dictionary of National Biography* and J. M. Ludlow's piece in the *Economic Review*, vi, 1896, are the basic secondary sources. Hughes has also been discussed frequently in both contemporary and recent books and articles. The footnotes list all such references as have been used. A good, but incomplete, bibliography of his writings can be found in *A Bibliographical Catalogue of Macmillan and Co's. Publications from 1843 to 1889* (London, 1891) and in *The Bookman's Journal*, 3rd Series, vol. xvii, 150–155 and 222–223.

INDEX

Acland, A. H. D., 261, 276
Adam, W. P., 20, 94
Adams, Charles F., 138, 143, 182
Adams, Henry, 136, 138, 139, 182
Adventures of Mr. Verdant Green, 113, 128-9
Agricultural and Horticultural Association, 153, 169
Ainger, Alfred, 107
Ainsworth, H., 8, 14
Ainsworth's Magazine, 10, 92
Airlie, Earl of, 231
Alabama Case, 139, 140, 141, 185, 189-192
Albert, Prince, 58
Alfred, King, 7, 81, 166, 172, 270, 279
Allan, Wm., 60, 122
Amalgamated Society of Carpenters and Joiners, 122; of Engineers, 66, 67, 123
America, United States of, 62, 89, 139-143, 148-9, 156, 174-194, 227-250, 265-6, 271
Applegarth, R., 122, 148, 157, 158, 159, 225
Arnold, Matthew, 15, 22, 23, 53, 62, 97, 121, 138, 166, 171, 188, 216, 244
Arnold, Dr. Thomas, 15, 21, 22, 23, 24, 25, 27ff., 35, 41, 43, 53, 64, 86, 87, 88, 92, 94, 96, 98, 100, 101, 133, 166, 200, 235, 270, 271
Arnold, Thomas, 15, 20, 26, 45
Athanasian Creed, 199, 201
Athenæum, 277
Atlantic Monthly, 128
Australia, 117
Austria, 154
Ayrton, W. E., 148

Balliol College, 27, 29, 40, 97
Barham, R. H., 7, 37
Bath, 200
Bayley, R. S., 77
Beach, D. N., 272
Beale, James, 153
Beales, E., 149
Beckett, Arthur à, 204
Bede, Cuthbert (Edward Bradley), 113, 128-9
Beesly, E. S., 158
Bellasis, Edward, 102
Bendyshe, Thomas, 126
Bentley, R., 108
Beresford Hope, A. J., 108, 127, 138, 218

Biglow Papers, 131, 132, 142
Bismarck, 182, 190
Blacklock, Dr., 247
Blackwood, A., 37, 38
Blackwood's Magazine, 10, 100, 103, 128
Blanc, Louis, 132, 152
Board of Aid to Land Ownership, 228, 229 ff., 231, 239, 246
Bolton, 39, 154, 202-3
Boston, 174, 179, 188, 228, 230, 289
Boutwell, 178, 273
Boxing, 28, 41, 79, 98, 287
Boyle, John, 228, 229, 230, 231, 236, 239, 242
Bradley, G. G., 58, 94, 95, 96, 102, 129
Brassey, T., 172, 213, 231, 248
Brewer, J. S., 73
Briggs, A., 155, 156, 214
Briggs, H., 120, 151, 154, 155, 156
Bright, J., 143, 150
Brighton, 38, 88, 119
Brontë, Charlotte, 91, 108
Brooke, Sir J., 69
Brown, Thomas Crowther, 129
Browning, Robert, 82, 105, 121, 188
Bryce, James, 186
Buchez, 59, 60
Buckingham, Duchess of, 9
Buckingham, Duke of, 193
Bury, 64, 65
Byron, 31, 94

Cabinet Makers, 170
Cadwallader, 290
Cambridge University, 39, 139, 144, 182, 280
Campbell, A. M., 57, 73
Canada, 176, 180, 192-3, 228
Carlingford, Lord, 186, 209
Carlyle, Thomas, 35, 41, 42, 61, 87, 93, 94, 99, 115, 133, 151, 155, 166-7, 172, 228, 270, 282
Central Co-operative Agency, 65, 70, 72, 76
Chamberlain, J., 200, 208, 222, 259, 261
Chambers, Sir T., 206, 207, 209
Chartists, 30, 39, 40, 55, 56, 57, 65, 117
Cheap Clothes and Nasty, 60
Chesson, F. W., 136
Chester, 253, 254 ff.
Chicago, 180, 189, 237
Christ Church, Oxford, 27
Christian Observer, 89, 103
Christian Social Union, 263
Christian Socialism, 53-75, 114, 156, 264

297